EXCAVATIONS
IN THE DARENT VALLEY, KENT

Plate I. *The Iron Age farmstead at Farningham Hill (from the air)*

EXCAVATIONS
IN THE DARENT VALLEY, KENT

The detailed reports on the discovery and excavation of a complete Iron Age Farmstead site at Farningham Hill; the excavation of important Prehistoric, Roman and Saxon sites at Darenth and the excavation of the south-east area of the Archbishops of Canterbury's medieval manor-house and Tudor palace at Otford.

BY

BRIAN PHILP

With main contributions by Joanna Bird, Alison Locker, Peter Couldrey, Derek Garrod, Peter Keller, Keith Parfitt, John Willson and Andrew Woodcock.

FOURTH RESEARCH REPORT IN THE
KENT MONOGRAPH SERIES (ISSN 0141 - 2264)

Published by:–
Kent Archaeological Rescue Unit
CIB Headquarters, Dover Castle, Kent.

1984

Dedicated to

DEREK GARROD and JOHN WILLSON for their enthusiasm, loyalty and dedicated work for the Kent Unit (CIB) and Kent Archaeology over very many years.

Produced for the Unit by Alan Sutton Publishing Limited, Gloucester
Printed in Great Britain

The Unit is greatly indebted to the **DEPARTMENT OF THE ENVIRONMENT, THE COUNCIL FOR KENTISH ARCHAEOLOGY, THE KENT COUNTY COUNCIL, THE KENT ARCHAEOLOGICAL TRUST** and **ESSO PETROLEUM Co. LTD.** for grants towards the cost of this publication.

CONTENTS

LIST OF FIGURES

LIST OF PLATES

ABOUT THIS REPORT

This Report is the fourth in the Kent Monograph Series. It largely follows the pattern set by the three previous volumes which were:

Vol. I Excavations at Faversham 1965 (published in 1968 by the C.K.A.)
Vol. II Excavations in West Kent 1960–1970 (published in 1973 by the Kent Unit)
Vol. III The Excavation of the Roman Forts of the Classis Britannica at Dover 1970–1977 (published in 1981 by the Kent Unit).

As with those Reports the entire proceeds from sales go to covering the costs of printing this volume, or into a fund for the publication of subsequent volumes. Other Reports are already in preparation.

The subject of this Report is work by the Unit on three major sites in the Darent Valley carried out in the period 1972–1975. Short interim accounts of this work have already appeared in the *Kent Archaeological Review, Britannia, Medieval Archaeology,* or in popular booklets produced for the general public.

As with previous Reports in this series, footnotes have been eliminated and the bibliographical references, numbered progressively throughout the text, are listed in that order at the back. These show as numbers placed in round-brackets and prefixed by the letters Ref. (e.g. Ref. 195). Similarly, the illustrated objects are also numbered progressively through the text, this time prefixed by the letters No. or Nos. so as to eliminate recurring finds-numbers and thus hopefully avoiding confusion. Coins (not illustrated) are noted in the text by the word 'Coin' followed by a number which refers to a register of coins. References to drawn sections and layers included in the text are shown in brackets prefixed by the letters S. and L., respectively (e.g. S.19, L.21). As with the other Kent Monographs the main text is set in 11 on 12 point Bembo typeface, at about 800 words to a page.

At the request of the Ancient Monuments Inspectorate of the D.o.E., several of the specialist reports have been reproduced in microfiche and are enclosed in the envelope attached to the inside back cover.

FOREWORD

This is the fourth volume published by the Kent Archaeological Rescue Unit and is like the others written by Mr. Brian Philp with contributions by members of the Unit and other specialists.

The sites so well reported in this book range from prehistoric to medieval times and all depended on the River Darent. It is thus a pointer to archaeologists, both professional and amateur, to pay particular attention to water. Rivers, streams and springs are all rich sources for us, but we must all remember that before large-scale modern water-extraction the rivers were larger and faster.

To all Men of Kent and Kentish Men this book is essential reading. Of very special interest is the account of the discovery and total excavation of the Iron Age Farmstead on Farningham Hill which was completed only two days before its final destruction by the contractors building the M20. With its detailed publication here it will long stand as the type-site for South East England. Of almost equal significance is the battle to preserve the south-east corner of the great palace at Otford, with its vast masonry and complex structural history, medieval and Tudor. The highly skilled and efficient excavation of this site by the Unit, in just 36 days non-stop, drew huge public and official support and resulted in the site being bought from the builders and thus saved for the Nation. So, too, were vital prehistoric, Roman and Saxon, structures and other evidence recorded ahead of total destruction by the sewerpipe contractors at Darenth.

We should all recognize what great work has been done by Mr. Brian Philp and the dedicated members of the Kent Archaeological Rescue Unit. Mr. Philp's success was foretold by Sir Mortimer Wheeler and in 1982 he was rightly honoured by membership of the Society of Antiquaries. His inspired leadership has been an example to many and particularly to the young students in the Unit's annual training digs in Kent. Some students have since gone on to read archaeology at university and others have become professional archaeologists. Thus, a body of opinion is being built up in the county which has a sound basic appreciation of the subject. The future, therefore, is assured.

Mr. Philp appears to be tireless without ever a day's rest. In addition to his fulltime duties, every Sunday he and many volunteers take part in rescue digs all over the county. He is a fighter who does not suffer fools gladly. He points his lance and goes straight forward to attain what he believes to be right. Certainly, without his major battle the Roman 'Painted House' at Dover would still be hidden underground. Unique in Britain it is the finest example here of a Roman domestic building with high, decorated walls.

In the past 20 years rescue archaeologists have found and dealt with many sites as a result of road-works, sewer-schemes and numerous other developments. That these sites have been interpreted so well and the finds processed and assessed so quickly, is remarkable. It is even more remarkable that Mr. Philp has been able to publish so soon. The whole pace of archaeological work has increased enormously and Mr. Philp is one of the few who can keep up with it. The very number of new sites shows how many more there are yet to be found in Kent. I know that Mr. Philp and the Rescue Unit will be in the vanguard of such new discoveries.

Monckton of Brenchley,
Runhams, Harrietsham.

November, 1983.

CHAPTER I.

INTRODUCTION

A. RESCUE WORK IN KENT AND THE DARENT VALLEY

The numerous official, commercial and private developments in busy, heavily populated Kent, since World War II, have destroyed dozens of important archaeological sites about the county. The scale of destruction, through mineral extraction; by motorway construction; during housing, factory and school-building programmes; by new farming methods and even coastal erosion, has steadily increased.

Almost nothing was done about this growing destruction, in the fifteen years following the War, either by local or county authorities, or by local or county history societies. Apart from occasional forays by the then Ministry of Works, the only real rescue effort came from a very few concerned local archaeologists, such as Ronald Jessup and Norman Cook at Snodland (Ref. 1), Sheppard Frere at Canterbury (Ref. 2) and the writer at Reculver (Ref. 3), all of whom not only carried out the fieldwork, but equally importantly, published the results.

The situation in Kent (at least) rapidly improved by the early 1960's with the formation of several local groups, mostly determined to give rescue-work first priority. The first was the Reculver Excavation Group formed in 1957, the second, the West Kent Border Archaeological Group formed in 1960 and the Lower Medway Archaeological Group formed in 1961. By 1964 some ten, or more, groups had formed into an active association under a new Council for Kentish Archaeology banner, which largely filled the considerable vacuum in Kent archaeology (Ref. 4). Large annual conferences were organised, the quarterly *Kent Archaeological Review* was launched and a county-wide emergency scheme launched under the direction of the writer. The latter worked well for several years, notably at Polhill in 1964 and 1967 (Ref. 5), Faversham in 1965 (Ref. 6) and Radfield (Ref. 7), though the system largely hinged upon the availability of experienced site-directors. By 1970, with the advent of the massive Dover town-centre programme and a marked increase in re-development generally and motorway construction in particular, the need for a fulltime team was clear and in 1971 the Kent Archaeological Rescue Unit was formed (Ref. 8).

By then rescue-work was needed over much of the county, both in areas where there was total inactivity and in some areas where local expertise and resources were hopelessly inadequate to deal with urgent large-scale situations. In West Kent one of the areas regularly threatened was the Darent Valley (Figs. 1 and 2), a strip of land following the River Darent from Otford to Sevenoaks, a distance of about 12 miles (about 20 km.). Here a variety of schemes was causing serious damage to known and new sites and all of these required urgent attention. Three of the major sites dealt with between 1972 and 1975 are covered by this volume and range in date from the Mesolithic of about 5000 B.C. to a Royal Palace of the 16th century. Prior to 1972 the major threats in the valley had been dealt with by the part-time West Kent Archaeological Group, under the direction of the writer, such as the Anglo-Saxon cemetery at Polhill, Operation Gaspipe in 1968 and the Darenth Roman Villa in 1969. All of these sites and many others were fully published in 1973 (Ref. 9).

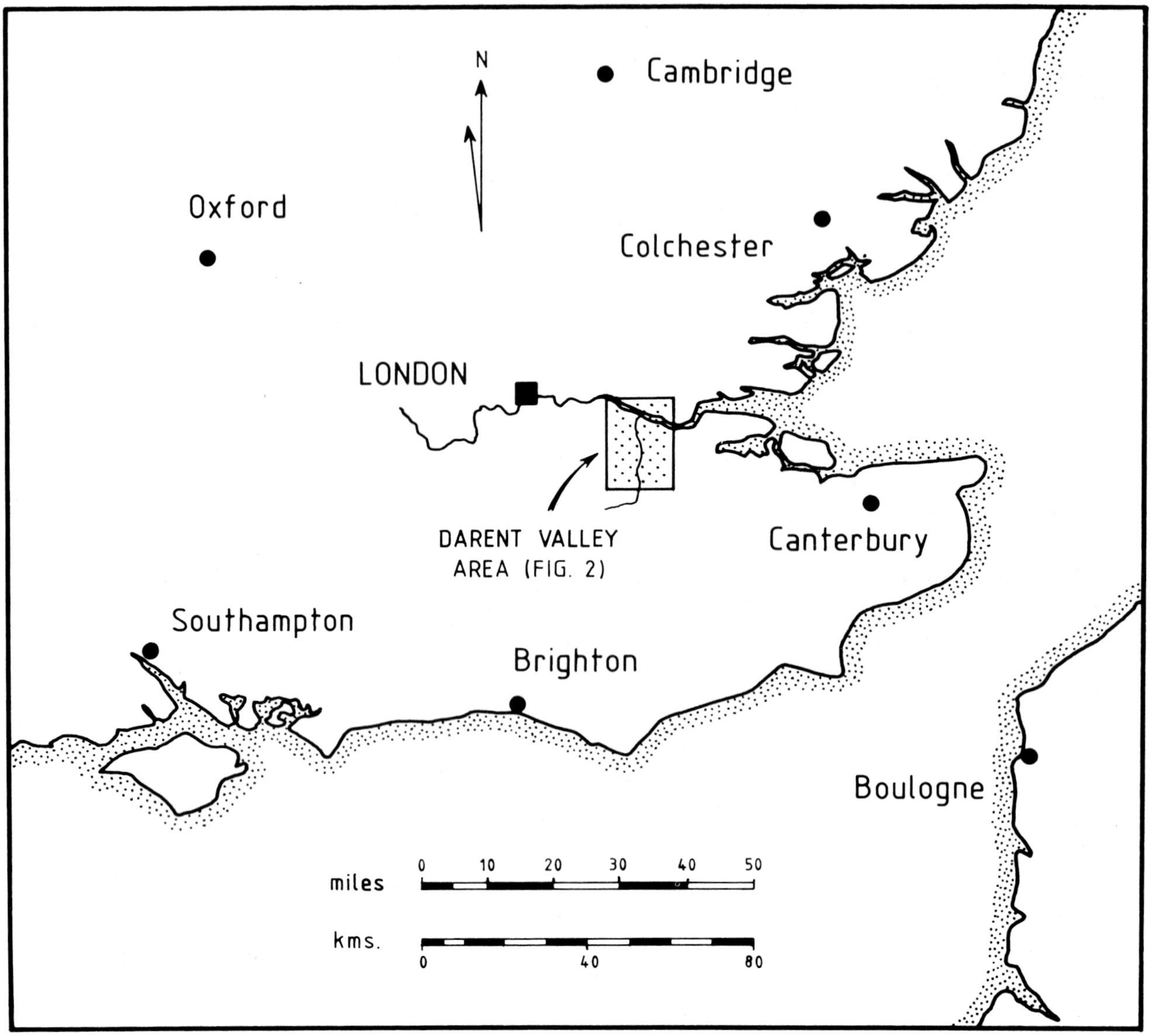

Fig. 1. *Map of Southern England showing the Darent Valley area.*

(1). The Darent Valley Sewer Pipeline

The first major full time situation arose in January, 1972 and lasted for six months. This was done on behalf of the Department of the Environment and involved a watching-brief, instant recording and several important excavations during the laying of a four mile length of sewer from Dartford to Farningham. A contractor, working for the West Kent Sewerage Board, was laying a new concrete sewer-pipe to replace an ancient large-diameter pipe that ran along the bottom of the valley (Plate II). Sometimes the new pipeline crossed fresh ground and occasionally new branch lines were laid. The greatest problem to all concerned was that the new pipe was mostly laid at a depth of about 16 ft. (5 m.), often below the water-table and frequently in loose gravel. As a result the contractors' trench was mostly about 20 ft. (6 m.) wide at the top, often flooded and largely populated with workmen, machines, large concrete pipes and pumps (Plate III). In addition, work was carried out simultaneously at various points and the trench was often dug and backfilled in the space of only two or three days.

The archaeological work involved constant watch along the whole length of the line and detailed survey work after areas had been topsoiled. Several sites were exposed at this stage and others as the pipe-trench was dug. All were dealt with under pressure, either by detailed recording or full excavation (Ref. 10). The most complex was that at the known Roman Villa complex at Darenth where evidence of Mesolithic, Neolithic, Bronze Age/Iron Age, Roman and Saxon settlements were located and excavated ahead of destruction (Ref. 11). This multi-period site is fully published in this volume, whilst the other sites on the pipeline are being published elsewhere (Ref. 12).

(2). The Kent Motorway Programme

Between 1974 and 1976 the same general area was subjected to an even greater threat, this time in the form of the construction of two lengths of 6-lane motorway. Both required fulltime work by the Unit, the first in 1974 on the Dartford-Swanley Link (M25) and the second in 1975–6 on the Swanley-West Kingsdown section of the M20 (Ref. 13). Again more sites were located and excavated ahead of destruction and the most significant, that of the Iron Age farmstead on Farningham Hill, is fully reported in this volume. The site lay totally within the motorway fences and it was fully excavated by the Unit just two days ahead of its destruction by the motorway contractors.

(3). The Royal Palace at Otford

In much the same period other rescue situations arose in the Darent Valley and were dealt with by the Unit. Of these the most important was the site of the medieval manor-house and Tudor Palace of the Archbishops of Canterbury at Otford. Here, in March 1974, the south-east corner of the palace was earmarked for instant destruction and only rapid large-scale excavations by the Unit non-stop for five weeks saved the day. This site is also fully reported in this volume.

B. AIMS AND METHODS

On all the sites the terms of reference were to record the archaeological features and structures ahead of destruction and to recover adequate dating evidence. Seldom was there much time to prepare a detailed plan of action and a highly flexible system had to be developed. Seldom were the circumstances ideal, seldom was the weather right and never was there adequate funding. Mostly, the work had to be fitted around the development projects which were themselves difficult and very costly if delayed. Accordingly, the system had to be one which worked effectively, was acceptable to everyone on the shared sites and allowed for all eventualities.

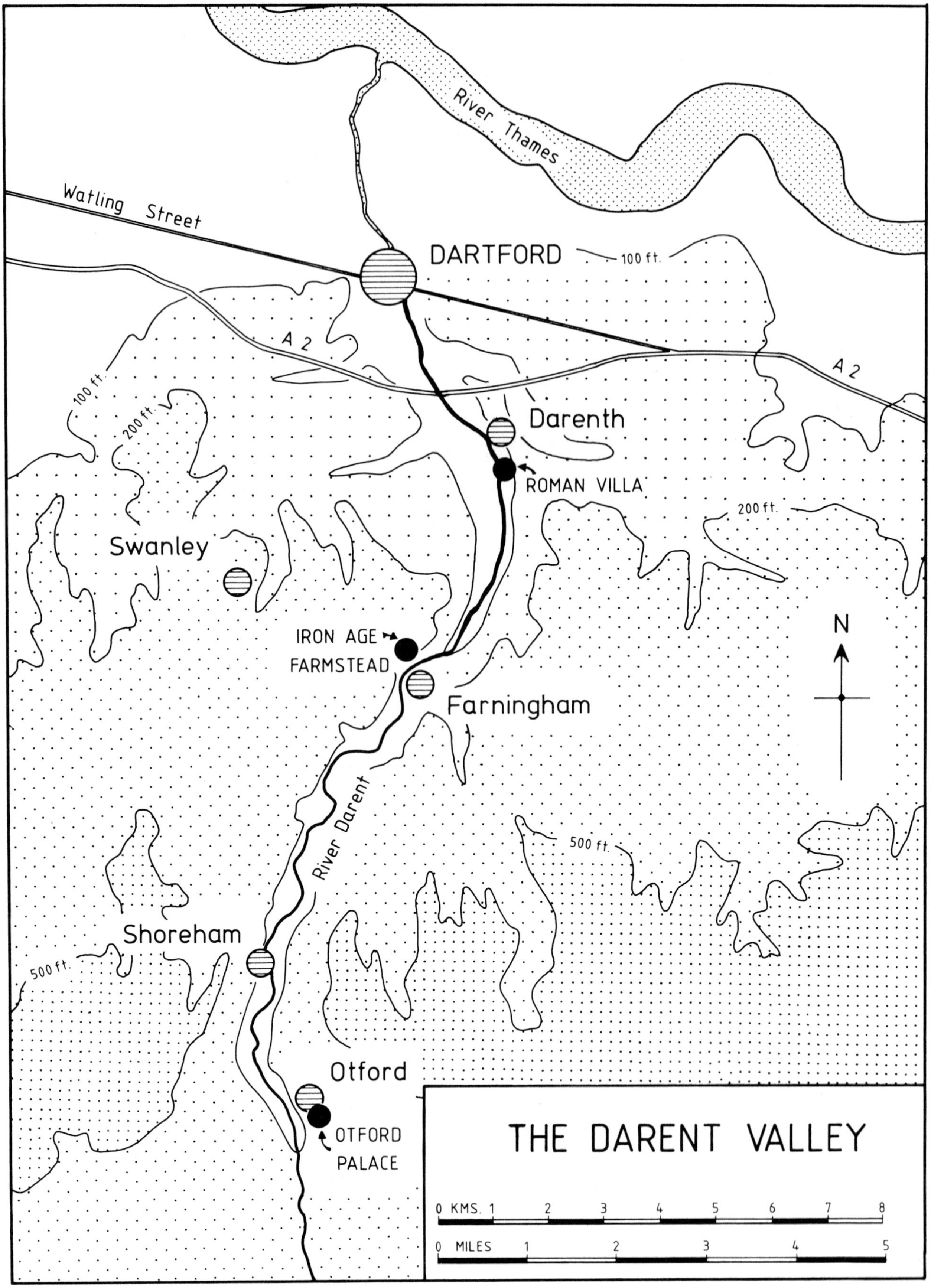

Fig. 2. *Map of the Darent Valley showing some present villages and the three excavated sites covered by this volume.*

Happily, the C.I.B. Unit had evolved such a system over many years of rescue-work in Kent. The first essential was to have teams of people able to work skilfully and well under difficult conditions. Here the Unit had several dedicated supervisors whom it had trained for these occasions. Similarly, it also had several excellent part-time staff and the loyal support of a large number of experienced volunteers, either members of the Unit, or of the West Kent Archaeological Group. On some sites, notably at Otford Palace, additional voluntary help was readily given by members of other responsible groups. The second essential was to have a full-time presence on the sites so that any new situation could be assessed and dealt with in the shortest possible time. This also allowed work in the intervals when the workmen stopped. Third, it was essential to have all the tools and recording equipment close at hand and this was best achieved by means of a mobile recording caravan which also served as a site office. Recording and excavation was then carried out and related to local datum-points which were fixed permanently when the contractors were finished. The finds from the site were quickly removed to the Unit's headquarters where the cleaning, marking and sorting took place.

Occasionally, it was possible to press for preservation where major sites were concerned. The sewer pipe-line was in fact moved by mutual consent off the walls of the Darenth Roman Villa. Subsequently, the Unit planned and carried out a programme of backfilling the 1894–5 excavation that had remained open for about 80 years. At Horton Kirby (publication pending) money was raised to move a branch-sewer to avoid the virtually complete destruction of the newly discovered Roman granary. At Otford three building plots were actually bought from the builder so that the south-east corner of the palace was not destroyed. All these sites now survive and details of the battle to save Otford Palace are given in the excavation Report.

C. ACKNOWLEDGEMENTS

Thanks, as always, must be due first and foremost to the large group of part-time and full time members of the C.I.B. teams who carried out the programmes of excavation over the three years covered by this Report. Without their hard work and enthusiasm nothing would have been achieved. More than 200 people helped with the various projects and the results stand as a tribute to them.

Although it is difficult to name them all, several do deserve a special mention. Of the many supervisors Pat Crozier, Jeanne Newbury, Edna Philp, Gerald Clewley, Howard Davies, Derek Garrod and Andrew Norris must be thanked for their excellent work. Of the many people who assisted with the excavations at least ten deserve a special mention for their hard work over extended periods. These include Miss Audrey Button, Messrs. Tim Allen, Peter Couldrey, Trevor Dennis, Anthony Emms, Maurice Godfrey, Peter Grant, Ronald Mummery, Keith Nicol and Edward Taylor. Many others are acknowledged in the text of the appropriate site.

Thanks are also due to several other people and organisations for their ready support. In particular to the Ancient Monuments Branch of the Dept. of the Environment for providing most of the funds for the three major excavations. Next to the West Kent Main Sewerage Board for its co-operation on the Darent Valley pipeline and to its main contractor A. Waddington & Sons Ltd., of London, S.W.10. Also to the Sevenoaks District Council for its agreement to purchase the site at Otford Palace and to the South East Road Construction Unit for its support on the M20 Motorway. Finally, the Council for Kentish Archaeology actively encouraged and supported all the excavations and many of its member-groups offered assistance with the work. Notable contributions were made by members of the Dover, Faversham, Reculver, Sittingbourne, Springhead, Upchurch and West Kent groups. To everyone concerned the writer extends his warmest thanks.

It is also a pleasure to acknowledge the help of various specialists for their contributions, notably Mrs. Joanna Bird for her report on the samian pottery from Darenth; Mrs. Alison Locker for her reports on the animal bones and soils from Farningham Hill; Mr. Peter Couldrey for his reports on the Iron Age pottery from Farningham Hill and Darenth; Mr. Derek Garrod for his report on the post-medieval pottery from Otford; Mr. Peter Keller for his report on the medieval pottery from Otford; Mr. John Willson for his report on the Roman and Saxon pottery from Darenth and to Dr. Andrew Woodcock for his report on the Mesolithic flints from Darenth. Other specialist contributions are acknowledged in the text.

Thanks are also due to the team who carried out the difficult programme of post-excavation work in readiness for publication. In particular Messrs. Mike Dutto, Colin Martin, John Willson and Trevor Woodman produced the finished maps, plans and sections from the site drawings. Mrs. Wendy Williams, Miss Joy Wheeler, Mr. Ralph Mills and Mr. Jonathan Joy kindly provided all the drawings of the illustrated objects. Miss Christine Rosa has acted as the editorial assistant throughout and Mrs. Pam Barrett has typed and re-typed the text and specialist reports. All the photographs were taken by the writer.

CHAPTER II.

THE IRON AGE FARMSTEAD ON FARNINGHAM HILL

SUMMARY

This late pre-Roman Iron Age farmstead, sited on a steep chalk hillside above the River Darent in West Kent, was totally excavated by the Kent Unit in 1975 ahead of motorway construction. A roughly pentagonal ditched enclosure of about 0·2 hectares (half an acre) had four original entrance causeways, one of which was later removed. Internally, a probable circular hut, about 5 m. in diameter and protected by a shallow uphill gully, and three groups of pits, largely filled the western part of the site. The largely open eastern side may have been used for storage, drying or for cattle and sheep pens.

Sixteen of the pits were substantial and were probably dug as underground silos, probably for storage of crops grown in small nearby fields. A minimum of 165 pottery vessels, found discarded in the pits and ditches, date between 50 B.C. and A.D. 50. The discarded meat bones show that cattle were the main source of meat, supplemented to a lesser degree by sheep, pig, red deer and roe deer. Barley and wheat seeds were found in some of the pits.

The farmstead probably represents a single family-unit, one of many suspected in the West Kent area. It is now the main type-site for late-Iron Age farmstead enclosures in S.E. England.

CONTENTS

A. INTRODUCTION

This site (NGR. TQ. 5451.6736) lay, until 1975, on open farmland on Farningham Hill in the parish of Farningham, some 500 m. north-west of the parish church (Fig. 3). It was then crossed by a public footpath and its centre lay about 80 m. from the hedge on the south side of the field. It is now occupied by a deep cutting carrying the M20 Motorway. The farmstead site occupied an exposed area of about half an acre on a marked south-facing slope nearly half way up the curving west side of the valley of the River Darent. The bedrock is Upper Chalk, capped by a thin layer of fine ploughsoil and it seems likely that continual ploughing over several centuries has cut into the site and reduced most of the features and possibly removed others. The top of the slope is crowned with a zone of Woolwich Beds which now supports Farningham Wood. The adjacent valley bottom is at about 35 m. O.D., the Iron Age farmstead between the 65 and 73 m. contours and the crest at about 120 m. The valley floor is about 150 m. wide here and the river, allowing for any movement since Iron Age times, would have been between 300 and 450 m. from the farmstead.

In 1973 it became clear that the construction of a 9 km. length of the Mid Kent Motorway (M20) between Swanley and West Kingsdown was imminent and that sites might be encountered along the route and rapidly destroyed. The fulltime K.A.R.U., responsible for motorway archaeology in Kent (Ref. 13), devised a programme of work with the support of the Council for Kentish Archaeology, the latter being the federation of responsible local groups. This included surveys from the air and on the ground and some preliminary excavation. One trial trench, some 30 m. in length, dug largely at random, in March, 1973 on Farningham Hill missed the farmstead enclosure by only 30 m. In March 1975, a detailed air survey by the Unit flying from Biggin Hill, of soil-marks in the Farningham Hill area, revealed the faint outline of a sub-rectangular enclosure exactly on the line of the proposed Motorway. This was provisionally identified as an Iron Age farmstead enclosure and as such well within the Unit's research policy for Iron Age settlements in Kent. This policy aims at substantially excavating both isolated farmstead sites and complex unenclosed settlements, where threatened by destruction and conforms with the recommendations of the regional rescue committee (Ref. 14). In the period 1972–1982 the Unit dealt with five Iron Age farmstead sites and also part of the major open settlement at Grain. The Unit obtained permission for 'entry' on the M20 in April, 1975 after the final crop had been lifted and then it excavated mechanically a trial-trench down the slope of Farningham Hill, roughly on the centre-line of the intended motorway. Within the first hour this located the ditches on both sides of the enclosure. Full-scale excavation started on 23rd April and continued non-stop for 94 days (13 weeks) ending on 25th July, 1975 (Plate I). During this time the main contractors, McAlpine Limited, stripped the topsoil off most of the motorway route east of the River Darent. During the latter part of the excavation it was also possible to carry out short rescue-excavations on two nearby sites threatened by the motorway construction and to patrol the whole route. In addition two more linear ditches (A and B on Fig. 3) were found west of the enclosure and six more ditches (C-H) east of the enclosure. These were either Romano-British or later. The excavation of the Iron Age farmstead was completed two days before the contractor's machinery moved into this area. As its ditches all lay within the motorway fences it was soon totally destroyed by a cutting some 2 to 8 m. deep created to take the two carriageways up Farningham Hill.

Ten members of the Unit, working on a fulltime basis, rotated to provide core-staff seven days a week for the whole period. These were supplemented by some 40 volunteer members of the Unit and the West Kent Archaeological Group and by another 31 students, who in July, took part in the third Darent Valley Archaeological Training School. The site was stripped mechanically on three widely-spaced days with plant hired casually and this work supplemented by manual excavation. As it was initially uncertain how long the site would be available the main effort was concentrated on examining all the features within the ditched area and on cutting across the ditches at two metre intervals. Eventually, it was possible to excavate the ditches entirely and thus the whole site (Ref. 15).

The excavation archive for this 13-week excavation consists of 44 site-plans and sections, 206 recorded contexts, 166 photographs, 23 boxes of finds and two site-notebooks. Of this three plans, 38 sections and eleven photographs covering almost all the features, are published here. The unpublished sections are mostly alternative sections across the enclosure ditches. All the pottery has been classified by fabric and is described here in detail as it provides vital dating evidence and also it represents the largest group of its type so far recovered from a controlled excavation in West Kent. All the animal bone, soils and seeds have been studied and are included here.

The post-excavation archive contains the analyses and summaries of features, contexts and finds. The archive is stored in the Kent Unit's security-controlled headquarters at Dover Castle to assist its ongoing work on Iron Age settlement sites in Kent, but where it may be consulted on request. Its final destination should be Rochester Museum, with copies placed in the National Monuments Record.

Acknowledgements

The writer wishes to acknowledge the large number of people who helped make both the excavation and the post-excavation work such a success. Thanks are firstly due to the South East Road Construction Unit for its ready co-operation at all stages of the work and also for supplying office facilities at Swanley. In particular Mr. Carss the Resident Engineer must be thanked for his interest and support. The Ancient Monuments Branch of the Dept. of the Environment, largely through the good offices of Dr. C. Young, kindly provided the finance for the operation. Mr. Kenneth McAlpine kindly provided his personal helicopter for photographing the overall site and generally encouraged the work.

On site the work was supervised by the writer and Mr. Derek Garrod, with supervision of selected areas carried out by Mrs. Pat Crozier, Mrs. Jeanne Newberry and Mrs. Edna Philp. The other fulltime members were Mrs. Miranda Saunders and Messrs. Anthony Emms, Keith Nicol and Andrew Norris, the latter being responsible for the excellent site-plans. Thanks are also due to the 71 volunteers who helped at various times and of whom the following deserve a special mention for particularly hard work. Mrs. K. Nurse, Misses Jane Gutteridge and Jean Taylor and Messrs. Tim Allen, David Bolton, Peter Couldrey, Richard Garnett, Maurice Godfrey, Peter Grant, Neil Lake, Ron Mummery, Edward Taylor and John Willson. The substantial support of the West Kent Archaeological Group and the Dover Archaeological Group, both active members of the Council for Kentish Archaeology, is also gratefully acknowledged.

Of the specialist help with the excavated material thanks are due to several people. Firstly, to Mr. Peter Couldrey for his excellent report on the pottery from the site and for his catalogue of the illustrated vessels; to Mrs. Alison Locker for her reports on the animal bone; to Mr. Terry O'Conner for his report on the mollusca; to Mrs. D. Vaughan for her comments on the charred grains and to Mr. Keith Parfitt for his notes on the small finds.

Of help with the preparation of this report for publication thanks are due to Mr. Jonathan Joy and John Willson for drawing most of the pottery; to Mrs. Wendy Williams for drawing the small finds; to Mr. John Willson for preparing the site-plan and the sections of the pits, post-holes and ditches and to Mr. Mike Dutto for the small-scale drawings. Mrs. Pam Barrett has kindly typed the text and Miss Christine Rosa has carried out various editorial duties.

B. THE EXCAVATED STRUCTURES AND FEATURES (Fig. 4)

The excavation revealed the enclosure ditches on all sides, four entrances and some 56 features within the area enclosed by the ditches. These included a shallow gully and a group of post-holes, concentrated slightly north-west of the physical centre of the site, which seem to represent a circular hut. Three small pits and eight small post-holes mostly lay along the eastern side of the site, whilst another 21 pits lay in three well-defined groups at the south end or on the west side. The various structures and features are described by type, beginning with the enclosure itself. Eight other ditches (marked A-H) found on Farningham Hill, either east or west of the enclosure during the contractors topsoiling operations, are described at the end.

(1). The Enclosure (Fig. 4)

The excavation revealed the entire plan of the enclosure and confirmed the outline suggested by the air photograph. The contractors subsequent large-scale soil stripping failed to produce related features immediately outside the enclosure, on either the east or west sides and it seems highly probable that substantially the whole site was excavated.

The work revealed that the site, almost certainly that of a farmstead, had been laid out entirely between the 65 and 73 m. contours on a north-south slope with a gradient of about one in eight. The enclosure had been created by the excavation of deep ditches on all sides with gaps left for four original entrances. Four (later three) distinct ditches, of varying lengths and form had created a broadly pentagonal plan. The internal length of the enclosure on the north-south axis was about 63 m. and the internal east-west width was about 40 m. Allowing for the pentagonal plan the internal area was about 0·2 hectares (about half an acre). The effective perimeter, with ditches and entrances combined, had a length of about 182 m.

As regards the interior of the enclosure it is clear that the known features largely cluster in the western half of the site, but it is likely that superficial features have been removed by ploughing over many years. Even so major features are largely absent from the eastern half of the site. Similarly, no major features occur along the inner lip of the ditch and generally there is a free zone 4 to 6 m. wide that seems unused. It seems possible that the chalk dug from the ditches could have been placed here to serve as an additional barrier to the ditch. Only in the south-west area did two small pits (Pit 7 and Pit 8) encroach on this free zone and anyway these could have been later features.

(2). The Ditches

Whilst it seems highly probable that the three main ditches forming the boundaries of the original enclosure were all dug at the same time, variations in their depths and profiles were recorded. Each ditch is described separately here.

THE SOUTH EAST DITCH (Fig. 5, Sections 1–4 and Plates II and III)

This ditch was broadly L-shaped in plan, with its two arms of widely differing lengths and the angle between them about 100°. The shorter north-east arm was about 18 m. long and the longer south-east arm about 54 m., thus producing a total length of about 72 m.

The ditch was largely V-shaped in profile, generally 2·00–2·50 m. wide at the top, only 20 to 40 cm. wide across its flat base and had survived to a depth of between 1·00 and 1·40 m. Both ends were partially squared-off and part of the southern end of the longest arm had been damaged by a recent disturbance.

Rather surprisingly there was no primary silting of fine soil in the bottom of the ditch and if this had formed then it must have been removed. Instead, rather more than half the depth of the ditch was filled with loose chalk rubble containing only small amounts of brown loam and flint (S.1, L.2; S.2, L.3; S.3, L.3; and S.4, L.6).

This lower filling contained animal bones, some 306 fire-cracked flints, a small chalk spindle-whorl (No. 2) and some 32 potsherds representing at least 12 vessels, of which three have been illustrated (Nos. 102–104). It seems highly probable that the chalk rubble had weathered and frosted off the upper sides of the ditch and fallen into the lower half. Indeed the various ditch profiles tend to support this suggestion, for although they start as distinct V-shapes they splay outwards near the top where the greatest degree of weathering would occur. If this is what happened, as appears very likely, then the original widths would have been about 1·40 to 1·75 m.

The upper filling of the ditch consisted of brown loam or alternate layers of brown loam and chalk rubble (S.1, L.1; S.2, L.1; S.3, L.1; S.4, L.2–4) all with occasional flint. In one place (S.1), where the west lip was square-cut, it is possible that the upper part of the ditch was re-cut. The upper filling contained quantities of Iron Age material including animal bones and some 531 potsherds representing a maximum of 106 pots, of which 30 have been illustrated (Nos. 105–134). It also contained fragments of quern, another chalk spindle whorl (No. 1), a carved chalk object (No. 3), a brooch pin (No. 5), a potin coin (Coin No. 1), 1424 fire-cracked flints, a fragment of a loomweight (No. 13) and a fourth century Roman Coin (Coin No. 3). Post-medieval roof tile was recovered from the disturbance near the south end.

THE SOUTH DITCH (Fig. 5, Section 5 and Plate IV)

This short ditch separated the two entrances at the south end of the site and had a total length of only 7.70 m. It was straight and had squared-off terminals. It had a sharp V-shaped profile, was mostly 2·30 m. wide at the top, about 40 cm. wide at the base and was up to 1·50 m. deep.

The base of this ditch was covered with a thin layer of fine soft chalk (S.5, L.9) and the lower third was filled with chalk rubble (S.5, L.8), probably formed as elsewhere on the site, by weathering of the upper sides. This was sealed by a band of charcoal (S.5, L.7), probably thrown in as domestic debris, which was in turn sealed by light brown loam (S.5, L.6) and more chalk rubble (S.5, L.5), here regarded as the middle filling. The upper filling contained layers of light brown loam and chalk rubble (S.5, L.2–4) and finally a layer of dark brown loam, carbon and chalk lumps (S.5, L.1). The primary and lower fillings contained 165 fire-cracked stones, 39 potsherds from a maximum of eight vessels, of which two have been drawn (Nos. 135 and 136). The layer of charcoal sealing the lower deposit contained 450 fire-cracked flints, 92 potsherds from a maximum of seven vessels, of which three have been illustrated (Nos. 137–139). The middle filling contained 79 fire-cracked stones, 22 potsherds from a maximum of seven vessels, of which two have been illustrated (Nos. 140 and 141). The upper filling contained animal bone, 3,217 fire-cracked flints, two fragments of a possible clay 'reel' (No. 9) and 394 potsherds from a maximum of 34 vessels, of which eight have been illustrated (Nos. 142–149). It also contained three fragments of quernstone (No. 10), a single piece of iron slag and a possible polished stone rubber (No. 12). The lower and middle fillings seem to represent weathered chalk and soil forming in the ditch and containing scattered domestic rubbish, but the upper filling included large quantities of rubbish.

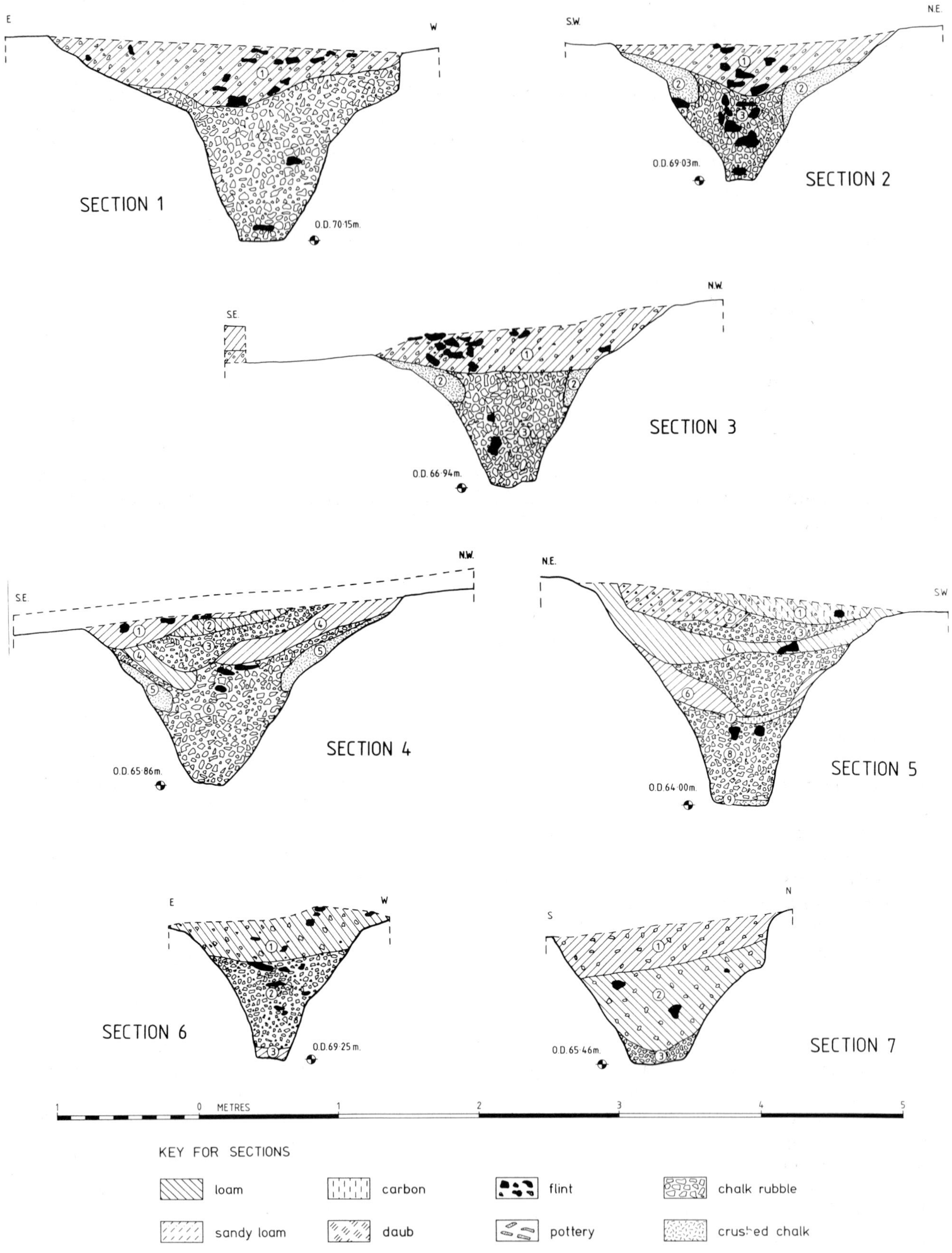

Fig. 5. *Sections across the Ditches of the Iron Age Enclosure, Farningham Hill.*

THE NORTH WEST DITCH (Fig. 5, Sections 6 and 7 and Plates V and VI)

This was the longest ditch found on the site and in plan it formed a broad arc along the north and west sides of the enclosure and it had a total length of about 86 m. In general it lacked the straightness and uniformity of the two other main ditches, except at its south-west end where it was largely straight and appeared as a likely continuation of the south-west side of the enclosure. The rest of the ditch then followed an uncharacteristic line and effectively destroyed the otherwise sub-rectangular arrangement and in effect created a fifth side. This tends to suggest that the northern arm of this ditch was dug with much less precision and that it could have been the last completed.

The variations in its width, depth and profile are here significant and close examination revealed that this ditch had originally been in two lengths, one divided from the other by an entrance causeway (North West Entrance), later removed. The evidence for this was that the chalk base here was at least 20 cm. higher, over a length of only 3·40 m., than the rest of the ditch. It seems clear that the deeper sections of ditch on each side represent the original ends. When the original chalk causeway between them was later moved the original ditches had already partially silted with weathered chalk rubble and the base of the newly cut section was simply and logically taken down to that level.

Allowing for the sloping ends of the original ditches it seems likely that the original entrance here was no more than 3 m. wide. This would leave the north-east ditch with a length of about 43 m. and the corresponding western ditch with a length of about 39·50 m. and thus the original entance lay roughly in the middle.

It was also clear that the south end of this ditch had been recut at least once. A marked cut on both sides at a point 12 m. from the South West Entrance (at Z on the plan), suggests that this length was at sometime recut. Similarly, a marginal increase in width over the next 13 m. suggests another recut at sometime. No stratigraphic differentiation was noted at these points, largely due to the fact that all the ditches were about half filled with uniform chalk rubble.

The original ditches (S.6) were about 1·50 to 2·70 m. wide at the top, about 0·90 to 1·15 m. deep and 22 to 40 cm. wide at the base. The later recuts (S.7) were 1·60 to 2·00 m. wide at the top, 1·05 m. in depth and up to 40 cm. wide at the base. In all cases the main lower filling consisted of chalk rubble (S.6, L.2 and S.7, L.2–3), again probably derived from weathering of the upper sides and again containing scattered domestic rubbish including animal bones and 46 potsherds the latter representing a maximum of 19 pots of which three have been illustrated (Nos. 150–152). The lower filling also contained a fragment of a quernstone and 753 fire-cracked stones. The upper part contained a mixture of brown loam and light chalk rubble (S.6, L.1 and S.7, L.1), again probably representing progressive silting and containing quantities of domestic rubbish. This included animal bones and some 182 sherds, representing a maximum of 38 vessels, of which eight have been illustrated (Nos. 153–160). The upper filling also contained a blue bead (No. 4), an iron brooch (No. 6), a bronze scabbard chape (No. 7) and 1,487 fire-cracked flints.

It is clear that all the ditches had partly filled with chalk rubble and it seems likely that this was caused by weathering, particularly frost-action, from the sides. However much the ditches may have been cleaned out initially it is certain that after an unknown period of time this was not done. Indeed some domestic rubbish, including animal bones and at least 118 potsherds, were thrown into the ditch whilst the chalk rubble was collecting. Subsequently, the ditches continued to silt with chalk, soil and more domestic rubbish, including another 1,222 potsherds. It seems clear that by this stage the ditches were no longer fulfilling their original function, but were being used as a dump for rubbish. Indeed by the time the settlement was eventually abandoned the ditches were no more than shallow hollows in the ground.

The bulk of the pottery in the upper part of the ditches was found in either the small South Ditch or the eastern arm of the South East Ditch. Similarly, the bulk of the fire-cracked stones came from the same general areas and this shows the main rubbish-dumping areas. Significantly, or not, this is well away from the Hut, but on its downhill side.

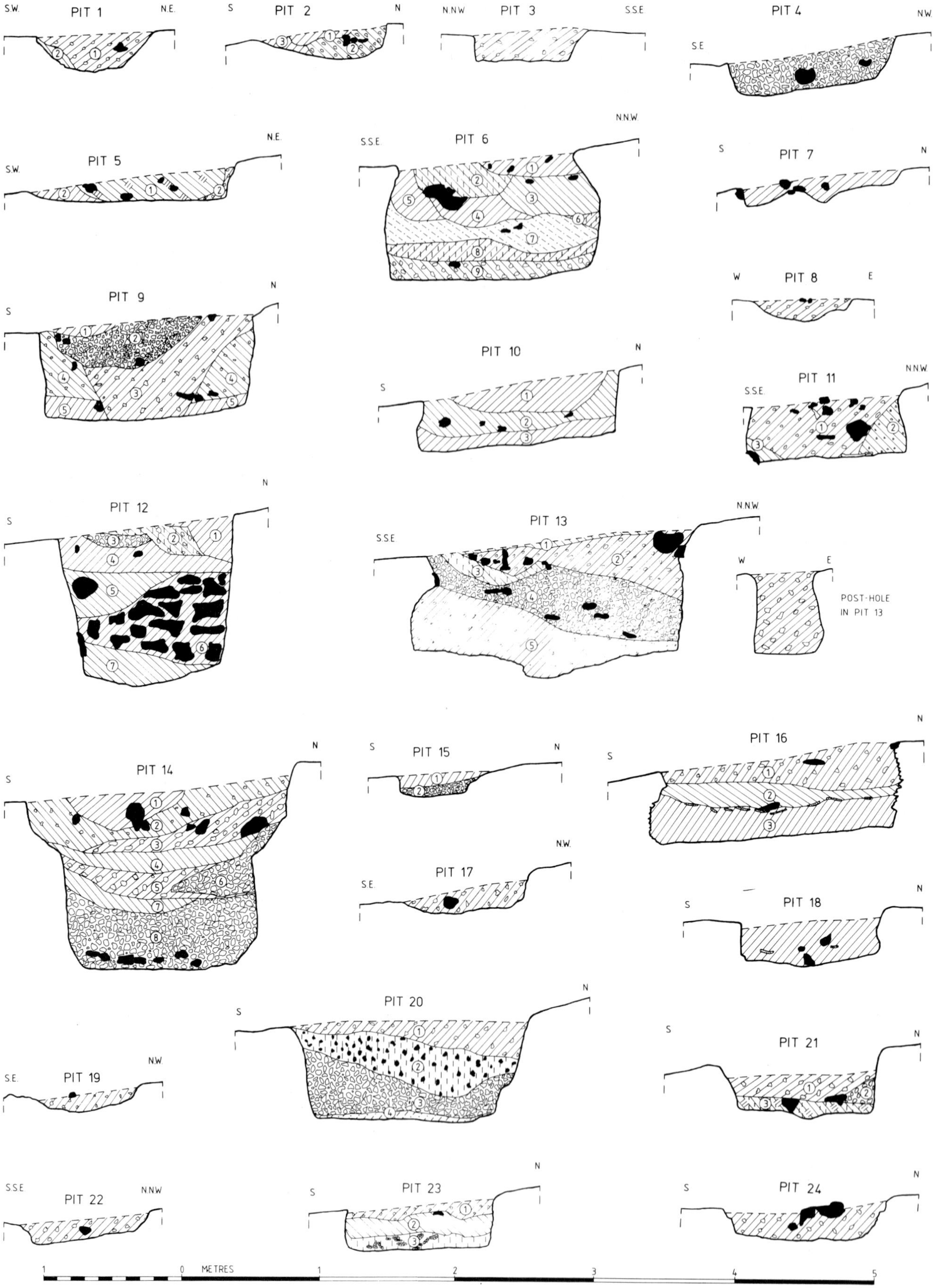

Fig. 6. *Sections across Iron Age Pits 1–24, Farningham Hill.*

(3). The Entrances (Fig. 4 and Plates VI and VII)

The excavation showed that the ditches marking the boundaries of the enclosure discontinued at three points where the solid chalk still survived. The three causeways thus created were clearly intended to serve as entrances through the ditches and it is likely that a fourth originally existed at the north-west corner. These four entrances are described below:–

The South Entrance was the largest of the three surviving and had a width of 7 m. Its width, taken with its position at the lower corner of the site and its situation on the site's broadly north-south axis, suggests it was the main entrance. A single post-hole (PH B7) found almost centrally on the axis of the entrance could have held a post that supported a gate.

The South West Entrance was 5·70 m. wide and was only separated from the South Entrance by the short South Ditch only 7·70 m. in length. Exactly why the site should need two entrances so close together is difficult to explain, but this was the downhill side nearest the river and thus the side likely to have had the greatest activity. No trace of any related post-holes were found, but again shallow holes could have been removed by ploughing.

The North East Entrance was the narrowest of the three surviving entrances with a width of just 3·30 m. No post-holes were found to suggest that it had been closed by a gate, though it is possible that shallow post-holes could have been removed by ploughing. This entrance lay broadly on the main north-south axis across the site and was clearly not the main one. Its narrow width and uphill location tend to suggest that it was something of a 'backdoor' for the site.

The North West Entrance seems to have formed part of the original scheme, but was later dug away to make the adjacent ditches continuous. Its original width is estimated to have been about 3 m. It seems clear from this that this narrow entrance was eventually abandoned and thus only served the earliest phase of settlement, when it gave access to the centre of the site. At some stage its internal approach was blocked by several storage pits and their construction could have been the reason for the original entrance being abandoned.

(4). The Pits (Pits 1–24, Figs. 4 and 6 and Plates VIII, IX and X)

The 24 pits found within the ditched enclosures varied considerably in size, form, depth and content. The great majority contained at least slight traces of Iron Age material and all are here regarded as forming an integral part of the Iron Age site. A small cluster of three pits lay about 8 m. inside the South Entrance. A second group of seven pits lay largely inside the west angle of the North West Ditch and 2–14 m. from its inner lip. A third group of eleven pits occupied a large area on the centre-west side, flanking the south side of the Hut. The three remaining pits were spaced across the eastern part of the site. Although broad types can be identified all three pit-groups contained pits of differing types. The pits are described below and initially, classified by size.

PIT 1

Small oval pit with bowl-shaped profile. Its filling of light brown loam and light chalk rubble contained an occasional flint, but no artefactual material.

PIT 2

Small oval pit with steep north face, cupped base and south side removed by ploughing or erosion. Its filling of dark brown loam and chalk contained no finds.

PIT 3

Small circular pit with nearly vertical sides and a flat base. Its filling of light brown loam and chalk contained no finds.

PIT 4

Small circular pit with steep sides and a flat base. Its filling of chalk rubble contained occasional flints, but no finds.

PIT 5

Large oval pit with steep north side, flat base and south-west side probably reduced by ploughing. Now very shallow. Its main filling (L.1) consisted of black-brown loam with chalk and daub specks, some 326 fire-cracked flints, ten fragments of baked clay, a fragment of quernstone (No. 11) and pottery. This sealed a deposit of weathered chalk at the sides (L.2). Some 33 sherds of pottery represented ten vessels, of which seven are illustrated (Nos. 14–20). This material must represent domestic rubbish and the pottery seems to be the earliest found on the site.

PIT 6

Large oval pit with undercut sides, a flat base and a surviving depth of 87 cm. The undercutting seems to have been deliberate and this pit was almost certainly dug for underground storage, thus being typical of the common 'Bee-hive' profile noted on many other Iron Age sites. The filling generally consisted of roughly horizontal layers of soil. The primary deposit (L.9) consisted of light-brown loam and chalk lumps. This was sealed by a thick layer (L.8) of black loam, which contained pottery and which appears to represent domestic rubbish discarded into the pit after it had gone out of use. This was in turn sealed by three layers (L.5–7) of light brown loam, chalk specks and potsherds. Fragments of the same vessels were found in both Layers 6 and 7 and it seems likely that both layers were deposited at much the same time. The final layers (L.1–4) perhaps representing a shallow recut, were mostly of black or brown loam and contained about 200 potsherds.

In all, this pit produced about 240 potsherds, from at least 26 pots, of which eleven are illustrated (Nos. 21–31). A total of 486 fire-cracked stones was recovered from the pit, with the majority from Layer 8.

PIT 7

Small circular pit with steep sides and undulating base and very shallow. Its filling of brown loam contained random flints, but no finds.

PIT 8

Small circular pit with bowl-shaped profile. Its filling of brown loam and chalk lumps contained no finds.

PIT 9

Large oval pit with vertical sides, a flat base and a depth of 72 cm. This seems to have been a carefully constructed pit, probably intended for underground storage. It had originally been filled with a deposit (L.5) of grey-brown loam and ash with chalk specks, sealed by a substantial deposit (L.4) of brown loam and chalk lumps. It seems that the pit had later been recut when a broadly V-shaped hole was made through the filling of the pit. This was filled (L.1–3) with brown loam and chalk rubble. Only 19 potsherds were recovered from this pit and two vessels are illustrated (Nos. 32 and 33). It also contained 245 fire-cracked stones.

PIT 10

Large oval pit with partly vertical and undercut sides, a flat base and 45 cm. deep. Probably another purpose-made storage pit. Its primary filling (L.3) consisted of a red-brown loam, which was sealed by a layer (L.2) of light brown loam and chalk specks. The top layer (L.1) consisted of mottled black-brown loam, again with chalk specks. These layers contained 83 fire-cracked flints, 25 potsherds and a potin coin (Coin No. 2). The pottery represents about 13 vessels of which seven are illustrated (Nos. 34–40).

PIT 11

A medium sized oval pit with slightly undercut sides, flat base and a depth of about 40 cm. Probably another purpose-built storage pit. The south-east corner of this pit (L.3) contained a deposit of dark-brown loam, whilst the opposite corner contained light-brown loam and chalk lumps (L.2). The main filling (L.1) consisted of brown loam and chalk lumps and it sealed both the other deposits. The pit contained 31 fire-cracked flints, about 62 potsherds of which three are illustrated (Nos. 41–43). The pottery suggests that this pit was one of the earliest on the site.

PIT 12

Medium-sized circular pit with slightly tapered sides and a cupped base and about 1·20 m. deep. Probably another purpose-built storage pit though without undercut sides and rather deeper than the others. The primary filling of brown loam (L.7) was capped by a deep layer of large dumped flints (L.6), in turn sealed by a deposit of dark brown loam (L.5). Four upper layers (L.1–4), of mixed soils, appear to have been thrown in from the north side. The upper filling contained 13 fire-cracked flints, 14 potsherds, a fragment of a quernstone and a significant group of mollusca. Six pots seem to be represented of which three are illustrated (Nos. 44–46) and again this pit appears to be one of the earliest on the site.

PIT 13

This very large pit was ovoid in plan and had both undercut and vertical sides. Its base was largely uneven and slightly east of its centre there was a circular hole about 40 cm. wide and about 69 cm. deep. The primary filling (L.5) consisted of brown loam and chalk lumps and this also filled the hole in the bottom of the pit. The middle filling (L.4) consisted of chalk rubble and flints, probably derived from an immediately adjacent area and perhaps resulting from the excavation of another pit. The upper layers consisted of black loam (L.3) and brown loam and chalk lumps (L.1 and 2). Some 78 fire-cracked flints and 24 potsherds were recovered from the filling. At least five vessels are represented and all are illustrated (Nos. 47–51). This pit also contained a number of bones, including those of a frog that had probably fallen in and occasional bones of a human infant aged about six months. The profile of the pit suggests that it was purpose-made, but its great width and the hole at the base make it unique on the site and it could thus have had a very specialised function. The hole could have held a post or it could have served as a drain-hole.

PIT 14

This large circular pit had largely vertical sides and a base with angled corners. Again this seems to have been purpose-built, but it is not similar to any other pit on the site. The upper sides were angled back, quite unlike any other pit and the outer lip so created thus produced a sub-rectangular plan. It seems probable that the upper part of the pit had suffered from weathering and this suggests that it had remained open for longer than any of the other pits.

The primary deposit (L.8) consisted of chalk rubble containing flints and it seems likely that this was dumped into the pit, the material perhaps derived from the excavation of a fresh pit nearby.

This was sealed by successive dumps of dark grey loam (L.7), chalk rubble (L.5–6), grey-brown loam (L.4), chalk rubble (L.3), brown loam and chalk lumps (L.2) and black-brown loam (L.1). The chalk rubble appears to have fallen from the upper sides and tends to support the suggestion of severe weathering.

The various layers contained 70 fire-cracked flints, some 82 potsherds, the skeletons of three dogs and a significant group of mollusca. At least 14 different pots seem to be represented and nine are illustrated (Nos. 52–60). Some 139 dog bones from three partially complete skeletons were recovered from different layers within the pit. Many of these were scattered in the chalk rubble at the bottom of the pit and most of the rest came from the centre of the pit (L.5 and 7). Only one substantially complete skull was found and it is clear that the dog bones in this pit were not articulated in any way. It seems likely that the dogs had been buried nearby and that their skeletons had been disturbed by pit or ditch-digging operations and discarded into this pit, whilst it was being filled.

PIT 15

Small circular pit with vertical and steep sides and a flat base. Its filling consisted of chalk rubble (L.2) and brown loam (L.1), but contained no objects.

PIT 16 (Plate X)

A large rectangular pit with both undercut and vertical sides, a flat base and about 55 cm. deep. This, too, seems to have been purpose-built, probably for storage. The primary fill (L.3) consisted of brown loam and chalk specks with very large quantities of broken pottery along its upper surface. About 629 potsherds formed an almost complete layer and at least 43 vessels are represented, of which 27 are illustrated (Nos. 61–87).

This deposit was sealed by a dark brown loam (L.2) and a light brown loam (L.1), both containing small chalk lumps. This pit also contained 20 fire-cracked stones, two fragments of a clay loom-weight (No. 8) and it appears to be one of the latest in date on the site.

PIT 17

Small ovoid pit with mostly steep sides and roughly flat base. Its filling of brown loam and chalk lumps produced five fire-cracked flints and 18 potsherds, the latter representing four pots of which one is illustrated (No. 88).

PIT 18

Medium-sized sub-rectangular pit with vertical sides and a flat base. Its filling of brown loam and chalk specks produced 23 fire-cracked flints and 84 potsherds, the latter representing eleven vessels of which five are illustrated (Nos. 89–93).

PIT 19

Small circular pit with sloping sides and cupped base. Its filling of brown loam and chalk lumps contained two small potsherds.

PIT 20

Large circular pit with steep or vertical sides and a flat base. Probably a purpose-built storage pit. Its primary filling of brown sandy loam (L.4) was sealed by a thick layer (L.3) of chalk rubble, possibly derived from weathering of the upper sides. This was covered by a thick dumped layer (L.2) of black sooty loam containing 2,487 fire-cracked flints, presumably debris thrown in from the adjacent Hut. The top layer (L.1) consisted of brown loam and chalk lumps. The pit also contained another 84 fire-cracked flints, some carbonised grains and 15 potsherds, representing seven pots of which three are illustrated (Nos. 94–96).

PIT 21

Large sub-rectangular pit with steep sides and a flat base. Its primary fill (L.3) consisted of brown loam containing fragments of daub and flints. A deposit (L.2) of chalk rubble lay on the north side and a layer (L.1) of brown loam and chalk lumps over this. The pit produced 75 fire-cracked flints and nine potsherds, of some four vessels, of which only one is illustrated (No. 97) and also about 130 fragments of burnt daub.

PIT 22

Small oval pit with sloping sides and a flat base. Its filling of brown loam and chalk lumps contained a single potsherd.

PIT 23

Medium-sized sub-rectangular pit with vertical sides and a flat base, but only 35 cm. deep. Its primary filling (L.3) consisted of fine black loam containing 42 fire-cracked flints. Its middle filling (L.2) was of dark brown loam and its upper filling (L.1) was brown loam and chalk lumps. The pit contained 27 potsherds, of at least three vessels all of which are illustrated (Nos. 98–100).

PIT 24

Medium-sized sub-rectangular pit with sloping sides and a flat base, but only 27 cm. deep. Its filling of brown loam contained five fire-cracked flints and four potsherds, one of which is illustrated (No. 101).

Even with many variations the 24 pits fall broadly into four main types, defined by plan-shape and depth. These are shown in the following table (Table A).

Type	Pit No.	Depth (m.)	Size (m.)	Area (sq. m.)	Volume (cu. m.)
Type A	6	0·87	1·30	1·33	1·15
	9	0·72	1·57 × 1·42	1·75	1·26
	12	1·12	1·25	1·23	1·37
	13	0·78	2·46 × 1·82	3·52	2·74
	14	1·34	1·95	2·99	4·00
	20	0·72	1·80	2·54	1·83
Type B	16	0·55	1·70 × 1·52	2·58	1·42
	18	0·35	1·50 × 0·95	1·42	0·50
	21	0·44	1·63 × 1·22	1·99	0·87
	23	0·35	1·07 × 0·96	1·03	0·36
	24	0·27	1·15 × 0·91	1·05	0·28
Type C	4	0·25	1·17 × 1·05	0·87	0·22
	5	0·23	2·40 × 1·50	3·60	0·83
	10	0·45	1·64 × 1·41	1·82	0·82
	11	0·40	1·18 × 1·06	0·98	0·39
	17	0·25	1·24 × 0·93	0·91	0·23
Type D	1	0·26	0·80 × 0·70	0·44	0·11
	2	0·21	0·92 × 0·75	0·54	0·11
	3	0·20	0·84 × 0·79	0·52	0·10
	7	0·15	1·09 × 1·03	0·88	0·13
	8	0·17	0·70 × 0·64	0·35	0·06
	15	0·17	0·66 × 0·61	0·32	0·05
	19	0·15	0·74	0·43	0·06
	22	0·17	0·90 × 0·84	0·59	0·10

Table A – Classification of Pits by Type

PIT TYPE A

This type consists of six large circular, or ovoid, pits that were generally the deepest on the site. The diameters ranged from 1·25 m. to 2·46 m. and the depth from 0·72 to 1·34 m. The largest Pit 13 was 2·46 by 1·82 m., but uniquely had a post-hole in its base and probably had a specialised function. Examples of Type A occurred in all three pit-groups.

PIT TYPE B

This type consisted of five large, or medium-sized pits that were basically rectangular or sub-rectangular in plan, mostly with rounded corners and of shallow depth. They ranged from 1·07 m. to 1·70 m. in length, from 0·91 m. to 1·52 m. in width and from 27–55 cm. in depth. All of these were situated in the large group of pits near the Hut. One, (Pit 5) contained the earliest group of pottery found on the site and another, (Pit 16) contained the latest group of pottery from the site.

PIT TYPE C

This type consisted of five large or medium-sized irregular, or ovoid, pits that were much shallower than Type B. They ranged from 1·17 to 2·40 m. in length, from 0·93 to 1·50 m. in width and from 23 to 45 cm. in depth. Examples of Type C occurred in all three pit-groups.

PIT TYPE D

This type consisted of eight small ovoid pits, all very shallow and with varying profiles. They were all within the range of 0·61 to 1·09 m. in both length and width and only 15 to 26 cm. deep. Two occurred at the edge of the north-west pit-group, three in the large pit-group by the Hut and three lay in a broad arc just east of the centre of the site.

There are also marked variations in the profiles of the pits (Fig. 7). Seven have profiles which show the sides to be partially undercut and are thus of the familiar bee-hive type, found on many Iron Age settlements sites. Of these, three (Pits 6, 13 and 16) are large, the other four (Pits 10, 11, 18 and 23) are medium-sized and both sub-rectangular and circular pits are represented.

Another four large pits (Pits 9, 12, 14 and 20) have vertical or slightly splayed sides and are again familiar as 'cylindrical' pits commonly found on Iron Age settlement sites. Another five (Pits 4, 5, 17, 21 and 24) are medium-sized and have sides that are generally splayed outwards, though weathering of the upper sides could have reduced vertical profiles to this form. Finally, the remaining eight (Pits 1, 2, 3, 7, 8, 15, 19 and 22) are mostly small pits, with bowl-shaped profiles or in two cases with near-vertical sides.

Whilst it is difficult to be certain about the precise function of the eight small pits, it seems clear that the first 16 were dug as silos for the underground storage of grain or other food-stuffs. These have been recorded at numerous Iron Age sites, including some hillforts, where they have been identified as pits for the storage of grain through the winter months (Ref. 16). The profiles of the pits at Farningham Hill are largely typical of similar pits found on Iron Age sites across much of Southern Britain.

Presumably the storage-pits at Farningham Hill served the needs of the farmstead there and reflect, in part at least, both the production, capacity and the needs of the farmer. Whilst all the pits are very unlikely to have been open at a single time, it is just worth commenting on the total

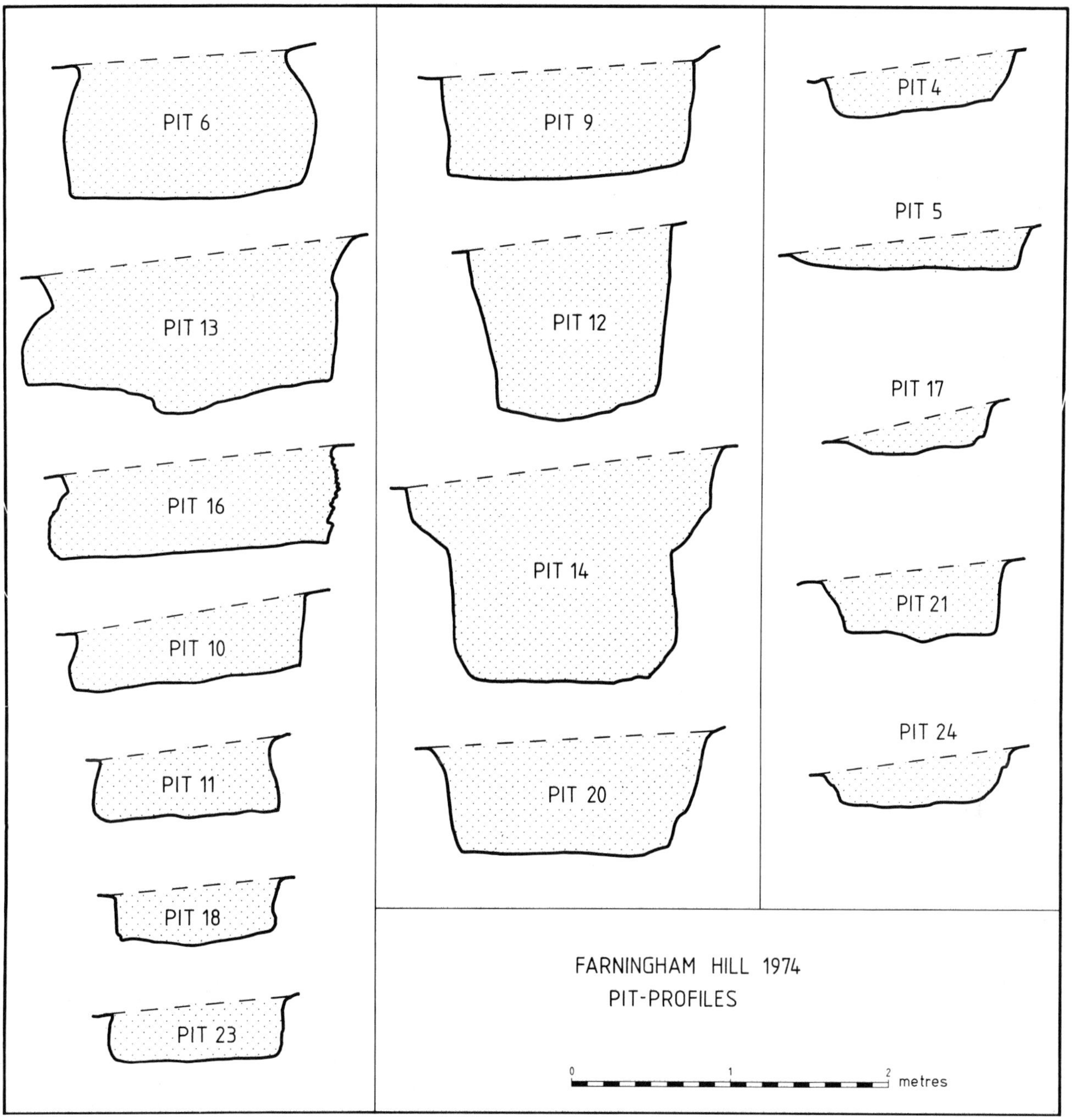

Fig. 7. *Profiles of the 16 main Iron Age Pits, Farningham Hill.*

storage capacity represented. Taking the main 16 pits together, their cubic volume totals about 18 cu. mts. With a very broad estimate of three-quarters of a tonne of grain per cubic metre, this produces a maximum total of about 13 tonnes. Estimates based on sensible experiments (Ref. 17) suggest that 1½ tonnes represent the likely yield from 1 hectare of land. Hence 13 tonnes might represent the yield from a maximum of about 8 hectares (say 20 acres). As eight Celtic fields are said to have occupied about one hectare, then a yield of 13 tonnes also represents an area covered by 64 nominal Celtic fields!

Although the many imponderables, such as precise use of each pit, possible linings, storage above ground, the length of times each pit was used and even the basis of calculation, make such absolute figures largely unhelpful, they do offer a useful comment on one aspect of such a farmstead. It suggests the total arable land under cultivation was never very large, but was more likely to have been small and compact and thus appropriate to a small family unit! It is clear that the pits eventually went out of use and became filled, partially through weathering, but mostly by deliberate act. Most contained domestic rubbish and it seems highly probable that they were dug and abandoned as required. It seems unlikely that more than a few were open at any one time.

As regards the pottery from the pits Peter Couldrey has shown that only five pits (Pits 5, 6, 10, 14 and 16) contained five or more vessels. However, his study of the pottery from each pit suggests that five (Pits 5, 9, 12, 15 and 21) could be regarded as the earliest on the site (a notional Phase I). Seven more (Pits 10, 11, 13, 18, 20, 23 and 24) could be regarded as of later date (a notional Phase IIA) and four others (Pits 6, 16, 14 and 17) the latest on the site (a notional Phase IIB). He has, however, stressed that only Pits 5 and 16 had sufficient pottery in them to make such an assessment valid. Pit 5 certainly seems to have been one of the earliest and Pit 16 one of the latest on the site.

The presence of pits of three possible phases appears to have little geographical significance. Nor do such phases appear to relate to size, shape or type of pit.

(5). The Probable Hut (Figs. 8, 9 and Plate XI)

A series of 23 post-holes (PH 1–26, three in series not used), was found concentrated in a limited area north-west of the physical centre of the site. It seems highly probable that most of these related to a single structure. Elsewhere Iron Age farmstead sites (see discussion below) contained one or more circular huts, of varying diameters, that were mostly evidenced by posts or gullies, or both. At Farningham the post-holes were framed in part by a shallow curving gully, but this was traced for only 5·60 m. on the north, uphill side. It is possible that this gully continued in both directions, but that it has since been ploughed away. On this evidence it seems likely that the post-holes here represent the site of a small hut.

If the gully had been pennannular in plan, then it would have had a diameter of about 8·50 m. and this would have enclosed all 23 post-holes, but its line would have cut through at least two of the pits. All that can be said about it with certainty is that a short gully had once existed, at least on the uphill side of the structure and that this probably served to collect surface water. The gully was generally 35 cm. wide, 5 to 25 cm. deep and was filled with brown loam and chalk rubble.

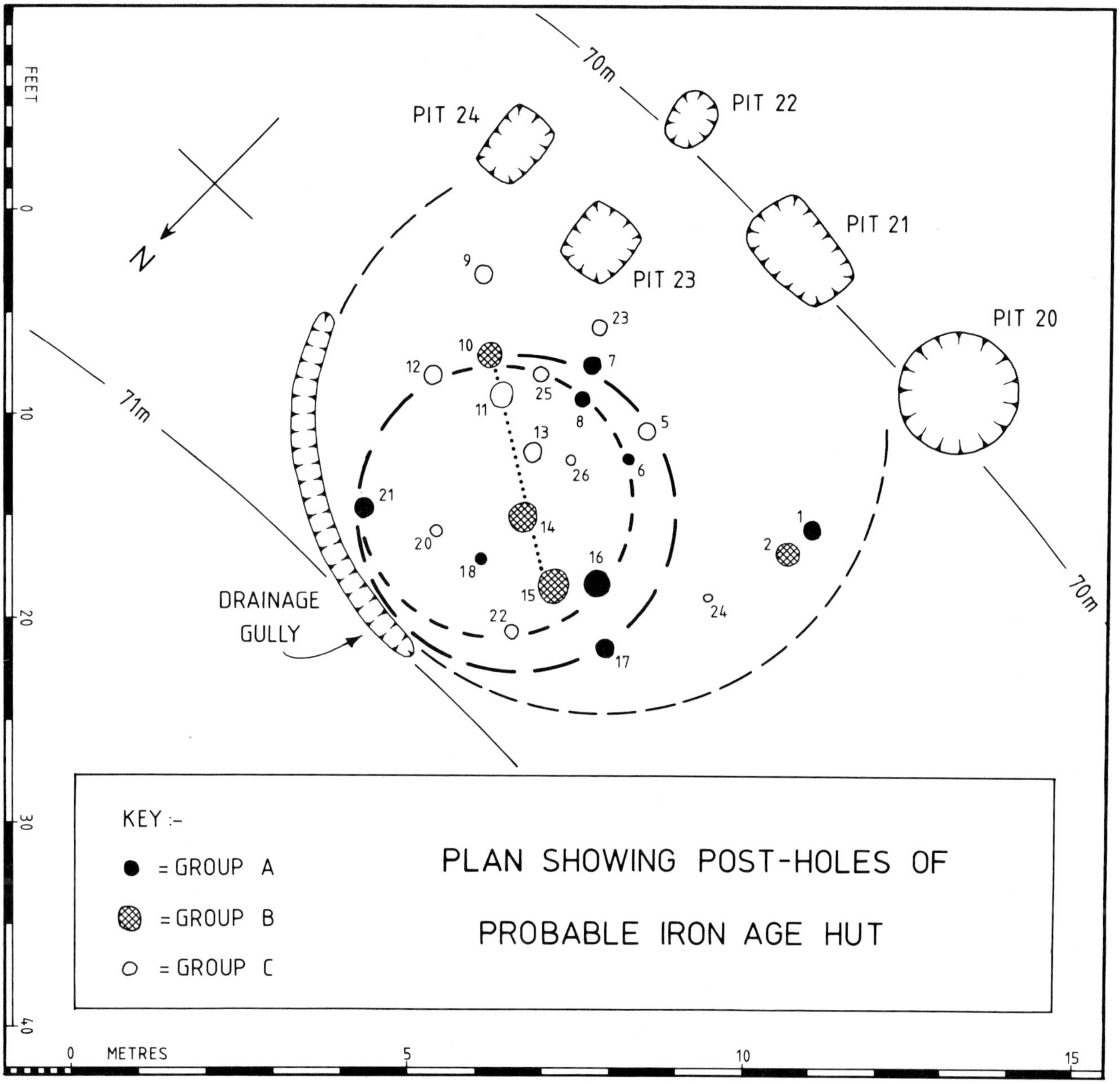

Fig. 8. *Plan showing post-holes of probable Iron Age Hut, Farningham Hill.*

With, or without, a penannular gully, it is difficult to produce a certain plan of a structure from the 23 post-holes. Indeed, it is possible that more than one phase of building is represented. Perhaps the easiest method of study is to divide the post-holes into broad types and from this two main groups emerge (Table B). Eight post-holes (Group A) were generally 17–35 cm. in diameter, 18–28 cm. deep and mostly had vertical sides and cupped bases. No regular plan can be

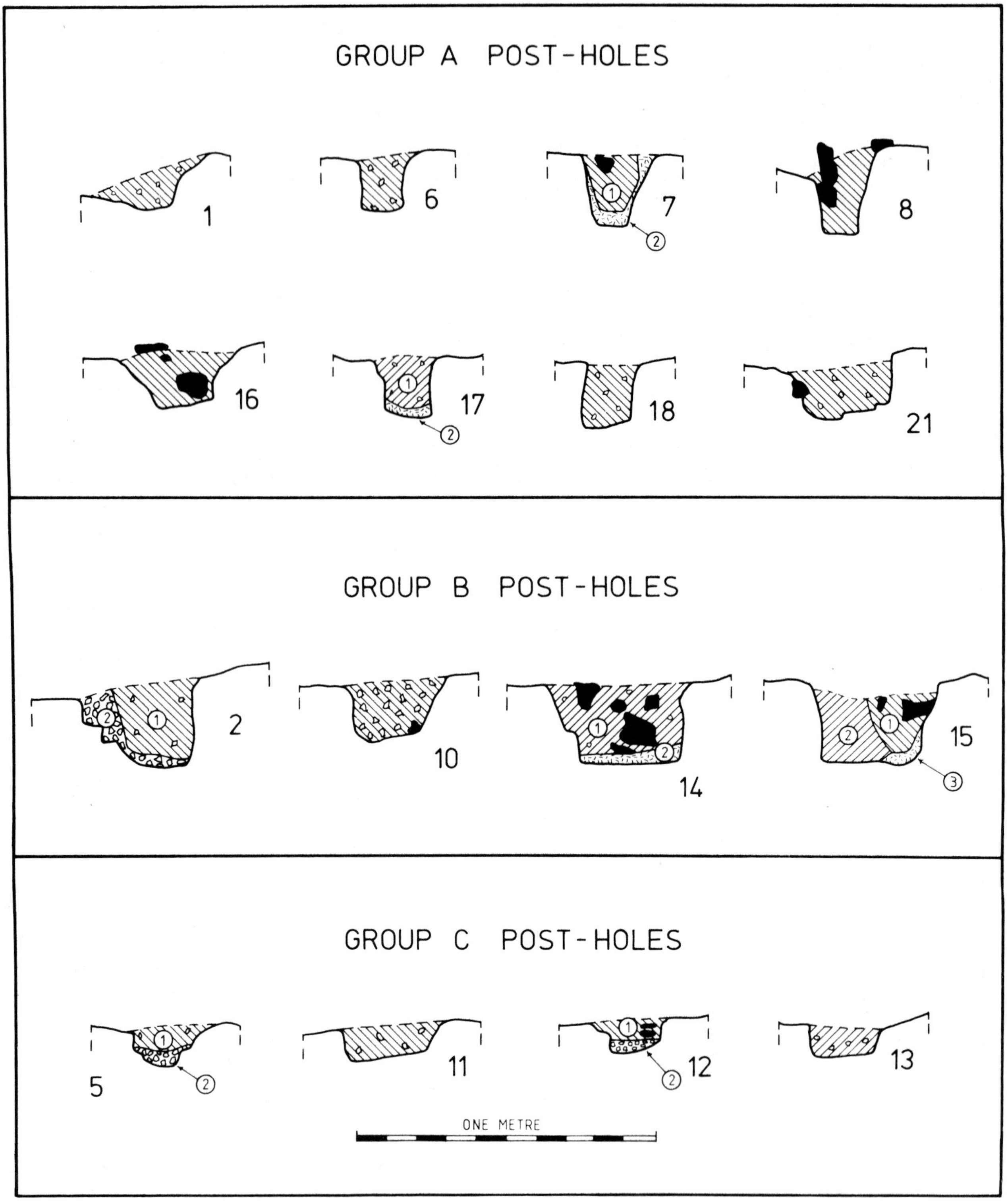

Fig. 9. *Sections of post-holes of probable Iron Age Hut, Farningham Hill.*

produced from these, although four (PH 6, 8, 16 and 21) seem to fall on the circumference of a circle with a diameter of about 4·00 m. Four more post-holes (Group B) were generally larger, being 37–42 cm. in diameter, 22–30 cm. deep and had vertical sides. Three of these fall in a straight line with the fourth at right angles to it. Finally, another eleven post-holes (Group C) are somewhat variable in character and may have been ploughed down. If deeper, then one (PH 11) could be placed in Group B where it also falls on the line created by the three big posts. The remaining ten post-holes in Group C, again if deeper, could be placed in Group A and if so then three (PH 12, 22 and 25) would then fall on the circumference of the Group A circle. A slightly larger circle, with a diameter of nearly five metres, can also be created by a line through five posts (PH 5, 7, 12, 17 and 21) in the combined Groups A and C.

Post-Holes	Diameter (cm.)	Depth (cm.)	Sides	Base	Notes
GROUP A					
PH 1	24	18	Vert.	Cup	Illustrated
PH 6	18	20	Vert.	Cup	Illustrated
PH 7	25	26	Steep	Cup	Illustrated
PH 8	23	28	Vert./Steep	Cup	Illustrated
PH 16	35	20	Sloping	Flat	Illustrated
PH 17	20	22	Vert.	Cup	Illustrated
PH 18	17	22	Vert.	Cup	Illustrated
PH 21	32	23	Steep	Uneven	Illustrated
GROUP B					
PH 2	40 × 34	30	Vert.	Uneven	Illustrated
PH 10	37	22	Sloping	Cup	Illustrated
PH 14	43 × 42	27	Vert.	Flat	Illustrated
PH 15	40 × 59	28	Vert.	Uneven	Illustrated
GROUP C					
PH 5	17 × 26	10	Sloping	Uneven	Illustrated
PH 9	24	7	Vert.	Flat	—
PH 11	27 × 37	13	Sloping	Uneven	Illustrated
PH 12	23	10	Sloping	Cup	Illustrated
PH 13	23	12	Vert.	Flat	Illustrated
PH 20	15 × 20	12	Vert.	Uneven	—
PH 22	20	14	Sloping	Cup	—
PH 23	15	22	Vert.	Cup	—
PH 24	15	5	Sloping	Flat	—
PH 25	18	12	Vert.	Cup	—
PH 26	15	22	Vert.	Cup	—

Table B – Post-Holes in Hut Area

Finally, by adding back the four large Group B posts (PH 2, 10, 14 and 15) to those describing the two circles, it can be seen that they fall broadly on the centre axis of the larger outline. One (PH 10) of these falls on the actual circumference of both circles and another (PH 14) falls close to the centre of both circles. It is anyway one of the largest on the site and could have served as a centre-post. Thus by ignoring five outlying holes (PH 1, 2, 9, 23 and 24) the remaining 18 all fall within a diameter of about 5·00 m. The probability is that this roughly equates with some main element of a circular hut, but the irregular spacing, the possibility that some were part of internal structures or represent different phases, prevents more than the tentative outlines offered here. The outlines created are largely parallel to the gully which thus neatly protects the uphill approach. On the surviving evidence, therefore, it is only possible to suggest the existence of a small circular hut about 4 to 5 m. in diameter, but also to admit that other possibilities could have almost equal merit.

(6). Other Post-Holes (B1 to B8)

Eight probable post-holes were located and these are tabulated below (Table C). All were circular or oval in plan, had steep or vertical sides and were all visibly smaller than the pits. They ranged from 21–55 cm. in diameter and from 7–43 cm. in depth. All were filled with brown loam and chalk rubble, but only one (B8) had flint packing. Four of the post-holes (B1 to B4) formed a group near the east angle of the enclosure which by its isolated position suggests that the post-holes related to each other in some way. Nos. B1, B2 and B3 seem to be at right-angles to each other, but an outline including B4 produces a trapezoidal plan. The arrangement does suggest some sort of large structure at this point, but with the probability that ploughing has reduced much of the evidence its function can only be guessed. If the surviving post-holes were the corner elements of a structure, then a small animal-pen could be indicated roughly 7 m. by 5 m. in area, but other possibilities remain.

Post-Hole	Diameter (cm.)	Depth (cm.)	Sides	Base
B1	21	14	Steep	Uneven
B2	25	7	Steep	Flat
B3	39 × 52	43	Vert.	Uneven
B4	47 × 42	22	Vert.	Cupped
B5	35	17	Steep	Uneven
B6	43 × 40	10	Sloping	Uneven
B7	24 × 18	13	Steep	'V' shaped
B8	55 × 50	25	Steep	Cupped

Table C. Post-holes beyond the Hut area.

A pair of post-holes (B5 and B6) with centres about 1·80 m. apart, was found near the southern end of the site and probably related to each other. Elsewhere on Iron Age farmstead sites pairs of posts of similar form are common and these are normally regarded as representing drying-frames for corn. A single post-hole (B7) within the South Entrance, probably related to a gate, whilst one more (B8) appears to have stood alone on the west side of the site.

(7). Ditches Outside the Iron Age Enclosure (A-H). (Fig. 10)

Varying lengths of eight chalk-cut ditches were located during the contractors topsoiling operations very shortly after the completion of the excavation of the Iron Age farmstead. Two (A and B) lay well to the west of the farmstead and six (C-H) lay to the east (Fig. 3). It was only possible to cut limited sections across most of these in the short time before their destruction. Most, however, extended across the width of the motorway and should still survive beyond.

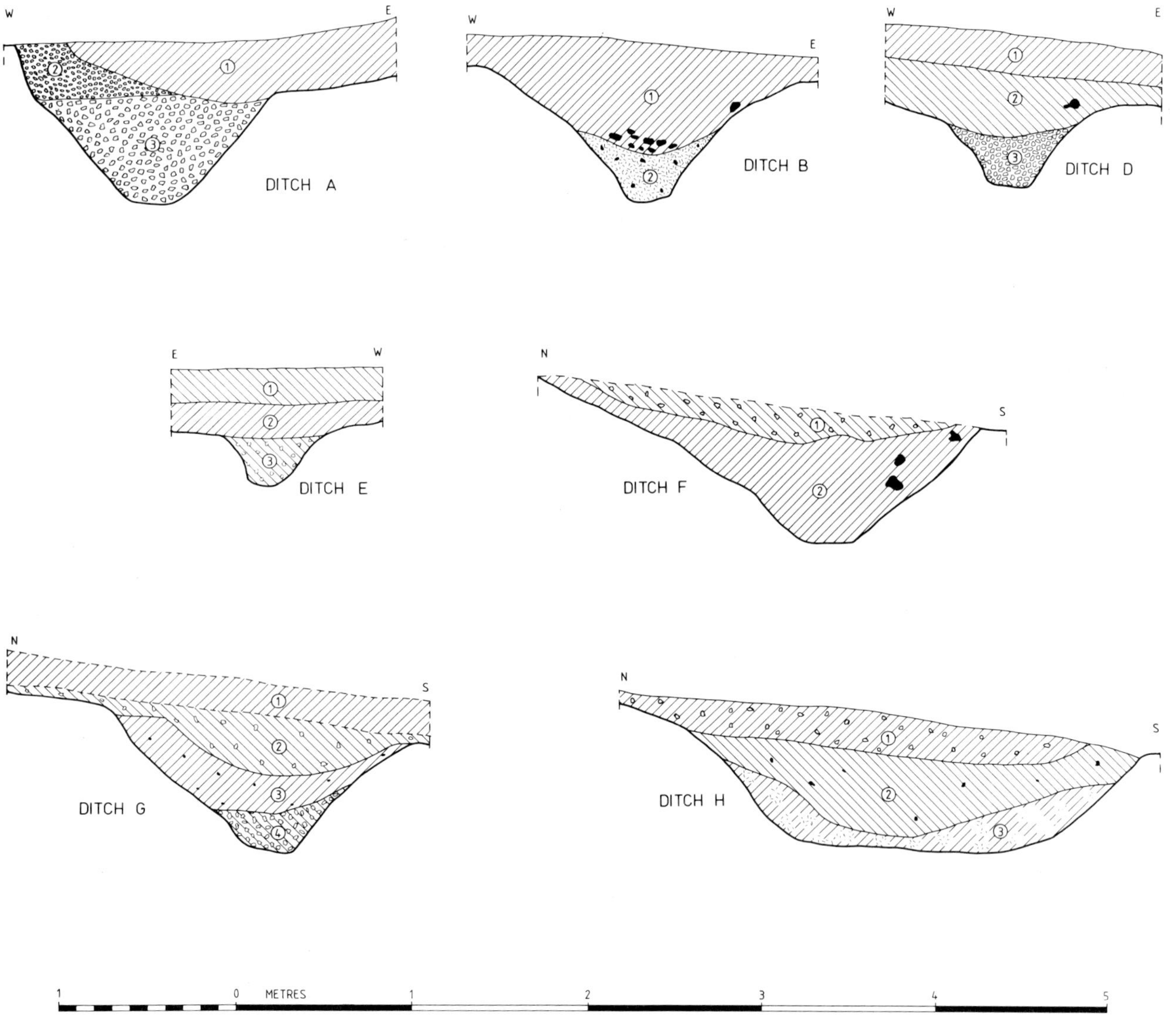

Fig. 10. *Sections across ditches outside the Iron Age Enclosure, Farningham Hill.*

DITCH A

This was about 240 m. west of the centre of the Iron Age enclosure and ran uphill on a broadly north-east by south-west axis for at least 27 m. It had a V-shaped profile, was 1·50 m. wide at the top, 25 cm. wide at the base and was 93 cm. deep. It was filled with chalk rubble, (L.2–3), but was cut away on the east side (L.1). One trench across the ditch produced sherds of second century Roman samian (Form 37) and a fragment of Roman glass. A second cut, however, produced a 17th or 18th century glazed potsherd and a fragment of an 18th century, or later, wine bottle. It seems likely that this ditch was dug in Roman times, perhaps as a distinct field boundary relating to one of the Roman sites in the area, and that it was partially disturbed in the 18th century.

DITCH B

This was about 170 m. west of the centre of the Iron Age enclosure and also ran uphill on a broadly north-south axis for at least 36 m. It had a wide V-shaped profile, was about 1·70 m. wide at the top, about 25 cm. wide at the base and was at least 80 cm. deep. Its lower filling (L.2) consisted of chalk wash and its upper filling (L.1) of brown loam, chalk specks and a group of large flints. No finds were recovered and this ditch is undated.

DITCH C

This ditch was found about 5 m. outside the South Entrance of the Iron Age enclosure and was traced for about 10 m. running on a broadly east-west axis. It was about 1·60 m. wide and contained fragments of roof-tile of post-medieval date. It was not examined in detail and its east end was not seen during the contractors topsoiling operations.

DITCH D

This ditch about 85 m. east of the Iron Age enclosure also ran uphill on a broadly north-south axis for at least 85 m. It had a splayed profile, was about 1m. wide at the top, was 25 cm. wide at the base and was about 50 cm. deep. Its primary fill (L.3) consisted of chalk rubble and its upper filling (L.2) was a light-brown loam with chalk specks, that also spread beyond the ditch. A group of 14 sherds of pottery was recovered from the upper fill of the ditch. Two sherds were of grit-loaded ware of Iron Age date and the others were from a cooking-pot and a storage jar, both of second century date. It seems probable that this ditch was dug in Roman times, again perhaps as a field boundary.

DITCH E

This small ditch was traced from about 50 m. to 185 m. east of the Iron Age enclosure. One arm, ran roughly east-west for at least 130 m. Its west end turned sharply to the south to give an angle of about 106° and this was traced for about 30 m. The ditch was broadly U-shaped in profile, about 60 cm. wide at the top, about 15 cm. wide at the base and only 35 cm. deep. It was filled with light-brown loam and chalk lumps (L.3) and sealed by brown loam layers of hillwash (L.2) and topsoil (L.1). A single sherd of Iron Age pottery came from this ditch though this could have arrived there at almost anytime. This ditch seems to have formed the north-west corner of an enclosure or field system and appeared to cut Ditch D which contained second century pottery.

DITCH F

This ditch was traced from 72 m. to 150 m. east of the Iron Age enclosure. One arm, about 36 m. in length, ran roughly north-south before turning through about 105° to run roughly east-west for about 60 m. It had a splayed profile and was about 2·60 m. wide at the top, about 30 cm. wide at the base and was mostly about 80 cm. deep. Its main filling of brown loam and chalk specks (L.2) was sealed by a light brown loam and chalk lumps (L.1) which contained a fragment of bone, an oyster shell and two struck flints. This ditch seems to have formed the north-east corner of an enclosure, or field system, but again of uncertain date. Its extreme north-east corner just missed the lip of Ditch E and it is possible that this was deliberate.

DITCH G

This ditch lay about 130 m. east of the Iron Age enclosure, where short lengths of two arms were set at about 105° to each other. A total length of 21 m. was recorded within the motorway fences. The ditch had a splayed profile, was about 1·80 m. wide at the top, 25 cm. wide at the base and was about 70 cm. deep. Its primary filling (L.4) of brown loam and chalk rubble was sealed by a deep deposit of brown loam containing some pebbles (L.3), whilst the upper fill (L.2) consisted of brown loam, chalk lumps and a very small chip of red tile. This ditch also seems to have been the north-east corner of an enclosure and it appears to have run parallel to both arms of Ditch F. If so, and the short length exposed makes certainty difficult, then both ditches could have formed part of a double-box enclosure, as noted on Romano-British sites elsewhere. This ditch is otherwise undated.

DITCH H

This large ditch lay about 135 m. to 225 m. east of the Iron Age enclosure and was traced on a broadly east-west axis for 105 m., though it re-aligned marginally near its centre. It had a very broad U-shaped profile, was 2·70 m. wide at the top, 1·20 m. wide at the base and was about 70 cm. deep. Its primary fill (L.3) of light-brown loam and chalkwash was sealed by a brown loam with flint (L.2). Its upper layer (L.1) consisted of brown loam with chalk lumps that contained a fragment of a red tile and a potsherd, probably of medieval date. The ditch cut through Ditches E, F and G and it appears to be the latest feature in that area, perhaps a medieval boundary ditch.

C. DISCUSSION (Fig. 11)

The Iron Age enclosure at Farningham Hill clearly belongs to a class of small ditched enclosures found widely across Southern Britain and mostly dated from the first century B.C. to the first century A.D. (Ref. 18). These have been identified as farmstead enclosures which may have evolved from large ditched settlements of the earlier Iron Age as at Little Woodbury (Ref. 19) and less certainly from Bronze Age antecedents (Ref. 20, p. 21). Those of the Farningham Hill type were probably small farmsteads, representing single-family units, that farmed and grazed adjacent land, but seldom on sites offering any degree of natural defence. Most seem to have had single ditches, one or more entrances, gates and internal huts and storage pits, or racks. In a few cases, mostly in woodland areas, slight traces of internal banks still survive. In some areas these enclosures appear to relate to adjacent field-systems or spaced groups of enclosures, or they may stand alone.

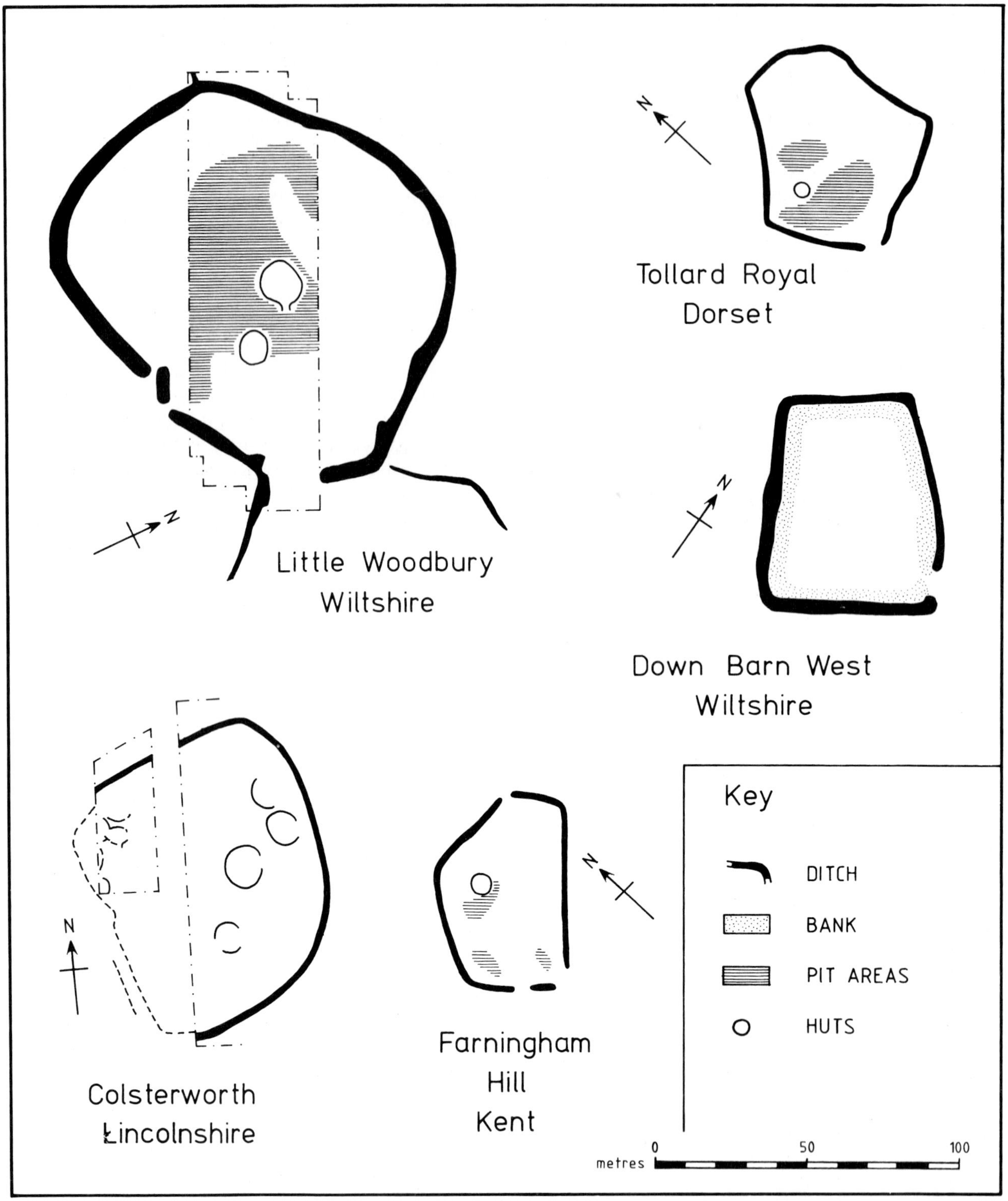

Fig. 11. *Comparative plans of iron Age Enclosures.*

The farmstead site at Little Woodbury, widely held to be a useful prototype, was excavated in 1938–39 and published in 1940. This was roughly circular in plan, enclosed about 1·6 hectares (4 acres) and certainly contained a large circular hut (or huts) and many storage pits. Even at Little Woodbury only half the area was excavated and it was not until 1965, when Wainwright excavated Tollard Royal, Dorset (Ref. 21) that a farmstead site of the Farningham Hill type was fully excavated. There, a kite-shaped enclosure of about 0·4 hectares (1 acre) measured 63 m. by 60 m. and contained a single hut, 34 storage-pits of different types and several above-ground granaries. These internal features were largely confined to the western half of the site. Notable broadly comparable enclosures, mostly of varying shapes, are known at Rotherley, Wilts. (Ref. 22), Woodcuts, Dorset (Ref. 23), Down Barn West, Wiltshire (Ref. 24), Worthy Down, Hants. (Ref. 25), Casterley Camp, Wilts. (Ref. 26) and Langford Down, Oxon. (Ref. 27). Another comparable site, almost completely excavated, occurs at Tallington, Lincs. (Ref. 28) where the enclosure measured 49 m. by 46 m., though no huts or underground pits were found. A larger sub-circular enclosure was excavated at Colsterworth, Lincs. (Ref. 29), measured 73 m. by 64 m. and contained circular huts, but no storage pits.

The importance of the Farningham Hill site in a national context is thus at once apparent for it seems to have been only the second total excavation of such a late-Iron Age farmstead site by 1975. So, too, does it contain most of the basic ingredients, such as the protecting ditch, the entrances, a probable circular hut and many pits, most of which were almost certainly used for storage. Its pentagonal form is within the range of known shapes, whilst its internal size at 0·2 hectares (half an acre) and 63 m. by 40 m. is also broadly typical. The general absence of structures along the eastern part of the site suggests open areas, perhaps for the storage of straw, hay and wood, or for cattle and sheep pens, or indeed for both. This matches the large open area noted at Tollard Royal and also highlights the dangers of partial excavation and the risk of unrepresentative sampling. The Farningham Hill farmstead enclosure may well prove to be the type-site for South East Britain, but was missed from a recent survey of archaeology in Kent published by the C.B.A. in 1982 (Ref. 30).

In detail the suggested circular hut, with a possible diameter of 4 or 5 m. was about the same size as that at Tollard Royal, which was also evidenced by a ring of post-holes. Similar circular huts, with a diameter of 4 to 8 m., have been found within corresponding isolated enclosures at Beard Mill, Stanton Harcourt and Stanlake (Refs. 31, 32 and 33). Elsewhere, huts with diameters of 5 to 15 m. have been recorded.

Of the 24 pits some 16 can be regarded as silos and dug for underground storage of grain and perhaps other foodstuffs. They are concentrated in three main groups, mainly at the centre on the south and west sides of the site and clearly they were not all in use at the same time as shown by the date of the pottery thrown into them. At least six were bee-hive shaped in profile, another five were cylindrical with near-vertical sides and five more were shallow and had splayed sides. These types are all paralleled on other Iron Age settlement sites on chalk, though seldom on sites liable to flooding. One probable corn-drying rack was found near the South Entrance and this type has also been found on many other Iron Age sites. No trace of the familiar 4-post, or 6-post, granaries was found at Farningham Hill. The ditches, generally about 2·00 m. wide and at least 1·20 m. deep, probably served for drainage, for simple protection from intruders and also for coralling animals. It seems likely that an internal bank had been built from the chalk dug from the ditches and if so this would have served as an additional barrier and also offered some degree of shelter from the wind and rain.

The largely non-defensive nature of the site is further evidenced by the multiple entrances (at least three), their considerable widths on the south side and the general lack of evidence of massive gates. The long axis of the site was broadly north-south and two of the entrances fall largely on this line. One, the largest entrance on the site, was on the downhill (river) side and must be regarded as the main entrance, whilst the other was the smallest and lay on the uphill side and may very usefully be regarded as the 'backdoor'. The third entrance lay strangely close to the main entrance on the downhill side and it seems from this that the south end of the enclosure took most of the traffic. Indeed, in this direction lay the river at a distance of at least 300 m. and considering the general absence of water on the site it seems likely that the river was an important supply. It seems probable that cattle and sheep, certainly represented by meat bones on the site, may have been herded to and from the enclosure both for pasturing on the lower slopes and watering at the river.

The animal bones from the site, whilst limited to under 1,000 fragments, show that the basic meat diet was cattle followed by sheep and pig, supplemented by red deer and roe deer. Preference for cattle was also noted at Tollard Royal, but most samples are too small for certainty. A small number of horse, dog, toad, frog and mouse bones were also recovered. The dogs may have been used for hunting and the frog and toad may have fallen into the pits.

Carbonised grain was recovered from four of the pits, but only in very small quantities. Wheat and barley were represented, both of which are commonly found on late-Iron Age sites (Ref. 34).

A total of over 12,000 fire-cracked stones was found on the site, about 8,000 from the ditches and about 4,000 from the pits, of which very large numbers came from the South Ditch and also Pit 20. Correspondingly large numbers of similar 'pot-boilers' have been found on other Iron Age sites where it has been suggested they were used to dry grain seed. No trace of hearths survive at Farningham Hill but clearly large quantities of these fire-cracked stones and black soil had been tipped into Pit 20 and the South Ditch, so it seems likely that any hearths would have been nearby.

The pits and ditches produced a total of 2,585 potsherds, from an absolute minimum of 165 vessels, almost as many as found at Tollard Royal. The total group is of outstanding importance and Peter Couldrey has placed it within the narrow-limits of 50 B.C. to A.D. 50 and this dating embraces both the two potin coins and the iron brooch. The date-range suggested by the finds allows for three or four generations of a single family, farming the hillside before moving at, or a few years before, the Roman Conquest.

Of special interest was the large group of pottery from Pit 16, which consisted of large fragments of many almost complete pots clearly thrown into the pit at one time. A mimimum of 43 pots was found and these include the latest vessels from the site, most of which are coarse wares. Such an unusual dumping of largely complete pots suggests unique circumstances. The most attractive suggestion is that this was done at the time the farmstead was abandoned and that these vessels, several large and coarse, could not be carried and were thus finally discarded. Significantly, perhaps, the pit used for the dumped pottery lay only 12·00 m. west of the circular hut and on the downhill side! Other possibilities (none ritual!) could also be considered.

In a local context the Farningham Hill farmstead and its associated landscape is now of prime importance as the only fully excavated and published site of its type in Kent. In West Kent alone some 20 late-Iron Age sites, probably mostly farmsteads, can be identified, mostly by the presence of ditches, either trenched or seen from the air. At least 20 more are implied by the presence of pottery and many others must remain to be found in a landscape only partially explored. Indeed one of the long-term research aims of the K.A.R.U., since its formation in 1972, is to give such Iron Age settlements high priority. Even with the clear obligation to deal with those threatened with imminent destruction it has been possible to deal substantially with five such sites in a span of seven years. Whilst the circumstances have precluded an examination of adjacent landscapes much fundamental data and important collections of artefacts have been recovered that greatly expand our otherwise limited regional knowledge. This will greatly facilitate the study of settlements in relationship to the ecological setting, the regional topography, the defensive systems and the suspected political and economic structures.

Caesar (Ref. 35) refers to Cantium (probably mainly East Kent) as being thickly studded with homesteads in the middle decades of the first century B.C. The density suggested for West Kent is thus not altogether unexpected and indeed helps confirm similar evidence from Hampshire (Ref. 36). The families in these farmsteads must have belonged to closely-knit tribal units that had their own political, social and military structures within a well-defined territorium. Perhaps some of their burials await discovery nearby?

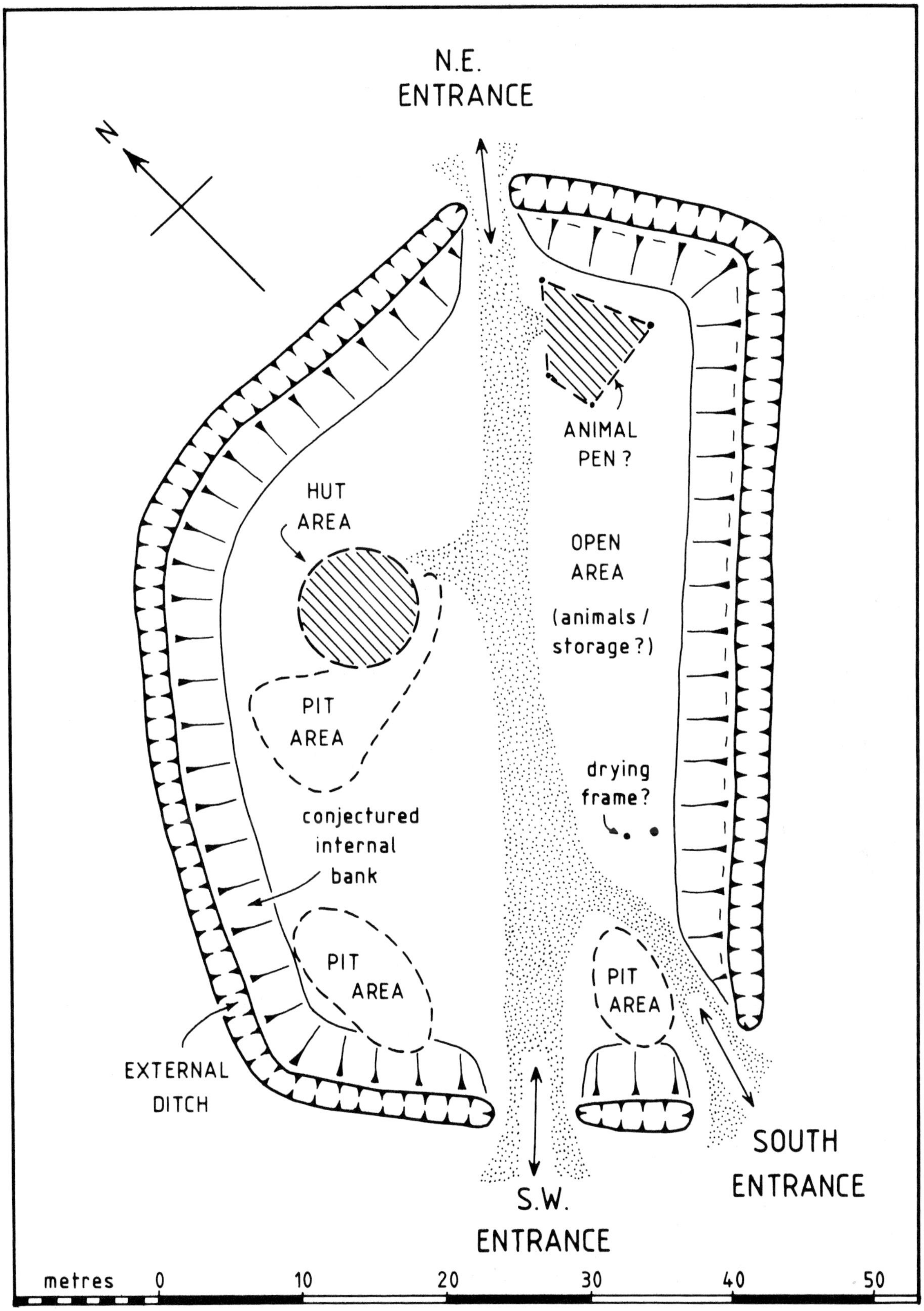

Fig. 12. *Actual and Notional Usage of the internal area of the Iron Age Farmstead, Farningham Hill.*

By West Kent standards the Farningham Hill site itself was largely typical. High ground, on chalk or on correspondingly light soils, was often chosen, though seldom a naturally defendable position. Certainly the Farningham Hill site was not the best defensive position available, for it lay about halfway up a steep slope widely dominated by higher slopes and also the crest of Farningham Hill. Its south-facing aspect gave it the benefit of long hours of daily sunshine and this advantage must have been considered preferable to the disadvantage of an elevated and more exposed site. Certainly many better-sheltered sites were available in the nearby valley bottom and close to the river. It seems likely that the shallow-soiled middle-slopes were preferred for growing crops or open grazing and may have been substantially covered with small-fields, though very few now survive. The nearest surviving early field-system occurs 2 km. to the south at Lullingstone Park and whilst even the date of that system is not known, it seems likely that it was Celtic in origin. No certain trace of adjacent fields was found at Farningham Hill.

The broadly pentagonal outline of the Farningham Hill farmstead is only one of several types that are known at nearby sites. Some other examples, as at North View, Sutton-at-Hone (Ref. 37) appear circular or eliptical. Later, excavated but unpublished examples as at Summerhouse Knoll, (Ref. 38) and Lullingstone Park (Ref. 39) are either rectilinear or circular. Others, mostly unexcavated, are ovoid, irregular or are of well-known banjo-type, as near Fawkham (Ref. 40).

The area within the enclosure ditches seems to have been divided for various functions (Fig. 12). A circular hut, about 4·00–5·00 m. in diameter seems to have occupied the area north-west of the physical centre of the site, protected on its uphill side by a small drainage gully. Three groups of pits occupied the south-west angle, the area south and west of the Hut and a small area by the south entrance, respectively. Most of the pits were probably dug for storage. A structure of some sort, seems to have stood near the north entrance, but apart from this and three small pits, the east side of the enclosure was largely clear. This area, at least 30 m. by 10 m., may have been used for surface storage or for cattle or sheep pens, or for both. Just possibly the ill-defined structure seen near the north entrance was a stall for cattle or sheep, or held feeding-stuffs.

The entrances indicate entry-points connected with local tracks which if projected across the enclosure, clearly gave access to the various internal elements and helped divide the area.

It seems clear that the ditches weathered and half filled with chalk rubble from the upper sides of the ditches. Subsequently, soil and chalk washed in and the ditches must have become largely filled even during the occupation of the site. Scattered domestic rubbish, meat bones, pottery and a few small finds, had been thrown into the ditches at various levels, but a large collection of domestic material had been thrown into the short South Ditch almost at ground-level. Clearly when this was thrown in the ditch was no more than a shallow hollow.

The pottery provides the main dating evidence for the site and suggests, if fully representative, a commencement at about 50 B.C. and an abandonment no later than the time of the Roman Conquest in A.D. 43. Much of the pottery had been thrown into the ditches and pits when these had gone out of use, particularly Pit 16 which contained the largest and latest group of pottery from the site. This had been thrown in at one time and this may represent a significant event in the history of the site, either a major re-organisation or even the final abandonment. What seems quite clear is that the site was abandoned no later than the middle of the first century A.D. The total absence of distinctive Romano-British pottery, or even of pre-Conquest butt-beakers or Gallo-Belgic wares is highly significant and a closing date of somewhere between A.D. 20 and 43 seems the most likely. It also seems highly probable that of the 14 fabrics identified all but one were local products, most likely from the immediate area of West Kent. Only one vessel (Fabric G)., a mica-dusted Fabric, has been identified as an import from Central Gaul.

D. THE EXCAVATED OBJECTS AND ENVIRONMENTAL MATERIAL

(1). THE COINS

Coin No. 1 Potin Coin Class II. Mack 17 (?). (Ref. 41). 0·97g. (N.559).
From upper filling of South East Ditch (KMW–12–148).

Coin No. 2 Potin Coin Class II. Mack 17, 0·51g. (fragment only). (N.562/3).
From Pit 10 (KMW–12–62).

Coin No. 3 Roman Coin Constantine I, A.D. 310.
From top of South East Ditch (KMW–12–49).

(2). THE SMALL FINDS (Figs. 13 and 14)

By Keith Parfitt, B.A.

No. 1 Chalk spindle whorl, weighing 21 grams, with central 'hour glass' perforation. The object is very crudely made and is of a roughly oval shape, with a sub-rectangular cross-section. From upper fill, South East Ditch (KMW–12–149).

No. 2 Chalk spindle whorl, weighing 18 grams. The central perforation has been formed by drilling in from both faces. The drills failed to meet up exactly in the centre, producing an angled hole and possibly a rather unsatisfactory end-product. From lower fill, South East Ditch (KMW–12–90).

No. 3 Small rectangular, carved chalk plaque. One side is decorated by incised lines in the form of a rectangle, enclosing a diagonal cross. The reverse side is plain. From the upper fill, South East Ditch (KMW–12–89).

No. 4 Half a small annular bead of pale blue glass. The bead has broken across the perforation, which is just off-centre. From upper fill, North West Ditch (KMW–12–14).

No. 5 Bronze brooch-pin, 71 mm. long, with spring in four turns. The pin is in excellent condition and probably formed part of a simple bow-brooch. From upper fill, South East Ditch (KMW–12–147).

No. 6 Iron brooch of involuted type, with spring in two turns and undecorated circular foot plate. The distribution of involuted brooches, often of bronze rather than iron, is wide, with examples coming from Yorkshire, Wales and much of Southern Britain, although they are not particularly common finds. The date of these brooches appears to be late-third to late-first century B.C. (Ref. 42). From upper fill, North West Ditch (KMW–12–24).

No. 7 Undecorated, bronze sword or dagger chape, with simple knobbed foot. A hole has been drilled through both walls just below the centre, probably to facilitate attachment to the upper part of the scabbard. The knob is filled with lead. The chape clearly does not belong to the elaborate Iron Age forms discussed by Jope (Ref. 43) and is probably late Iron Age or Roman, although no good parallels have been found. From upper fill, North West Ditch (KMW–12–70).

No. 8 Two fragments, of fired clay probably from a large triangular loom-weight. Coarse sandy fabric unlike any of the pottery from the site. A typical Iron Age form. From Pit 16 (KMW–12–107).

No. 9 Two fragments of fired clay which appear to belong to the solid base of a 'reel' shaped object. Sandy fabric with inclusions of chalk unlike any of the pottery from the site. Similar objects were found associated with Belgic type pottery at Borden, Kent (Ref. 44). From South Ditch (upper). (KMW–12–35).

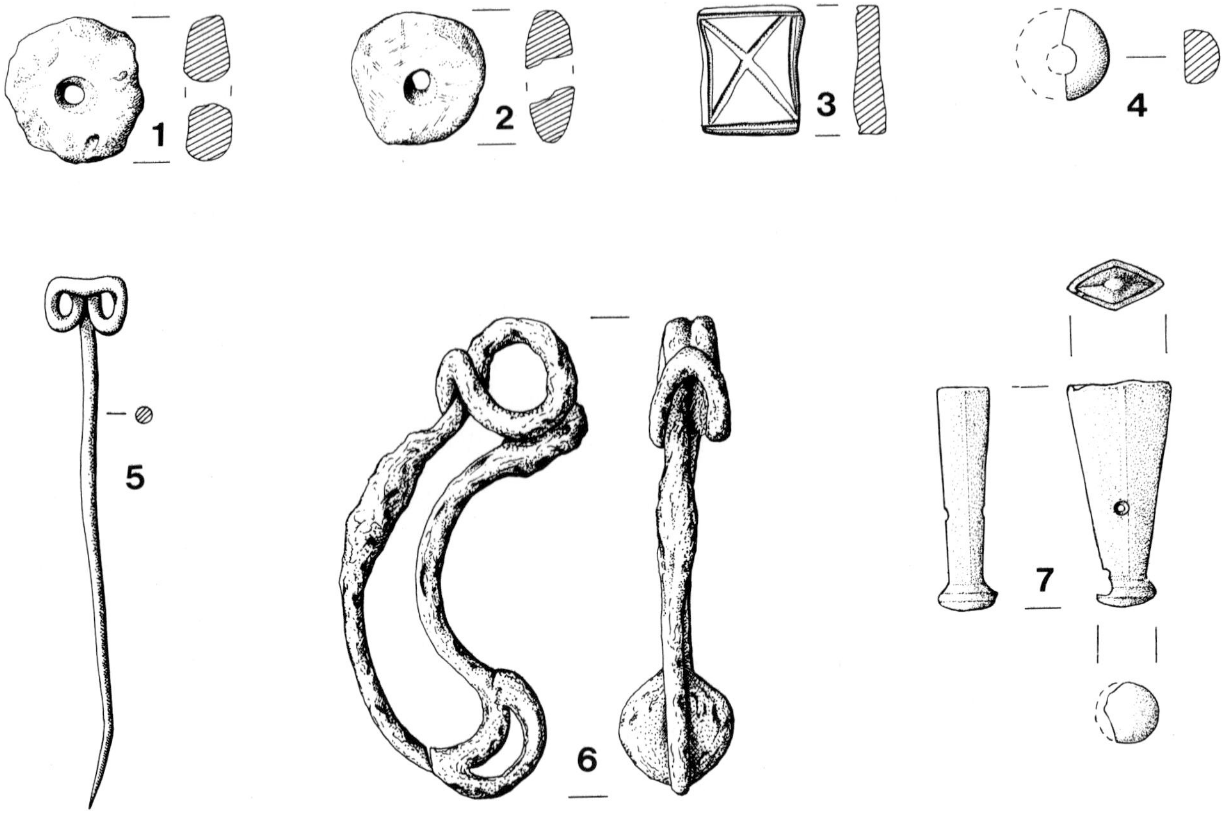

Fig. 13. *Chalk objects (½), a glass bead, bronze pin and iron brooch (1/1) and a bronze sword or dagger chape (½), Farningham Hill.*

(3). THE QUERNSTONES AND STONE-WEIGHT (?) (Fig. 14)

By Keith Parfitt, B.A.

The site produced fragments of eight definite quernstones of which two are illustrated (Nos. 10 and 11). All of these appear to be of rocks obtainable fairly locally; seven are probably Greensand and one is of a dense iron-stone. All the fragments except No. 11 are probably from rotary querns. No. 11 seems to be part of a Greensand saddle-quern. Eight other small stone fragments are too fragmentary to be identified as parts of querns. Most of these are, again, of Greensand but also included is a fragment of probable sarcen stone and a small piece of pebble conglomerate, which is not of local origin. In addition, a single stone rubber was recovered.

No. 10 Fragment of the upper stone of a rotary quern. Fine grained Greensand. The lower side has been dressed by rough pecking, whilst the upper side has been smoothed, perhaps by pounding. From upper fill of South Ditch (KMW–12–29).

No. 11 Small part of the lower stone of a Greensand saddle-quern. The two faces have been dressed by rough pecking. The concave upper one has been subsequently smoothed through use. From fill of Pit 5 (KMW–12–45).

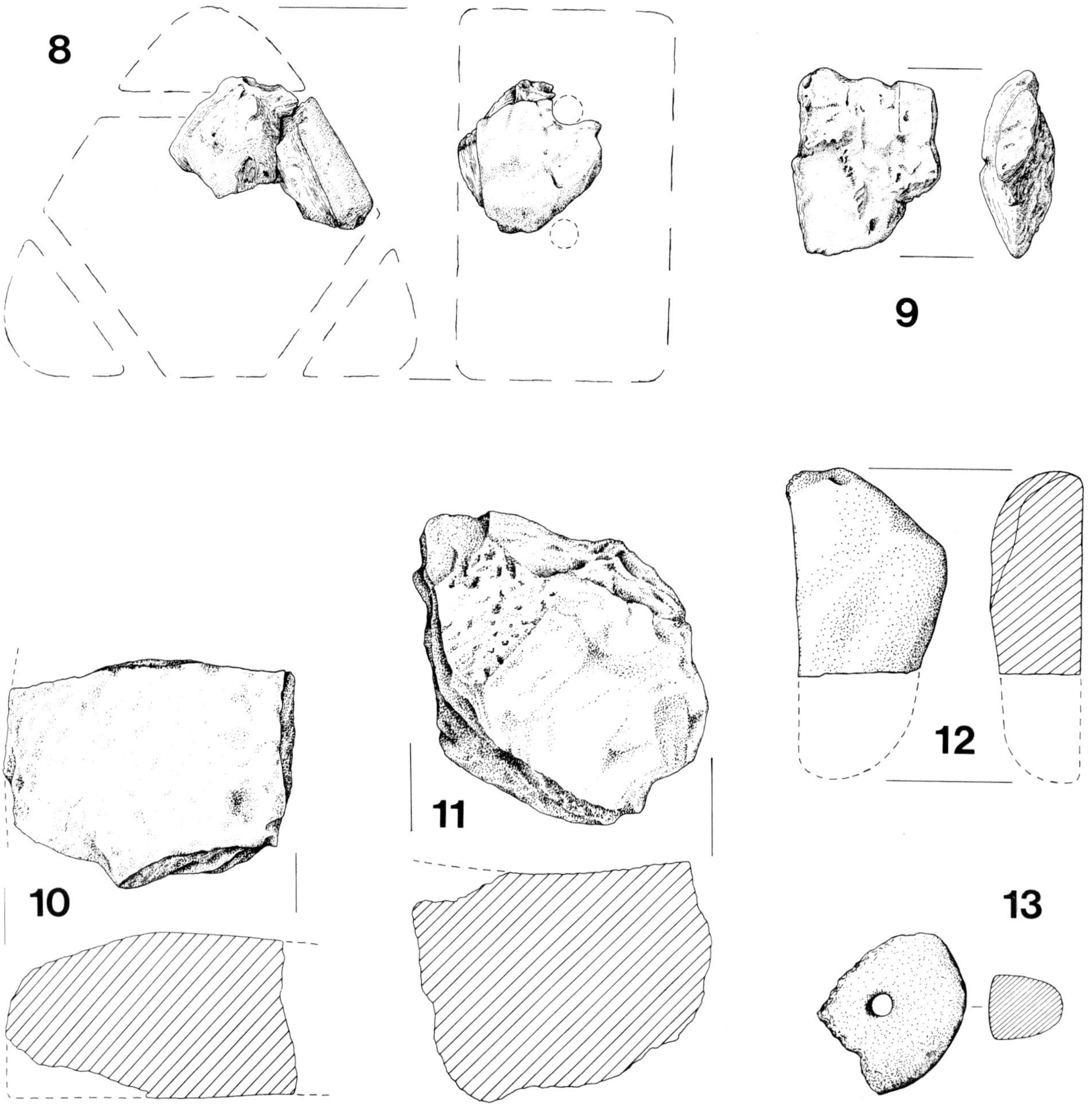

Fig. 14. *Baked-clay objects, quernstones and possible stone weight* ($\frac{1}{3}$) *Farningham Hill.*

No. 12 Part of a small stone rubber of fine hard orange-brown sandstone. One end has broken away. On one side the two facets appear to have been smoothed by use. From upper fill, South Ditch (KMW–12–35).

No. 13 Roughly oval sandstone (loom?) weight, with off-centre perforation. The shape suggests that it represents a quarter segment from a larger rounded stone object, later reworked and drilled. Weight 125 grams. From upper fill, South East Ditch (KMW–12–83).

(4). THE IRON AGE POTTERY (Figs. 15 to 21)

By Peter Couldrey, B.Sc.

As the Iron Age farmstead on Farningham Hill was subjected to total excavation it was possible to recover all the pottery that had survived on the site. This came from either the three enclosing ditches, or from the 24 pits found within the enclosure. In all some 2,585 sherds, weighing about 90 kg., were recovered and these represent an absolute minimum of 165 vessels, of which 148 have been illustrated (Nos. 14 –161).

While the quantity of pottery is not very large, it does provide the most extensive assemblage of late-Iron Age pottery so far recovered from closed groups in West Kent. It is dated from 50 B.C. to about A.D. 50.

The primary aim of this pottery report is to present the material for comparative purposes. Extensive parallels are not quoted and references are generally restricted to local published examples.

The method of study was as follows:– within each deposit sherds were grouped into a minimum number of vessels distinguished by fabric, form and extreme variations in wall thickness. Within some pits, sherds from the same vessel were found in different deposits. In these cases the deposits were merged. Some fabrics or forms were sufficiently distinctive or rare to enable sherds from the same vessel to be recognised in more than one feature. In many cases however, as with wall sherds of the ubiquitous shell-tempered fabric (H3–H8), this was not possible. Using this method, the resulting estimate of the number of vessels was 405. Each vessel was numbered and a record made of the weight, wall thickness, number of non-fitting sherds and the percentage of the total circumference represented by the surviving rims or bases (rim and base equivalents – Ref. 45). A catalogue was drawn up containing this data for all vessels from the site. A copy of this catalogue is held with the pottery.

This report describes the fabrics, forms and styles of decoration and then examines the internal chronology of the site, the date of its occupation and ends with a brief discussion of the material.

FABRICS

Fourteen fabric groups were identified macroscopically and have been distinguished on the basis of their primary inclusions. They have been designated A-P ('I' and 'O' were not used) and are described below. Some of these groups are homogeneous (A, B, C, F and G) while others include a wide variety of inclusions or size of inclusions. These have been sub-divided in order to indicate the extent of the variation; though it is acknowledged that these sub-groups may merely reflect points imposed on a continuous distribution rather than discrete groups. The term 'tempering' is used to describe inclusions in the clay matrix. It does not necessarily imply that these inclusions were added deliberately. Twenty sherds were submitted to Dr. I. Freestone of the British Museum Research Laboratory for thin-section analysis. Preliminary results have broadly confirmed the groups described below and have also served to identify the tempering of Fabric P as limestone. A detailed report is being prepared and a copy will be held with the excavation archive.

The distribution of fabrics by weight throughout the features is shown in Table D.

Fabric A

This is characterised by abundant inclusions of black rounded grains of glauconite between 0·2 and 0·3 mm. in diameter, and rare inclusions of sub-rounded grains of white translucent quartz, up to 2 mm. in size. Most of the sherds have a dark grey (N3) or black (N2) surface and grey (5YR6/1) core, though a few are light brown (7.5YR7/5) probably as a result of refiring. This fabric has been sub-divided into two groups on the basis of surface treatment:

A1 Sherds are burnished on both surfaces.

A2 Sherds are burnished on the external surface only. The internal surface remains smooth and the same colour as the core. One example (No. 91) has been attributed to A2, though the grains of glauconite are marginally larger, up to 0·35 mm., and slightly more widely spaced.

	Fabric															
Feature	A	B	C	D	E	F	G	H	J	K	L	M	N	P	Total	%
Pit 5	778	95		1073				114							2060	2·3
Pit 6		1		5	135			866	56	100	12		36		1211	1·3
Pit 9		7						121							128	0·1
Pit 10				11		9		292		65				15	392	0·4
Pit 11		9		92	24			2780		3					2908	3·2
Pit 12	33	2			43			14		7					99	0·1
Pit 13				20	3			122	4				110		259	0·3
Pit 14	10	2	14	5	2			1219	68				6		1326	1·5
Pit 15								38							38	0·04
Pit 16		10		5	137		3	6262	29		11		46217		52674	57·7
Pit 17								56					870		926	1·0
Pit 18	31	11						3288							3330	3·6
Pit 19													4		4	0·004
Pit 20	4	4		32	22			36	240						338	0·4
Fig 21	17			20				82							119	0·1
Pit 22				6											6	0·007
Pit 23	16	52			14			170		10					262	0·3
Pit 24								42							42	0·05
S.E. Ditch (Lower)	47	47			6			90	16	21		11			238	0·3
S.E. Ditch (Upper)	9	17		48	113	190		4501	243	144	7	40	1479		6791	7·4
South Ditch (Low/Mid.)		151		7				1051	90	10	3				1312	1·4
South Ditch (Top)	55	112		13	315	62		14016	21		4	71	5		14674	16·1
N.W. Ditch (Lower)	12				8			301	37	58	20				436	0·5
N.W. Ditch (Upper)	90			90	309	46		1093	48			11	26		1713	1·9
Total	1102	520	14	1427	1131	307	3	36554	852	418	57	133	48753	15	91286	
%	1·2	0·6	0·02	1·6	1·2	0·3	0·003	40·0	0·9	0·5	0·06	0·1	53·4	0·02		

Table D – The Distribution of Fabrics by Weight (gm.)

Fabric B

This, like Fabric A, is characterised by abundant inclusions of black sub-rounded grains of glauconite, but these are finer, less than 0·2 mm. in size. In addition moderate inclusions of vegetable tempering are represented by voids of up to 0·5 mm. in size. The surfaces are generally smooth or lightly burnished. This fabric has been sub-divided into two groups:–

B1 Sherds generally have a dark grey (N3) burnished exterior surface and smooth interior surface with a grey (5YR6/1) core.

B2 Similar to B1, but in addition, sherds have common inclusions of iron oxides up to 2 mm. in size; and these often result in a brown (2.5YR5/6) colouring of the core and surfaces.

Fabric C

A hard sandy fabric with burnished surfaces. No inclusions are visible. Only two vessels (Nos. 52 and 60) were found in this fabric, both fired light brown (7.5YR7/5) throughout.

Fabric D

A very hard sandy fabric with smooth burnished surfaces. This is characterised by abundant rounded grains of black glauconite, about 0·1 mm. in size, and common rounded grains of translucent quartz about 0·1–0·2 mm. in diameter. The colours vary from brown (5YR5/6) to light or dark grey (5YR6/1–N3). This fabric is distinguished from Fabric B1 by its hardness, though this may be due to refiring.

Fabric E

Miscellaneous sandy wares. This group contains a variety of sandy fabrics, some of which are represented by only one vessel. Grog is present in three (E4, E5 and E7) but their predominantly sandy texture has been responsible for their inclusion in this group.

E1 A hard burnished fabric characterised by common inclusions of very fine quartz, 0·2 to 0·4 mm. in size and sparse to moderate inclusions of iron oxides between 0·5 and 1·5 mm. in size. Sherds are generally grey or dark grey (N3) throughout, though some have brown (5YR5/6) patches on the surface, possibly as a result of refiring.

E2 A hard burnished fabric characterised by moderate grains of fine white translucent quartz (0·5 mm.), rare grains of medium quartz (1–2 mm.) and rare grains of iron oxides up to 1 mm. in size. Sherds are generally grey (10YR4/1) or dark grey (N3).

E3 A hard burnished fabric characterised by abundant grains of very fine quartz (0·2 mm.). Sherds are generally grey (10YR4/1) or dark grey (N3) throughout.

E4 A hard highly burnished fabric characterised by abundant very fine grains of glauconite (0·1 mm.), common grains of iron oxides (up to 1 mm.), and opaque light brown grains of grog up to 1 mm. in size. Only one vessel, a carinated bowl (No. 79), was found in this fabric. Colours varied from light grey (N5) to black (N2.5).

E5 A soft sandy fabric with abundant very fine grains of quartz (0·1 mm.), moderate fragments of shell (up to 2 mm.), sparse grains of iron oxides (1 mm.), and moderate inclusions of black grog (1 mm.) and vegetable tempering, represented by black voids up to 2 mm. in length. Apart from one very worn sherd, all examples of this fabric had combed decoration on an orange-brown (10R5/6) external surface and a grey to brown (5YR3/1 – 5YR4/2) internal surface and core (e.g. No. 27). Some sherds from Pits 6 and 16, the South East Ditch and the South Ditch may come from a single vessel.

E6 Shell in sandy matrix: a soft fabric characterised by sparse to moderate inclusions of shell (generally less than 1 mm., rare up to 4 mm.) moderate inclusions of quartz (0·2 mm.) and sparse inclusions of iron oxides (0·5 mm.). Colours vary from brown (5YR5/6) to dark grey (N3).

E7 A very hard burnished fabric, represented by one wheel-turned everted rim vessel (No. 29). Common small black inclusions (less than 0·3 mm.) may represent grog. Inside the rim, where the surface has not been burnished, the fabric feels sandy. No other inclusions are visible. The colour is generally grey (10YR4/1) to dark grey (N3).

E8 A hard burnished fabric, represented by one everted rim (No. 38). This has common inclusions of quartz (up to 0·2 mm.), sparse inclusions of iron oxides (up to 1 mm.) and abundant very fine black grains (up to 0·1 mm.) possibly of glauconite. This one sherd has been fired light brown (7.5YR5/2) throughout.

E9 A general category to cover medieval and later intrusive material. This includes tile, hard sandy wares and stoneware.

Fabric F

This group covers wares with grog tempering in a sandy matrix. All the vessels represented are hard, well fired and had smooth surfaces. The colours vary from grey (10YR4/1) to dark grey (N3). All include common to abundant grains of quartz between 0·5 and 1·00 mm. in size. This group has been sub-divided according to the size of inclusions:–

F1 Characterised by abundant black grains of grog (0·5 to 1·00 mm.), common inclusions of iron oxides (2 mm.) and moderate inclusions of shell (1 mm.).

F2 Characterised by abundant black grains of grog (0·5 to 1·00 mm.).

F3 Characterised by abundant black grains of grog (0·5 to 1·00 mm.), and common inclusions of iron oxides (2 mm.).

Fabric G

A fine 'mica-dusted' fabric, represented by one wheel-turned vessel (from feature Pit 16, not illustrated). Dr. Paul Tyers has examined this fabric and reports as follows:–

"Two sherds (probably from the same vessel) in a fine micaceous orange-brown fabric represent a type of vessel which has been previously recognised at a number of Late Iron Age sites in S.E. England (Ref. 46 and 48).

The examples from Camulodunum fall into two broad form categories – the Cam. 262, an ovoid jar with a thickened and heavily moulded rim and the Cam. 102 which has a thinner wall, a single rim-moulding and an angle at the shoulder (Ref. 47). Many of the Cam. 262 are in a coarsely tempered dark grey-brown or red-brown fabric with prominent angular pink and white feldspar and biotite mica inclusions (the latter is also applied as a surface wash in some instances) and sparser quartz and small black and red grains. The Cam. 102 is typically in a finer textured orange-brown ware with a golden-brown micaceous slip on the rim and shoulder, and this is the fabric represented here.

The Farningham Hill sherds have a grey-brown core (10R 5/1) with orange-brown margins (10R 5/8) and lighter orange surfaces (2.5YR 6/6 – one of the sherds has a grey discolouration on the external surface). The fabric is hard and fairly smooth and tempered with moderately abundant white or glassy quartz (0·1–0·2 mm.), occasionally up to 0·5 mm. diameter; sub-angular and sparser feldspar (0·1–0·4 mm. angular), white and gold mica (0·1–0·7 mm., particularly prominent in the surface) and small black and red inclusions (up to 0·5 mm. – probably including iron ores and volcanic or ferro-magnesian minerals). Cam. 102 jars in an apparently identical fabric have been identified at Camulodunum and Skeleton Green and analysis of thin-sections suggests a source in an area of plutonic and volcanic rocks. It is likely that at least some of the British examples of Cam. 102 and 262 jars originate in Central France, perhaps towards the Morvan area where vessels of similar form and fabric are known (Ref. 48).

These Central Gaulish imports are an interesting addition to our data on the relations between Britain and France towards the middle of the first century A.D. and a useful counterbalance to the considerable evidence for commercial relations with the 'Gallo-Belgic' regions of Northern Gaul."

Fabric H

Shell tempered fabric with occasional inclusions of vegetable tempering. Vessels in this fabric occur in a wide range of colours from light brown to dark grey or black (7.5YR7/5 – N2) and may be soft or hard, reflecting variable firing conditions. The surfaces of most of the vessels have been wiped smooth, allowing the shell tempering to remain visible. Slurry has been used in some instances (*cf.* No. 21) to cover the shell, and a few examples have been burnished. This group has been sub-divided into two categories:– one with a sandy matrix, the other with a smooth soapy feel. Quartz grains are common or abundant in the former but rare in the latter. Grog is visible in some of the soapy examples. Each of these categories has been sub-divided according to the size of inclusion.

Shell in sandy matrix

H1 A hard fabric with common inclusions of shell up to 1 mm. in size. This is represented by one vessel (No. 125) with stamped and grooved decoration.

H2 A hard fabric with abundant inclusions of shell fragments up to 3 mm. in size. Larger fragments are rare. This fabric was restricted to one storage vessel (No. 144).

H3 Common to abundant inclusions of shell up to 5 mm. in size.

H4 Common to abundant inclusions of shell up to 7 mm. in size.

H5 Common to abundant inclusions of shell greater than 7 mm. in size.

Shell in soapy fabric.

H6 Common to abundant inclusions of shell usually between 2 and 3 mm., but with rare examples up to 5 mm. in size.

H7 Common to abundant inclusions of shell up to 7 mm. in size.

H8 Common to abundant inclusions of shell greater than 7 mm. in size.

Samples of this fabric were examined by Dr. John Cooper who reports on the molluscan evidence, as follows:–

"Sample 1 (Fabric H2) South Ditch, upper. (No. 144)

Medium-finely crushed shell fragments, mostly of bivalves, in a brownish matrix. Shows parallel alignment of ?grass stem impressions on exterior and some carbonised plant remains and ?grass impressions within the matrix on the interior. There are a few quartz sand grains in the matrix. This ware could have been fired at a higher temperature than the other two samples, but is essentially of the same original material.

Sample 2 (Fabric H7) South Ditch, upper.

Coarse shell fragments, mostly of the corbiculid bivalve *Polymesoda cordata* (Morris). The lighter coloured interior surface shows some ?grass stem impressions, and may be a "slip" applied to the coarse black core.

Sample 3 (Fabric H8) Pit 10.

Coarse to very coarse shell fragments, mostly of corbiculid bivalves and the apex of the gastropod *Brotia melanioides* (J. Sowerby). Coarse wares, seemingly with the original shaly bedding unaltered by pre-mixing. The black shelly clay is fairly plastic and without much preparation of it, a sort of dish or platter could be cut from it and fired; as the clay contains much organic matter it may even be self-firing (tests on fresh clay could be made to establish this). These remarks could also apply to Sample 2. The fabric and contained molluscs are similar to those reported in 1977 from Bishopstone, Sussex (Ref. 49).

All three samples are made from the so-called Black Shelly Clays of the Woolwich Beds, which represent an estuarine phase of this Formation in the Palaeocene (about 55–60 million years ago). This material would be found locally – for instance, it occurs in road cuttings on the A2 at Swanscombe Hill and Cobham, and probably much nearer to Farningham itself. Locally made ware from local materials, probably not suitable for small vessels without much previous grinding."

Fabric J

Fabric tempered with calcined flint. Most of the vessels in this group are well fired and hard. Colours vary from light brown to dark grey (7.5YR7/5 – N3) and the surfaces are often burnished. The group has been sub-divided according to the size of flint and the presence of other inclusions.

J1 Abundant inclusions of angular flint up to 3 mm., rare up to 5 mm., in a sandy matrix. Surfaces are hard and burnished.

J2 Moderate to abundant inclusions of angular flint up to 2 mm. in size. Surfaces are hard and may be slipped or burnished.

J3 Sparse inclusions of flint less than 1 mm. in size, in a sandy matrix. The surfaces are smooth.

J4 As for J3 but with additional inclusions of iron oxides up to 1 mm. in size.

Fabric K

Vegetable tempered fabric. This group is characterised by the presence of voids with black edges, representing the remains of vegetable material. Most of the surviving sherds are hard and the surfaces are smooth or burnished. The colours vary from brown to dark grey (7.5YR7/5 – N3). The group has been sub-divided according to type, quantity and size of inclusion.

K1 Common black voids up to 3 mm. in length with common inclusions of white rounded quartz up to 1 mm. in size.

K2 Common black voids up to 5 mm. in length with common grains of translucent quartz up to 0·2 mm., moderate inclusions of iron oxides (0·5 mm.) and rare inclusions of flint (1 mm.).

K3 Common voids up to 17 mm. (average 5–9 mm.) with other inclusions as for K2. Each example is worn and the surfaces sandy.

K4 Sparse to moderate voids up to 6 mm. with moderate inclusions of iron oxides (1 mm.) and moderate inclusions of translucent quartz up to 1 mm. in size.

Fabric L

Flint and shell tempered fabric, with occasional inclusions of vegetable tempering. Vessels in this fabric occur in a wide range of colours from light brown to dark grey (7.5YR7/5 – N3) and may be soft or hard. The matrix is generally sandy and the surfaces may be smooth or burnished. The group has been sub-divided according to the size of inclusions.

L1 Flint: common inclusions of 6–9 mm. and moderate inclusions of 1–2 mm.
Shell: moderate inclusions of 3–4 mm. and rare inclusions of 5–6 mm.

L2 Flint: common inclusions of up to 1 mm. and moderate inclusions of 4–5 mm.
Shell: sparse inclusions of 1–5 mm.

L3 Flint: abundant inclusions of up to 1 mm. and rare inclusions up to 3 mm.
Shell: moderate inclusions of up to 2 mm.

L4 Flint: common to abundant inclusions of up to 2 mm.
Shell: moderate inclusions of 3–4 mm.

L5 Flint: moderate to common inclusions of 1–2 mm.
Shell: moderate inclusions of 1–2 mm.

L6 Flint and shell: sparse inclusions of less than 1 mm.

Fabric M

Vegetable and shell tempering. This is distinguished from Fabric H by the more abundant use of vegetable tempering. The colours vary from light brown to dark grey (7.5YR7/5 – N3). The matrix is sandy and the surfaces have been smoothed. This group has been sub-divided according to the inclusions.

M1 Vegetable: moderate to common up to 8 mm. long.
Shell: moderate between 3 and 9 mm., common 4–6 mm.

M2 Vegetable: moderate inclusions about 3 mm. long.
Shell: sparse to moderate inclusions of 2–4 mm.
Iron oxides: moderate inclusions of 1–2 mm.

Fabric N

Grog tempered fabric. No single grog tempered fabric was found; rather a range of fabrics whose primary inclusion was grog. Colours varied; but the small and medium sized vessels tended to be grey, often with a dark grey burnished surface, while the larger storage jars exhibited a range of colours from dark grey to brown (N3–5YR5/3). The fabric is generally soft and feels soapy. The sherds from one storage jar (No. 83) were extremely crumbly, suggesting that the vessel had been underfired. The group is sub-divided according to the inclusions and their size.

N1 Abundant inclusions of grog of 1–2 mm. and sparse inclusions up to 3 mm. These generally appear as dark grey inclusions in a light grey core. (Found as Forms 7 and 8).

N2 A coarser version of N1 with abundant inclusions of grog up to 8 mm. in size. This is found on thick-walled vessels (generally greater than 7 mm. – forms unknown).

N3 Abundant inclusions of grog up to 1 mm. in size and common inclusions of iron oxides up to 2 mm. (found as Forms 7 and 8).

N4 A coarser version of N3 with abundant inclusions of grog up to 2 mm. and moderate to common grains of iron oxides up to 3 mm., rarely up to 8 mm. (Found as thick-walled storage jars – Form 12).

N5 Abundant inclusions of grog, up to 1 mm. in size, moderate inclusions of iron oxides, up to 0·5 mm. and sparse to moderate inclusions of flint up to 2 mm. (Found as Form 10C).

N6 Abundant inclusions of grog, up to 2 mm. and sparse inclusions of shell up to 1 mm. (Found as Form 9A).

N7 A coarser version of N6 with inclusions of grog up to 3 mm. and moderate inclusions of shell up to 3 mm., sparse up to 5 mm. (Found as Form 10A).

N8 Common inclusions of grog up to 2 mm., sparse to moderate inclusions of shell up to 3 mm. and moderate inclusions of iron oxides up to 1 mm. (Found as Forms 7, 9 and 10).

N9 Moderate to common inclusions of grog up to 1 mm., sparse to common inclusions of iron oxides up to 3 mm., sparse inclusions of shell up to 2 mm., and moderate to abundant inclusions of vegetable tempering, represented by voids up to 3 mm. in length. (Found as Forms 8 and 9).

Fabric P

A very hard fabric with abundant inclusions of limestone up to 2 mm. in size. The surfaces are burnished and the fabric fired dark grey (N3) to brown (7.5YR5/2). This is represented by one vessel only (No. 37).

TYPOLOGY

The typological division set out below is intended to reflect the range of forms represented and to act as an aid to discussion. Complete profiles were rare and most of the classification is based on rims. In particular, Forms 1–3 cover a wide range of mainly irregular hand-made vessels which are sub-divided on the basis of detailed differences in rim profiles. As a result, some rims are grouped with more than one form (Nos. 92, 114 and 161). Some forms are clearly 'Belgic' and, where appropriate, reference is made to Dr. Isobel Thompson's type series (Ref. 50).

The association of fabrics and forms is shown in Table E, and the distribution of forms throughout the features in Table F.

FORM 1A Upright Rims with Rounded Tops (No. 127).

i Open bowls and jars with rim diameter greater than 16 cm. (Nos. 22, 56, 75, 136, 139, 156).
ii Cup or beaker with rim diameter less than 16 cm. (No. 124).
iii Jar or bowl with a thinned rim (No. 140).
iv Jar or bowl with a rim with external thickening (No. 138).
v Jar with cuts across the rim (No. 36).

FORM 1B Upright Rims with Flat Tops (No. 103).

i Storage jar (No. 76).
ii Open bowls or jars (Nos. 19, 40, 93).
iii Upright thickened rims with flat tops (Nos. 21, 50, 97, 150).
iv Upright rim with flat top and external expansion (Nos. 20, 51).

	Fabric													
Form	A	B	C	D	E	F	G	H	J	K	L	M	N	P
1								25		2				
2		1						23						
3								5						
4	5	6	1	6	4				1	1				
5				1				8		2		1		
6								1						
7					1	2		1					5	
8									1				7	
9			1		1								5	
10								2	1				4	1
11								1						
12													5	
13					1									
14													1	
15	1													
16									1		1			

Table E. The association of forms with fabrics. Each value refers to the number of vessels.

FORM 1C **Shouldered Jars**

- i With plain rim (Nos. 35, 39).
- ii With internally-bevelled rim (No. 42).

FORM 2 **Closed Jar Forms.** Within this group can be seen developing bead and recessed rims, both of which were to become common in the post-Conquest period. Three examples show the recessed rim emerging almost by accident from other forms (Nos. 92, 114 and 161).

2A
- i Small jar with plain rounded rim (No. 78).
- ii Small jar with prominent shoulder (No. 80).
- iii Large jar with plain rounded rim (No. 147).
- iv Large jar with plain slightly everted rim (No. 101).

2B
- i Bead rim with external expansion and groove (Nos. 74, 89, 92).
- ii Bead rim expanded both internally and externally (No. 122).

2C
- i Incurving rim with flattened top and external expansion (Nos. 43, 47, 54, 114, 148, 161).
- ii Incurving rim with flattened top and external projection (Nos. 99, 110, 160).
- iii Incurving rim with recessed top and external expansion (Thompson's type L5–1). (Nos. 24, 92, 114, 134, 161).
- iv Incurving rim with recessed top and external projection (No. 53, 48).

2D
- i Incurving rim with flat top and internal expansion (Nos. 73, 98).
- ii Incurving rim with flat top and internal projection (Nos. 71, 94).
- iii Incurving rim with internal bevel (No. 72).

FORM 3A **Open Bowl or Jar Forms**

i Out-turned rim with flat top (No. 23).
ii Out-turned rim with flat top and internal projection (No. 112).
iii Rim with rounded top and internal projection (No. 128).
iv Rim with rounded top and external expansion (Nos. 129, 131).

FORM 4 **Everted Rim Jars.** This group covers jars with everted rims which rise in a smooth curve from the neck and have a gentle internal swelling. They are generally plain, often with highly burnished surfaces, though burnished 'decoration' does occasionally occur beneath the base (see comments on decoration Type b below) and wall sherds with curvilinear grooves probably belong to this group (decoration Type d). This form was used by Ward Perkins as the type-fossil of his 'Wealden' Culture (Ref. 51) and is now known to have a widespread distribution from Sussex to Essex (Ref. 52). Local examples are known from Greenhithe (Ref. 53), Caesar's Camp, Keston (Ref. 54), Crayford (Ref. 55), Hulbury and Oldbury (Ref. 56). (Nos. 16, 17, 18, 26, 38, 41, 45, 46, 49, 52, 57, 84, 95, 100, 104, 121 and 155). These may be sub-divided according to the type of base:–

4A Widely splayed low pedestal (Nos. 14, 102).

4B Less widely splayed foot-ring (Nos. 90, 119, 153, 154).

4C Slight foot-ring (No. 15).

FORM 5 **Other Plain Everted Rim Forms.** This group contains miscellaneous forms which cannot be placed with those in Group 4, though some may be copies of that form.

5A Jar with sharply everted rim (No. 151).

5B Rim is thin at the neck and thickens towards the top (No. 34).

5C Everted rim with flat top (Nos. 58, 135, 141).

5D Coarse everted rims of irregular profile. (Nos. 32, 33, 137, 142, 143, 149, 157).

FORM 6 **Saucepan Pot.** This form is rare in Kent and more characteristic of groups to the south and west in central Southern England (Ref. 57). The occurrence of this form in a shell tempered fabric with a decorated base may be regarded as a local copy (No. 28).

FORM 7 **Necked Bowls.** These are distinguished by having a cordon or groove on, or at the base of, the neck below a thickened, externally-projecting or slightly everted rim. (Thompson's type D1–1). (Nos. 65, 130, 133, 146 and 158). They may be sub-divided according to the type of base:–

7A Foot-ring base (No. 63).

7B Flat base (Nos. 61, 62). (Thompson's types E2–3 and D1–4).

FORM 8 **Pedestal Jars.** These are distinguished by having a pedestal base; but the group also includes those jar forms with grooves or cordons on the body. Four examples have been wheel-turned (Nos. 64, 69, 115 and 132).

8A Grooves on the neck and shoulder (Nos. 64, 69).

8B Multiple cordons on the wall (Thompson's type A3). (Nos. 67, 107).

8C Quoit-shaped pedestal base (Thompson's type A1). (Nos. 68, 115).

8D Substantial pedestal base hand-made with a coil (No. 96).

8E Solid pedestal with flat foot (Thompson's type A8). (No. 132).

FORM 9 **Everted-Rim Jars or Bowls with Cordons or Grooves on the Neck or Shoulder.** This group includes forms that cannot be attributed with certainty to Forms 7 or 8. Two examples have been wheel-turned (Nos. 31, 70).

9A Grooves on neck and shoulder (Thompson's type B2–1). (Nos. 31, 66, 70, 120, 159).

9B Cordon on neck (Thompson's type B1). (Nos. 29, 60).

FORM 10 **Globular Jars.** These are distinguished from Form 2 by having a more regular profile.

10A Beaker or small jar with short everted rim. (Nos. 109, 123).

10B Jar with externally projecting rim (Nos. 25, 37).

10C Large jars with everted rims (Thompson's type B1–7). (Nos. 30, 105, 113, 118).

FORM 11 **Storage Jar** with a thickened flat-topped rim on an upright neck (No. 144).

FORM 12 **Storage Jar** with a thick bead rim. This form continued into the post-Conquest period, though often with everted rim (*cf.* Calfstock Lane, Farningham, Ref. 58). (Thompson's type C6–1).

12A Stabbed decoration on a raised cordon around the shoulder (Nos. 82, 83, 88).

12B Stabbed chevron decoration around the shoulder (No. 81).

12C Grooved (chevron?) decoration around the shoulder (No. 116).

FORM 13 **Carinated Bowl or Beaker.** (Thompson's type E1–2?). (No. 79).

FORM 14 **Small Bowl or Cup with Omphalos Base.** Small cups with omphalos bases occur occasionally in 'Belgic' contexts in the South-East (Thompson's type E2–4), but a closer parallel to this form with a constricted bead rim is found at Dragonby, Lincs. (Ref. 59). (No. 77).

FORM 15 **Bowl with Omphalos Base,** or thumb-impressed decoration on the wall. (No. 91).

FORM 16 **Lids**

16A Thick almost flat (could be a shallow dish). (No. 106).

16B Raised. (No. 152).

DECORATION

In addition to the forms described above, some of the vessels were decorated and this decoration has been divided into fourteen categories.

(a). Finger Nail Impressions (No. 36).
The use of finger-nail and finger-tip impressions on the rim or shoulder of vessels is well known from late-Bronze Age/early-Iron Age contexts; but the oblique columns on this example are hard to parallel. The size and condition of these sherds provide no reason to suppose that the pot is residual. The use of finger-nail impressions on the rim is found on a vessel associated with the primary defences at Oldbury (Ref. 60).

(b). Decorated Bases (Nos. 14, 15, 28, 57, 102, 153).
With the exception of No. 28, this decoration appears on footring bases. Similar examples are known from Essex to Sussex associated with Type 4 everted rim footring jars (e.g. Mucking, Ref. 61 and The Caburn, Ref. 62). Local published examples from West Kent have been found at Greenhithe (Ref. 63) and Oldbury (Ref. 64). These fall within Cunliffe's Mucking-Crayford style, (Ref. 65), dated from the third to the first centuries B.C.

(c). A Single Groove Forming a Wave Pattern, Bordered by Two Horizontal Grooves (No. 28).
This style of decoration is commonly found on saucepan pots and comparable designs are known from Surrey (e.g. Hawk's Hill, Ref. 66) and Sussex (e.g. Bishopstone, Ref. 67) and dated from the third to first centuries B.C.

(d). Two or More Curvilinear Grooves (No. 41).
The full design is not known, but similar examples forming part of a scroll pattern have been found at Greenhithe (Ref. 68) and Caesar's Camp, Keston (Ref. 69), where they were associated with Type 4 everted-rim footring jars. The occurrence of this example in Fabric D tends to support this association (see below).

(e). Stamped and Grooved Designs (Nos. 91 and 125).
This general style of decoration is now well known and examples from the Thames Estuary and the Lower Thames regions have been discussed by Elsdon (Ref. 70). No. 91 is hard to parallel in detail. No. 125 however, has interlocking arcs and what appears to be a roundel motif flanked by triangular stamps. Interlocking arcs occur throughout the region, and the association of roundels and triangular stamps is found on a vessel from Canvey Island (Ref. 71).

(f). 'Comb'-Stamped or Rouletted Decoration around a Row of Lozenges (No. 145).
The use of comb-stamped decoration to fill panels is rare in the South East but appear to be related to rouletting which is more common in Lincolnshire or the South West (Ref. 72). One similar example can be cited, again from Canvey Island (Ref. 73).

(g). Circular Stamp with Incised Line (No. 126).
Circular stamps are known from the Lower Thames region, but they usually appear in groups; are smaller than this example, and are not linked by incised lines.

(h). Lattice Pattern (Nos. 37 and 44).
Burnish lattice decoration is found on a small globular vessel (No. 37) and one wall sherd. One sherd with similar decoration was found at Little Waltham in a period III, pre-'Belgic' context (Ref. 74). Other local examples are more commonly associated with 'Belgic' forms, and the pattern became popular in the post-Conquest period.

(j). Open Lattice Decoration (No. 61).
Burnished open lattice decoration is here found on a necked bowl; is known from 'Belgic' contexts, e.g. Aylesford (Ref. 75), and was popular in the post-Conquest period.

(k). Oblique Lines (No. 60).
Burnished oblique lines are here associated with a vessel with a horizontal cordon. Similar examples are known from 'Belgic' contexts, e.g. Southend (Ref. 76).

(l). Horizontal Cordons or Grooves (Nos. 29, 31, 37, 60, 61, 62, 63, 64, 66, 67, 69, 70, 105, 107, 108, 118, 120, 146, 158 and 159).
This type of decoration is commonly associated with 'Belgic' wheel-thrown pottery, to the extent of being almost diagnostic of the group (Ref. 77).

(m). Combed Scored Surfaces. These vary considerably and may be sub-divided as:–
Light: Nos. 27, 117.
Medium: Nos. 59, 156
Coarse: Nos. 105, 111, 118, 122.
These are associated with closed and globular forms (Form 2Bii-No. 122 and Form 10C Nos. 105 and 118). The contexts of these examples, Pits 6, 14 and the upper fills of the ditches, support a 'Belgic' date for this form of decoration.

(n). Stabbed Chevrons in Horizontal Bands around the Shoulder (Nos. 81, 82, 83, 88).
These occur on Form 12 storage vessels and are well known from the 'Belgic' and post-Conquest periods, e.g. at Gun Hill, Essex (Ref. 78).

(p). Linear Design incised after Firing (No. 85).
The full pattern represented on this sherd is unknown. Indeed these marks could be regarded as accidental scratches acquired during the life of the pot rather than deliberate decoration.

The evidence for the internal chronology of the site is based on the stratigraphy within the ditch fills and the seriation of the pit groups. Although many pits contained more than one deposit, some contained very little pottery; some contained sherds from the same vessel throughout their fill; and others reveal no significant change in the forms between levels. Stratigraphy within the ditch fills was more useful. Comparison of the contents of the lower and upper fills shows that distinctions can be made between the distribution of forms (Table F) and fabrics (Table G). In the discussion which follows these two phases of ditch fill are treated separately and the fill of each pit is considered as a whole.

Form	Pit 5	Pit 12	South East Ditch Lower	Pit 15	Pit 21	South Ditch Lower	North West Ditch Lower	Pit 9	Pit 23	Pit 11	Pit 18	Pit 10	Pit 20	Pit 24	Pit 14	Pit 13	South Ditch Top	North West Ditch Upper	Pit 6	South East Ditch Upper	Pit 16	Pit 17
4	5	2	2						1	1	1	1	1		2	1		3	1	2	1	
1	2		1	1	1	4	1			1	1	4			1	3		1	2	1	2	
5						3	1	2				1			1		3	1				
16							1													1		
2									2	1	2		1	1	2	2	2	1	1	4	6	
10												1							2	5		
15											1											
8													1							3	4	
9															1			1		1	2	
7																	1	1	2	3	4	
12																				1	3	1
3																			1	4		
6																			1			
13																					1	
14																					1	
11																	1	(1)				
Total	7	2	3	1	1	7	3	2	3	3	5	7	3	1	7	6	7	9	10	25	24	1

Table F. Distribution of Forms throughout the Pits and Ditches.

CHRONOLOGY

Table F shows the distribution of forms among features. Only five pits (Pits 16, 10, 6, 5 and 14) contained more than five vessels with recognisable forms. This sample is too small to allow detailed assessment of the relative chronology of all the features. Nevertheless, it does permit some general comments to be made.

Forms 1, 4, 5 and 16 (upright rims, everted rims and one lid) were found in the lower fills of the ditches. Pits 5, 9, 12, 15 and 21 contained only these forms and are here regarded as belonging to Phase 1. In practice, only Pit 5 contained a sample large enough to enable it to be considered early. Forms 1, 4 and 5 occurred in most pottery groups from the site in residual contexts, and the other features have been included in this phase because they lack later forms.

The remaining features are attributed to Phase 2. The distribution of forms within this second group however, does suggest that a further sub-division into Phases 2A and 2B is possible. Seven of these Pits (10, 11, 13, 18, 20, 23 and 24) contain the early forms and one other form (2, 10 or 8). Forms 2 and 10 are closely related and this group appears to represent the new use of closed forms. Pit 18 is included here because its additional form (15) is unique and its appearance in Fabric A suggests an early date (see below). These features could be interpreted as representing an intermediate period, Phase 2A.

Pits 6, 14, 16 and 17, together with the upper fills of the ditches, contain a wider range of vessel forms and may represent a final phase (2B) in the use of the site. The differences between these last two phases however need reflect no more than the widespread use of Form 2 and the relatively small size of the sample from the intermediate group.

An examination of the distribution of fabrics enables the sample size to be increased to include all sherds rather than just those with identifiable forms. First it is necessary to identify those fabrics which are chronologically distinct. Table E shows the association of forms with fabrics. Of the forms identified as belonging to Phase 1, Form Nos. 1 and 5 are found mainly in shell tempered fabric (H), which is used for many other forms and is too common to reflect chronological variation (Table D). Form 4, the everted-rim footring jar, occurs in sandy fabrics of which A, B and D are not also associated with later 'Belgic' forms.

Of the remaining fabrics, only Fabric N is associated exclusively with 'Belgic' forms and may be used to identify a later group.

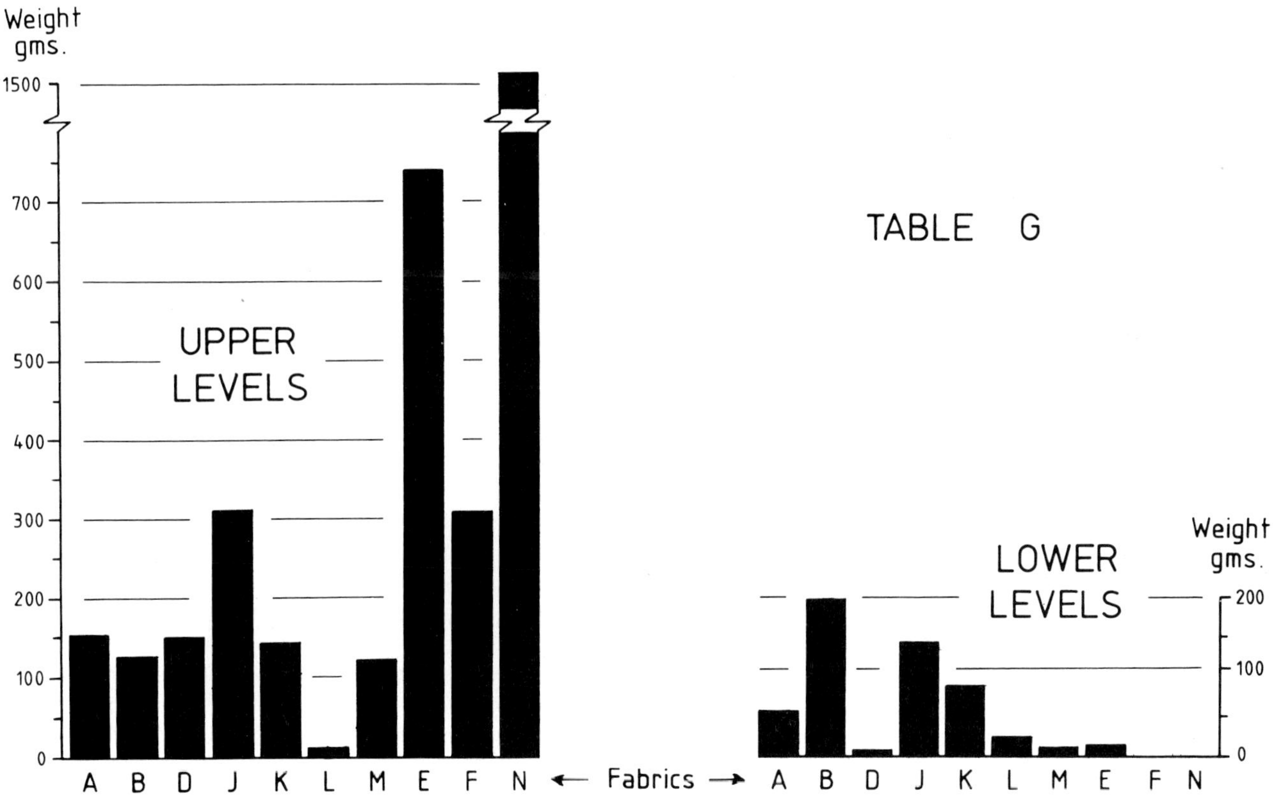

TABLE G

Graph showing distribution of fabrics by weight (gms) in the upper and lower levels of the ditches

The distribution of fabrics within the ditches supports this division: Fabrics A, B and D appear in the lower fills (264 gm. 13·3% of weight) and less frequently in the upper fills (434 gm., 1·9%). Fabric N however is present only in upper fills (1510 gm. 6·5%).

The distribution of Fabrics A, B, D and N, shown as a percentage of the weight of pottery from each feature, is illustrated in Table H. This confirms the broad grouping into Phases 1 and 2 identified above by the distribution of forms. Phase 2A is here characterised by the total lack of grog (Fabric N) and very low percentages of Fabrics A, B and D. This is due to the relatively high percentage of shell and flint tempered fabrics, as a result of the small sample size (Table D).

Having outlined the evidence for the internal chronology of the site, the date of occupation may now be considered. Phase 1 is characterised by the everted-rim footring jar and may be attributed to Cunliffe's Mucking-Crayford style (Ref. 79), dated from the third to mid-first centuries B.C. It is unlikely that the settlement began before about 50 B.C. since the quantity of pottery from features attributed to Phase 1 is small (4302 gm., 4·7% of the total weight of pottery from the site) and was followed by later forms apparently without a break.

The estimate of the date of abandonment is based on comparison with other local assemblages and the presence of an imported vessel in mica-dusted fabric (G) in the fill of Pit 16 – probably the latest group on the site. In his discussion of this fabric (see above), Dr. Tyers has placed it towards the middle of the first century A.D. The small quantity (3 gm.) found could be regarded as residual but comparison of the remaining 'Belgic' forms with other local assemblages confirms this date.

The use of some native forms and fabrics is known to have continued into the second half of the first century A.D. At Calfstock Lane dated 50–100 A.D., half a mile to the east of Farningham Hill (Ref. 80), shell tempered and grog tempered fabrics were found together with bead and recessed-rim jars (*cf.* Forms 2B and 2C), associated with a Colchester BB brooch, and a storage jar with chevron decoration on the shoulder (*cf.* Form 12). Examination of the complete range of forms, which include native copies of Gallo-Belgic forms, shows that there is little overlap between the two assemblages. Similarly, comparison with material from the villa sites of Frank's Hall (Ref. 81) and Farningham Villa II (Ref. 82), both within half a mile of Farningham Hill, shows that most of the Belgic forms represented at Farningham Hill have fallen out of use by the second half of the first century A.D. Thus Farningham Hill is likely to have been abandoned by about 50 A.D.

Few sites with large groups of 'Belgic' pottery are known from West Kent (Ref. 83). The absence of pre-Conquest Gallo-Belgic imports or their copies may be characteristic of the area as a whole. Similarly, the absence of jars decorated with vertical burnished lines on their necks, a stylistic trait shared with Essex (Ref. 84), and apparently confined to late sites: Stone (A.D. 25–45), Springhead and Orsett (both post-Conquest), may also represent a restricted distribution. Future excavations should reveal whether this has any chronological significance at Farningham Hill.

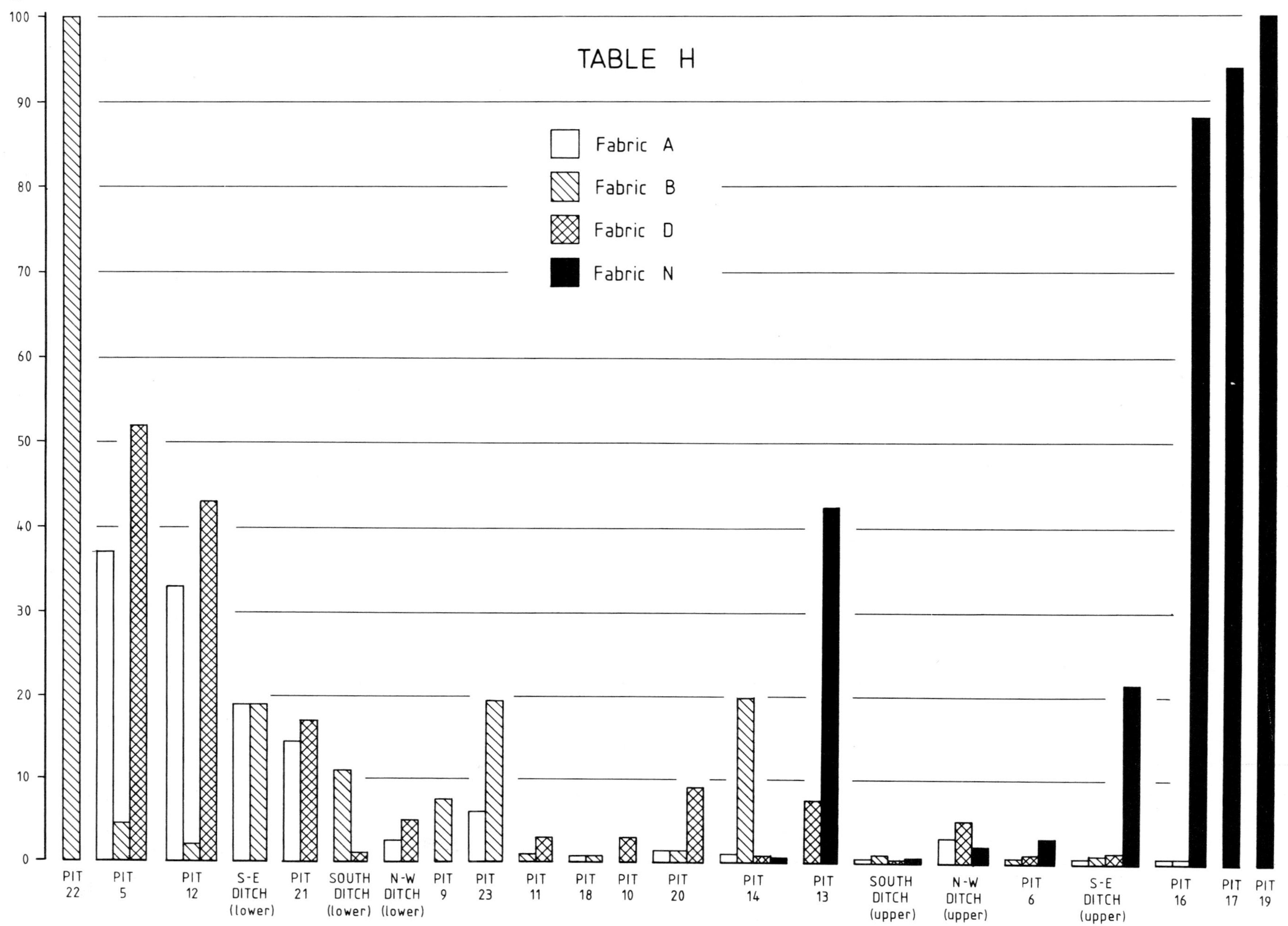

Graph showing distribution of fabrics A, B, D and N throughout features as a percentage of weight per feature. (Pits 15 and 24 contained only shell-tempered sherds).

DISCUSSION OF THE POTTERY

The main intention of this report is to present the material for comparative purposes. Detailed discussion of affinity must await the future excavation and publication of more closed groups. In particular, examination of the sources of the fabrics requires further work on the characterisation of the clays and the distribution of the fabrics themselves. Parallels for specific forms and decoration have been indicated above and only brief comments are offered here.

During Phase 1 the pottery forms consisted of everted-rim footring jars (Forms 4 and 5) and coarse shell tempered vessels with upright rims (Form 1). This range was increased during Phase 2A to include closed forms (Form 2). The association of vessels in coarse shell tempered fabrics with finer quality everted-rim jars is known from other sites; but because the shell tempered vessels are often fragmentary, they have rarely been considered. Precise parallels for these irregular handmade vessels are unlikely to occur, but broadly similar examples are known from Oldbury where upright rims were found associated with the construction of the primary defences (Ref. 85), and from the pre-Roman settlement at Greenhithe where closed forms (Form 2) were recorded in a pre-Belgic context (Ref. 86).

Dr. John Cooper has confirmed that the shell tempered fabric derives from the Woolwich Beds (see report on Fabric H, above). Local outcrops of Woolwich Beds occur at the top of Farningham Hill, 300 metres from the site, and in the Darenth and Lords Woods, 5 km. to the north-east; though the existence of satisfactory clays remains to be confirmed.

The distribution of everted-rim footring vessels is now known to span Sussex, Kent and Essex. Associated with these Form 4 jars, is the use of glauconite tempered Fabrics A and B. Fabric A at Farningham Hill is macroscopically indistinguishable from Fabric A at Little Waltham (Ref. 87). In their report on this fabric, Peacock and Williams suggested that the Essex and Kentish examples examined could have derived from a single source and that suitable clay could have been found in Greensand, Thanet Sands, Reading Beds or London Clay (Ref. 88). The appearance of a similar fabric associated with 'Belgic' forms in a restricted area around Maidstone and the Medway valley supports the suggestion that the Greensand was used in the later period (Ref. 89) and this may represent the continuation of a tradition.

In addition to the everted-rim footring vessels, stylistic links with Essex recur with the use of stamped and grooved decoration (Type e). This general style falls within Elsdon's Thames Estuary and Lower Thames Region. Two vessels with this decoration from Farningham Hill were found in features assigned to Phases 2A (No. 91 from Pit 18) and 2B (No. 125 from the top of the South East Ditch), though the sherds were small and probably residual. The occurrence of No. 64 in Fabric A suggests that it precedes the final 'Belgic' phase.

The presence of a saucepan pot (No. 28) shows that some sporadic contact did exist with groups further to the south or west, though this was rare. The survival of the complete profile and the weight of the sherds (306 gm.) suggest that this pot was still in use until shortly before its burial in Pit 6, and thereby indicates continuity between stages 2A and 2B.

In the final 'Belgic' Phase 2B a wider range of vessel forms appears together with the use of grog tempered fabrics and the first certain evidence for the use of the fast wheel. The variety of grog tempering (Fabrics N1–N8) and the evidence for one vessel being underfired (No. 83) suggests that pots in this fabric were manufactured locally; though no direct evidence of pottery making was found on the site. Many of the stylistic links during this phase were shared with East Kent, Essex and Herfordshire (compare the distribution of Thompson's types A1, A3, A8, B2–1, C6–1 and E1–2 which correspond to Farningham Hill Forms 8C, 8B, 8E, 9A, 12 and 13). Some of the rarer vessels in fine fabrics – such as Form 13 in Fabric E4 – may represent 'imports' from Essex or Hertfordshire; and it is likely, given the large quantity of continental 'mica-dusted' ware at Skeleton Green and Camulodunum (Ref. 90) that Fabric G arrived from north of the Thames rather than direct from the continent.

CATALOGUE OF THE ILLUSTRATED POTTERY (Figs. 15–21, Nos. 14–161)

Farningham Hill has produced an important collection of pottery from closed groups and this is illustrated in full here. All rims, non-flat bases and decorated wall sherds have been drawn, apart from some 'Comb'-decorated sherds, which were often small and uninformative. A sample of these 'comb'-decorated sherds has been illustrated to show the range of variability.

All vessels are grouped in feature number order – the pits followed by the ditch fills in clockwise direction (South East Ditch, South Ditch and North West Ditch). Within the ditches, pots from the lower fills are illustrated before those from the upper.

The colours of the vessels are described verbally and with the use of Munsell colour codes which are shown in parantheses. All vessels are regarded as handmade unless described otherwise.

Pit 5 (KMW–12–45).

No. 14 An everted-rim jar in hard sandy fabric. The footring base is decorated with burnished arcs depicting a three-armed cross. Both surfaces are hard and smooth and were originally highly burnished. The core is light grey (2.5YR6/0) and the surfaces are dark grey (N3). (Form 4A, Fabric A1).

No. 15 An everted-rim jar in hard sandy fabric. The footring base has a burnished cross underneath. The internal surface is brown (5YR5/6). The external surface is burnished and the colour varies from grey to brown (N3 – 5YR5/6) and the core is grey (N5–N3). (Form 4C, Fabric D).

No. 16 An everted-rim jar in hard sandy fabric. The surfaces are dark grey (N3) with patches of brown (N3); and the core is grey (N4). Traces of burnishing are still visible on the external surface. (Form 4, Fabric B2).

No. 17 An everted-rim jar in hard sandy fabric. The external surface has been burnished and is dark grey. The internal surface is brown (5YR5.5/6) with grey patches (N3) and the core is grey. (Form 4, Fabric D).

No. 18 An everted-rim in hard sandy fabric. The surfaces are smooth and dark grey (N3) with brown patches (5YR5/4) and the core is grey (5YR5/1). (Form 4, Fabric B1).

No. 19 An open bowl in shell tempered fabric. The top of the rim has been smoothed flat with the result that some of the clay overhangs the inner surface. The external surface has been wiped leaving broad shallow grooves. The core is grey (5YR3/1) and the surfaces are brown, the inner being (5YR5/4) than the outer (2.5YR4/4). (Form 1Bii, Fabric H3).

No. 20 A coarse shell tempered vessel with externally expanded rim. The fragment is too small to allow the angle or diameter to be determined with any certainty. The surface has been wiped smooth and the sherds fired dark grey throughout (N3). (Form 1Biv, Fabric H6).

Pit 6 (KMW–12–46, 104, 105 and 108)

No. 21 An upright thickened rim in shell tempered fabric. The thickening of the rim is due both to the flattening of the top and the use of a wider coil. The external surface has been smoothed with a slurry and is dark grey (N3). The top of the rim and the internal surface are light brown (5YR6/4) and the core varies between the two. (Form 1Biii, Fabric H4).

No. 22 A plain upright rim of shell tempered fabric. There are faint traces of a light horizontal groove beneath the rim. The colour of the surfaces varies from light brown to grey (5YR6/4 – N4) and the core is dark grey (N3). (Form 1Ai, Fabric H3).

No. 23 A plain out-turned rim of shell tempered fabric. Both the surfaces have been wiped smooth and the colour varies from black to orange brown throughout (N2.5 – 2.5YR5/6). (Form 3Ai, Fabric H3).

No. 24 An in-turned, externally thickened and recessed rim in shell tempered fabric. A slight horizontal groove runs beneath the rim. Both surfaces have been wiped. The external surface is dark grey (N4–N3) and the internal surface varies from orange brown to light brown (5YR6/4 – 10YR6/6). (Form 2Ciii, Fabric H4).

No. 25 A globular jar with externally projecting rim in shell tempered fabric. The external surface is dark grey (N3); the internal surface is light brown (5YR6/4); and the core is grey (5YR4/1). (Form 10B, Fabric H3).

No. 26 A worn fragment of an everted rim in hard sandy fabric. Both surfaces show signs of having been burnished and their colour varies from orange to light sandy brown (2.5YR6/6 – 7.5YR7/6). The core is grey (N3). (Form 4, Fabric D).

No. 27 A wall sherd of hard sandy fabric. The external surface has been covered with a slurry and then with a fine combed decoration. The external surface is orange (10R5/6); the internal surface is dark brown (5YR3/1) and the core brown (5YR4/2). (Fabric E5).

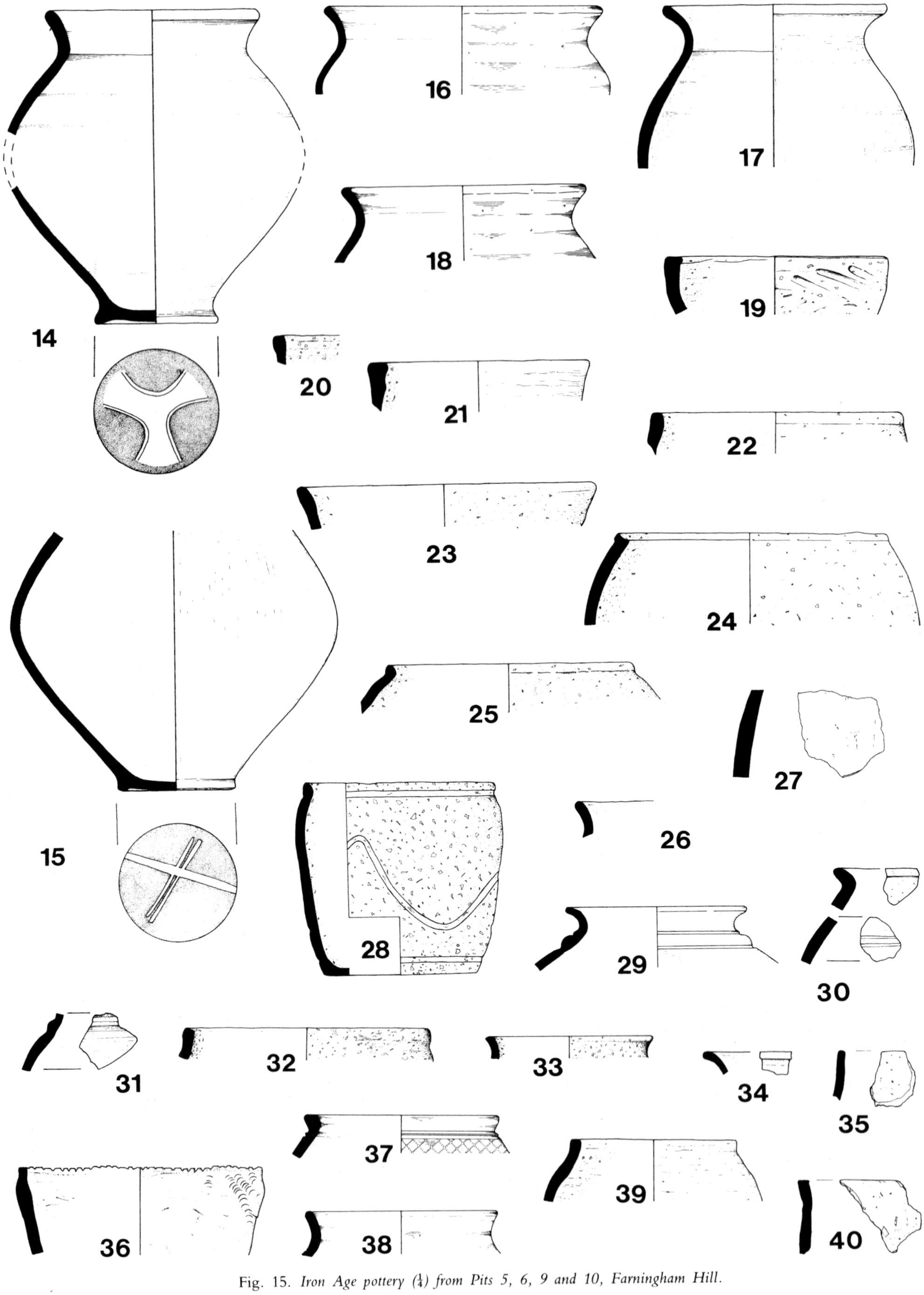

Fig. 15. *Iron Age pottery* (¼) *from Pits 5, 6, 9 and 10, Farningham Hill.*

No. 28 A saucepan pot of shell tempered fabric. There is a horizontal groove just below the rim and another above the base. Between these a single groove follows a curvilinear wave pattern. The surviving sherds show a single grooved line radiating from the centre of the base (not illustrated). The colour varies from dark grey to brown (N4 – 7.5YR5/2) with light brown patches (7.5YR6/4). (Form 6, Fabric H3).

No. 29 A wheel-made cordoned bowl in hard sand and grog tempered fabric. The core is grey (N4) with a margin of brown (5YR5/4). The external surface and rim are dark grey (N3) and highly burnished, and the internal surface beneath the rim is grey (10YR4/1). (Form 9B, Fabric E7).

No. 30 Two sherds probably belonging to the same globular jar of fine flint tempered fabric. Both surfaces are burnished. The external surface and core are black (N2.5) and the internal surface is brown (7.5YR5/2). Two burnished grooves run around the shoulder. (Form 10C, Fabric J2).

No. 31 A fragment of neck with two horizontal grooves, in grog and vegetable tempered fabric. The grooves have been burnished and the surface below them is smooth. Fine horizontal striations suggest that the vessel was wheel-made. The external surface is brown (7.5YR6/2); and the core and internal surface are black (N3) with a margin of brown (2.5YR6/6). (Form 9B, Fabric N9).

Pit 9 (KMW–12–64).

No. 32 An irregular everted rim in shell tempered fabric. The angle and diameter are uncertain. It has been fired dark grey (N3) throughout. (Form 5D, Fabric H3).

No. 33 An everted rim in shell tempered fabric. The angle and diameter are uncertain. The core is dark grey (N3) and the surfaces are brown (5YR6/4). (Form 5D, Fabric H3).

Pit 10 (KMW–12–61 and 62).

No. 34 An everted rim, thickening towards the top, in fine sandy fabric. Faint striations on the external surface suggest that this might have been wheel-made. The colour varies from light to dark grey throughout (N4–N3). (Form 5B, Fabric D).

No. 35 A shouldered vessel with a plain almost upright rim in shell tempered fabric. The angle and diameter are uncertain. The surfaces are smooth and the sherd has been fired brown (5YR5/4) with a darker patch near the rim (2.5YR4/2). (Form 1Ci, Fabric H3).

No. 36 A coarse jar in vegetable tempered fabric. The external surface has been wiped and is decorated with oblique columns of finger-nail impressions. There are cuts about 2 mm. deep across the rim. The internal surface and rim are brown (7.5YR6/4) and the external surface and core are grey (N4–N3). (Form 1Av, Fabric K4).

No. 37 A globular jar with externally projecting rim of limestone tempered fabric. Both the surfaces are hard and smooth. There are two horizontal grooves on the neck and beneath these is a lightly-grooved lattice decoration. The external surface and core are dark grey (N3) and the internal surface is brown (7.5YR5/2). (Form 10B, Fabric P).

No. 38 An everted rim in fine sandy fabric with smooth surfaces, fired light brown throughout (7.5YR6/4). (Form 4, Fabric E8).

No. 39 A small shouldered jar or beaker with a plain upright rim in a vegetable tempered fabric. The surfaces are smooth and the sherd has been fired orange-brown throughout (5YR6/6). (Form 1Ci, Fabric K4).

No. 40 A plain flat-topped rim in shell tempered fabric. The surfaces are smooth and brown (5YR6/4). The core is dark grey (5YR3/1). (Form 1Bii, Fabric H3).

Pit 11 (KMW–12–68).

No. 41 An everted-rim jar in fine sandy fabric. Both surfaces are heavily burnished. One wall sherd of the same fabric, shown here as belonging to the same vessel, is decorated with two curvilinear grooves. The colour of the surface varies from black to brown (N2–7.5YR5/4) and the core varies from dark grey to light brown (N4–7.5YR6/4). (Form 4, Fabric D).

No. 42 A shouldered jar with upright neck and internally bevelled rim in a coarse shell tempered fabric. The colour of the internal surface varies from light brown to orange brown (5YR6/4 – 2.5YR5/6) and that of the external surface from dark grey to orange brown (7.5YR4/2 – 2.5YR5/6). The core is grey (N4–N3). (Form 1Cii, Fabric H5).

No. 43 A fragment of a flat-topped rim with external expansion in shell tempered fabric. The core is dark grey (N3) and the surfaces are brown (5YR6/4). The angle and diameter are uncertain (Form 2Ci?, Fabric H5).

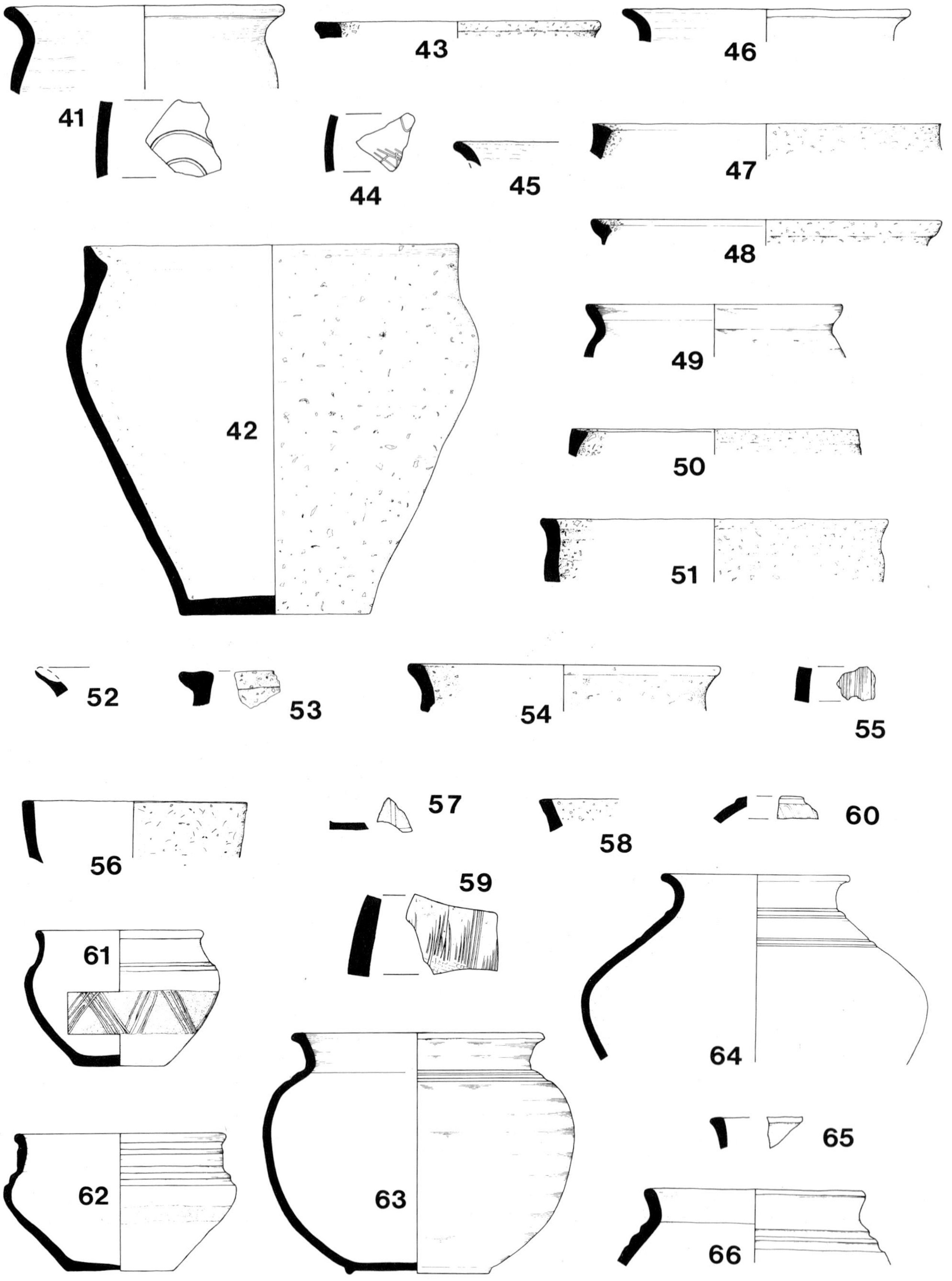

Fig. 16. *Iron Age pottery* ($\frac{1}{4}$), *from Pits 11, 12, 13, 14 and 16, Farningham Hill.*

Pit 12 (KMW–12–58 and 59).

No. 44 A wall sherd in a hard sandy fabric. Both surfaces are burnished and the external surface has burnished decoration consisting of a wavy line above a lattice pattern. The sherd has been fired dark grey to black throughout (N3–N2). (Fabric E1).

No. 45 An everted rim in a hard sandy fabric. It has been burnished on both surfaces and is dark grey (N3) with one brown (10YR4/1) patch on the external surface. (Form 4, Fabric E1).

No. 46 An everted rim in glauconite tempered fabric. Both surfaces have been burnished. The colour of the external surface varies from reddish-brown to light grey (2.5YR5/6 – 10YR5/1); and that of the core and internal surface is a paler brown to grey (7.5YR6/4 – 10YR5/1). (Form 4, Fabric A1).

Pit 13 (KMW–12–91, 92 and 93).

No. 47 A fragment of an inturned rim with flat top and external expansion. The angle and diameter are uncertain. It has been fired dark grey (N3) throughout. (Form 2Ci, Fabric H3).

No. 48 A fragment of a recessed rim with external projection in shell tempered fabric. It has been fired brown (2.5YR4/4) throughout. (Form 2Civ, Fabric H5).

No. 49 An everted rim in a hard sandy fabric. The core is light grey (N6) and the surfaces vary from grey to dark grey (N5–N4). Beneath the internal surface is an orange-brown (10R6/6) margin. (Form 4, Fabric D).

No. 50 A fragment of an upright thickened rim with flat top. The angle and diameter are uncertain. It has been fired dark grey (N3) throughout. (Form 1Biii, Fabric H3).

No. 51 An upright rim, probably from an open bowl, in shell tempered fabric. The external surface of the rim has been destroyed. The colour varies from brown (5YR6/4) to dark grey (N3). (Form 1Biv, Fabric H5).

Pit 14 (KMW–12–126, 131, 133 and 135).

No. 52 A fragment of an everted rim in hard sandy fabric. Most of the inner surface has been destroyed. It has been fired light brown throughout (7.5YR7/5). (Form 4, Fabric C).

No. 53 A large jar with an inturned, slightly recessed, rim with external projection in coarse shell tempered fabric. Sherds from this vessel were distributed throughout the pit. The core is dark grey (N3) and the surfaces vary from grey-brown (2.5YR6/4) to red (2.5YR5/6). (Form 2Civ, Fabric H4).

No. 54 An externally projecting rim with flat top in shell tempered fabric. The angle is uncertain. The core is dark grey (N3) and the surfaces vary from brown (2.5YR5/6 – 5YR6/4) to dark grey (N3). (Form 2Ci, Fabric H4).

No. 55 A wall sherd in shell tempered fabric with deep scored decoration. The external surface is red-brown (2.5YR5/6) and the core and internal surface are dark grey (N3). (Fabric H6).

No. 56 A plain upright rim of a small open bowl in hard shell tempered fabric. The external surface has been destroyed and the angle and diameter are uncertain. The colour varies from light grey to light brown throughout (10YR5/1 – 7.5YR6/4). (Form 1Ai, Fabric H3).

No. 57 A small fragment of the base of a footring jar in a hard sandy fabric. The underside is light brown (7.5YR6/4) and shows traces of burnished cruciform design. The core and upper surfaces are grey (10YR5/1). (Form 4, Fabric B2).

No. 58 A plain everted rim with flat top in shell tempered fabric. The surfaces have been wiped smooth, and the sherd has been fired dark grey throughout (N3). (Form 5C, Fabric H3).

No. 59 A wall sherd in a hard sand and vegetable tempered fabric. The external surface shows the edge of a 'combed' pattern. The alignment of the ends of the grooves suggests that they were applied in groups of seven or eight. The core is dark grey (N3) and the surfaces are dark brown (5YR5/3 – 5YR5/4). (Fabric K4).

No. 60 A fragment of a shoulder in fine sandy fabric. This has a burnished cordon and the wall beneath the cordon is decorated with burnished oblique lines. The sherd has been fired light brown throughout (7.5YR6/4). (Form 9B, Fabric C).

Pit 16 (KMW–12–97 and 107).

No. 61 A necked bowl in grog tempered fabric. There are horizontal grooves on the neck and shoulder. Beneath the shoulder is a band of decoration consisting of groups of four or five burnished lines forming an irregular open lattice pattern against a matt background. The remainder of the external surface is burnished down to and including the base. The surfaces and core are dark grey (5YR2.5/1) with brown patches (5YR5/4). (Form 7B, Fabric N1).

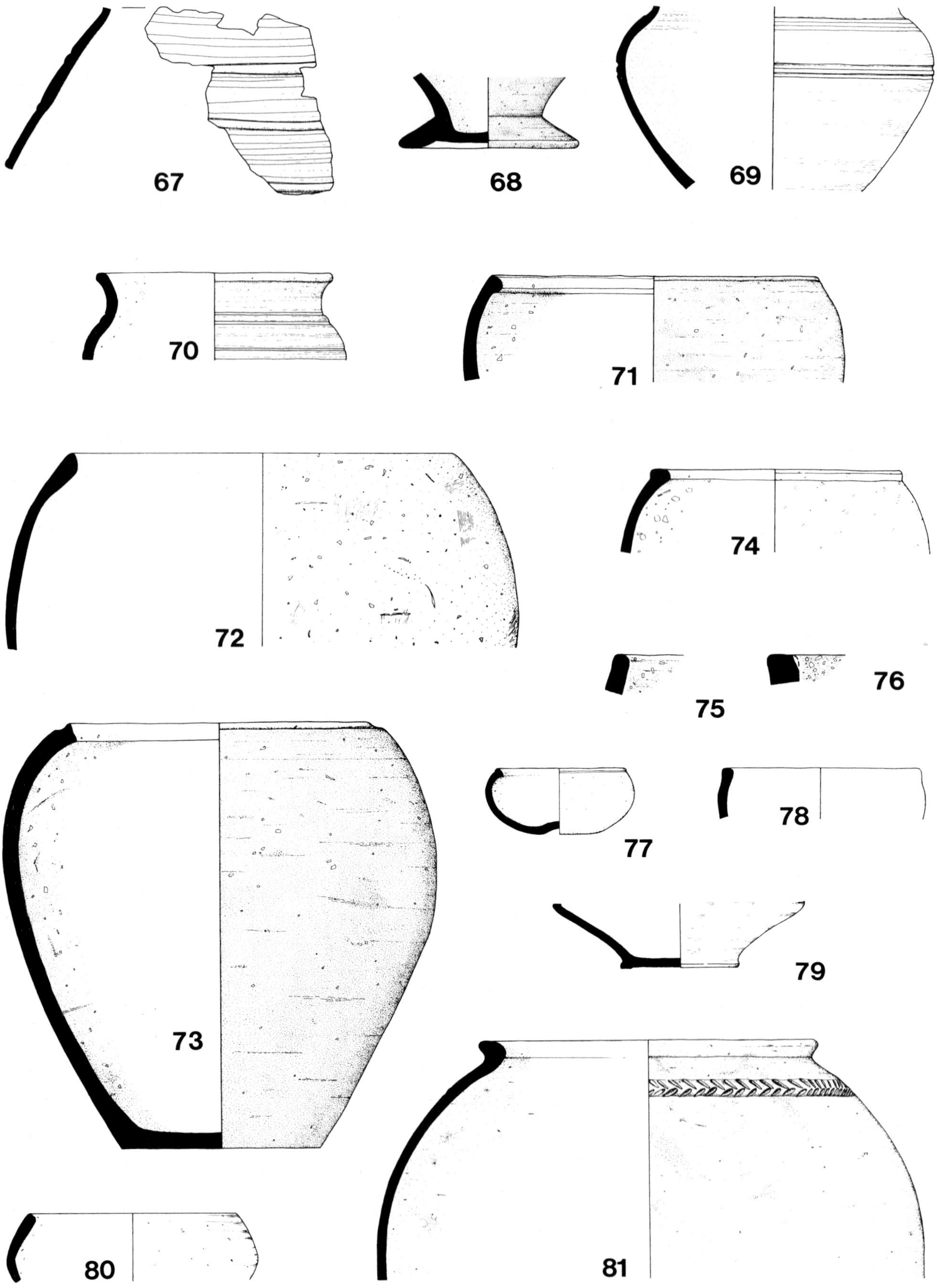

Fig. 17. *Iron Age pottery* ($\frac{1}{4}$), *from Pit 16, Farningham Hill.*

No. 62 A necked bowl in grog tempered fabric. There are horizontal grooves on the neck and shoulder. Internally the wall beneath the neck is smooth, and the neck and rim are burnished. The external surface is burnished with the exception of an irregular horizontal band beneath the shoulder which has been left smooth. The core is brown (5YR5/4) and the surfaces vary from dark grey to brown (N3–5YR5/4). (Form 7B, Fabric N8).

No. 63 A large necked bowl with a thickened flat-topped rim in grog tempered fabric. The base has a shallow footring. There are two broad horizontal grooves; one at the base of the neck and one on the shoulder, with other lighter ones in between. Burnishing occurs all over the external surface and down to just beneath the neck internally. The surfaces and core are generally dark grey (5YR2.5/1) with brown patches (7.5YR5/4). (Form 7A, Fabric N3).

No. 64 An everted-rim jar in smooth grog tempered fabric. This probably had a pedestal base. There are two pairs of horizontal grooves widely spaced on the shoulder. The inner surface is badly worn, but the fine striations that do survive suggest that the vessel was wheel-made. The external surfaces are dark grey (N3) and the core is light grey (N4) with a margin of brown (5YR6/4). (Form 8A, Fabric N1).

No. 65 An upright flat-topped rim with external projection in grog tempered fabric. This is likely to belong to a necked bowl similar to No. 63 above. The surfaces have been burnished dark grey-brown (5YR3/1) and the core is orange-brown (2.5YR6/6). (Form 7, Fabric N3).

No. 66 A bowl of grog tempered fabric with an everted rim and two broad grooves on the neck. The external surface and rim are burnished and brown (5YR4/2). The internal surface beneath the rim is dark grey (N3) and the core is brown (5YR4/2) with abundant black flecks and an orange-brown margin (2.5YR5/6). (Form 9A, Fabric N9).

No. 67 Wall sherds probably from a pedestal jar, in a grog tempered fabric. Decoration consists of horizontal zones of irregular lightly grooved lines bordered by cordons. The surfaces and core are grey-brown (5YR4/1.5) with a margin of brown (2.5YR5/6). (Form 8B, Fabric N9).

No. 68 A quoit-shaped pedestal base in grog tempered fabric. The surfaces and core are grey (N3) with patches of brown (5YR5.5/4). (Form 8C, Fabric N4).

No. 69 Wall sherds probably from a pedestal jar, in grog tempered fabric. There are grooves on the neck and shoulder. Fine striations on the internal surface suggest that the neck and rim may have been finished on a wheel. The external surface is dark grey-brown (10YR3/1) and has been burnished all over. The core varies from dark grey to brown (N3–5YR3/1) and the interior is dark rusty brown (2.5YR4/2). (Form 8A, Fabric N9).

No. 70 A bowl in grog tempered fabric with an everted rim and cordons on the neck and shoulder. The external surface is burnished to half-way up the neck. Above that level and over the rim are fine striations suggesting that the top of the rim at least may have been finished on a wheel. The surfaces and core are dark brown (10YR3/1) with lighter patches (5YR5/4). (Form 9B, Fabric N8).

No. 71 A jar with in-curving rim in shell tempered fabric. A slight groove runs along the top, formed as a result of smoothing the clay of the external surface up onto the rim. The internal surface has been burnished and the external surface left smooth. The internal surface is light brown (10YR6/3) and the external surface and core vary from dark grey to brown (N3 – 5YR5/3). (Form 2Dii, Fabric H6).

No. 72 A jar with in-curving internally bevelled rim in shell tempered fabric. Both surfaces have been wiped, but fragments of shell protrude. The colour varies from red-brown to dark grey throughout (10R5/6 – N3). (Form 2Diii, Fabric H5).

No. 73 A jar with a plain in-turned rim in shell tempered fabric. The surfaces have been covered with slurry and few of the shell fragments are visible. Faint horizontal striations near the rim suggest that the rim may have been finished on a wheel. From the base to the shoulder the surfaces are light orange-brown (5YR6/4). Above the shoulder the surfaces become grey (5YR3.5/1), though most of the rim and the internal surface is orange-brown. The core is dark grey (N3). (Form 2Di, Fabric H7).

No. 74 A bead rim bowl in coarse shell tempered fabric. Both surfaces have been smoothed but shell fragments remain visible. The external surface shows some burnishing. The internal surface is a deep red-brown (10R4/4). The core is dark grey (N2.5) and the external surface and rim are black (5YR2.5/1). (Form 2Bi, Fabric H5).

No. 75 A coarse plain rim of shell tempered fabric. The angle and diameter are uncertain. The colour consists of grey and brown patches throughout (N2.5 and 5YR6/6). (Form 1Ai, Fabric H3).

No. 76 A thick flat-topped rim of coarse shell tempered fabric, probably belonging to a storage jar. The angle and diameter are uncertain. The surfaces and core vary from dark grey to brown (N3 – 5YR5/3). (Form 1Bi, Fabric H4).

No. 77 A small bead rim bowl or cup with omphalos base in grog tempered fabric. The surfaces and core vary from dark grey to brown (N3 – 5YR5/3). (Form 14, Fabric N1).

No. 78 A small jar or bowl with a plain in-turned rim in a hard sandy fabric. Surface marks suggest that this could have been finished on a wheel. The surfaces are dark grey (5YR3/1) with a brown margin (5YR5/6), and the core is grey-brown (7.5YR5/2). (Form 2Ai, Fabric B2).

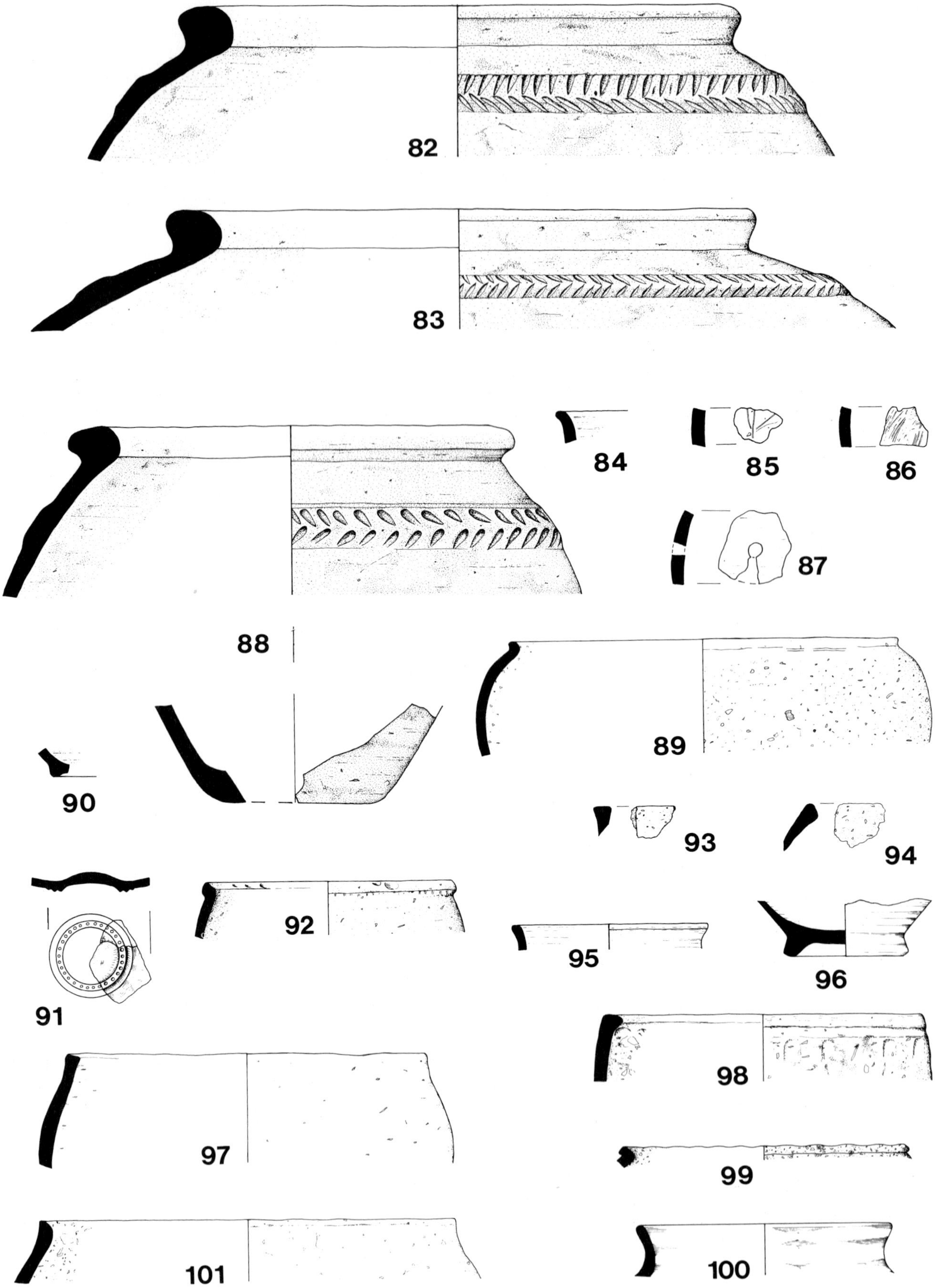

Fig. 18. *Iron Age pottery ($\frac{1}{4}$), from Pits 16, 17, 18, 20, 21, 23 and 24, Farningham Hill.*

No. 79 The base of a carinated bowl with a low footring in grog tempered fabric. The external surface and base are highly burnished and black (N2.5). The internal surface and core are light grey (N5). (Form 13, Fabric E4).

No. 80 A shouldered jar or bowl with a plain in-turned rim with slight internal thickening, in shell tempered fabric. The surfaces have been smoothed. The core is dark grey (7.5YR3/1) and the surfaces vary from dark grey to brown (7.5YR3/1 – 7.5YR6/4). (Form 2Aii, Fabric H6).

No. 81 A storage jar with a thickened bead rim in coarse grog tempered fabric. There is a row of stabbed chevron decoration around the base of the neck. Above this decoration the external surface has been burnished, and beneath it the surface is smooth. A light groove, visible at the bottom of the burnished zone, preceded and probably served to align the stabbed chevrons. The external surface varies from red-brown to grey (10R5/6 – N4). The internal surface varies from dark brown to grey (2.5YR4/2 – N4) and the core is dark grey (N3). (Form 12B, Fabric N4).

No. 82 A storage jar with a thickened bead rim in coarse grog tempered fabric. A cordon around the base of the neck is decorated with a stabbed chevron design. Above this decoration the external surface has been burnished, and beneath it the surface is smooth. Marks on the inner surface of the base show that this was made on a wheel, but these marks do not occur on the wall which was probably coil built. The surfaces vary from red-brown (10R5/8) to dark grey (N3), and the core varies from brown (2.5YR4/2) to grey (N4). (Form 12A, Fabric N4).

No. 83 A storage jar with a thickened bead rim in coarse grog tempered fabric. A cordon around the base of the neck is decorated with a stabbed chevron design. This vessel is similar to No. 82 above, except that the base is handmade. The core is dark grey (N3) and the surfaces vary from grey to brown (10YR4/1 – 2.5YR5/4). Some of the rim sherds are extremely friable, possibly as a result of being under-fired. (Form 12A, Fabric N4).

No. 84 A fragment of an everted rim in a hard sandy fabric. The surfaces appear to have been slipped and burnished. The external surface is brown (5YR5/6) and the internal surface and core are very dark grey (N2). (Form 4, Fabric D).

No. 85 A wall sherd of shell and grog tempered fabric. The external surface has an incised design applied after firing. The internal surface is brown (5YR5/3). The core is brown-grey (5YR5/1) and the external surface is orange-brown (2.5YR6/8). (Fabric H6).

No. 86 A wall sherd of shell and grog tempered fabric. The external surface is decorated with narrow grooves producing a roughly wiped rather than a combed effect. The internal surface is orange-brown (2.5YR6/6). The core is grey (N4) and the external surface is brown-grey (5YR5/3). (Fabric H6).

No. 87 A wall sherd in grog tempered fabric. A hole has been drilled through it from the external surface after firing. The edges of the sherd remain rough. The surfaces are dark grey (N3) and the core is grey-brown (2.5YR4/2). (Fabric N8).

Pit 17 (KMW–12–118).

No. 88 A large storage jar with a thick bead rim and flat base in grog tempered fabric. The shoulder is decorated with a raised cordon which bears a stabbed chevron design. All the sherds found have been fired red throughout; the core being lighter (10R5/8) than the surfaces (2.5YR5/6). (Form 12A, Fabric N4).

Pit 18 (KMW–12–119).

No. 89 A large jar with inturned, externally expanded bead rim in shell tempered fabric. An irregular groove runs beneath the rim. The internal surface is red-brown (2.5YR5/4) with brown patches (5YR6/3) and the core and external surface are dark grey (N3) with brown patches (5YR5/3). (Form 2Bi, Fabric H4).

No. 90 Fragments of a footring base in a hard sandy fabric. The internal surface is smooth and the external surface has been burnished. The colour of the core and the internal surface is dark brown (5YR3/1) and that of the external surface black (N3). (Form 4B, Fabric B2).

No. 91 Two sherds of very hard glauconite tempered fabric. Decoration consists of curvilinear grooves with a parallel line of impressed dots curving round a deep thumb impression. These sherds have been interpreted as forming an omphalos base, though they could belong to a wall. The external surface and core are dark grey (N3) and the internal surface is grey-brown (N3 – 7.5YR6/4). (Form 15, Fabric A2).

No. 92 An inturned recessed rim with external projection in shell tempered fabric. The external profile of the rim varies from a gentle swelling to a sharp projection. The recessed groove is made up of a series of finger depressions, and at one point these are spaced apart so that the groove disappears. The sherds have been fired dark grey throughout (N3). (Form 2Bi – 2Ciii, Fabric H6).

No. 93 A plain rim with flat top in shell tempered fabric. The angle and diameter are uncertain. The core and external surface are dark grey (N3) and the internal surface and top of the rim are light brown (5YR6/6). (Form 1Bii, Fabric H3).

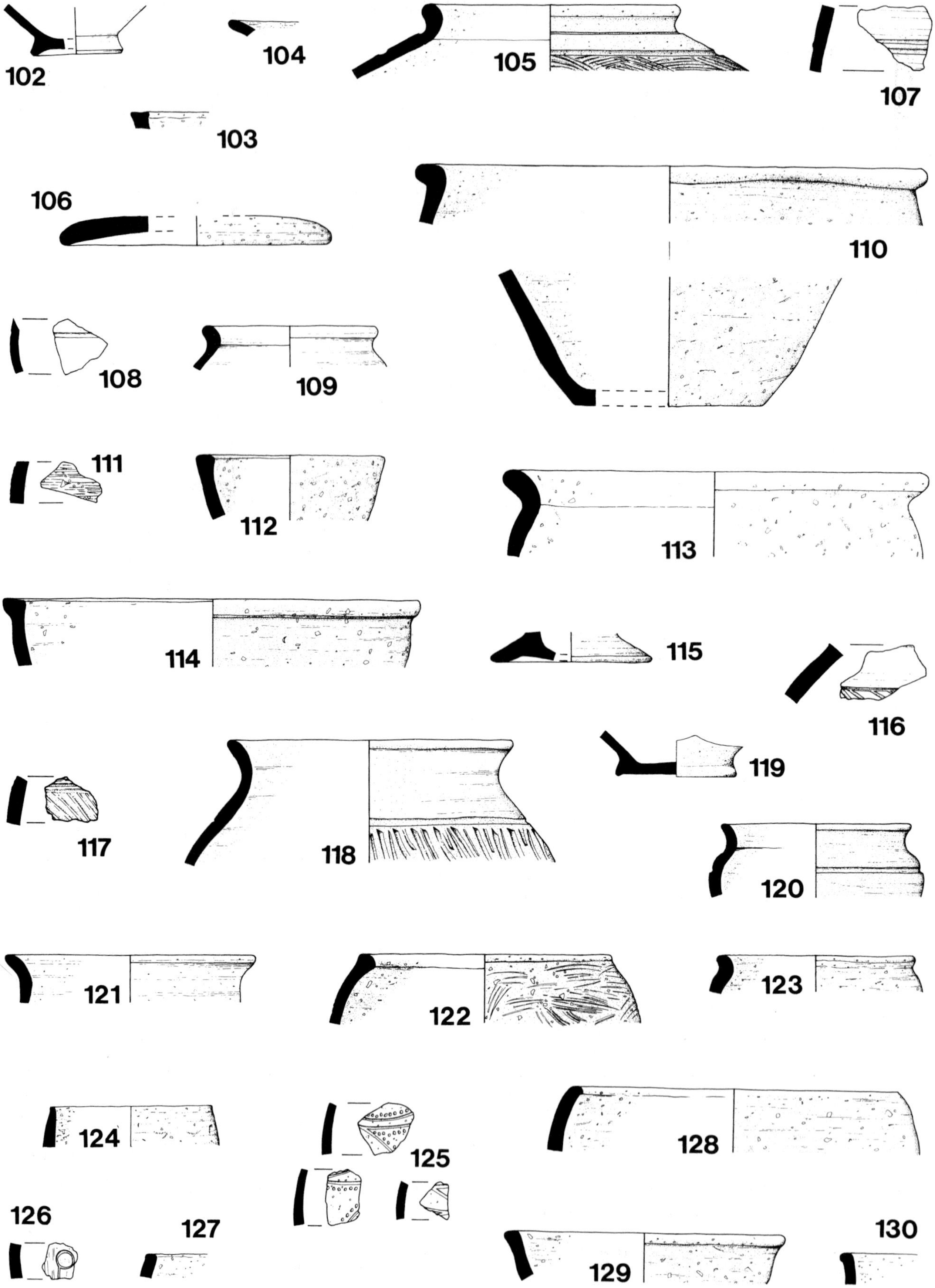

Fig. 19. *Iron Age pottery (¼), from South East Ditch, Farningham Hill.*

Pit 20 (KMW–12–121, 127 and 137).

No. 94 A thickened inturned rim in shell tempered fabric. The top has been smoothed down so that some clay overlaps the inner edge of the wall. The colour varies from brown to dark grey (2.5YR4/4 – N3). (Form 2Dii, Fabric H3).

No. 95 A fragment of an everted rim in hard sandy fabric. The core is grey (N4) and the surfaces are black (N3) and burnished. (Form 4, Fabric A1).

No. 96 A pedestal base in hard flint gritted fabric. The internal surface is smooth and dark grey (N2) and the external surface is burnished and its colour varies from light brown to dark grey (5YR6/6 – N2). The foot appears to have been added as a coil to the bottom of the base. (Form 8D, Fabric J2).

Pit 21 (KMW–12–122).

No. 97 A thickened flat-topped rim in shell tempered fabric. The rim is irregular, with the expansion occurring over the inner surface at one point and over the external surface at another. The external surface has been coated with a thick slurry and fired dark grey (N3). The inner surface has been wiped smooth and the colour varies from dark grey to brown (N3 – 2.5YR4/4). The core is dark grey (N3). (Form 1Biii, Fabric H7).

Pit 23 (KMW–12–124).

No. 98 An incurving rim with flat top in shell tempered fabric. Both surfaces have been wiped, but shell protrudes. The diameter is uncertain. The colour varies from orange-brown (10R5/6) to dark grey (N3) throughout. (Form 2Di, Fabric H5).

No. 99 A fragment of a flat-topped rim with external projection in shell tempered fabric. The angle and diameter are uncertain. The core is dark grey (N3) and the surfaces are orange-brown (10R5/6) with a grey (N3) patch along the outer edge of the rim (Form 2Cii?, Fabric H3).

No. 100 An everted rim in a sandy fabric. The surfaces have been burnished and the sherds are dark grey (N3) throughout. (Form 4, Fabric B1).

Pit 24 (KMW–12–125).

No. 101 A plain slightly everted rim of a jar in shell tempered fabric. The surfaces have been wiped smooth and the sherds have been fired dark grey (N3) throughout. (Form 2Aiv, Fabric H5).

South East Ditch, Lower (KMW–12–52, 115 and 139).

No. 102 A low pedestal base in a hard glauconite tempered fabric. There are traces of a burnished cruciform design underneath (not illustrated). The sherd is worn and the detail of this decoration is unclear. It has been fired dark grey throughout (N3). (Form 4A, Fabric A1).

No. 103 A flat-topped rim in shell tempered fabric. The sherd is small and the angle and diameter are uncertain. The internal surface is brown (2.5YR5/4) and the core and external surfaces are black (N2.5). (Form 1B, Fabric H3).

No. 104 An everted rim in a hard glauconite tempered fabric. The core is grey-brown (10YR4/1) and the burnished surfaces are dark grey (N3) over a margin of brown (2.5YR5/6). (Form 4, Fabric B2).

South East Ditch, Upper (KMW–12–3, 53, 55, 83, 85, 102, 114, 134, 140, 147, 148 and 149).

No. 105 A large globular jar with a short everted rim in a grog and flint tempered fabric. On the shoulder are two horizontal grooves. Above these the surface has been smoothed; below them the surface is decorated with rough scoring. The core and internal surface are grey-brown (5YR5/3), with an orange-brown margin (2.5YR5/6), and the external surface is grey (N4). (Form 10C, Fabric N4).

No. 106 A lid or shallow dish in flint tempered fabric, with smooth surfaces. The sherd has been fired dark grey throughout (N3). (Form 16A, Fabric J1).

No. 107 A wall sherd possibly from a pedestal jar, of grog tempered fabric, with grey-brown core (10YR3/1) and dark grey surfaces (N3). The external surface is decorated with a light cordon between two horizontal grooves. On either side of this is a series of light grooves, similar to those found on No. 67 in Pit 16. (Form 8B, Fabric N7).

No. 108 A wall sherd of fine flint tempered fabric. The external surface is decorated with a shallow linear groove, and has been burnished. The sherd has been fired light brown throughout (5YR5/6), with a patch of dark grey (N4) on the external surface. (Fabric J2).

No. 109 A thickened everted rim of a small globular jar in grog tempered fabric. Both surfaces are smooth and the interior shows signs of burnishing. The core is light grey (N4); the internal surface dark grey (N3) and the external surface and rim are brown (5YR5/3). (Form 10A, Fabric N7).

No. 110 A large jar with a flat-topped, externally projecting rim and a flat base. The fabric is tempered with shell and grog. Both surfaces have been smoothed. The core is dark grey (N3); the internal surface is orange-brown (2.5YR5/8) and the external surface is light brown (7.5YR6/4) with grey (N4) patches. (Form 2Cii, Fabric H6).

No. 111 A wall sherd in shell tempered fabric. The external surface is decorated with a rough scored design. The external surface is brown (7.5YR5/4), and the core and internal surface are black (N2.5). (Fabric H3).

No. 112 An open bowl with an internally projecting flat-topped rim, in shell tempered fabric. Both surfaces have been wiped smooth. The sherd is dark grey throughout (N3) with patches of brown (7.5YR6/4). (Form 3Aii, Fabric H6).

No. 113 A large globular jar with a thick everted rim in shell tempered fabric. The core is dark grey (5YR3/1) and the surfaces are brown (5YR6/6). (Form 10C, Fabric H4).

No. 114 A coarse jar with a slightly in-turned externally projecting rim in shell tempered fabric. The profile of the rim varies from being flat to recessed. The internal surface is red-brown (10R4/6) and the core and external surface are dark grey (N3). (Form 2Ci-2Ciii, Fabric H7).

No. 115 A quoit-shaped pedestal base in grog tempered fabric. Very faint striations on the surface suggest that this was made on a wheel. It has been fired grey (N3) throughout with some patches of brown (5YR5/3). (Form 8C, Fabric N7).

No. 116 The neck of a storage jar in grog tempered fabric. A horizontal groove runs along the top of a band of diagonal grooves, which possibly represent the top of a band of chevron decoration. The surface above this decoration has been burnished. The core is dark grey (N3) and the surfaces are grey (5YR4/1), with an orange-brown (2.5YR5/6) patch over the decoration. (Form 12C, Fabric N4).

No. 117 A wall sherd in shell and grog tempered fabric. It has two panels of light combed decoration. The core is dark grey (N3) and the surfaces vary from dark grey (N3) to brown (7.5YR6/4). (Fabric H6).

No. 118 A large globular jar with a wide everted rim in grog tempered fabric. An irregular horizontal groove runs around the bottom of the neck. Below this the surface is decorated with roughly scored diagonal grooves. The rim and neck appear to have been covered in a grey slip (10YR4/1), though most of this has now worn off, leaving a grey-brown surface (7.5YR6/4). The core is dark grey (10YR4/1). (Form 10C, Fabric N8).

No. 119 A footring base in a hard sand and vegetable tempered fabric. Both surfaces of the base and wall have clear wheel marks. The external surface is dark grey (N3), and the core and internal surface are grey (10YR5/2). (Form 4B, Fabric K4).

No. 120 A small bowl or jar with an everted rim in grog tempered fabric. There is a horizontal groove on the shoulder. The core and surfaces are dark grey (N3) with a margin of brown (2.5YR5/6). (Form 9A, Fabric N9).

No. 121 A jar with everted rim in flint tempered fabric. Very little of the flint tempering is visible through the surfaces which are hard and burnished. The core is light grey (10YR6/1) and the surfaces are dark grey (N3). (Form 4, Fabric J1).

No. 122 A jar with a thickened bead rim in shell tempered fabric. Light horizontal wipe marks are visible on the neck and roughly scored grooves produce an irregular 'combed' effect on the shoulder. The internal surface varies from light brown to grey (7.5YR6/4 – 10YR4/1) and the core and external surfaces are dark grey (N3). (Form 2Bii, Fabric H6).

No. 123 A small globular jar with a short everted rim in shell tempered fabric. The external surface has been coated with slurry. The internal surface is brown (7.5YR5/2 – 6/4) and the core and external surface are dark grey (N3). (Form 10A, Fabric H6).

No. 124 A beaker or small jar with a plain almost upright rim in shell tempered fabric. The thickness of the wall increases rapidly beneath the rim. The sherd has been fired black (N2.5) throughout. (Form 1Aii, Fabric H6).

No. 125 Three wall sherds in fine hard shell tempered fabric with stamped and grooved decoration. The grooved design incorporates interlocking arcs and roundels. Flanking some of these lines are triangular stamp marks, each with a maximum size of between 2 and 3 mm. The sherds have been fired dark grey to brown throughout (N3 – 7.5YR6/4). (Fabric H1).

No. 126 A wall sherd in shell and grog tempered fabric. The external surface has been lightly scored and then decorated with an impressed circle (external diameter 13 mm.) joined by a grooved line. The internal surface is black (N3) and the external surface and core are grey-brown (5YR4/1 – 2.5YR4/2). (Fabric H6).

No. 127 A small fragment of a plain upright rim in shell tempered fabric. The diameter is uncertain. It has been fired black throughout (N2). (Form 1A, Fabric H6).

No. 128 An open bowl with a plain rim in shell tempered fabric. Both surfaces have been smoothed, but the treatment is irregular with the result that the rim occasionally overhangs the inner surface. The core is dark grey (5YR3/1) and the surfaces vary from light grey to orange (5YR5/1 – 2.5YR6/6). (Form 3Aiii, Fabric H6).

No. 129 A rounded-topped rim with external expansion from an open bowl in shell tempered fabric. The internal surface is light brown (5YR5/3) and the core and external surface are dark grey (N3). (Form 3Aiv, Fabric H6).

No. 130 A fragment of rim, possibly from a necked bowl, in shell tempered fabric. The core is dark grey (N3) and the surfaces are brown (5YR5/3). (Form 7, Fabric H3).

No. 131 A rounded-topped rim with external expansion, possibly from an open bowl, in shell tempered fabric. The core is dark grey (N3) and the surfaces vary from dark grey (N3) to brown (7.5YR6/4). (Form 3Aiv, Fabric H3).

No. 132 A worn fragment of a pedestal base in grog tempered fabric. The surfaces of the walls, though worn, have faint horizontal striations and they may have been wheel-made. The base however, is flat and has been smoothed by hand. The core is light grey (10YR5/1); the internal surface is grey (10YR4/1) with a margin of brown (2.5YR5/6), and the external surface is dark grey (N3). (Form 8E, Fabric N3).

No. 133 An upright thickened rim with a flat top, possibly belonging to a necked bowl similar to No. 63, in grog tempered fabric. The external surface has been burnished. The core is dark brown (2.5YR4/2) and the surfaces are dark grey (N3). (Form 7, Fabric N3).

No. 134 A jar with a slightly in-turned recessed rim in shell tempered fabric. The core is dark grey (N3); the internal surface varies from brown to dark grey (5YR6/4 – N3) and the external surface is brown (5YR6/4). Both the surfaces have been covered with slurry. (Form 2Ciii, Fabric H7).

South Ditch, Lower (KMW–12–31 and 146).

No. 135 A worn sherd from a gently everted rim in shell tempered fabric. The external profile is irregular and the diameter unknown. The rim has been formed by smoothing the clay down from the top with the result that an irregular hollow runs beneath the rim. Under this is a second irregular groove. Most of the sherd is dark grey (N3), though the upper part of the external surface and top of the rim are dark brown (5YR5/3). (Form 5C, Fabric H3).

No. 136 A plain upright rim in shell tempered fabric. The external surface is orange-brown (2.5YR5/6); the core is grey (5YR4/1) and the internal surface varies from brown to grey (2.5YR5/6 – 5YR4/1). (Form 1Ai, Fabric H8).

South Ditch, Hearth (KMW–12–37).

No. 137 A coarse everted rim in shell tempered fabric, fired dark grey throughout (N3). (Form 5D, Fabric H4).

No. 138 An upright externally thickened rim in shell tempered fabric. The external surface has been coated with slurry which conceals most of the shell fragments. The internal surface remains rough. The colour of the surfaces varies from orange-brown to grey (2.5YR6/6 – 5YR5/1) and the core is grey (N4). (Form 1Aiv, Fabric H8).

No. 139 A plain rim in shell tempered fabric. The angle and diameter are uncertain. The sherd is brown (5YR5/4) with a darker patch (2.5YR4/2) near the rim. (Form 1Ai, Fabric H3).

South Ditch, Middle (KMW–12–34).

No. 140 A plain rim in a shell tempered fabric. The profile is irregular, but for most of its length, the top coil used to create the rim is narrower than the wall beneath. The colour of the surfaces varies from orange-brown to grey (2.5YR5/6 – 2.5YR4/1) and that of the core is brown (2.5YR4/2). (Form 1Aiii, Fabric H7).

No. 141 An everted rim with flattened edge in a vegetable tempered fabric. Both surfaces show traces of having been burnished. The core and internal surface are dark grey (N3) and the external surface varies from brown to grey (2.5YR5/6 – 10R2.5/1). (Form 5C, Fabric K2).

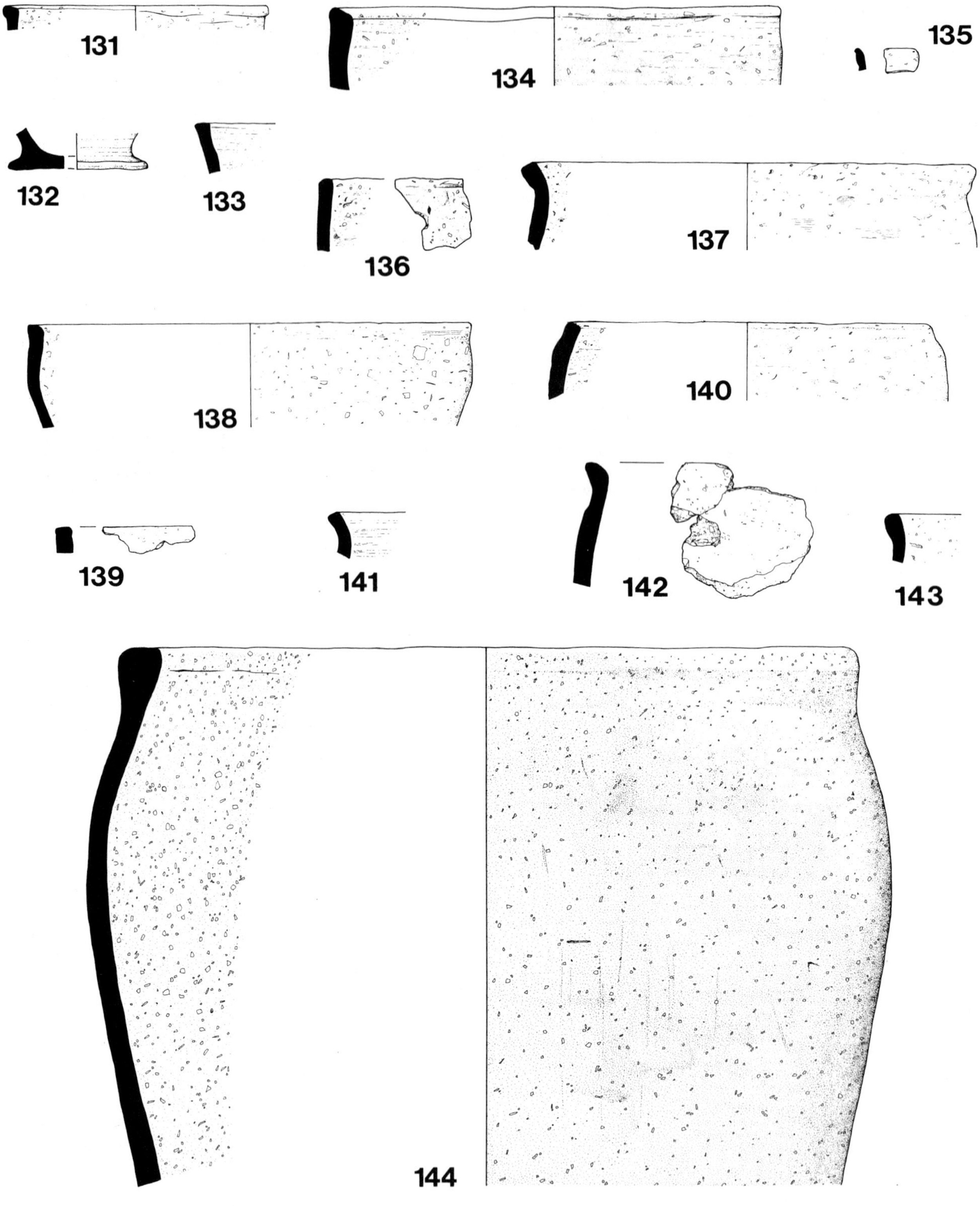

Fig. 20. *Iron Age pottery ($\frac{1}{4}$), from the South East and South Ditches, Farningham Hill.*

South Ditch, Upper (KMW–12–11, 10, 32 and 35).

No. 142 A coarse everted rim in shell tempered fabric. There is a groove beneath the rim. The core is dark grey (N3) and the surfaces are covered with smooth brown slip (5YR5/3 – 2.5YR5/6). (Form 5D, Fabric H7).

No. 143 A coarse everted rim in vegetable and shell tempered fabric. The core is dark grey (N3) and the internal surface is light brown (7.5YR6/4). The external surface varies from brown (2.5YR5/6) to grey (7.5YR3/1). (Form 5D, Fabric M2).

No. 144 Storage jar with globular body, vertical neck and thickened rim with flat-top, in shell tempered fabric. The external surface varies from light brown to orange (5YR6/4 – 10R5/8) with one patch of dark grey (N3), and the internal surface and core are dark grey (N3). Sherds of this vessel were also found in the upper level of the North West Ditch. (Form 11, Fabric H2).

No. 145 A worn wall sherd in flint and grog tempered fabric with stamped decoration. The decoration consists of three horizontal rows of dotted lines above a row of lozenges. Within these lozenges the surface is plain, but between and beneath them the rows of dotted decoration continue. The sherd is small and very worn and as a result it is not possible to determine whether the dots were applied individually; were applied with a 'comb' or a roulette wheel. The dots are approximately 1·2 – 1·3 mm. across and they appear to be round or triangular rather than square. The external surface is orange-brown (10R5/6); the internal surface is light brown (5YR6/6) and the core is grey (N4). (Fabric N5).

No. 146 A necked jar or bowl in a fabric tempered with grog and grit. It has an everted rim and widely spaced broad grooves on the shoulder. The grooves are about 5 mm. wide and up to 1·5 mm. deep, with a U-shaped profile. The sherds are dark grey throughout (N4). (Form 7, Fabric F1).

No. 147 A large jar with a plain slightly in-sloping rim in shell tempered fabric. Irregular depressions on the top of the rim and around the wall of the vessel probably reflect the irregular width of coils rather than deliberate decoration. The internal surface is light brown (5YR6/4) and the core and external surface are dark grey (5YR4/1). (Form 2Aiii, Fabric H5).

No. 148 An in-turned externally thickened rim with flat top in shell tempered fabric. The angle is not certain. The internal surface is brown (5YR5/4) and the core and external surface are dark grey (5YR2.5/1). (Form 2Ci, Fabric H6).

No. 149 A coarse everted rim in shell tempered fabric, fired dark grey throughout (N3). (Form 5D, Fabric H3).

North West Ditch, Lower (KMW–12–19, 21 and 28).

No. 150 A jar with an almost vertical, externally thickened flat-topped rim in shell tempered fabric. The inner surface is smooth, but the external surface is rough with vertical wipe marks. The sherds are dark grey (N2.5), with one patch of brown (5YR5/3) on the external surface. (Form 1Biii, Fabric H4).

No. 151 A small jar with a sharply everted rim in a sandy vegetable tempered fabric. It appears to have been burnt and is now coloured light brown to grey (7.5YR6/4 – N4) with patches of dark grey (N3). (Form 5A, Fabric K3).

No. 152 A lid in a sand and flint tempered fabric. The diameter is uncertain. The sherd is dark grey (5YR4/1) with brown patches (7.5YR6/4). (Form 16B, Fabric L5).

North West Ditch, Upper (KMW–12–6, 8, 12, 20 and 30).

No. 153 A footring base in a sandy fabric. The external surface is burnished and the underside of the base has a design scratched on after firing. The vessel appears to have been burnt. The colour of the surfaces vary from pale grey to dark grey (10YR5/1 – N3), and the core is brown (5YR5/3). (Form 4B, Fabric E1).

No. 154 A footring base in a sandy fabric. The external surface is highly burnished and the internal surface is smooth. The core and internal surface are grey (10YR4/1) and the external surface is dark grey (N3). (Form 4B, Fabric E2).

No. 155 A jar with an everted rim in a hard sandy fabric. Both surfaces have been burnished and the sherds have been fired dark grey throughout (N3). (Form 4, Fabric A1).

No. 156 A bowl with a plain rim in a shell and grog tempered fabric. Beneath the shoulder, near vertical wipe marks create a 'combed' effect. The internal surface is brown (5YR5/3) and the core and external surface are dark grey (5YR3/1) with a patch of orange-brown (2.5YR6/8) on the external surface. (Form 1Ai, Fabric H7). Sherds of this vessel were also found in the top of the South Ditch.

No. 157 A large jar with an everted rim in a shell and vegetable tempered fabric. The internal surface and core vary from brown to dark grey (7.5YR5/2 – 2.5YR3/1) and the external surface is brown (2.5YR5/6). (Form 5D, Fabric H3).

No. 158 A necked bowl in a sandy fabric tempered with grog and shell. The neck is decorated with horizontal grooves. The sherds have been fired grey (N4) throughout. (Form 7, Fabric F1).

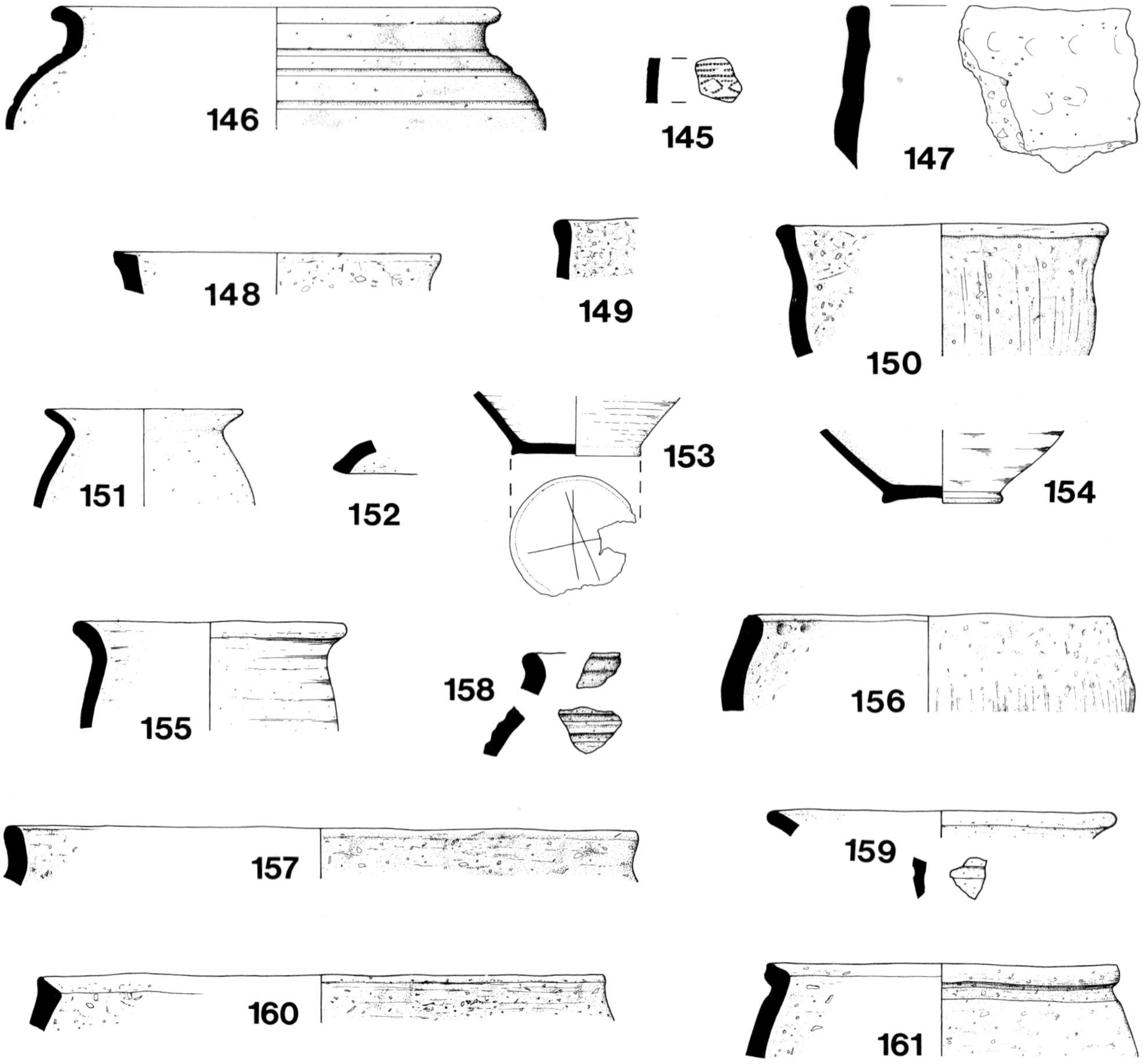

Fig. 21. *Iron Age pottery (¼), from the South Ditch, the North West Ditch and an Unstratified deposit, Farningham Hill.*

No. 159 Two sherds, possibly from the same vessel, in a grog and shell tempered fabric; an everted rim with a squared top and a wall sherd with a horizontal groove. Both sherds have been fired grey-brown throughout (2.5YR4/1). (Form 9A, Fabric N6).

No. 160 An in-sloping rim with external projection in shell tempered fabric. The colour varies from grey to orange-brown throughout (5YR3/1 – 2.5YR4/6). (Form 2Cii, Fabric H7).

Unstratified. (KMW–12–51).

No. 161 An in-sloping rim with external projection in shell tempered fabric. The profile of the rim varies: at one point it is convex, at another it is concave, bearing a marked recess. Beneath the rim is a wide shallow groove. The external surface has been coated with slurry which covers the shell fragments. This and the core are black (N2.5) and the internal surface is dark brown (2.5YR4/2). (Form 2Ci-2Ciii, Fabric H8).

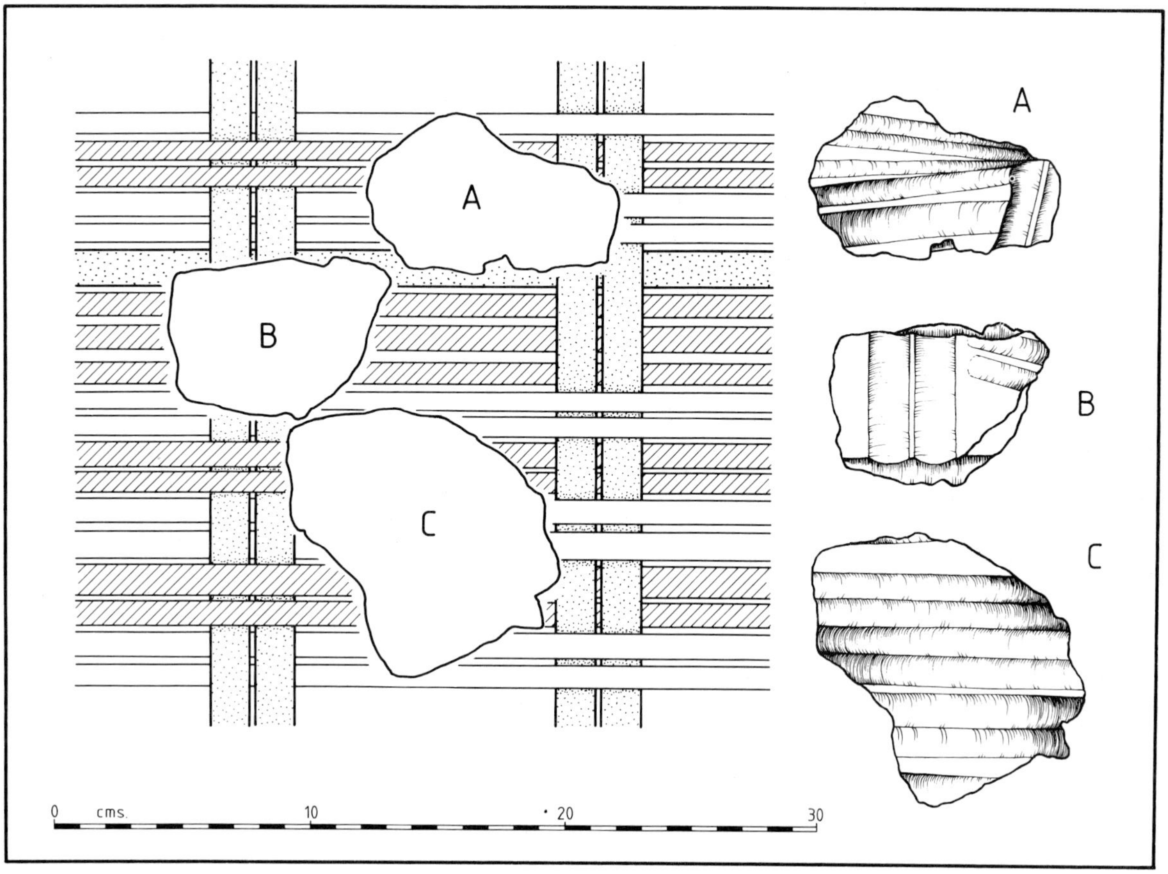

Fig. 22. *Tentative reconstruction of wattle frame based on fragments of daub from Pit 21, Farningham Hill.*

FINDS AND ENVIRONMENTAL REPORTS 5 – 8

The following specialist reports have been produced on microfiche and are to be found in the envelope attached to the inside back cover of this volume.

(5). The Animal bone by Alison Locker, B.Sc., (Nos. M1–M6).
A report on the total animal bones recovered from the ditches (Table I) and the pits (Table J). Cattle were the main source of meat at Farningham, followed by sheep and pig. Hunting for red deer, roe deer and wild boar supplemented the domestic supply. Cattle and sheep were kept at least until sub-adulthood and mainly until maturity, suggesting that their primary purpose was for milk and wool.

(6). The Charred Grains by Mrs. D. Vaughan, (Nos. M7 and M8).
A short report on the carbonised plant remains found in the pits.
Grains of wheat and barley were found in four pits (Table K).

(7). The Mollusca by T.P. O'Conner, (Nos. M9–M11).
A short report on 20 samples taken from the pits (Table L) and the mollusc remains found in them and also a list of mollusca recovered during the excavation (Table M).

(8). The Fragments of Daub, (No. M12).
A brief note on the collection of daub fragments found in Pit 21 and a reconstruction of the wattle-frame (Fig. 22 printed).

CHAPTER III

THE PREHISTORIC, ROMAN AND SAXON SITES AT DARENTH

SUMMARY

Rescue excavation by the Kent Unit ahead of rapid pipe-laying operations revealed clear evidence of a wide-ranging multi-period landscape across the west side of the well-known Darenth Roman Villa site. This produced the first evidence of prehistoric activity and included a concentrated assemblage of Mesolithic flint; Neolithic pottery and possible related features; a probable Late Bronze Age pit and Iron Age pottery. Several second-fourth century Roman features included a substantial wood-lined water-channel; a flint boundary wall and several chalk rafts and ditches. The Roman aisled building (Room 65), found in 1894–5, was found to butt a pre-existing structure. Two certain and two possible Saxon sunken-floored huts and a large posted-structure were found and confirm a major fifth-sixth century Saxon settlement site in the south-west corner of the Roman complex.

CONTENTS

A. INTRODUCTION

The prehistoric, Roman and Saxon sites lie partially superimposed upon each other within the limits of the palatial Roman Villa on Darenth Court Farm (NGR. TQ. 5635. 7065, Fig. 23). The villa was excavated by George Payne in 1894–5 (Ref. 100) when some 71 rooms or buildings, mostly in long ranges around two large courtyards, were revealed. In 1969, rescue-excavations directed by the writer, for the West Kent Archaeological Group, revealed a detached bath-house and large aisled building, both south-west of the main villa-block (Ref. 101).

The 1894–5 excavation was left open for public viewing, but gradually became overgrown and was later abandoned. By 1970, the site, by then a Scheduled Ancient Monument, was covered by a dense wood. Everywhere within, the Roman walls lay exposed and high spoil-heaps provided excellent facilities for regular illicit digging by school-masters 'teaching' history!

Early in 1972 the farmer was able to get a local contractor to clear the larger trees and the Unit was able to hire large mechanical excavators, on a casual basis, to help level some of the spoil-heaps and bury some of the walls. It was also able to persuade the sewer-pipe contractor to drop his surplus soil into the deepest part of the old excavation. Finally, in 1974 the Unit persuaded the D.O.E. and the farmer to finance a short operation to remove all the tree stumps and to level the spoil-heaps. This was achieved by the Unit in ten days at a cost of about £400 when all the Roman masonry was buried and the site left level. Part of the area was taken into cultivation, but the greater part has again become overgrown.

In January, 1972 it became known that the West Kent Main Sewerage Board was re-laying the main Darent Valley sewer between Dartford and Farningham and Unit members immediately checked the plans. It was at once clear that this cut right through the extreme west range of the Darenth villa and across the scheduled area. It seems that the water-authority did not know of the scheduling and that the D.O.E. had not been informed of the intended pipe-line! The Unit immediately informed both parties and the engineers offered to re-align their pipe-trench, some four weeks ahead of the work. This moved the intended line off the Roman masonry and onto the narrow strip of unexcavated ground between the villa and the river (Ref. 102).

The Unit offered to excavate some of the pipe-trench, ahead of the contractors, so that any archaeological features could be located, excavated and recorded ahead of certain destruction. This offer was accepted by the West Kent Sewerage Board and limited finance provided by the Ancient Monuments Branch of the Dept. of the Environment. The work was directed by the writer, supported by a team of two, working on a full time basis and with the support of volunteer members of the West Kent Archaeological Group.

Even with such limited resources it was possible to excavate mechanically about 450 ft. (137 m.) of trench, mostly 5 ft. (1·50 m.) wide, from north to south across the site. This was then supplemented by manual excavation at the critical points. Three main areas of interest were located and it was possible to open up small area-excavations here (North Area, Centre Area and South Area) to allow more extensive work. In all this work revealed some 32 features of Neolithic, Roman and Saxon date (Features 1–32). It was also possible to locate the north and west walls of "Room 65" and part of "Room 58" of the 1894–5 excavation so that the new features could be tied into the previous plans. The hectic archaeological work lasted four weeks and was completed just as the contractor's constantly advancing operation reached the north end of the site (Plate XII). All the features and structures on the line were then totally destroyed by the pipe-laying operation, which generally removed a width of about 20 ft. (6 m.) at ground-level.

The trench excavated by the Unit began at the hedge marking the northern end of the main site at the point marked 0 ft. on the Datum-line (Fig. 24). This extended southwards to a point close to the fence marking the southern limits of the main site, there bordered by a public-footpath. The Unit continued the trench for another 325 ft. (99 m.) into the field south of the footpath, passing parallel to and about 80 ft. (24 m.) east of the Roman-aisled building found in 1969. This work failed to locate any significant Roman features and apart from recording a small pit (F33) of Late Bronze Age date and a light scatter of Roman debris, no further work was possible in the time available (Ref. 103).

The excavation archive for this four-week excavation consists of 20 sheets of plans and sections, 115 recorded contexts, 64 photographs, 13 boxes of finds and the site-notebook. Of this, four plans, six sections and six photographs covering all of the main features are published here. All the prehistoric, Roman and Saxon pottery has been classified by fabric and is included here, as it forms the crucial dating evidence. The Mesolithic flints and later small-finds are also included here.

The post-excavation archive contains the correlation of contexts and features and also lists of finds. The archive is on short-term storage in the Kent Unit's security controlled archive at Dover Castle where it may be consulted on request. Its final destination should be Dartford Museum, with copies placed in the National Monuments Record.

Acknowledgements

The writer wishes to extend his warm thanks to a number of people who helped in many different ways. Firstly, to Mr. Alec Fishlock and Mr. Steve James the engineers in charge of the pipe-line programme. Next, to Mr. Edward Weekes for his help with backfilling the 19th century excavations and to Miss Sarnia Butcher of the Dept. of the Environment for her helpful support. Also to the site-contractors, A. Waddington & Sons Ltd. for their ready co-operation.

Thanks are also particularly due to Mr. Gerald Clewley and Mr. Howard Davies for their fulltime work on the excavation and to Edna Mynott, Mr. and Mrs. D. Broadfoot, Mr. R. Gierth, Mr. J. Willson and Mr. J. Williams for extended work at weekends. Thanks are also due to another 60 volunteers, mostly members of the West Kent Archaeological Group, but also others being members of the Dover, Fawkham Historical, Faversham, Otford, Reculver, Sittingbourne, Springhead and Upchurch Groups, combining under the auspices of the Council for Kentish Archaeology.

Grateful thanks are also due to various specialists for their reports on the excavated finds. Mrs. Joanna Bird has reported on the samian; Miss Brenda Dickinson on the three samian stamps; Mrs. Katherine Hartley on the mortaria; Dr. Isobel Smith on the Neolithic pottery; Mr. Peter Couldrey on the Iron Age pottery; Dr. Donald Harden on two glass fragments; Mr. Keith Parfitt on most of the small-finds; Mr. John Willson on the Roman and Saxon coarse pottery and Dr. Andrew Woodcock on the Mesolithic flint assemblage and axes.

B. THE EXCAVATED STRUCTURES AND FEATURES

The 33 features described here are listed in feature number order, beginning at the north end of the main trench but also including those found in the extended areas. These include 22 Romano-British features, five Anglo-Saxon features, a Late Bronze Age pit (south of the main trench), a low-lying peat deposit, an area producing Mesolithic material and probable prehistoric gullies and a pit. All measurements are given initially in feet, with metric equivalents in brackets, to assist comparison with the earlier excavations on this site.

Feature 1 (Chalk Raft 1, Fig. 24).

A layer of chalk rubble had been compacted onto the surface of the natural gravel at about 5–18 ft. (1·5–5·5 m.) on the Datum. This only appeared in the east face of the trench and it was not thus possible to determine its width. It was 2 ins. (5 cm.) thick and presumably about 13 ft. (4 m.) in length, if it was rectangular in plan and on the same broad axis as the adjacent chalk rafts on its south side.

Feature 2 (Chalk Raft 2, Fig. 24 and Plate XIII).

A second, much larger, layer of chalk rubble had been compacted on the natural gravel at 24–58 ft. (7·3–17·5 m.) along the Datum, thus giving a total length of about 34 ft. (10 m.). There was a space of about 6 ft. (2 m.) between its north end and the south end of Chalk Raft 1. Both its east and west sides were found and these showed that it had been oblong in plan and only about 2 ft. 6 ins. (75 cm.) wide and 2 ins. (5 cm.) thick. It sealed the Roman North Ditch (F5) which contained second century pottery, but was sealed by the Roman oven (F6).

Feature 3 (Chalk Raft 3, Fig. 24).

A third layer of chalk had been compacted on the natural gravel at 36–57 ft. (11–17 m.) along the Datum, thus giving a total length of about 21 feet (6·5 m.). Its east side was found in the pipe-trench whilst its west edge was beyond the edge of the excavation. It was oblong in plan, at least 2 ft. 6 ins. (75 cm.) wide and also 2 ins. (5 cm.) thick. Its east side was about 1 ft. 6 ins. (0·5 m.) from the west side of Chalk Raft 2 and it, too, sealed the Roman North Ditch. The soil above this chalk raft contained 13 sherds of Roman pottery (No. 169), including a samian F.15/17 of early-second century date and dishes of second century type, a late-Neolithic sherd (No. 333b) and one flint awl (No. 316).

Feature 4 (Chalk Raft 4, Fig. 24).

A fourth layer of chalk had been compacted onto the natural gravel to the east of Chalk Rafts 2 and 3. This was only exposed in the east extension of the North Area from 44–60 ft. (13·4–18·28 m.) on the Datum, thus having a minimum length of 16 ft. (4·88 m.). Both its east and west sides were found and its actual width was about 3 ft. 5 ins. (1 m.). Again an oblong form is indicated with the space between it and Chalk Raft 2 being just 3 ft. (91 cm.). The soil above this chalk raft contained nine sherds of Roman pottery of late-first or second century date.

Feature 5 (Roman North Ditch, Figs. 23, 24 and 25, Section A).

A small east-west ditch was found crossing the pipe-trench at 57 ft. (17·37 cm.) on the Datum and then traced in the North Area extension for a total length of 16 ft. (4·88 m.). It was U-shaped in profile, at least 4 ft. (1·22 m.) wide and about 2 ft. (60 cm.) deep. It had been dug into the natural gravel and had eventually silted with deposits of grey and black loam (L.7–10). These were sealed by three of the Chalk Rafts (F2–4), which had generally slumped into the ditch (L.6) when the underlying silt had contracted. The ditch contained 22 sherds of Roman pottery (not illustrated) mostly of second century date and not later than A.D. 200, a sherd of late-Neolithic pottery (No. 328) and a flint core (No. 249).

Feature 6 (Roman Oven, Fig. 24 and Plate XIV).

A tile-built rectangular oven was found in the North Area at 47 ft. (14·32 m.) on the main Datum and completely excavated. It was laid out on an approximate north-south axis and was 5 ft. 8 ins. (1·72 m.) by 2 ft. (60 cm.) overall. Its narrow walls were built of fragments of broken tile and included several lumps of chalk and these defined an internal area of 3 ft. 10 ins. (1·16 m.) by 11 ins. (0·28 m.). Its north end had been blocked off.

The oven rested on a black loam deposit some 5 ins. (13 cm.) thick containing Roman material. This black soil sat directly over the rammed Chalk Raft (F2) and contained a fragment of a glass vessel (No. 165), one flint axe flake (No. 325) and about 50 sherds of Roman pottery (Nos. 171

and 172). These included a samian F.31 dated Antonine and dishes, bowls and cooking-pots dating from the late-second century to at least the fourth century. Significantly, this pottery included flanged bowls probably not earlier than A.D. 250 in date.

The black loam above the oven contained 14 sherds of Roman pottery (Nos. 173–175) including one sherd of second century samian, two fourth century flanged bowls and a fourth century bowl of Oxfordshire Ware. It seems likely from this that the oven was probably constructed during the first half of the fourth century.

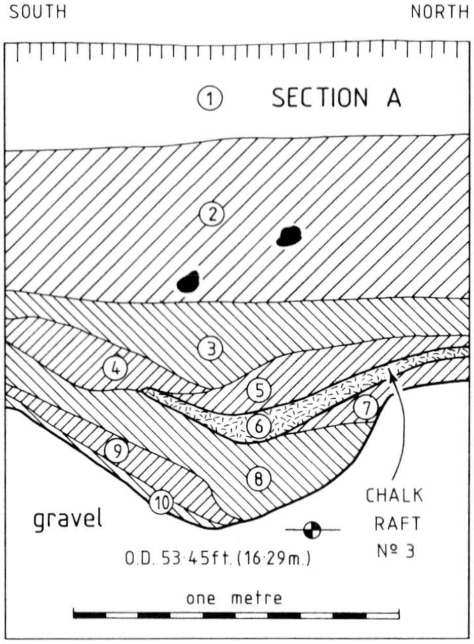

Fig. 25. *Section A, through Roman North Ditch (F5), Darenth Roman Villa.*

Feature 7 ("Room 58" Excavated 1894–5, Fig. 24).

No attempt was made to excavate this structure, but as it was open to the sky its position was plotted onto the small-scale site-plan. This enabled all the new features to be related to the 19th century excavations and ensured that the pipe-trench was kept some 45 ft. (14 m.) to the west. This room and other exposed adjacent masonry from the original excavation was buried by the Unit during the pipe-line excavation.

Feature 8 (Pit, Fig. 24).

This small pit was found on the east side of the pipe-trench at Datum 93 ft. 6 ins. (28·5 m.). It was sub-circular in plan, with a diameter of 2 ft. 6 ins. (76 cm.) and a depth of about 2 ft. (60 cm.). It was bowl-shaped in section and its filling of black loam contained Roman tile and pottery, flint and shell. The pottery consisted of 29 sherds (Nos. 176–180) of vessels mostly of late-second or early-third century date and none later than about A.D. 250.

Feature 9 (Pit, Fig. 24).

This large, sub-rectangular pit was found on the west side of the pipe-trench at Datum 88–100 ft. (27–30·5 m.) though only its east side was uncovered. It was at least 12 ft. (3·65 m.) long, at least 3 ft. (91 cm.) wide and some 4 ft. 6 ins. (1·37 m.) deep cut into the natural gravel. Its filling of black loam contained 14 sherds of Roman pottery (No. 181) of late-second century or early-third century date and also a stone hone (No. 247A).

Feature 10 (Pit, Fig. 24).

This pit was only seen in section in the east face of the pipe-trench at Datum 125 ft. (38 m.). It was about 7 ft. 6 ins. (2 m.) long, of uncertain width and only 10 ins. (25 cm.) deep into the natural soil. Its filling of grey-black loam and some flints contained Roman tile, but no pottery.

Feature 11 (The Peat Deposit, Fig. 24).

At about Datum 100 ft. (30·5 m.) the surface of the natural gravel began to drop and reached its lowest point at about Datum 150 ft. (46 m.) where it was some 3 ft. (91 cm.) lower. Beyond this point it rose steadily southwards to form a low spur, capped by brickearth and occupied by the Mesolithic site. This resulted in a broad natural hollow, centred on about Datum 185 ft. (56·5 m.) that was found to contain grey clay, sandy silts and peat. The peat, mostly up to 6 ins. (15 cm.) thick, was confined to a 25 ft. (7·62 m.) wide zone between Datum 175 (53·34 m.) and 200 ft. (61 m.). This contained a small fragment of a probable late-Neolithic vessel (No. 330) and it seems likely that this deposit was forming in late-Neolithic times. This is to some extent confirmed by the presence of two shell-loaded potsherds (No. 342) of Iron Age date in the black loam layer that sealed the peat. Dumps of Roman tiles and flint above this show that this particular spot was consolidated during the villa period. Even so the zone remained lower than the areas to the south and north and the post-Roman hillwash deposits were correspondingly deeper directly over this natural hollow.

The peat itself suggests water-logged conditions and indeed the trench remained flooded here throughout the excavation. Further, George Payne's plan shows a small stream flowing from the bank just below this point into the main river and traces of this survive today in spite of extensive gravel quarrying. It seems likely that a small underground spring may still feed the hollow from the east side and indeed it may be significant that in Roman times the large pool (Room 42) and the 'water shrine' (Room 66), both needing an adequate water-supply, were about 150 ft. (46 m.) east of this precise point and could have been fed from such a spring.

Feature 12 (Metalling, Figs. 24 and 26).

An area of compact metalling was found in the east extension of the Centre Area, between Datum 313 (95·4 m.) and 328 ft. (100m.), but clearly continuing to the north, east and south (Fig. 27, Section B, L.5). Unusually on this site, it sloped to the east due to differential make-up. This consisted of a thick layer of chalk, flint and tile up to 10 ins. (25 cm.) thick on the west side, but mostly of fine gravel, tile chips and occasional potsherds only 3–9 ins. (8–23 cm.) thick on the east side. Neither layer reappeared some 20 ft. (6 m.) to the north, nor obviously some 50 ft. (15 m.) to the south. In the absence of other evidence it seems likely that this metalling was somewhat localised, perhaps relating to the adjacent north end of the large aisled building (Room 65). It seems to have been cut by the small east-west Roman Centre East Ditch (F13). A primary layer of fine metalling was noted beneath the main metalling in one place, but this was not examined in detail. The soil between the two layers contained one flint scraper (No. 285) and 34 sherds of Roman pottery (Nos. 182 and 183), mostly of late-second and early-third century date. This suggests that the upper metalling, at least, could not have been laid earlier than about A.D. 220.

Feature 13 (Roman Centre East Ditch, Figs. 24 and 26).

A short length of a small north-south ditch was recorded at about 315–328 ft. (96–100 m.) on the main Datum, in the east extension of the Centre Area (Fig. 27, Section B, L.6–12). This had cut through the metalled surface (F12), but had itself been cut by the Roman Water Channel (F14) and by at least one post-hole of the Saxon Structure (F23).

This was not examined in any detail, but generally it was about 4 ft. 6 ins. (1·4 m.) wide, 2 ft. (60 cm.) deep and contained deposits of loam, flint and pebble. The filling contained eleven sherds of pottery (not illustrated) including a samian F.31 dated Antonine and vessels probably dating from the end of the second century.

Feature 14 (Roman Water Channel, Figs. 24 and 26 and Plate XV).

A wide, shallow cut was found in the gravel at Datum 270–327 ft. (82·3–99·6 m.). This was about 8 ft. (2·5 m.) wide at the top, had sloping sides and a flat base about 6 ft. (1·8 m.) wide (Fig. 27, Section B, L.13). Its maximum depth was about 18 ins. (45 cm.) and both sides had been lined with small wooden posts, the sockets of which were clearly visible. Twenty-one post-sockets were located (Table A) and of these 18 were rectangular and three were circular. It seems clear that these posts retained the sides of the cut and it is likely that they held vertical boards, or some other form of lining. This would have created a parallel sided channel some 5 ft. 6 ins. (1·7 m.) wide and at least 18 ins. (45 cm.) deep. There can be little doubt that natural water would have collected in this channel for some, or all, of the time. Indeed there seems little doubt that this man-made channel, running on the same axis as the adjacent river, was specifically constructed to carry running water across the site. Its primary filling consisted of some 3 ins. (8 cm.) of washed gravel, whilst the remaining fill was a black loam containing Roman tile, pottery and a coin (Coin No. 1). The filling was cut through by at least one of the large posts of the Saxon Structure (F23).

The pottery (Nos. 184–191 and 235) consisted of about 135 sherds representing at least 20 vessels. These included a samian F.31 dated Antonine and four other samian sherds dated mid-second to mid-third century. The coarse pottery included several sherds of cooking-pot, two mortaria and at least 14 dishes, the latter including both flanged, plain and bead-rim vessels. It also included a derived Neolithic sherd (No. 333a) and six small sherds of Saxon pottery (No. 345), the latter from the slumped upper deposits. The Roman pottery mostly dates from about A.D. 150–250, but the presence of fourth century dishes suggests that the Channel was not filled with soil and rubbish before at least the early-fourth century. The Saxon material was probably discarded into a slight hollow over the line of the channel. The single coin of Victorinus (A.D. 265–270), agrees with the dating suggested by the pottery. A thin layer of black loam that sealed the filling of the Water Channel, produced three Roman coins (Coin Nos. 2–4). One was a barbarous radiate (A.D. 270–300), and the other two corroded coins of the House of Constantine (c. A.D. 320–350). If these coins were lost in the second quarter of the fourth century then this would suggest that the Channel was finally filled no later than the middle of the fourth century.

The pipe-trench cut the Water Channel at an acute angle and virtually followed its length for a distance of at least 57 ft. (17 m.). From the row of posts on the west side it seems likely that at least two alignments are represented. If so, then the Channel had been diverted marginally towards the north-west somewhere about Datum 303 ft. (92 m.). Assuming a northwards flow, which considering the topography and the northward flow of the adjacent river is probable, then a source somewhere to the south-west is likely. Indeed the edge of what may have been a continuation of the Channel was found in the north-west corner of the west extension of the South Area (F25), but lack of time prevented the excavation here from being extended. If this was the continuation then another 60 ft. (18 m.) may be added to the known length of the Channel. It is clear that this was a planned feature requiring a considerable amount of labour and materials and thus reflecting an important element of the Roman site. It could have served a water-mill or had a variety of other functions, (see discussion on page 89).

		Size of Post		Spacing		Depth	
No.	Shape of Post	inches	cm.	Feet and inches	m./cm.	Ft. Ins.	cm.
R1	Rectangular	5″ × 5″	13 × 13	–	–	2″	5 cm. (min.)
R2	Rectangular	7″ × 6½″	18 × 16·5	2′10″ from Post R1	86 cm.	2″	5 cm. (min.)
R3	Rectangular	3″ × 6″	8 × 15	2′10″ from Post R2	86 cm.	2″	5 cm. (min.)
R4	Rectangular	5″ × 5½″	13 × 14	2′10″ from Post R3	86 cm.	2″	5 cm. (min.)
R5	Rectangular	5″ × 5″	13 × 13	3′5″ from Post R4	1·04 m.	2″	5 cm. (min.)
R6	Rectangular	5″ × 5″	13 × 13	5′5″ from Post R5	1·65 m.	2″	5 cm. (min.)
R7	Rectangular	4″ × 6″	10 × 15	3′5″ from Post R6	1·04 m.	2″	5 cm. (min.)
R8 to R10	Missing – not seen	–	–	–	–	–	–
R11	Rectangular	5″ × 4½″	13 × 11·5	12′9″ from Post R7	3·88 m.	2″	5 cm. (min.)
R12	Rectangular	5″ × 6″	13 × 15	3′4″ from Post R11	1 m.	2″	5 cm. (min.)
R13	Rectangular	5½″ × 5½″	14 × 14	3′6″ from Post R12	1·06 m.	2″	5 cm. (min.)
R14	Rectangular	5″ × 5″	13 × 13	2′11″ from Post R13	88 cm.	1′ 0″	30 cm.
R15	Rectangular	5″ × 5″	13 × 13	2′5″ from Post R14	74 cm.	1′ 0″	30 cm.
R16	Rectangular	5½″ × 6½″	14 × 16·5	1′1″ from Post R15	33 cm.	1′ 2″	36 cm.
R17	Rectangular	5″ × 5½″	13 × 14	1′1″ from Post R16	33 cm.	2″	5 cm. (min.)
R18	Rectangular	6″ × 6″	15 × 15	3′7″ from Post R17	1·1 m.	2″	5 cm. (min.)
R19	Rectangular	6″ × 5″	15 × 13	6′5″ from Post R18	2 m.	2″	5 cm. (min.)
R20	Circular	6″ × 6″	15 × 15			1′ 6″	45 cm.
R21	Circular	5½″ × 5½″	14 × 14	3′2″ from Post R20	96 cm.	1′ 0″	30 cm.
R22	Circular	7″ × 7″	18 × 18	3′6″ from Post R21	1·06 m.	1′ 4″	40 cm.
R23	Rectangular	4″ × 4″	10 × 10	1′4″ from Post R22	40 cm.	8″	20 cm.
R24	Rectangular	6″ × 6″	15 × 15	3′4″ from Post R23	1 m.	12½″	32 cm.

Table A – Posts along the Roman Water Channel.

Feature 15 (Tile Base, Fig. 26).

A broadly rectangular area of broken Roman tiles and pebble was found on the west side of the pipe-trench at 290–299 ft. (88·4–91 m.) on the main Datum. This was about 9 ft. (2·7 m.) long, about 2 ft. 6 ins. (76 cm.) wide and only 3 ins. (8 cm.) deep. There were some signs of burning across the top of the tiles and it is possible that they had served as the base of an oven, but the area was too disturbed to be certain. The tile base overlay the Chalk Raft (F16) and was in turn sealed by black loam containing Roman and Saxon material. The soil beneath the tiles contained part of an antler (No. 240) and some 50 potsherds (Nos. 192–194) which included one samian F.44 and two samian F.33, of Antonine to mid-third century date. The coarse pottery included two bead-rim cooking-pots and at least five bead-rim dishes, all probably of second or early-third century date. From this it seems clear that the tile base could not have been constructed much before about A.D. 225. In the circumstances it is difficult to say more than this.

Features 16 and 17 (Chalk Rafts, Fig. 26).

Two areas of rammed chalk were found in the west extension of the Centre Area. The north one (F16) was 2 ins. (5 cm.) thick and about 14 ft. (4·3 m.) in length. The south one (F17) was generally thicker and at least 12 ft. (3·65 m.) long. (Fig. 27, Section B, L.14). Their precise outlines could not be determined as they were mostly cut away by later features. They are likely to be of early-Roman date and to correspond in some way with the Chalk Rafts (F1–4) at the north-end of the trench. The south one, at least, was later in date than the underlying gully (F19) through which it had been cut at one point.

Feature 18 (Pit, Fig. 26).

An oblong pit was found in the west extension of the Centre Area at about 314 ft. (96 m.) on the main Datum. It was cut roughly east-west, into the underlying gravel and much later had been cut into by a post-hole of the Saxon Structure (F23, P.H.S6).

It was 4 ft. 2 ins. (1·27 m.) in length, 2 ft. 6 ins. (76 cm.) in width and just 14 ins. (36 cm.) deep. Its sides were sloping, its base flat and it was filled with orange-grey clay containing fire-cracked stones, a flint scraper (No. 260), a flint axe (No. 321) and a single sherd of flint-gritted pottery of possible Neolithic date. The pit is clearly pre-Roman and the evidence may favour a Neolithic date, thus corresponding with late-Neolithic sherds from the site. However, this depends on the dating of the sherd and this cannot be regarded as conclusive.

Features 19 and 20 (Gullies, Fig. 26).

These two small gullies joined together at right-angles to produce a T-shaped plan, across the west extension of the Centre Area at 292–315 ft. (89–96 m.) along the main Datum.

The north-south gully (F19) was traced in a straight line for 24 ft. (7·32 m.) until both ends had been cut away by later features. The east-west arm (F20) only survived for a distance of 3 ft. 9 ins. (1·14 m.). Both gullies appeared to be of identical construction with vertical sides, flat bases and 12–14 ins. (30–36 cm.) wide. Each was filled with a brown clay loam containing fire-cracked stones, some 25 struck flints including a fine scraper (No. 270) and six sherds of flint-tempered pottery. The latter is mostly too fragmentary for illustration, but one sherd has faint cord impressions and appears to be of late-Neolithic date (No. 329). It was not possible to examine these gullies in detail and it is difficult to suggest their precise function.

The few dateable finds all appear to be of Neolithic date and if so then the gullies are both likely to be of that date. However, the dating evidence is limited and as the gullies were not examined in detail it is clearly impossible to offer a precise date. They could have related to the adjacent pit (F18). It is also just possible that the gullies related to the Iron Age material found elsewhere on the site but either way they certainly seem to be of pre-Roman date.

Feature 21 (Roman Boundary Wall, Figs. 24, 26 and 27).

A mortared flint wall was located in the west extension of the Centre Area at a point about 288 ft. (88 m.) and 324 ft. (98·75 m.) on the Datum. This ran almost north-south, roughly parallel to, and about 53 ft. (16·15 m.) from, the west wall of 'Room 65' excavated in 1894–5 (see below). It was traced for 36 ft. (11 m.) and clearly continued to the north, though it did not survive where its projected line crossed the pipe-trench. Its south end was cut by the lip of a large feature, perhaps a wide ditch (F22) and its line cut by one of the large post-holes of the Saxon Structure (F23, P.H.S4).

Its foundation consisted of a single course of unmortared flints just 24 ins. (60 cm.) wide. The wall proper was built of flints set in yellow mortar, some 22 ins. (56 cm.) wide and surviving only one course high.

In the absence of related floors, or other walls, it seems likely that this wall served as a boundary wall on the west side of the villa complex. There was no direct evidence as to its precise date, but it must be earlier than the wide feature (F22) that cut its south end which contained coins and pottery of third century date. The wall also appears to run parallel to the Roman Water Channel (F14) and if they do respect each other then they may be partly of contemporary date.

Feature 22 (Roman Centre West Ditch, Figs. 24 and 26).

The northern lip of a large feature was found at Datum 327 ft. (99·66 m.) and traced across the west extension of the Centre Area. It seems probable that this was part of another shallow ditch. It was traced, running roughly east-west, for a distance of about 21 ft. (6·4 m.). It was at least 3 ft. (91 cm.) wide and only 14 ins. (36 cm.) deep. Its base was flat and its north side steep.

It cut through a rammed Chalk Base (F17), the silted Water Channel (F14) and the flint boundary wall (F21). Clearly, it had been excavated sometime after the construction of these features. Its filling of black loam contained Roman pottery, tile and two coins (Nos. 5 and 6). The pottery consisted of some 20 Roman potsherds that included a samian F.45 dated late-second to early-third century. The coarse sherds date from the mid-second to mid-third century, whilst the coins were a barborous radiate (c. A.D. 270–300) and a corroded bronze. It seems likely that this ditch was not filled before the end of the third century. This filling was in turn cut through by one of the large post-holes of the Saxon Structure (F23, P.H. S4).

Feature 23 (Saxon Structure, Figs. 24, 26 and 27).

A series of 13 large post-holes was found in the west extension of the Centre Area and the details of these are tabulated below (Table B). Most of the post-pits were 14–26 ins. (36–66 cm.) in diameter, had vertical sides, flat bases and were 10–24 ins. (25–60 cm.) deep. There was clear

No.	Diam. of Post Pit	Packing	Diam. of Post	Fill of Post-Hole	Depth	Shape of Post-Hole
S1	18″ 45 cm.	Flint, tile and grey black loam	10″ 25 cm.	Black loam	21″ 53 cm.	Vertical sides, flat base
S2	25″ 63 cm.	Flint, tile and grey black loam	10″ 25 cm.	Black loam	24″ 61 cm.	Vertical sides, flat base
S3	23″ 58 cm.	Flint, tile and grey black loam	12″ 30 cm.	Black loam	18″ 45 cm.	Vertical sides, flat base
S4	24″ 61 cm.	Flint, tile and grey black loam only at top	9″ 23 cm.	Black loam	19″ 48 cm.	Vertical sides, pointed base
S5	E/W 17″ × 14″ 43 × 36 cm.	Flints, 1 tile and 2 Roman pots	8″ 20 cm.	Black-brown loam	17″ 43 cm.	?
S6	18″ 45 cm.	Grey black loam, flint and samian	9″ 23 cm.	Grey-brown loam	7″ 18 cm.	?
S7	E/W 20″ × 15″ 50 × 38 cm.	Brown loam, flint and tile	8″ 20 cm.	Black loam	16″ 40 cm.	Vertical sides, flat base
S8	18″ 45 cm.	Flint and tile	8″ 20 cm.	Black loam	7″ min. 18 cm.	?
S9	15″ 38 cm.	Flint and tile	8″ 20 cm.	Black loam	16″ 40 cm.	Circular, vertical sides, flat base
S10	14″ 36 cm.	Brown loam and chalk specks	?	Grey-brown loam	11″ 28 cm.	Circular, steep sides, cupped base
S11	26″ 66 cm.	Flint, tile and mortar	8″ 20 cm.	Black loam	12″ 30 cm.	Circular, vertical sides, flat base
S12	17″ 43 cm.	Flint, tile, grey-brown loam	8″ 20 cm.	Black-brown loam	10″ 25 cm.	Circular, vertical sides, flat base
S13	13″ 33 cm.	Flint and tile	6″ 15 cm.	Black-brown loam	12″ 30 cm.	Circular, vertical sides, flat base

Table B – Posts Relating to the Saxon Structure (F23)

evidence of central, circular posts mostly 8–10 ins. (20–25 cm.) in diameter. Several of the posts had been packed with flints and broken Roman tile. The packings also contained about 45 Roman potsherds (No. 195) including a samian F.33 and a samian F.38, both of Antonine date and coarse potsherds, mostly of second century date. Two fragments of glass (No. 167), one the base of a small vessel, the other window-glass and a late-Neolithic sherd (No. 332) were also found in the post-holes.

The majority of these formed two clear lines, a northern line consisting of at least three post-holes (P.H. Nos. S9, 10 and 11) and a southern line of at least five more (P.H. Nos. S1–4 and 8). In general the larger posts were spaced at intervals of about 5–6 ft. (1·5–1·8 m.), but the pair of western ones were about 9 ft. (2·7 m.) beyond the others. The two lines were almost parallel, being 17 ft. (5·18 m.) apart at the east end and 16 ft. 4 ins. (4·97 m.) at the west end.

The general absence of similar post-holes anywhere else in the area examined and the concentration of posts at this one point, suggests that all or most related to a single structure. Indeed the roughly regular spacing, the straightness of the two main lines of posts and the fact that the latter were almost parallel, suggests that the structure was a wooden building about 17 ft. (5·18 m.) wide and at least 23 ft. (7 m.) long. If so, then a broadly east-west axis is indicated.

As regards dating this wooden structure is clearly later than all the other features on this particular site. One post-hole (P.H. S2) had been dug through the fill of the Roman Water Channel. Another (P.H. S4) cut through the fill of the Centre West Ditch which was itself cut through the flint boundary wall and filled in by about A.D. 300. Hence, the structure must be later in date than the third century.

Of greater significance was a thin layer of black-brown loam that covered all the other features and seemed to represent an occupation soil relating to the posted-structure. This contained four small sherds of coarse hand-made pottery, Anglo-Saxon in character and perhaps made in the 5th or 6th centuries A.D. It seems clear that this layer formed in the post-Roman period and its association with the posted-structure strongly suggests that the latter was constructed at this time. The discovery of at least two Saxon (perhaps four) sunken-huts some 65 ft. (19·8 m.) to the south and of Anglo-Saxon pottery and loomweights some 100 ft. (30·48 m.) to the south-east (in 1969) makes this identification both reasonable and indeed likely.

Feature 24 ("Room 65" Excavated 1894–5, Fig. 24 and Plate XVI).

In order to ensure that the pipe-trench did not gradually encroach on to the villa as it progressed southwards, a trench was opened up at the presumed north end of "Room 65" excavated by George Payne. This was located largely in the correct position and it demonstrated that the repositioned pipe-trench would miss it by about 30 ft. (9 m.). However, at the south end of the Roman building the gap had narrowed to only 15 ft. (4·57 m.) and it is certain that a large part of this building would have been destroyed had the original line been completed.

No attempt was made to examine this area in detail, but several interesting points emerged. The first was that the outer west wall of "Room 65" was built of flints set in yellow mortar and was 26 ins. (66 cm.) wide. Second, the north wall of this building was built of flints set in orange mortar and was 28 ins. (71 cm.) wide. Third, the north wall butted to the west wall at an angle of about 92°. It seems clear from all this that the west wall was a pre-existing wall and that the north wall, as indeed "Room 65" itself, was added to it sometime after its construction. Perhaps the west wall had originally served as a long boundary wall.

The internal wall was just 18 ins. (46 cm.) wide and formed an integral part with the north wall. The area between the two north-south walls, in effect the west aisle of the building, was 10 ft. 9 ins. (3·27 m.) wide and this showed traces of a pebble floor, whilst chalk was just visible in the angle of the next compartment to the east.

Feature 25 (Pit (?), Figs. 24 and 28).

The east side of a broad, shallow feature was revealed on the west side of the South Area, but the rest of it lay beyond the limit of excavation. It had a sloping side, a flat base and was about 1 ft. 6 ins. deep (45 cms.). Its axis was north-east by south-west and thus it could have formed the continuation of the Roman Water Channel (F14) found in the Centre Area. It could equally well have been another Saxon hut, being immediately adjacent to Saxon Huts A and C.

The filling of this consisted of black loam containing fragments of Roman tile and 34 sherds (No. 196) of Roman pottery of second to fourth century date. It also produced a single sherd of Saxon grass-tempered pottery, but this lay at the top of the feature and thus its precise significance is uncertain. The rest of the feature lay beyond the area threatened by the pipe-line and no attempt was made to excavate it further. With such limited evidence it seems best to simply regard this feature as either of Roman or Saxon date and to leave its function an open question.

Feature 26 (Roman South Ditch, Figs. 24, 28 and 30).

This was located in the west extension of the South Area at about 370–400 ft. (113–122 m.) on the main Datum. Its axis was north-north-east by south-south-west and it was traced for about 40 ft. (12 m.). It did not appear in the east face of the pipe-trench and it must have ended at about this point. It was 4 ft. (1·21 m.) wide at the top, had a U-shaped profile and had been dug about 2 ft. 6 ins. (76 cm.) into the natural brickearth and gravel (Fig. 29, Section C).

Its filling consisted of slumped brickearth, grey-brown loam and grey-black sandy loam and some flints (L.4–8). In this was Roman tile and pottery. The ditch had been partially cut away by one of the Saxon sunken huts (Hut A). (Fig. 30, Section D, L.7–8, cut by L.3).

The Roman pottery from this ditch consisted of about 150 sherds representing about 28 vessels (Nos. 197–207 and 236). Five samian vessels included three F.31, an F.30 and an F.38, all Antonine to early-third century in date. The coarse pottery included at least ten dishes, the majority of second century date, but two probably dating from the first half of the third century.

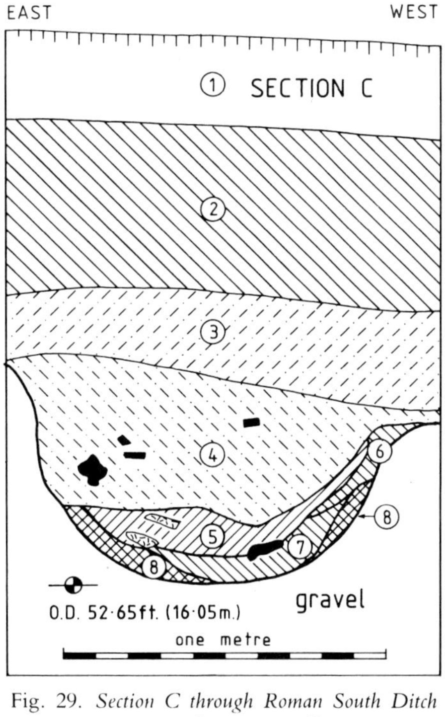

Fig. 29. *Section C through Roman South Ditch (F26), Darenth Roman Villa Site.*

Another twelve vessels were cooking-pots, that seem to range throughout the second century. A sherd of a castor-ware vessel is probably of late-second or early-third century date and two mortaria are of third century date. The ditch also contained parts of two deer antlers (Nos. 241 and 242), fragments of a small stone hone (No. 247b) and a retouched flint (No. 326). From this evidence it seems likely that the ditch was filled completely no later than the middle of the third century. If this was so then the ditch may have been dug late in the second century.

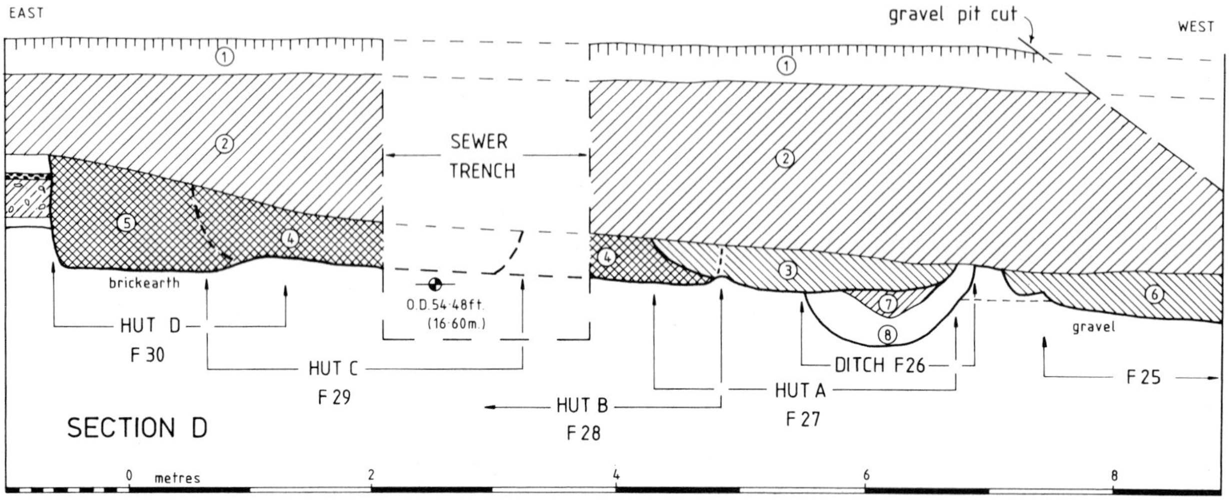

Fig. 30. *Section D, through the Saxon Hutx (F27–30) Darenth Roman Villa Site.*

Feature 27 (Saxon Hut A, Figs. 24, 28, 30 and 31).

A large sub-rectangular pit was found in the west extension of the South Area at a point about 390 ft. (119 m.) on the main Datum. Its axis was roughly north-south and it had sloping sides and a flat base. It was 12 ft. 9 ins. (3·88 m.) long, 7 ft. 6 ins. (2·28 m.) wide and had been cut at least 2 ft. 6 ins. (76 cm.) through the natural brickearth and just into the underlying gravel (Fig. 30, Section D, L.3).

It was filled with mixed grey-black loam silt containing potsherds and a sandstone block. The pottery included 74 Roman sherds of second to fourth century date and some 40 sherds of Anglo-Saxon pottery (Nos. 346–351), probably of fifth or sixth century date. In addition the pit produced a bone handle (No. 246) and the tip of a deer antler (No. 243). No internal post-hole was found, but a post-hole was detected on both the north and south sides. The north post-hole was circular, 10 ins. (25 cm.) in diameter, 18 ins. (46 cm.) deep and had vertical sides and a flat base. The black loam filling contained several small Roman potsherds, probably derived from the Roman ditch through which it was cut, but there was no trace of packing.

The south post-hole was also circular, 10 ins. (25 cm.) in diameter and had been cut through the fill of the Roman ditch and 9 ins. (23 cm.) into the underlying brickearth. Its original depth was probably about 15 ins. (38 cm.) and it had steep sides and a flat base. Its black loam filling contained no finds, nor was there any trace of packing.

The shape and dimensions of the pit are very similar to those of a Saxon sunken-hut, or grubenhaüs. Indeed taken with the presence of the Saxon pottery from the filling and the known Anglo-Saxon material from the adjacent area in 1969 (Ref. 101), there can be very little doubt that this was a Saxon hut. In addition the two post-holes almost on the short axis, are fairly standard features of such sunken-huts and many parallels are known (see discussion below).

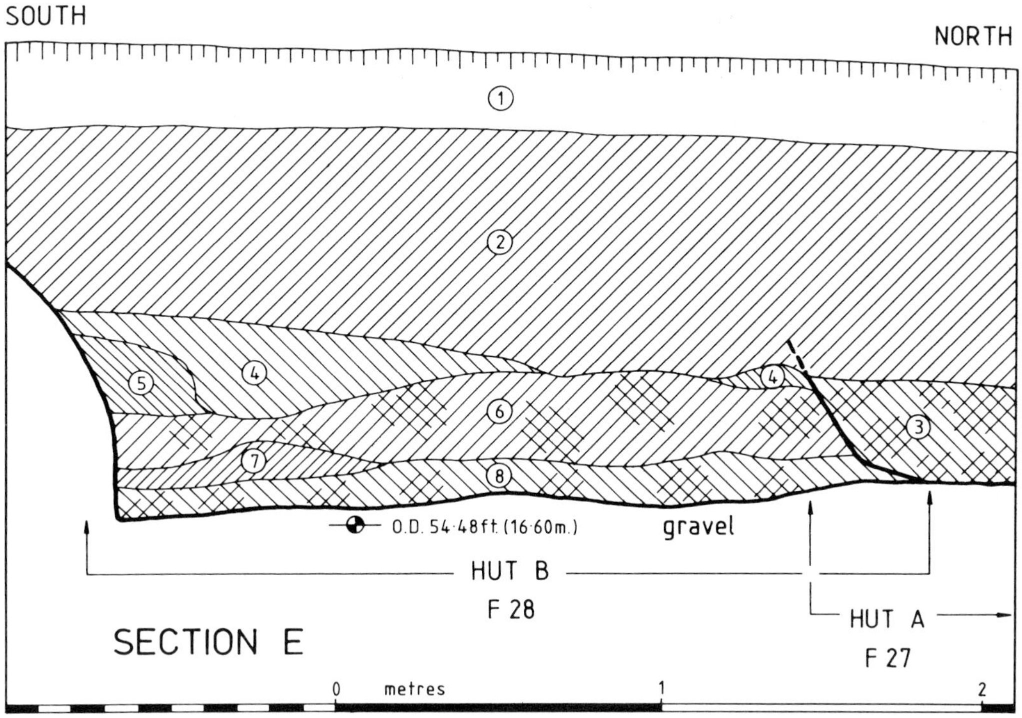

Fig. 31. *Section E, through Saxon Huts A and B (F27 and F28), Darenth Roman Villa Site.*

Feature 28 (Saxon Hut B, Figs. 24, 28 and Plate XVII).

Another, deep rectangular pit was found cut by the pipe-trench about 395 ft. (120 m.) along the main Datum, (Fig. 31, Section E). Its axis was north-south and it had vertical sides and a flat base. It was partly cut by Hut A (Fig. 30, Section D). It was 8 ft. 2 ins. (2·48 m.) long and at least 4 ft. (1·22 m.) wide, though neither the east nor the west sides survived. In all probability it had been roughly square. It was cut into the natural deposits to a depth of 2 ft. 9 ins. (83 cm.) and was just 3 ins. (8 cm.) deeper than Hut A. It was filled with a mixed deposit of orange brickearth and brown loam and appeared to have been deliberately backfilled. The filling produced only two sherds of Romano-British pottery and a single flint truncated blade (No. 296).

Feature 29 (Saxon Hut C, Figs. 24 and 28).

Another large sub-rectangular pit was cut by the pipe-trench immediately east of Saxon Hut A and traces of it were found on each side of the trench. It was 14 ft. (4·27 m.) long, 8 ft. 6 ins. (2·59 m.) wide and had been dug through at least 34 ins. (86 cm.) of stratified prehistoric and Roman deposits. It was filled with a mixture of hard orange clay and chalk and it gave the appearance of having been deliberately backfilled, (Fig. 30, Section D, L.4). In its base were at least ten mainly circular hollows, mostly only 2–6 ins. (5–15 cm.) deep and of uncertain purpose. There was a single flint-packed post-hole (East Post-Hole) near the south-east corner, which was oval in plan, 24 ins. (61 cm.) in length and 10 ins. (25 cm.) deep. It was bowl-shaped in section with the flint-packing mostly on the east side. There were no finds.

The size, depth and form of this large pit suggest that this too had been a sunken Saxon hut of the Grubenhaüs type.

Feature 30 (Saxon Hut D, Figs. 24 and 28).

A fourth pit was found in the east extension of the South Area immediately east of Hut B where it had been cut by Hut C (Fig. 30, Section D, L.5). It was only 7 ft. (2·13 m.) long, 6 ft. 3 ins. (1·9 m.) wide and it had been excavated at least 3 ft. (91 cm.) into the earlier stratified deposits. It had a flat base, nearly vertical sides and was partially cut away by an ovoid pit of much later date. It was filled with hard orange clay and chalk rubble and this had the appearance of representing a deliberate backfilling. No finds were recovered from the filling.

Feature 31 (Chalk Raft 5, Fig. 24).

This was cut by the pipe-trench at about 395 ft. (120 m.) to 429 ft. (130·7 m.) along the Datum and it clearly continued beyond the south end of the trench (Fig. 32, Section F,L.3). Although its south-west side was found in the trench a north-south length of about 34 ft. (10·36 m.) was exposed and an east-west width of at least 20 ft. (6·1 m.). It consisted of chalk rubble brought onto the site and rammed into a compact layer. At its north edge it was 2 ins. (5 cm.) thick and this increased to a maximum of 10 ins. (25 cm.) towards the centre. Presumably this was laid to form a hard-standing or loading platform adjacent to "Room 65", though the relationship of the two was not determined. This chalk platform directly sealed a thick layer of rammed flint and pebble which had itself served as a prepared surface. It also sealed the brown sandy-loam deposits that contained the Mesolithic material.

Feature 32 (Mesolithic Deposits, Fig. 24).

As the excavation reached the south end of the site it located deposits of soil containing quantities of worked flints (Fig. 32, Section F, L.5–6). The trench was expanded on its east side, between Datum 402–432 ft. (122·5–132 m.) to allow a wider examination and to recover a large sample of material. An area 30 ft. (9·1 m.) by 11 ft. (3·35 m.) was thus excavated here, giving a total area of about 330 sq. ft. (30 sq. m.). It was not possible to extend the limits of the excavation, nor to spend more than 10 man-days on this part of the site.

The disturbed topsoil deposits were removed by machine and these were found to seal the Roman Chalk Raft (F31) and an underlying layer of pebble and flint, also of Roman date. These two Roman deposits sealed a layer of brown sandy loam, some 11 ins. (28 cm.) thick, beneath which was a white-brown sandy loam over the natural orange brickearth. Both the layers above the brickearth contained large quantities of prehistoric material including over 2,000 pieces of worked flint, about 90 flint tools (Figs. 40–43, Nos. 250, 254–256, 258, 259, 261, 262, 264, 266, 268, 269, 272, 274, 277–284, 287, 291, 292, 294, 297–300, 302–307, 309–314, 317 and 324) and several very small sherds of flint-tempered pottery (Nos. 340 and 341). The flints have been studied by Dr. A.W. Woodcock who reports that the bulk of the material is probably Mesolithic and of one date.

What may be significant is that the concentration of material (for very little was recovered from the rest of the excavation), was found on top of a small cap of natural brickearth overlying the gravel. This brickearth started at about Datum 350 ft. (106·6 m.) and had risen 3 ft. (91 cm.) in height by Datum 410 ft. (125 m.) where it was about 2 ft. (60 cm.) thick. This partly coincided with a rise in natural gravel, which started at about Datum 150 ft. (46 m.) and had risen by 5 ft. (1·53 m.) by Datum 410 ft. (125 m.). In effect this created a low spur, which probably ran on a roughly east-west axis, to a point close to the present river bank. The northern edge of this spur was flanked by the peat-filled hollow (F11), but its southern limit was not determined owing to the presence of a track used by contractors as a major entry-point.

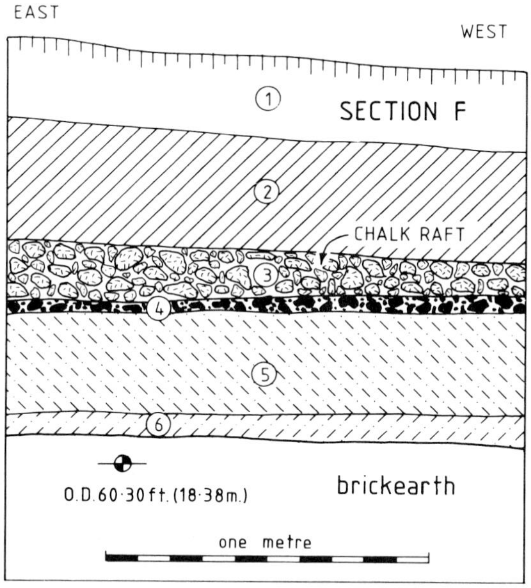

Fig. 32. *Section F through Roman (L.3 and 4) and Prehistoric deposits (L.5 and 6), Darenth Roman Villa Site.*

Other Deposits

Some 17 stratified deposits at various points along the main trench, generally unrelated to specific features, produced about 280 potsherds representing at least 68 vessels (Nos. 162–164 and 208–214). These included four small sherds of Saxon pottery. The Roman pottery included ten samian vessels, mostly second century; four cooking-pots dated late-first or second century; 15 dishes dated mid-second to mid-third century; 26 cooking-pots or jars dated second to third century and four colour-coated and one indented beaker of third century date. Pottery of fourth century date was largely absent. These deposits also produced fragments of three glass vessels (Nos. 166 and 168) and part of a stamped tile (No. 248).

Another 17 groups from unstratified contexts on the site produced a further 210 potsherds, perhaps representing another 80 vessels (Nos. 215–234, 237–239 and 343–4). Ten of these were samian vessels of second or early-third century date; two of these were bead-rim cooking-pots dated late-first or early-second century; eight were straight-sided dishes mostly dated mid-second to late-third century; nine were bead-rim dishes mostly dated mid-second to early-third century; at least another 27 were cooking-pots of second, third or fourth century date; three were mortaria of third century date; five were flanged dishes dated early-third to mid-fourth century and six more were colour-coated vessels, mainly of third century date and two were Anglo-Saxon jars probably dating to the fifth and sixth centuries. The unstratified groups also contained fragments of three antlers (Nos. 244, 245A and 245B), several sherds of Iron Age pottery (No. 339) and several flint axes and other tools (See pages 109, 125 and 112).

Five Roman coins (Coin Nos. 7–11) were also recovered from the unstratified deposits. These include one of Tetricus I (A.D. 270–275), two illegible, one of Arcadius (A.D. 383–408) and one of Arcadius or Honorius (A.D. 383–410). The latter two are the latest known from the whole site and were found together in the field on the pipeline about 60 ft. (18 m.) south of the fence flanking the main villa-block.

Feature 33 (Late Bronze Age Pit, field south of main trench (DRV–445)).

A bowl-shaped pit, or hollow, some 6 ft. (1·83 m.) wide and 2 ft. 6 ins. (76 cm.) deep, was recorded in the east face of the machine-cut trench, some 59 ft. (18 m.) south of the fence marking the outer limit of the wooded area. Its fill of dark-brown loam contained about 80 potsherds of hand-made, shell or grit-tempered pottery. This represents a minimum of ten vessels (Nos. 334–338) which may date somewhere within the range 900–600 B.C. (see page 125). This is the only evidence of Late Bronze Age/Early Iron Age material so far recorded on the Darenth site.

C. DISCUSSIONS

(1). The Mesolithic Material.

The concentration of struck flint at the south end of the main trench (F32) contained over 2,200 items in an area of only 37 sq. yds. (34 sq. m.). This gives a high density of about 60 flints per sq. yd. (64 per sq. m.). Another 400 flints were also recovered from various deposits across the site and of the combined total of about 2,600, some 95 (4%) have been classified as implements. The whole assemblage has been identified (see below) as probably Mesolithic and of one date. It included axes, axe-sharpening flakes, microliths and microburins. None of the previous excavations had produced Mesolithic material.

Whilst the limited time and very difficult circumstances prevented a comprehensive examination of this particular area, the excavation succeeded both in discovering the Mesolithic site and in providing a substantial sample of material evidence. Indeed the flints found represent one of the largest assemblages of Mesolithic flint so far found and published in Kent. The work demonstrated the potential of this and corresponding areas.

It also seems clear that the Mesolithic site sat on a low spur of brickearth and gravel, close to the river and just south of a low-lying water-filled hollow, at one time fed by a small spring. The flint material was found over a distance of only 30 ft. (9·1 m.) but clearly this cannot have been its full extent. It must be that the soil containing the material extends someway to the east and to the south of the pipeline. However, the area to the west was extensively disturbed by the contractors' operations and much earlier by the gravel pits and it is unlikely that much survives there. On the present evidence it is difficult to comment more on the precise nature and extent of the site. Whilst it is possible that it was visited by various groups of people over a considerable time, the bulk of the material was probably deposited at one time.

(2). The Late-Neolithic Material.

Only 13 potsherds of late-Neolithic date were recovered during the excavation and these have been examined by Dr. I. Smith (See below), who suggests dates within the first half of the second millenium B.C. No other Neolithic pottery had previously been reported from any of the earlier excavations, including the very extensive work of 1894–5.

Of the sherds found in 1972, six small ones came from the straight gullies (F19 and F20); one was found in the adjacent oblong pit (F18); one came from the peat deposit (F11) some 120 ft. (36·57 m.) to the north and the remainder mostly from Roman or Saxon deposits across the site.

From this slight evidence it does seem certain that a late-Neolithic settlement had existed on the Darenth Roman Villa site, but little can yet be said as to its nature, form or extent. It seems likely that more evidence could survive to the east of the pipeline where it may be sealed by the Roman deposits. The minor features (F18–20) that produced seven of the sherds also produced several struck flints. Even so, the features need not be Neolithic, though it seems clear that they are pre-Roman. Nor is their function clear. On the available evidence, however, it is now possible to identify a Neolithic settlement site at Darenth and to highlight its presence in terms of future action.

(3). The Late Bronze Age and Iron Age Material.

The 158 sherds of Late Bronze Age and Iron Age pottery recovered during the 1972 excavations is again the only material of this date known from this site, in spite of extensive earlier excavations. Sherds of about ten vessels were found in a pit (F33) south of the main trench and these have been identified as Late Bronze Age, or just possibly Early Iron Age, but generally within the date range of 900–600 B.C. A scatter of small sherds, mainly from the southern half of the main trench, are probably of the middle pre-Roman Iron Age and thus within the date-range of 300–50 B.C. The pottery has been examined by Mr. P. Couldrey (see below).

Apart from noting the presence of this material on the site and its implication of settlement, or settlements, ranging through part or all of the first millenium B.C., it is difficult to comment on their nature, form or size. It does, however, extend the range of known prehistoric material from the site and demonstrates the potential of these riverside situations. Even so the concentration of material of widely differing dates, including of course Romano-British and Saxon, within such a relatively small area suggests a special significance for this particular site. Taken together with the documented late-Saxon, medieval and present (small) settlement, centred on the nearby church at Darenth, then the spectrum of activity at Darenth generally seems to span a range of more than 6,000 years. It suggests the presence of a major archaeological landscape.

(4). Romano-British

The many Romano-British features found along the length of the pipe-trench are perhaps typical of what might be found closely adjacent to most very large villas. Of the features at the north end of the trench the earliest is the east-west ditch (F5) which contained pottery of second century date. This may have formed part of an enclosure, field-system or drainage-system relating to an early phase of the site. Certainly its relationship to the West Range of the villa is not known. The filling of the ditch was sealed by three of the Chalk Rafts (F2–4). In all, four rafts form a close group with three being parallel and generally rectangular in plan. Although their form tends to suggest some sort of structural function, there was no trace of related walls either of wood or stone and their precise function must remain open. They were covered by black soil, by the rectangular Roman oven (F6) and then by more black soil. The pottery recovered from this soil was mostly of third and fourth century date. The oven, situated only about 40 ft. (12 m.) from the West Block of the villa, may have been used for domestic purposes or was perhaps used for corn-drying.

At the centre of the site was the Roman Water Channel (F14), at least 57 ft. (17·37 m.) long and 5 ft. 6 ins. (1·67 m.) wide between its posted sides and at least 18 ins. (46 cm.) deep. This is somewhat similar in form to the water channels found associated with the fourth century watermill at Ickham, Kent (Ref. 104). There, the larger tail-race was about 10 ft. (3 m.) wide and planked on bottom and sides, whilst the head-race was only about 5 ft. (1·5 m.) wide. The Darenth channel may well have served a similar purpose and indeed the discovery of very large millstones at Darenth in 1969 (Ref. 101), strongly suggested then the presence of a nearby mill.

However, this channel may have been carrying water across the site for a variety of purposes! The channel also ran roughly parallel to the west wall of the walled-garden ("Room 64") found in 1894–5 and about 30 ft. (9 m.) from it. Part of the area between the two was metalled (F12) and it seems likely that this surface may have served an access into the adjacent aisled building ("Room 65"). The upper metalling here seems to have been laid after A.D. 220, and it was soon cut by a small ditch (F13), which was in turn cut by the channel. The latter had silted and been filled by the early-fourth century.

To the west the newly-found flint boundary wall (F21), again roughly parallel to both, may represent either a riverside wall, or even a new boundary wall to replace the one adapted to help create "Room 65". Both this flint wall and the Water Channel appear to have been cut by a wide east-west ditch (F22), of uncertain size and purpose, perhaps in the fourth century A.D. Near the south end of the site another small Roman ditch (F26), with second and third century material in it, again may have formed part of an enclosure, field-system or drainage-system. It also seems to have run roughly parallel to the Water Channel. Finally, at the extreme southern end of the trench an extensive area of rammed chalk rubble (F31) over flints, may represent a loading-platform, or raft, again adjacent to "Room 65". Elsewhere along the trench two ill-defined pits (F8 and F9) produced late-second to early-third century pottery and were probably not filled before about A.D. 220.

What is also of interest is the new information on "Room 65", (found by George Payne in 1894–5), a large oblong building incorporating flanking aisles and about 108 ft. (33 m.) in length. The 1972 excavation proved conclusively that the north and west walls of this building were not built integrally. The west wall had certainly pre-existed and in the absence of any obviously connecting wall, may simply have served as a boundary-wall on the west side of the site. The north wall, differently constructed, clearly butted to and was later in date than the west wall, though it was integrally connected with the west aisle wall as shown on the site-plan. From this it seems certain that "Room 65" was constructed by incorporating the earlier, west wall.

This new information provides significant fresh evidence for the relative dating of these two elements in the structural history of the site. It clearly contradicts a survey published by E.W. Black in 1982 (Ref. 105) which tried to identify eight main periods of construction within the main complex found in 1894–5 and devoid of stratigraphical recording or critical excavation. Somehow he fitted these around the five major periods identified within the adjacent aisled building scientifically excavated in 1969. The 1982 survey, based largely on circumstantial evidence and no field-work, also failed to properly acknowledge the large amount of work that went into 1894–5, 1969 and 1972 excavations! Even so it was a useful exercise though its qualified conclusions make the suggested periods highly speculative. Indeed it has now failed its first test by the spade. Its claim that "Room 65" (given as Period 4) was *earlier* than the west boundary wall (given as Period 6) is now shown to be entirely wrong. Whatever the actual phasing of these elements may have been, the 1972 excavation has shown that the west wall was in fact earlier than "Room 65".

Finally, it seems appropriate to summarise some general points about the whole complex. It is at once clear that in scale and area the Darenth villa represents one of the very largest Roman villas known in Britain and is still the largest so far found in Kent. In size (Fig. 33) it compares favourably with Bignor, Sussex (Ref. 106), Brading, Isle of Wight (Ref. 107) and Woodchester, Gloucestershire (Ref. 108) in Britain and even with Winkel-Seeb in Switzerland (Ref. 109). Its buildings cover an area about 738 ft. (225 m.) north-south by at least 492 ft. (150 m.) east-west, including at least one more building not shown on the plan. Doubtless others remain to be found.

With so many structural elements the social and organizational development of Darenth is clearly of great interest and potential. However, the absence of essential detail from the 1894–5 excavation account makes such interpretation very difficult and almost impossible.

What can be said is that the overall plan must represent, to a greater or lesser extent, a composite picture of the site development from at least the second to fourth centuries A.D. The actual sequence of building was largely missed by the 19th century excavations and even the basic

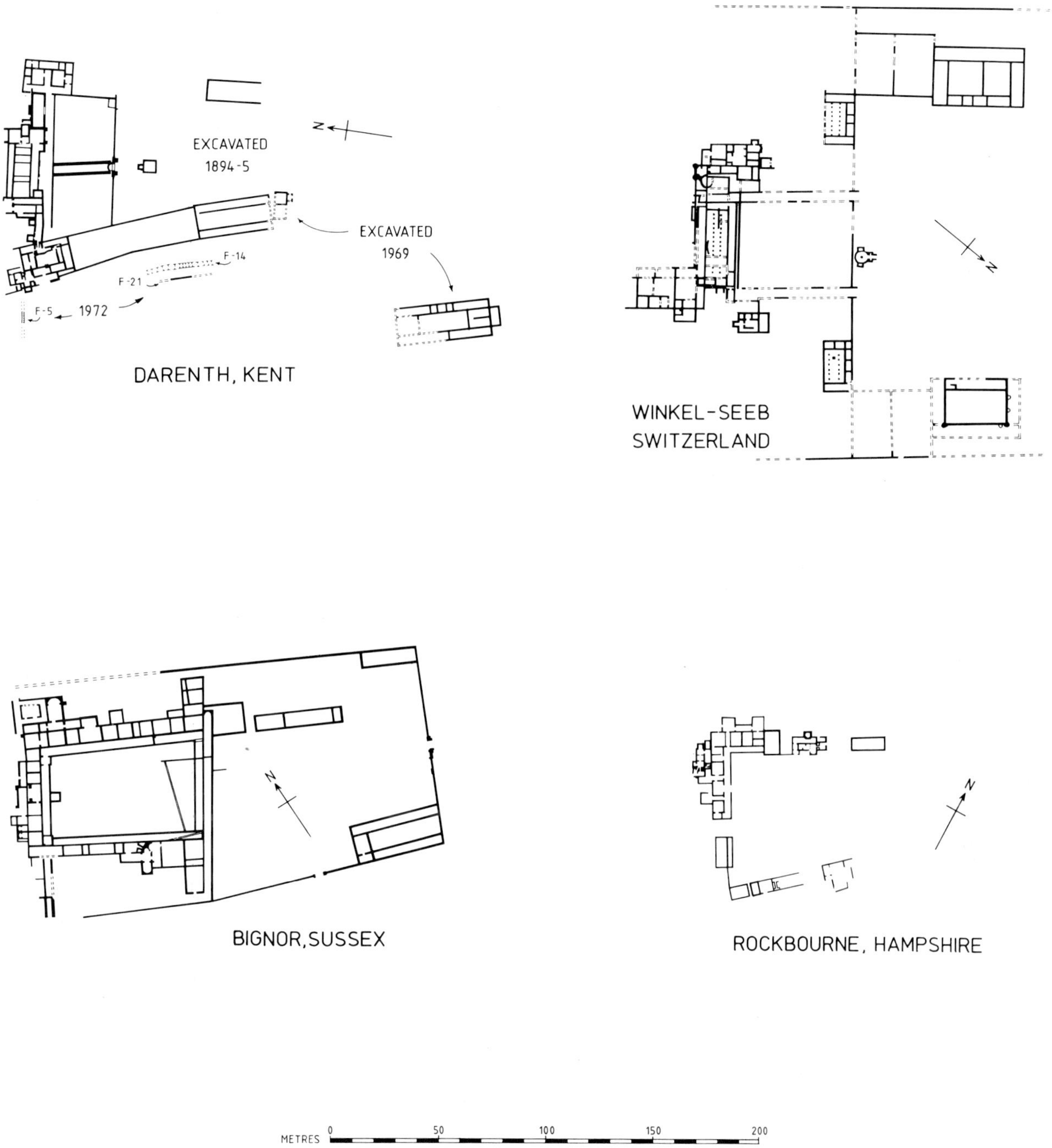

Fig. 33. *Comparative-Plans of Large Villas.*

stratification ignored. Three large blocks (North, East and West) stand out as the major elements and it seems clear that the North Block was always the main house facing south. It has been suggested by J.T. Smith (Ref. 110) that multiple-house villas reflect joint proprietors and certainly the duality of Winkel-Seeb is architecturally very clear. The East Block at Darenth has been identified as a second house, whilst the West Block has been identified as a work-hall.

Whatever the precise function of the various elements the East and West Blocks roughly balance and both are set acutely to the North Block. With projected boundary walls this produces an unusual tapered fan-shaped plan, seen otherwise in Britain at Rockbourne, Hants. (Ref. 111) in contrast to the rather more orthodox rectangular plans seen frequently elsewhere (Fig. 33). This fan-shape is largely continued at Darenth by the outlying buildings such as 'Room 65' and 'Room 71', with what seems to be a walled-garden joining the former with the West Block. The area within this overall framework, often identified as a courtyard, is clearly divided into two major elements. That at the northern end is partly flanked by the three main blocks, is walled and measures 206 ft. (63 m.) by 88 ft. (27 m.) internally. It is divided internally by a large walled pool about 84 ft. (25·6 m.) by 11 ft. (3·35 m.) internally which was clearly intended as a major feature of the whole complex and lying roughly on the central axis of the villa. Such pools are unusual in Britain, though an obvious example at Eccles (Room 94) is situated only 12 miles south-east of Darenth. Its excavator (Ref. 112) identified it in 1971 as 'for the stalling of cattle or as stables', thus failing to understand the precise function of the large corner drain or the prime position of the structure within the villa-complex. The pool at Eccles also fronted the main house and at 83 ft. (25·29 m.) by 11 ft. 6 ins. (3·50 m.) internally it was only marginally smaller than that at Darenth.

The south end of the pool at Darenth was overlooked by what is generally described as a monumental entrance, again on the main axis of the villa. Just south of this, in what may conveniently be regarded as an outer courtyard, was a substantial shrine enclosing a well and yet again on the main axis of the villa. Shrines also occur at Chedworth (Ref. 113) and Winkel-Seeb in Switzerland.

The great aisled building found in 1969, well to the south-west of the main complex seems to have been a major working element of the farming estate, perhaps both the bailiff's house and work-building. It seems to have been situated close to the river, perhaps to facilitate the transport of produce away from this major agricultural site. The small bath-house also found in 1969 is slightly nearer the aisled building than the main complex, but could have served either, or even an unidentified building nearby.

(5). Anglo-Saxon.

The Saxon material was confined to the southern end of the 1972 trench where a group of sunken-huts (F27–30) and a large post-built structure (F23) were found. To this can be added the pottery and loom-weights found in 1969 (published in 1973) at the north end of 'Room 65' (Ref. 114). Hence all the provenanced Saxon evidence has come from the south-west corner of the main villa-complex and is so far within an area about 100 ft. (30 m.) north-south by about 110 ft. (33 m.) east-west.

The largest Saxon structure so far recorded is the post-built structure found in the Centre Area which was laid out on an east-west axis and above several large Roman features. Its length was at least 23 ft. (7 m.) and its width about 17 ft. (5·2 m.) with a slight taper towards the west end. In size and form it seems to fit within the range of comparable buildings recorded at Chalton, Hants. (Ref. 115) and Bishopstone, Sussex (Ref. 116). It seems likely that the Darenth structure was a timber-framed building of at least three bays, with gable ends and a ridged roof.

About 120 ft. (36 m.) south of this structure was a line of four large pits, also laid out on an east-west axis and thus largely parallel to it. Certainly the two larger pits (Huts A and C) were sunken-huts of typical Saxon type, whilst the other two were both much smaller and also earlier in date and are less readily identified. The certain huts were 12 ft. 9 ins. by 7 ft. 6 ins. (3·9 by 2·3 m.) and 14 ft. 0 ins. by 8 ft. 6 ins. (4·27 by 2·6 m.) respectively and their sides nearly touched at one point.

The limited pottery evidence from Darenth comes mostly from Hut A and from the 1969 excavation. This is tentatively dated to the 5th or 6th centuries A.D. and certainly within the broad range of A.D. 450–600, though the 1969 finds alone seem to favour a 6th century date. Whatever the precise date it is now clear that an early Saxon settlement existed at Darenth, at least occupying the south-west corner of the main Roman villa-complex. Predictably, this was missed in the 1894–5 excavation and thus its full extent is not yet known. Already with a framed building, at least two (perhaps four) sunken-huts, pottery and loom-weights the evidence is substantial and an important settlement site seems to be indicated. At once it constitutes the most significant early Anglo-Saxon settlement site so far found in West Kent. The presence of Saxon huts well within the boundaries of a large Roman villa is unusual and twenty years ago it was virtually unknown. In 1970 the West Kent Archaeological Group found a single sunken-hut containing Saxon material, close to the centre of the Roman villa complex at Lower Warbank, Keston (Refs. 117 and 118), some 10 miles (16 km.) south-west of Darenth. Then, in 1975, the Kent Archaeological Rescue Unit found another single sunken-hut at the eastern edge of the Roman villa complex at Franks, Horton Kirby only about 2 miles (3 km.) south of Darenth (Ref. 119). The one at Keston measured 13 ft. 3 ins. by 11 ft. 8 ins. (4 by 3·6 m.) and the one at Horton Kirby about 10 ft. 6 ins. by 12 ft. (3·20 by 3·60 m.).

Thus in a span of only five years three major villa sites in West Kent have been found to contain early Saxon structures. All were discovered during programmes of rescue-excavation ahead of various developments and none could have been predicted in advance! In much the same period more sunken-huts were found at Dover (Ref. 120) and others at Canterbury in both 1979 and earlier (Ref. 121 and 122), both well within the limits of Roman urban sites. Clearly, other early Saxon structures must remain to be found in Kent and it seems highly likely that properly conducted large-scale villa excavations will eventually reveal more.

From all this it is now very clear that some early Saxons were consciously deciding to settle within the limits of ruined Roman villas when many more open sites were equally available. Contrary to the traditional view these sites must have had certain attractions, perhaps in terms of shelter, good soil or readily available materials. Equally, elsewhere, largely open sites such as Mucking, Essex (Ref. 123); Chalton, Hants. (Ref. 124) and West Stowe, Suffolk (Ref. 125) were chosen at much the same time by other early Saxon settlers. The settlements within the villas immediately raises the popular debate of continuity from Roman times. It seems most unlikely that all the West Kent villa-estates were totally abandoned during the first half of the fifth century and the likelihood is that some at least continued their essential farming functions, if on a much reduced scale, until perhaps A.D. 450.

In broader county terms it is clear that Germanic mercenaries were already in East Kent during the first half of the 5th century and material evidence has come from Richborough (Ref. 126), Wingham (Ref. 127), Milton Regis (Ref. 128) and Chatham (Refs. 129 and 130). In contrast there is no evidence yet of their presence in Kent west of the River Medway and in this there is an important and lasting distinction for it seems that the Medway was to serve as a major political boundary. Jutish migrants had established their Kingdom in East Kent by the end of the fifth century, whereas West Kent seems to have been settled via the Thames and its tributaries by people who may be regarded as Saxons. Just possibly the Saxon expansion into West Kent was partly a process of replacement and re-occupation of some abandoned Roman sites with, presumably, some settlement on new open sites mostly not yet found. Into this picture must be fitted the early Kentish traditions reported in the Anglo-Saxon Chronicles with Hengest and Horsa (perhaps identifiable as Germanic Mercenaries (Ref. 131)), winning battles at Aylesford and Crayford, nominally in A.D. 455 and 457, respectively. Thereafter, "The Britons then forsook the land of Kent and in great consternation fled to London" (Ref. 132). These traditions, although probably recorded some 400 years after the events, effectively reflect the likely end of any sub-Roman elements in Kent. On the limited evidence they also effectively mark the extension of Saxon domination into West Kent.

The three new sites at Horton Kirby, Keston and Darenth clearly add significantly to the number of early Saxon settlement sites in West Kent. Evidence for others was found at Cliffe in 1920 (Ref. 133), Northfleet in the 1930's (Ref. 134) and at Dartford in 1955 (Ref. 135), but none by controlled scientific excavation. To these may be added early cemetery sites at Orpington (Ref. 136), Cliffe (Ref. 137), Higham (Ref. 138), Northfleet and Horton Kirby (Riseley) again (Ref. 139). All of these early sites lie within easy reach of the Thames and its tributaries. The cemetery found at Riseley in 1938 lies only 800 m. east of the Frank's Saxon hut and there is every likelihood that the two sites correspond. The contrast with roughly contemporary cemeteries in East Kent, both in terms of numbers and quality of grave-goods, is sharp and highly significant. Later cemeteries in both East and West Kent help fill in the picture.

Of equal interest is the duration of Saxon settlement on the three villa sites. On none is there any significant archaeological evidence of occupation after the sixth century and all three sites seem to have been permanently abandoned thereafter. Presumably the people living on these sites moved to more suitable places and indeed nearby late-Saxon villages are known in each case and still survive well over 1,000 years later. Again the origins of these villages are not clear, but all three could date from the 7th or 8th centuries A.D. The village at Darenth lies only 700 m. north of the early-Saxon settlement; that at Keston only 500 m. south-east of Warbank and that at Farningham only 800 m. south-west of the Saxon hut found at the Frank's villa site. Whether these early villages actually replaced the settlements in the ruined villas is still very much an open question. One attractive notion is that the introduction of Christianity at the beginning of the 7th century somehow led to the creation of new villages slightly removed from what were pagan sites. Certainly the pagan cemetery sites were largely abandoned and replaced by burial-grounds close to smaller churches and the communities that needed them.

D. THE EXCAVATED OBJECTS.

(1). THE ROMAN COINS

Coin	Obverse	Date	Feature	Deposit Code
1	Victorinus	265–270	F14 Upper Fill of Roman Channel	DRV–465
2	Bar. radiate	270–300	Black loam over water-channel (F14)	DRV–503
3	Corroded	c.350	Black loam over water-channel (F14)	DRV–503
4	Corroded	c.350	Black loam over water-channel (F14)	DRV–503
5	Bar. radiate	270–300	F22 Roman Centre West Ditch	DRV–466
6	Corroded	c.350	F22 Roman Centre West Ditch	DRV–466
7	Tetricus I	270–275	Unstratified	DRV–400
8	Corroded	–	Unstratified (Field South of Villa)	DRV–444
9	Corroded	–	Unstratified (Field South of Villa)	DRV–455
10	Arcadius	383–408	Unstratified (Field South of Villa)	DRV–455
11	Arcadius (?) or Honorius	383–410	Unstratified (Field South of Villa)	DRV–455

Table C – Roman Coins from the Darenth Villa Site.

(2). THE SAMIAN WARE (Fig. 34, Nos. 162–164).

By Joanna Bird, B.A., F.S.A.

(Information on the Potters' Stamps kindly provided by Miss Brenda Dickinson, B.A.).

Feature 3 (DRV–411)
Dr. 15/17, Les Martres, early C2.

Above Feature 6 (DRV–403).
Central Gaulish sherd, C2.

Under Feature 6 (DRV–404).
Dr. 31, Central Gaul, mid-late Antonine.

Feature 13 (DRV–507)
Dr. 31, Central Gaul, Antonine.

Feature 14 (DRV–465 and 468).
Dr. 31, Central Gaul, Antonine.
Three Central and one East Gaulish sherd; mid C2–mid C3.

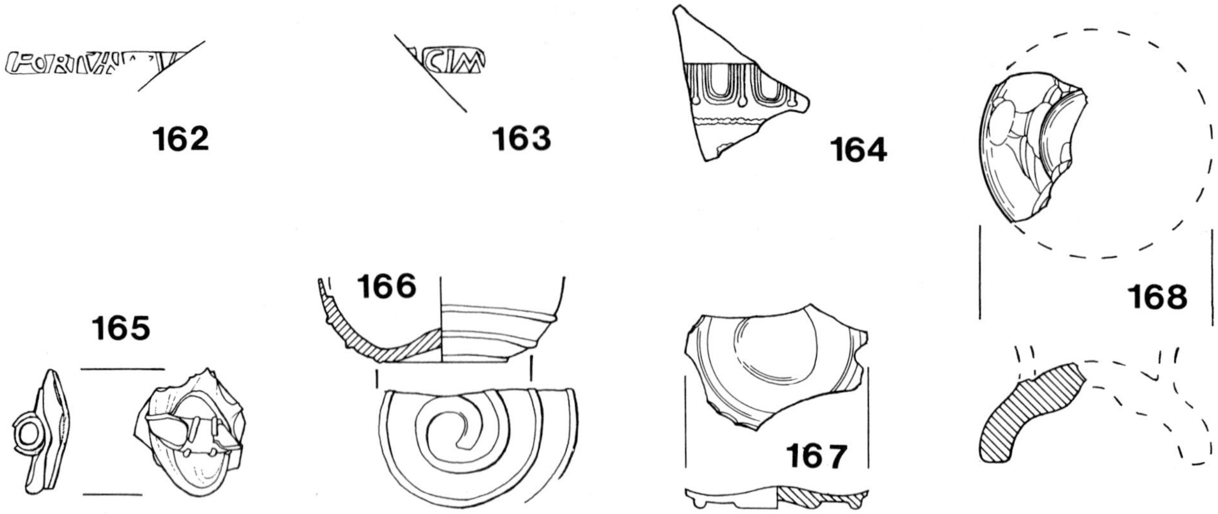

Fig. 34. *Roman Samian Stamps (1/1), decorated sherd, and vessel glass (1/2), Darenth Roman Villa Site.*

Under Feature 15 (DRV–483).
Dr. 33, Central Gaul, Antonine.
Dr. 33, East Gaul, later C2-mid C3.

Feature 15 (DRV–511).
Dr. 44, East Gaul, later C2-mid C3.

Above Feature 17 (DRV–472).
Dr. 33, Central Gaul, Antonine.

Feature 22 (DRV–466).
Dr. 45, East Gaul, late C2-mid C3.

Feature 23 (DRV–475 and 513).
Dr. 33, Central Gaul, Antonine.
Dr. 38, Central Gaul, Antonine.

Feature 25 (DRV–460).
Central Gaulish sherd, C2.

Feature 26 (DRV–427 and 431).
Two × Dr. 31, Central Gaul, later C2.
East Gaul (Argonne) rim, probably Dr. 38; later C2-early C3.
Dr. 30, Central Gaul, Antonine.
Dr. 31, Central Gaul, Antonine.

Stratified from Main Trench (DRV–418, 419, 423, 425, 482, 494 and 503).

No. 162 Stamp of Fortunatus ii 1a, Dr. 31 FORTVNΛTV[S.] Trier. There is very little dating evidence for Fortunatus ii, but his use of forms 18/31R and 32 suggests that he worked in the Antonine period.

No. 163 Stamp of Musicus ii 2a, Dr. 33 [MVS]ICIM Lezoux. Musicus' stamps occur on Hadrian's Wall and in a pit of the 150s at Alcester. His forms include 18/31R, 27 and 38 *c.* A.D. 140–170.
Dr. 36 probably, Central Gaul, C2.
Dr. 31R, Central Gaul, later C2.
Dr. 18/31 or 31, Central Gaul, Antonine.
Dr. 33, Central Gaul, Antonine.
Burnt Central Gaulish sherd, Hadrianic–early Antonine.
Dr. 18/31, Central Gaul, first half C2.
Dr. 36, Central Gaul; (*cf.* Ref. 141, pl. 53, No. 20, for square rim profile). First half C2.

No. 164 Dr. 37, Central Gaul; ring-tongued ovolo with astragalus border. Antonine.
Central Gaulish sherd, C2.

Unstratified. (DRV–407, 408, 428, 448 and 462.
Dr. 30 or 37 rim, Central Gaul, Antonine.
Dr. 31, Central Gaul, Antonine.
Dr. 31R, Central Gaul, later C2.
Dr. 38 probably, Central Gaul, Antonine.
Dr. 38, East Gaul, later C2-early C3.
Dr. 45, Central Gaul, late C2.
Dr. 37 or 30 rim, Central Gaul, Antonine.
Dr. 31 or 18/31, Central Gaul, Antonine; sherd from a second.
Cordoned jar shoulder (*cf.* Ref. 141, pl. 79, No. 14), East Gaul, late C2–early C3.
Jar of beaker foot, East Gaul, later C2–early C3.
Dr. 38, Central Gaul, Antonine.

(3). THE VESSEL GLASS (Fig. 34, Nos. 165–168).

Four fragments of glass, from separate vessels, were recovered during the excavation and these are listed below and illustrated. Dr. Donald Harden has very kindly examined the first two and has provided detailed comments.

No. 165 From black loam below Feature 6 (DRV–404). This fragment comes from the curving shoulder of a vessel of greenish glass and the seemingly colourless appliqué attached to the fragment lies with its thicker end rising appreciably from the shoulder of the vessel at the top, while its thinner end is at the bottom. The thinner end splays out at three places, as it were to grip the wall of the vessel. This is characteristic of similar splays at the bottom of many Roman jug and bottle handles. I cannot cite parallels for the shape of this appliqué. Passing to the horizontally-placed tubular piece attached on top of this, we enter an unknown *milieu.* I have never seen such a tube, even without the added complication of its being surrounded by spiral trailing in relief, on any glass of Roman or any other date. It reminds me, faintly, of the fishes and snails which are to be seen in relief on a cage-cup from Hungary which was published in my article on the Rothschild Lycurgus cup (Ref. 142). But these fishes and snails are carved in openwork relief from the body of the cup, and are not made, as this appears to have been, by being blown and trailed as a separate piece and then attached to the vessel. I do not understand this piece, nor does anyone else to whom I have shown it. It must be Roman, late-3rd to mid-4th century, but no parallel can be cited either for the appliqué or for the trailed tubular piece applied on top of the appliqué.

No. 166 From soil sealing Roman deposits in Centre Area (DRV–482). This fragment of bottom is bluish-green and extremely bubbly, both of which might suggest that it is Saxon, and, if so, a pouch-bottle or squat jar of the late-6th or the 7th century. But another factor, its trailing, starting from a drop-on on the bottom and winding spirally upward, is not characteristically Saxon and is very common on Roman vessels of many dates. I expect, therefore, that it is Roman and, if so, that the profusion of bubbles would suggest that it is a late-Roman, 4th century piece. I cannot be sure of what the upper part of the vessel would have been – perhaps a handleless flask or jug. The body was most likely bulbous; higher up all is guesswork. Note that the pontil-mark on the bottom lies over the trailing, so that this trailing was applied before the vessel was attached to the pontil, having been knocked off the blowing-iron (which is what one would expect).

No. 167 From fill of Post-hole F23 (DRV–467). Part of a base of a small circular jar or bottle, in pale greenish-white glass. It has a small leaded footring and a raised central thickening.

No. 168 From soil sealing Roman metalling F12 (DRV–504). Fragment of thick pale-green glass, perhaps a pedestal base of a small circular cup or jar.

(4). THE ROMANO-BRITISH COARSE POTTERY (Figs. 35–37).

By John Willson.

A total of 1,214 Romano-British coarseware potsherds was recovered from the excavation from both stratified and unstratified deposits and these represent a minimum of 146 different vessels, of which 66 (Nos. 169–234) have been illustrated. Although this pottery may not be a representative sample its classification provides some useful information. Five main groups emerge. These are shown in Table D and are discussed briefly below:–

	Patch Grove Ware	Shell Tempered Ware	Coarse Sandy Ware	Colour Coated Ware	Late Grog Tempered Ware	Totals
Pots	12	2	115	10	7	146
Percentages	9%	1%	79%	6%	5%	100%

Table D – Classification of Roman Coarse Pottery (excluding mortaria), from Darenth.

GROUP A – Patch-Grove and Related Wares.

The vessels in this group are basically a native ware with a porridgy fabric, generally grey in colour, speckled with dark grey or black inclusions. The surfaces are generally orange, brown, buff, grey or even black in colour and have a faint polished finish. The ware is soft and has a soapy feeling to the touch.

A total of 127 sherds was recovered from the excavation which represents a minimum of twelve vessels. This total includes five jars, some carinated and others with cordoned necks (Nos. 206 and 230) and seven storage jars generally with outcurved rims and stick-stabbing decoration on the shoulder (No. 204).

This ware would seem to appear at or about the Conquest (A.D. 43), becoming extremely common during the second half of the first century. It survived into the second century, but was largely superseded by the mass-produced and harder Romanised wares by the mid-second century. Storage jars and cinerary urns in this fabric do seem to have survived at least until the end of the second century (Ref. 143).

GROUP B – Shell-Tempered Ware.

This native ware contains crushed shell added to the clay before firing as a temper. It is normally quite soft to the touch and sometimes of vesicular appearance where the shell has burnt out during firing. It comes in a wide range of colours, varying from orange to brown, grey or even black. It is common in West Kent in tandem with the Patch-Grove Wares and has a wide distribution, normally in the form of bead rim cooking-pots and large bead or roll rim storage jars. It appears in pre-Conquest Late Iron Age contexts and is common on many sites throughout the second half of the first century to about the early-second century. It appears to have largely ceased production by the mid-second century, when the typical mass-produced Roman sandy wares replaced it. (See Ref. 144).

Only ten sherds of shell-tempered ware were recovered during the excavation and these represent a minimum of two vessels, of which one bead rim cooking-pot and a single large rolled rim storage jar (No. 205) can be identified.

GROUP C – Coarse Sandy Wares.

This group consists of a very wide range of vessels. They are generally typical Romanised wares, being hard and sandy to the touch and better fired than the Patch-Grove or shell-tempered native wares. The fabric is generally sandy, hard and comes in a variety of colours with the forms and functions varying widely.

A total of 982 sherds was recovered and these represent about 115 different vessels, of which 60 have been illustrated. The range of types is considerable and consists of a single cheese press (No. 200), two lids, two flagons, two amphorae (No. 180), two beakers, six mortars (Nos. 235–239). Eleven bowls of which two are early types with broad flanged rims (No. 224) and nine are typical third and fourth century flanged bowls (Nos. 175, 189, 190, 191, 213, 214, 223, 225 and 226). There are at least 13 jars, of which two have everted rims, three are narrow-necked vessels, four are recessed rim jars (Nos. 177, 183, 211 and 212) and four have outcurved rims (No. 207). There are at least 35 dishes, of which four have upright and grooved rims, eight have plain upright rims (Nos. 184, 188, 199, 208, 217 and 222) and 23 have bead rims (Nos. 169, 173, 178, 181, 182, 185, 186, 187, 192, 193, 195, 197, 198, 215, 216, 218, 219, 220 and 234).

Of 41 cooking-pots, four have squared rims (Nos. 179, 210 and 228), four have cavetto rims, nine have beaded rims (Nos. 170, 194, 202 and 209), ten have everted rims (Nos. 203 and 229) and 14 others have either outcurved, thickened or rolled rims (Nos. 171, 176, 201 and 223).

As regards dating, early-first century wares are absent; a few vessels date from the second half of the first century to the mid-second century; but the majority however, would seem to date from the mid-second to the mid-third centuries, with some vessels dating to the late-third and fourth centuries.

GROUP D – Colour-Coated Wares.

A total of 54 sherds representing some ten different vessels was recovered from the excavation. Three sub-groups have been recognised, as follows:–

RHENISH WARE: Only a single sherd of this ware was recovered and this represents a fragment of a beaker dated to the late-second or early-third centuries A.D.

NENE VALLEY WARE: The vessels in this ware generally have a white fabric with a dark brown or grey-black slip. Represented are a single flanged bowl (No. 231); a 'Hunt Cup' and two 'bag' beakers with cornice rims and rough-cast decoration. The majority of the vessels date from about the mid-second century with the exception of No. 231 which dates to the late-fourth century.

OXFORDSHIRE WARE: Some five vessels are represented in this ware and generally they have an orange fabric and a red colour slip. They consist of a single jar with an outcurved rim and four bowls, of which two have flanged rims, one having white paint decoration on the flange (No. 174). One has a bead rim (No. 232), whilst another has rows of stamped demi-rosettes as decoration. As regards dating most would appear to date from about A.D. 240 although at least one could date from about c. A.D. 325. However, an overall date range of A.D. 240 to A.D. 400+ would seem acceptable.

GROUP E – Late-Grog Tempered Ware.

A total of 41 sherds representing a minimum of seven vessels in this group was recovered from the excavation. The ware generally has a grey fabric with dark grey and off-white grog inclusions, the surfaces of the vessels are generally grey or grey-brown, with most of the vessels burnished black on the rim and neck, or in some cases all over. The surface finishes are generally poor as are the general shapes of the vessels, this reflecting the hand-made nature of the ware.

Included in this group are two cooking-pots with outcurved rims (No. 227), four flanged rim bowls (Nos. 172, 196 and 228), and a single 'dog' dish with a plain upright rim.

As regards dating, the outcurved rimmed cooking-pots, flanged bowls and upright rimmed 'dog' dish appear to be the basic forms in this ware and all appear in late-fourth century contexts at Bekesbourne, Canterbury and Richborough as well as 'Franks' Roman Villa site at Farningham.

CATALOGUE OF THE ILLUSTRATED COARSE POTTERY (Figs. 35–37, Nos. 169–234).

This catalogue contains illustrations and descriptions of some 66 coarse pottery vessels from the excavation, excluding samian and mortaria.

The dating of the coarse pottery described here is largely supported by parallels drawn from 14 publications dealing with Romano-British coarse pottery from many sites, both local and distant.

Abbreviations.

The following terms have been used in the catalogue to identify pottery types of similar form.

SOUTHWARK	Nos.	(Ref. 145)
WEST KENT	Nos.	(Ref. 146)
ROCHESTER	Nos.	(Ref. 147)
GREENHITHE	Nos.	(Ref. 148)
RICHBOROUGH III	Nos.	(Ref. 149)
BEKESBOURNE	Nos.	(Ref. 150)
FAVERSHAM	Nos.	(Ref. 151)
OXFORDSHIRE	Types	(Ref. 152)
JOYDEN'S WOOD	Nos.	(Ref. 153)
DOVER	Nos.	(Ref. 154)
RICHBOROUGH II	Nos.	(Ref. 155)
GILLAM	Types	(Ref. 156)
RICHBOROUGH IV	Nos.	(Ref. 157)
CANTERBURY	Nos.	(Ref. 158)

Feature 3 (DRV–411).

No. 169 Dish with triangular rim of sandy ware. Grey-brown fabric with a dark grey burnished surface. Similar to Southwark No. 1051 dated to the second century.

Over Feature 5 (DRV–406).

No. 170 Cooking-pot with a flattened bead rim of sandy ware. Grey fabric and a dark grey surface. Similar to vessels from Darenth (West Kent No. 360), Rochester (No. 12) and Greenhithe (No. 222) where they are dated to the second century.

Under Feature 6 (DRV–404).

No. 171 Cooking-pot with outcurved moulded rim of hard sandy ware. Pinky-buff fabric and a creamy-white surface. A similar vessel from Richborough (III (Pit 54) No. 336) is dated circa fourth century.

No. 172 Hand-made bowl with bulbous sides and a flanged rim of grog tempered ware. Dark grey fabric with dark grey and off-white grog particles, dark grey-black surface. Burnished internally and on flange with an uneven surface finish. A similar vessel from Bekesbourne (No. 8) is dated to the fourth century.

Over Feature 6 (DRV–403).

No. 173 Dish with heavy bead rim of sandy ware. Grey fabric and a dark grey surface, burnished all over. Similar to Darenth (West Kent No. 333) and Faversham (No. 264), dated A.D. 200–240.

No. 174 Shallow bowl with out-turned rim, upturned at tip, of colour-coated ware. Orange fabric and surface, the vessel is decorated with a red colour-slip all over, with painted scroll and dot pattern and a thin zone of rouletting on the rim. This vessel is a product of the Oxfordshire Kilns and can be paralleled to Oxfordshire Type C.50.4 and is dated between A.D. 325–400+.

No. 175 Dish with an upturned flanged rim of sandy ware. Grey fabric and surface, fourth century.

Feature 8 (DRV–441).

No. 176 Cooking-pot with an outcurved rim of sandy ware. Grey fabric and surface.

No. 177 Jar with recessed rim of sandy ware. Grey fabric and a dark grey surface. An almost identical vessel from Darenth (West Kent No. 342) is dated A.D. 140–260.

No. 178 Dish with heavy bead rim of sandy ware. Light grey fabric and a grey surface, burnished all over. Similar to No. 173, A.D. 200–240.

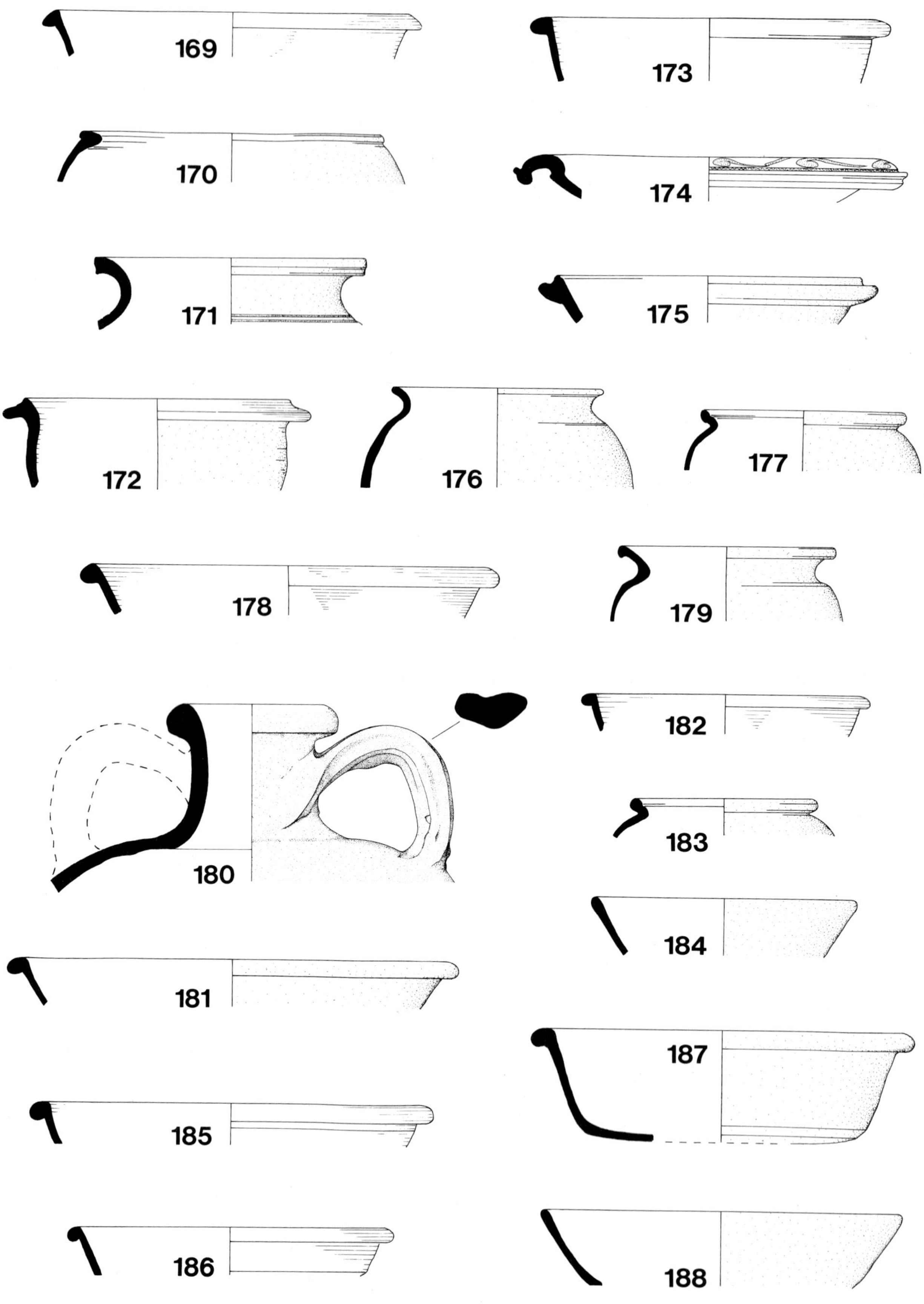

Fig. 35. *Romano-British Coarse Pottery (¼), Darenth Roman Villa Site.*

No. 179 Cooking-pot with squared rim of sandy ware. Grey fabric with a brown surface. Similar to a vessel from Darenth (West Kent No. 441) dated late-second, or early-third century.

No. 180 Amphora with outcurved, thickened rim of sandy ware. Pinky-buff fabric and a creamy-buff surface. Two-ribbed handle attached to neck and shoulder and the stub end of a second handle opposite.

Feature 9 (DRV–415).

No. 181 Dish with heavy bead rim of sandy ware. Dark grey fabric, grey-black surface. Dated A.D. 200–240.

Feature 12 (DRV–512).

No. 182 Dish with bead rim of sandy ware. Grey fabric and a dark grey surface with traces of burnishing all over. Similar to Darenth (West Kent No. 355) dated A.D. 200–240 and at Southwark (No. 1258) later-second century.

No. 183 Jar with recessed rim of sandy ware. Grey-brown fabric with a dark grey surface. Similar to No. 177, A.D. 140–260.

Feature 14 (DRV–435, 465, 468 and 478).

No. 184 Straight sided dish with a plain upright rim of sandy ware. Dark grey fabric and surface. Similar to a vessel from Darenth (West Kent No. 429) probably early-third century.

No. 185 Dish with a heavy bead rim of sandy ware. Grey fabric and a dark grey surface, burnishing to exterior and on rim. Similar to No. 173, dated A.D. 200–240.

No. 186 Dish with chamfered base and a bead rim of sandy ware. Dark grey-black fabric and surface with traces of black burnishing. Similar to No. 182, late-second to mid-third century A.D.

No. 187 Dish with chamfered base and a bead rim of sandy ware. Grey fabric with a dark grey surface. Similar to No. 173, dated A.D. 200–240.

No. 188 Dish with straight sides and a plain upright rim of sandy ware. Grey fabric and a dark grey plain surface. Very similar to No. 184 dated to the early-third century.

No. 189 Dish with a flanged rim of sandy ware. Buff-orange fabric and surface. Similar to a vessel from Darenth (West Kent No. 416), dated late-third and fourth centuries.

No. 190 Dish with a flanged rim of sandy ware. Light grey fabric and a grey surface. Similar to No. 189. Late-third and fourth centuries.

No. 191 Dish with a flanged rim of sandy ware. Dark grey fabric and surface, black burnish all over. A similar vessel from Darenth (West Kent No. 437) is dated to the second half of the third, or fourth centuries.

Feature 15 (DRV–511).

No. 192 Dish with a bead rim of sandy ware. Dark grey fabric and surface, lightly burnished all over and decorated with burnished diagonal lines. Similar vessels from Darenth (West Kent No. 317) and Greenhithe (No. 178) are dated late-second to mid-third century.

No. 193 Dish with a slightly hooked rim of sandy ware. Red fabric and surface, plain. Probably dates from the mid-late second century.

No. 194 Cooking-pot with bead rim of sandy ware. Light grey fabric and a dark grey surface. Similar vessels from Darenth (West Kent No. 331) and Joyden's Wood (No. 11) are dated to the second century.

Feature 23 (DRV–513).

No. 195 Dish with a slightly hooked bead rim of sandy ware. Grey-brown fabric, grey surface with burnishing all over and decorated with burnished diagonal lines. A similar vessel from Southwark (No. 1189) is dated from the mid-second century.

Feature 25 (DRV–460).

No. 196 Dish with a flanged rim of grog-tempered ware. Dark grey fabric with grey and off white grog particles, dark grey surface with traces of black burnishing on flange. Similar to No. 172, fourth century.

Feature 26 (DRV–427, 431 and 459).

No. 197 Dish with a slightly beaded rim of sandy ware. Dark grey fabric with a creamy-brown surface, with a faint groove below rim. Similar vessels from Dover No. 851, Joyden's Wood No. 32 and Rochester No. 50 are dated to the second century.

No. 198 Dish with a heavy bead rim of sandy ware. Light grey fabric and surface, burnished all over and decorated with diagonal line pattern. A larger version of No. 192 that can be paralleled at Southwark (No. 1092) dated from the mid-second century.

No. 199 Shallow dish with straight sides, chamfered base and a plain upright rim of sandy ware. Grey-brown fabric and a dark grey surface, decorated with wavy line pattern. Similar vessels from Dover No. 880, Richborough (II, No. 154) and Southwark No. 1194 are dated from A.D. 130 and on.

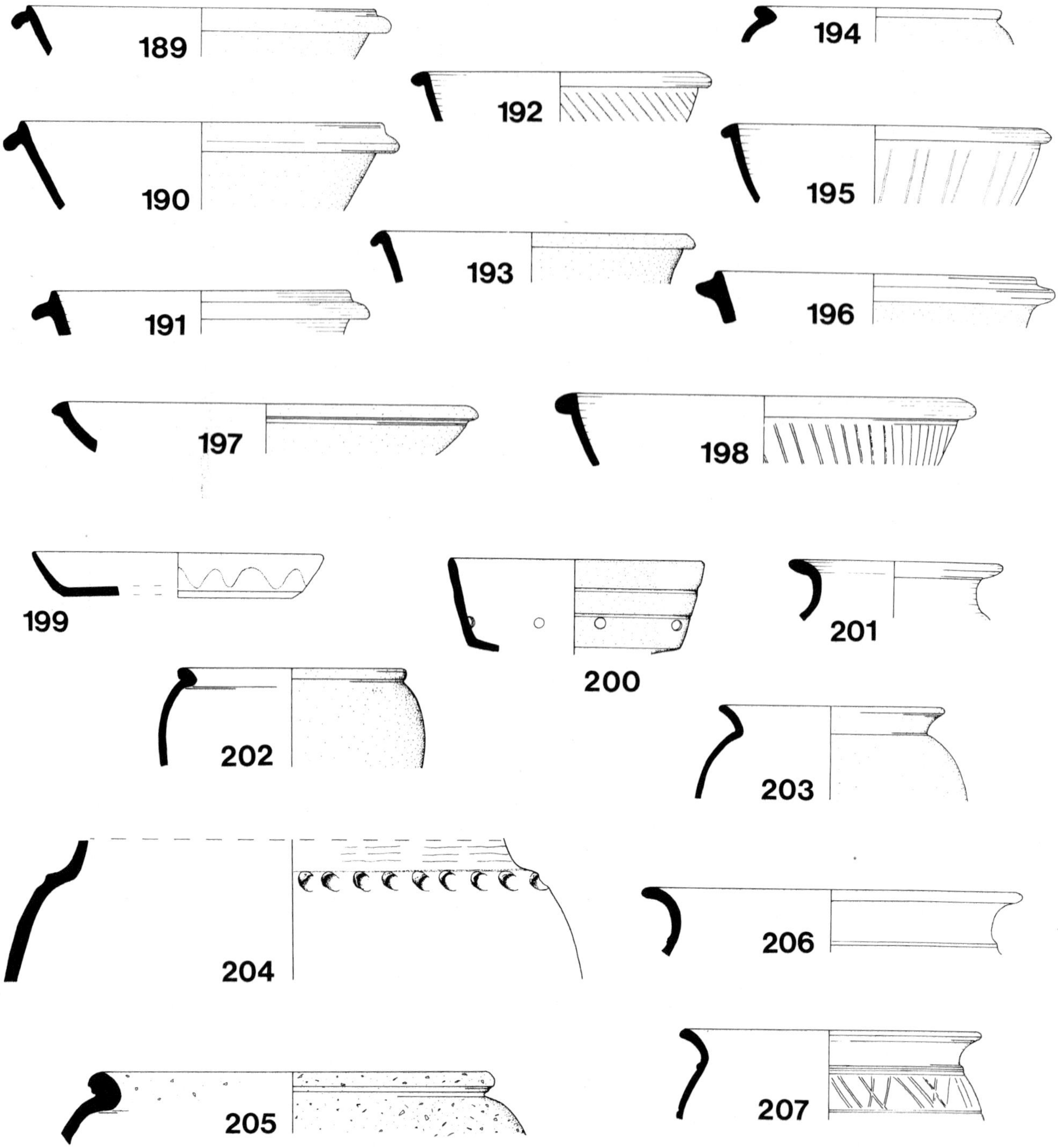

Fig. 36. *Romano-British Coarse Pottery* (¼), *Darenth Roman Villa Site.*

No. 200 Cheese-press with straight sides and an upright rim of sandy ware. Dark grey-black fabric, grey-brown surface. The sides are pierced at intervals with small circular holes, the base is unfortunately missing but it is normally ridged and pierced. Two faint horizontal grooves on body exterior. A very similar vessel from Richborough (II, Pit 18, No. 152) is dated to A.D. 268–270. Whilst at Mumrills (Gillam Type 350) another very similar vessel is dated A.D. 140–200. The form would seem therefore to have a wide date range.

No. 201 Cooking-pot with an outcurved thickened rim of sandy ware. Grey-brown fabric with a dark grey surface, faint traces of burnishing to exterior and inside rim.

No. 202 Cooking-pot with bead rim of sandy ware. Dark grey fabric and surface. Similar vessels from Darenth (West Kent No. 361) and Joyden's Wood No. 12 are dated to the second half of the first century and second century A.D.

No. 203 Cooking-pot with everted rim of sandy ware. Grey-brown fabric, grey surface. Similar to vessels from Joyden's Wood No. 22, Southwark No. 930 and Darenth (West Kent No. 316) where their date range is late-second to early-third centuries A.D.

No. 204 Storage-jar (rim missing) of Patch Grove ware. Speckled grey fabric with dark grey-black grog inclusions and a creamy-buff surface. Decorated with a zone of stick-stabbing on shoulder. Similar to vessels from Hayes (West Kent No. 249) and Joyden's Wood Nos. 2–4. Dated from the second half of the first century or second century.

No. 205 Storage-jar with a rolled rim of shell-tempered ware. Grey fabric with crushed shell tempering, orange-brown surface. A similar vessel from Southwark No. 762 dates to the Flavian period. However, this type of vessel has a wider date range and can occur throughout the first and second centuries.

No. 206 Jar with outcurved rim of Patch Grove ware. Grey speckled fabric with dark grey-black grog particles. Creamy-brown soapy surface, faint trace of a cordon on neck. Similar to Greenhithe No. 237, second century.

No. 207 Jar with outcurved rim of sandy ware. Brown fabric with a dark grey surface. Decorated with a cordon at base of neck, followed by a zone containing diagonal line pattern followed by a groove below, probably produced at Highgate Wood. Similar vessels at Southwark Nos. 1466 to 1470 and Greenhithe No. 147 are dated from the late-Flavian to late-Hadrianic period.

Stratified from Main Trench (DRV–422, 423, 482 and 503).

No. 208 Dish with straight sides and a plain rim of sandy ware. Grey fabric with a dark grey surface, smooth or lightly burnished finish. Similar to Darenth (West Kent No. 350) and Faversham (No. 268), where they are dated to the early-third century.

No. 209 Cooking-pot with a slightly recessed bead rim of coarse sandy ware. Grey fabric with a dark grey gritty surface. Similar vessels from Joyden's Wood (No. 13) and Greenhithe (No. 119) are dated to the second century.

No. 210 Cooking-pot with outcurved squared rim of sandy ware. Grey fabric and a dark grey surface. Similar to Darenth (West Kent No. 382) and Faversham (No. 257), dated late-second to early-third century.

No. 211 Jar with recessed rim of sandy ware. Grey-brown fabric and a grey surface. Similar vessels from Dover (No. 765) and at Richborough (IV, No. 405) where they are dated A.D. 75–100.

No. 212 Jar with recessed rim of coarse sandy ware. Blue-grey fabric and a grey surface. Similar to No. 177, A.D. 140–260.

No. 213 Dish with flanged rim of sandy ware. Grey fabric with a dark grey surface. A transitional type between the bead rim dish and the flanged dish.

No. 214 Dish with a flanged rim of sandy ware. Dark grey-black fabric, brown-grey surface. Burnished all over. This is an early transitional type between the bead rim dishes and the later properly flanged bowls and is probably dated to the mid-third century A.D. A similar vessel from Darenth (West Kent No. 368) can be compared.

Unstratified (DRV–407, 408, 428, 447, 449 and 462).

No. 215 Straight sided dish with a faint bead rim of sandy ware. Grey fabric and a dark grey plain surface. A similar vessel from Darenth (West Kent No. 404) is dated to the late-third or fourth century, and at Southwark (Nos. 1762–1768) in contexts dated to the second half of the third century.

No. 216 Dish with a bead rim and chamfered base of sandy ware. Grey fabric and a dark grey surface with traces of burnishing all over. Similar to No. 182, A.D. 200–240.

No. 217 Dish with straight sides and an upright rim of sandy ware. Light grey fabric, dark grey surface with a faint groove below rim. A similar vessel from Darenth (West Kent No. 429) dated probably, early-third century.

No. 218 Dish with bead rim of sandy ware. Dark grey-black fabric and surface, traces of black burnishing all over and decorated with acute lattice pattern. Similar vessels from Dover No. 553, Southwark Nos. 1646–1653 and Greenhithe No. 184, are dated A.D. 150–240.

No. 219 Dish with large bead rim of sandy ware. Grey fabric and a dark grey surface, burnished all over. Dated A.D. 200–240.

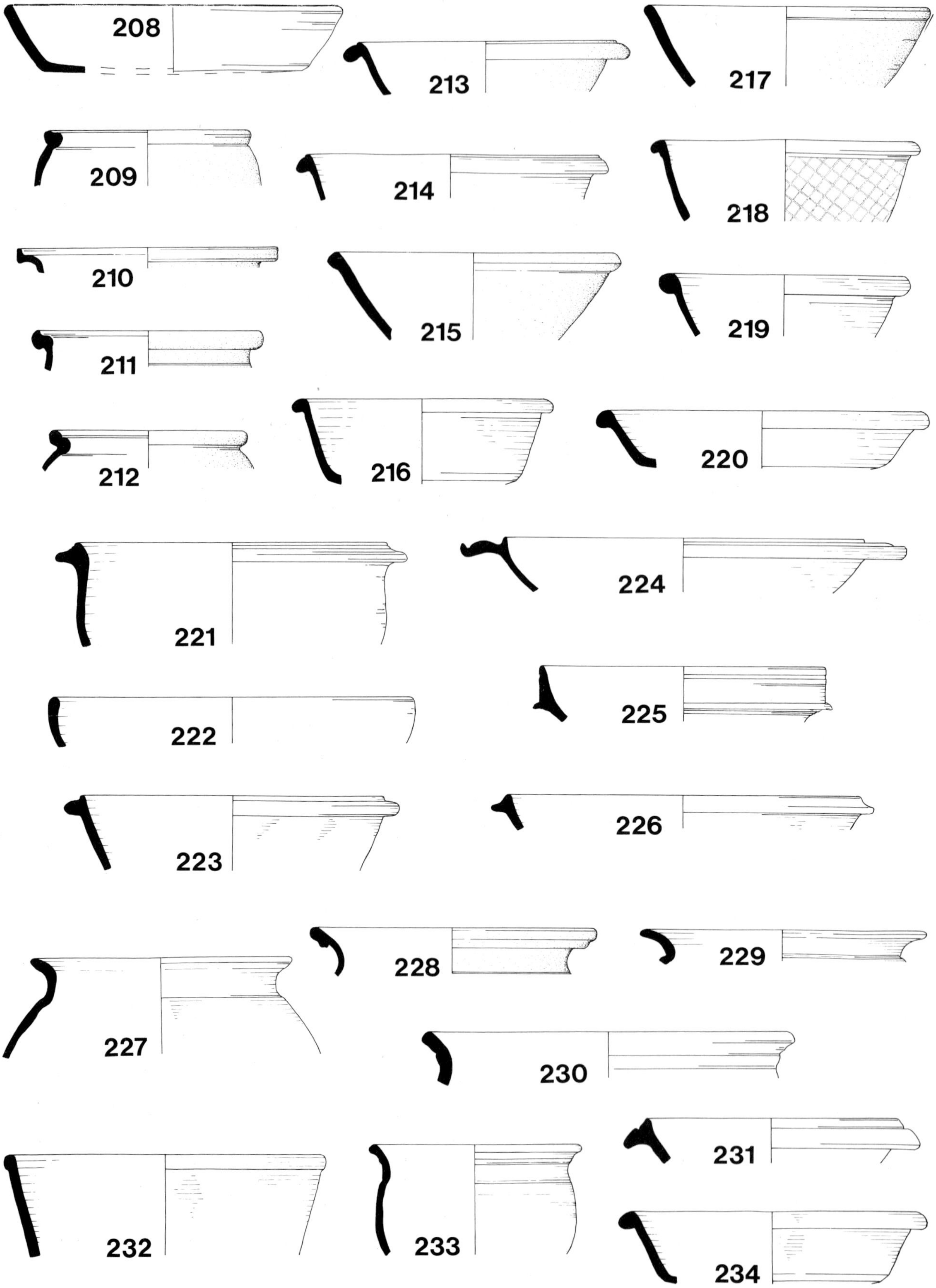

Fig. 37. *Romano-British Coarse Pottery* (¼), *Darenth Roman Villa Site.*

No. 220 Dish with bead rim and chamfered base of sandy ware. Dark grey fabric and surface, black burnished all over. Similar to vessels from Joyden's Wood No. 31, Southwark Nos. 1254–1255 and Dover No. 418 dated A.D. 120–240.

No. 221 Hand-made dish with bulbous sides and a flanged rim of grog-tempered ware. Dark grey fabric with dark grey and off-white grog particles, dark grey-black surface. Burnished internally and on flange with an uneven surface finish. Similar to No. 172, fourth century.

No. 222 Shallow bowl or dish with curved sides and a thickened rim of sandy ware. Grey fabric and a grey and orange-brown surface, lightly burnished interior.

No. 223 Dish with a rounded flanged rim of sandy ware. Grey fabric, grey-brown surface, burnished all over. Similar to Darenth (West Kent No. 368) early to mid-third century.

No. 224 Bowl with a moulded flange rim of smooth sandy ware. Dark grey fabric with a grey-brown surface. The fabric of this vessel appears to be what is commonly known as 'London Ware', although in this particular case the vessel was probably manufactured in the Medway Marsh area. A similar vessel from Southwark No. 1579 is dated A.D. 90–130.

No. 225 Unusual bowl with a walled side and the trace of a small flange of sandy ware. Grey fabric and surface with traces of a grey-white slip. Probably third century (Alice Holt ware?).

No. 226 Dish with a flanged rim of sandy ware. Grey fabric with a dark grey surface, burnished all over. Similar to No. 214, mid-third century.

No. 227 Hand-made cooking-pot with an outcurved rim in grog tempered ware. Grey fabric with grey and off-white grog particles, greyish-brown surface. Lightly burnished exterior and inside rim with an uneven surface finish. Similar vessels from Richborough III, (No. 334) and at Canterbury (Nos. 76–80) are dated to the fourth century.

No. 228 Cooking-pot with a squared outcurved rim of sandy ware. Orange fabric and surface.

No. 229 Cooking-pot with everted rim of sandy ware. Grey-brown fabric, dark grey surface, burnish to exterior and inside rim. Similar to vessels from Darenth (West Kent No. 366), Dover No. 660 and Faversham No. 255, where they are dated to the first half of the third century.

No. 230 Jar with a thick outcurved rim of Patch Grove type ware. Light grey speckled fabric with dark grey-black grog inclusions, creamy-grey soapy surface. Slight cordon on neck. A similar vessel from Calfstock Lane, Farningham (West Kent No. 297) is dated to the late-first century A.D.

No. 231 Bowl with downturned flanged rim of colour-coated ware. White fabric and surface, covered with a dark grey-brown colour slip all over. A Nene Valley product that can be paralleled at Southwark (No. 371) dated to the late-fourth century.

No. 232 Bowl with bead rim of colour-coated ware. Orange fabric and surface with an orange-red colour slip all over. Oxfordshire Type C55, dated A.D. 240–400+.

No. 233 Cooking-pot with outcurved rim of sandy ware. Grey-brown fabric, dark grey surface with a burnished zone on neck and shoulder. Similar to Southwark Type IIE dated from the late-Flavian to late-Hadrianic period.

No. 234 Dish with heavy bead rim and a chamfered base of sandy ware. Dark grey fabric and surface, burnished all over. Similar to No. 185, A.D. 200–240.

(5). THE ROMAN MORTARIA (Fig. 38, Nos. 235–239).

By Katharine F. Hartley, B.A., F.S.A.

Feature 14 (DRV–465).

No. 235 A collared mortarium in slightly granular pink-brown fabric with browner surface and a good amount of quartz and occasional black and red-brown inclusions; flint, red-brown and quartz trituration. Made in Kent, probably within the period A.D. 190–260.

One rim-sherd and two body sherds from the same mortarium; in fine textured, off-white fabric with very fine inclusions, probably quartz and red-brown in colour; black ironstone trituration. Made in the Castor-Stibbington area of the lower Nene valley, probably in the late-third or fourth century.

Feature 26 (DRV–427).

No. 236 A mortarium in granular, buff-pink fabric, fired cream at the surface; the clay is packed with quartz and occasional black and red-brown inclusions. Probably made in a local workshop in the third century.

A flange and spout fragment in slightly sandy, buff fabric with fine quartz inclusions. Probably made in Kent in the third century.

Feature 23 (DRV–513).

A body and base fragment in soft, fine-textured, cream fabric with quartz, occasional black and pale brown trituration. Probably made in Colchester or in the Canterbury area. From Saxon Post-hole S8.

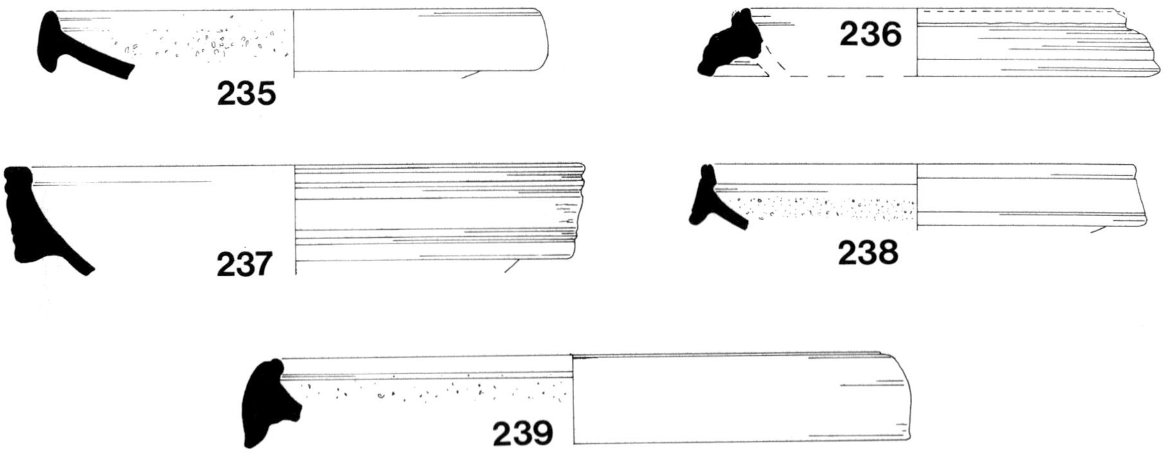

Fig. 38. *Romano-British Mortaria (¼), Darenth Roman Villa Site.*

Unstratified (DRV–408, 422 and 462).

No. 237 A mortarium fragment with powdery surface, in fine-textured, cream fabric with very little trituration composed of flint, quartz and red-brown material. No exact parallel is known for this mortarium but the basic type to which it belongs was made at and near Colchester and at a workshop at Canterbury. Probably made within the period A.D. 200–250.

No. 238 A wall-sided mortarium in fine-textured fabric with dark grey core, fired somewhat paler at the surface, and with very tiny quartz inclusions; flint and quartz trituration. Made in Kent in the third century, probably before A.D. 260.

No. 239 A collared mortarium near to several from Colchester (Ref. 159), in fabric basically similar to No. 237 but with occasional, ill-sorted quartz, flint and red-brown inclusions and similar trituration. Probably made at Colchester, A.D. 180–240.

(6). ANTLER TOOLS, BONE HANDLES, HONES AND A STAMPED TILE (Fig. 39, Nos. 240–248).

By Keith Parfitt, B.A.

Seven pieces of antler from the 1972 excavation are illustrated and all appear to be the by-products of the manufacture of hand-tools, such as rakes, handles and hammers. A number of antler tools were found on the Darenth Villa complex in 1894–5 (Ref. 160) and again in 1969 (Ref. 161).

The work in 1972 also produced one bone handle, two small stone hones and a fragment of a stamped tile. These are illustrated here and briefly described.

From the soil beneath Tile Base. F15. (DRV–511).

No. 240 Part of an antler tine with broken tip. Two shallow saw cuts occur at the opposite end, which is also broken.

From Roman South Ditch. F26. (DRV–459).

No. 241 Part of the main shaft of a red deer antler sawn off at both ends. A knife has been used to remove the original surface along one side.

From Roman South Ditch. F26. (DRV–459).

No. 242 Part of a red deer antler tine with broken tip. The opposite end has been partly sawn then broken off. In two areas the original surface of the antler has been cut away.

From Saxon Hut A. F27. (DRV–489).

No. 243 Part of an antler tine. Several cuts were made to allow the piece to be broken away from the main antler.

Unstratified. (DRV–452, 458 and 400).

No. 244 Part of the main shaft of a red deer antler, sawn off at both ends. A knife has been used to remove a large slice at one end.
The original surface of the antler has been removed in two other areas, using a knife.

No. 245a Part of the main shaft of a red deer antler, sawn off at both ends.
A large, adjoining tine has also been removed with a saw. Multiple saw cuts occur on both sides of the piece.

No. 245b Part of the main shaft of a red deer antler, sawn off at both ends.
An adjoining tine has also been removed with a saw. A knife has been used to remove the original surface of the antler on two opposite sides.

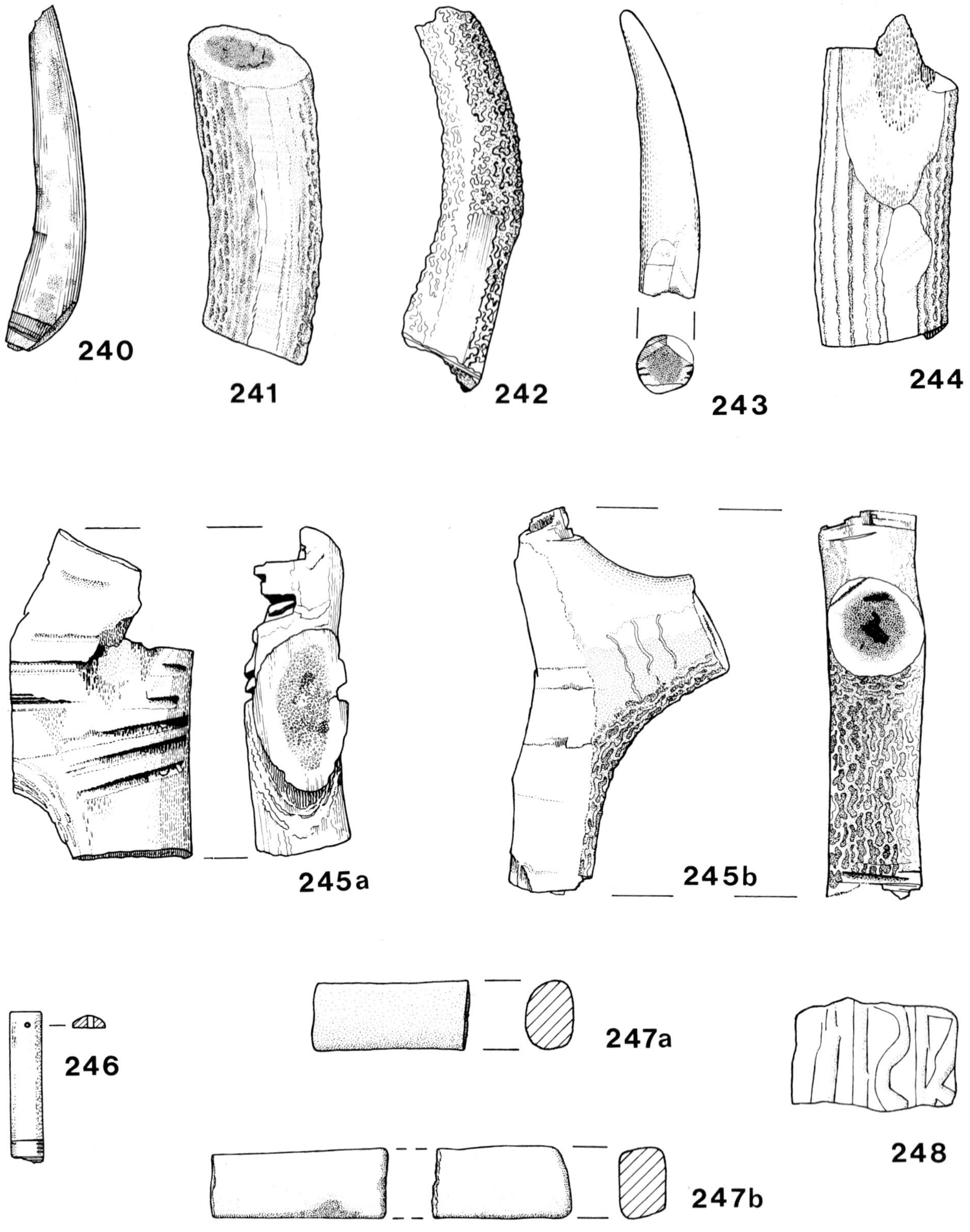

Fig. 39. *Antler tools, bone objects, hones and tile stamp (all ½), Darenth Roman Villa Site.*

From Saxon Hut A. F27. (DRV–489).

No. 246 Fragment of probable facing-plate from knife-handle. Bone, D-shaped in section, perforation at end and trace of incised decoration.

From Pit F9. (DRV–415).

No. 247a Central portion of a small hone of light grey fairly coarse sandstone, sub-rectangular in cross-section.

From Roman South Ditch. F26. (DRV–427).

No. 247b The two ends of a small hone of grey sandstone, rectangular in cross-section.

From stratified deposit at the north end of the Main Trench. (DRV–410).

No. 248 Fragment of tile bearing the letters ABR of Cabriabanus, applied with a wooden roller die. Excavations at Darenth in 1969 produced a fragment of a voussoir-tile with an identical stamp applied several times (Ref. 162) and other similar examples came from Plaxtol, Kent in 1857 (Ref. 163). On the present example the 'C' and first half of the first 'A' have missed the edge of the tile, when the die was applied. The second half of the first 'A' and the following 'BR', however, survive.

(7). THE PREHISTORIC FLINT.

By Andrew Woodcock, B.Sc., M.A., Ph.D., A.M.A., M.I.F.A.

All the flint material from the 1972 excavation was submitted to me for comment and consisted of 2,477 pieces of worked flint including 95 tools (Figs. 40–43, Nos. 249–327).

Of these the great majority came from two layers sealed by Roman deposits at the southern end of the main trench (page 86). However, of the seven axes only one came from these layers and the rest came from unrelated points along the length of the site, or from unstratified deposits. Too much significance should not be attached to this point since it might be expected that the larger, less easily buried, material would be that most readily incorporated into later contexts. A good example is the association of a Mesolithic tranchet axe (No. 321), truncated scraper (No. 260), also probably of Mesolithic date, and a fragment of Neolithic pottery in the fill of a pit (F18).

It also has to be recognised that, because of the limited amount of time available for the excavation, it was not possible to record the artifacts in their exact relationship to their horizontal stratigraphy with the same precision as would have been the case had there been unlimited time. Any conclusions are therefore based on a consideration of the artifacts as a whole. Furthermore, since the deposits were not sieved, it is just possible that some of the smaller components of the industry, such as the microliths and small blades, might have been missed, although alternatively their absence could be explained by suggesting that seasonal flooding may have removed some of the lighter material from the site.

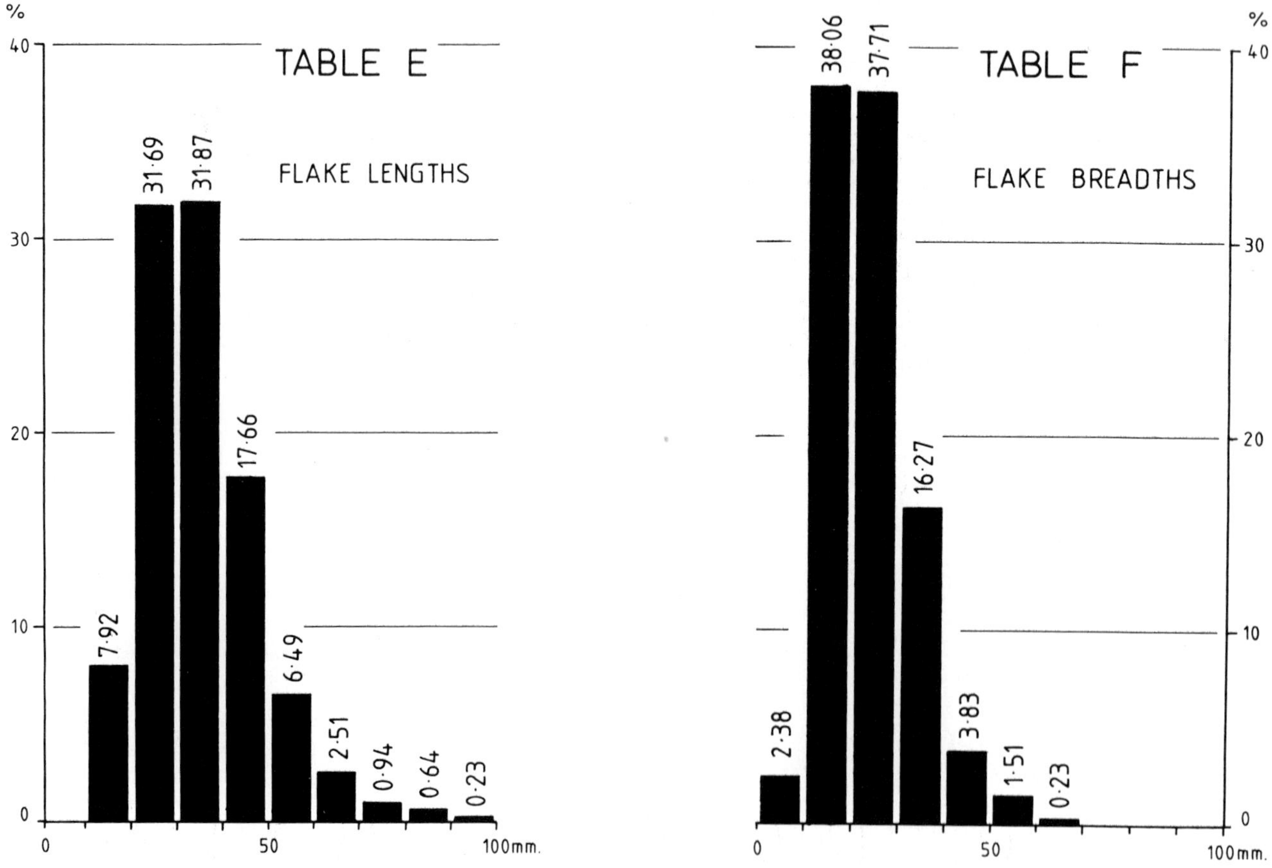

Percentage histograms of flake lengths and breadths.

The raw material consists almost entirely of flint derived from local sources (e.g. from the Chalk, or the Coombe-Rock or Clay-with-Flints which sometimes caps it, the River Gravels, or more rarely from Tertiary deposits). The majority of the flintwork is in a fresh and unabraded condition, with little or no patination. Some ochreous straining has occurred however, importing a brownish tint to much of the flint. A number of pieces show a greater degree of patination, and amongst these are some with at least two phases of working. Although an attempt was made to categorise the flint by colour, texture, nature of the cortex etc., this proved to be too subjective an exercise to be statistically useful.

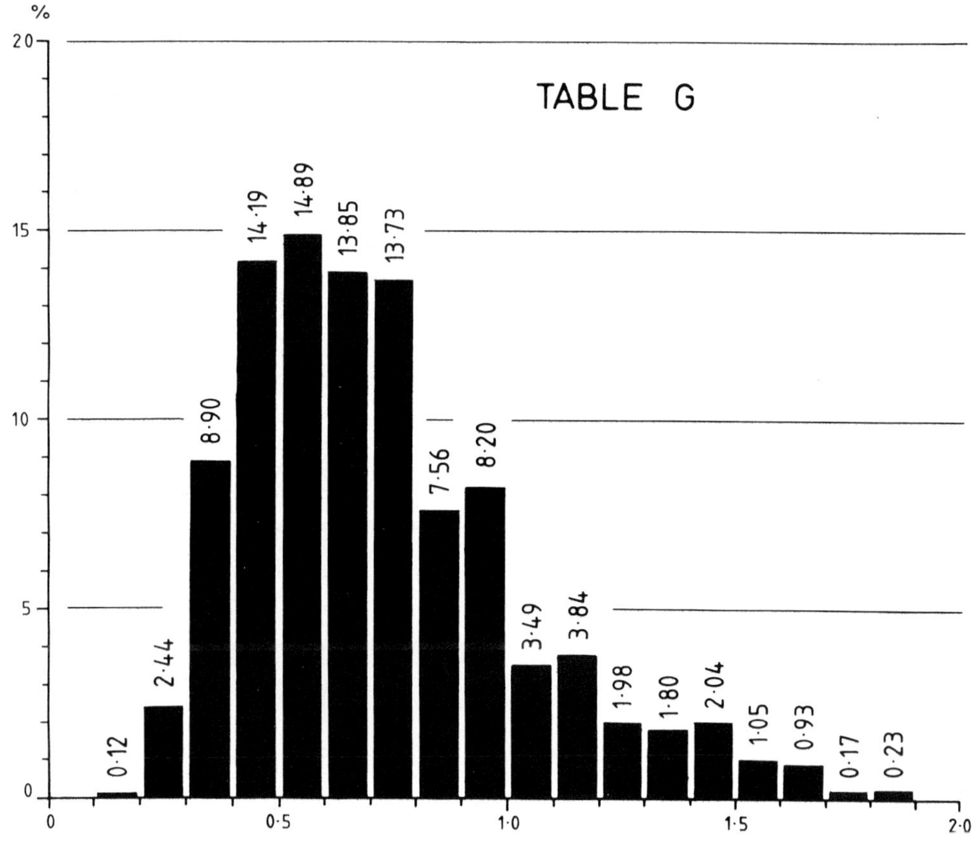

Percentage histogram of breadth/length ratios.

a). BLADES AND FLAKES (2,166)

Out of the 2,382 pieces of debitage from the site, 2,166 were blades or flakes. Of these 1,720 were sufficiently complete for their lengths and breadths to be measured. This information is presented as a series of percentage histograms showing values of length, breadth, and breadth to length ratio (Tables E-G). These show that whilst the values of length and breadth demonstrate strong unimodal size distributions (63·6% of the flakes being between 20 and 40 mm. long and 75·8% between 10 and 30 mm. in width) the breadth to length ratio has a greater spread of values, with comparatively few blade-like flakes being present (only 25·6% of the flakes having a value of B/L less than 0·5 and 2·5% less than 0·3). Remarkably few flakes (less than 2%) exhibit positive signs of abrasion or damage through use.

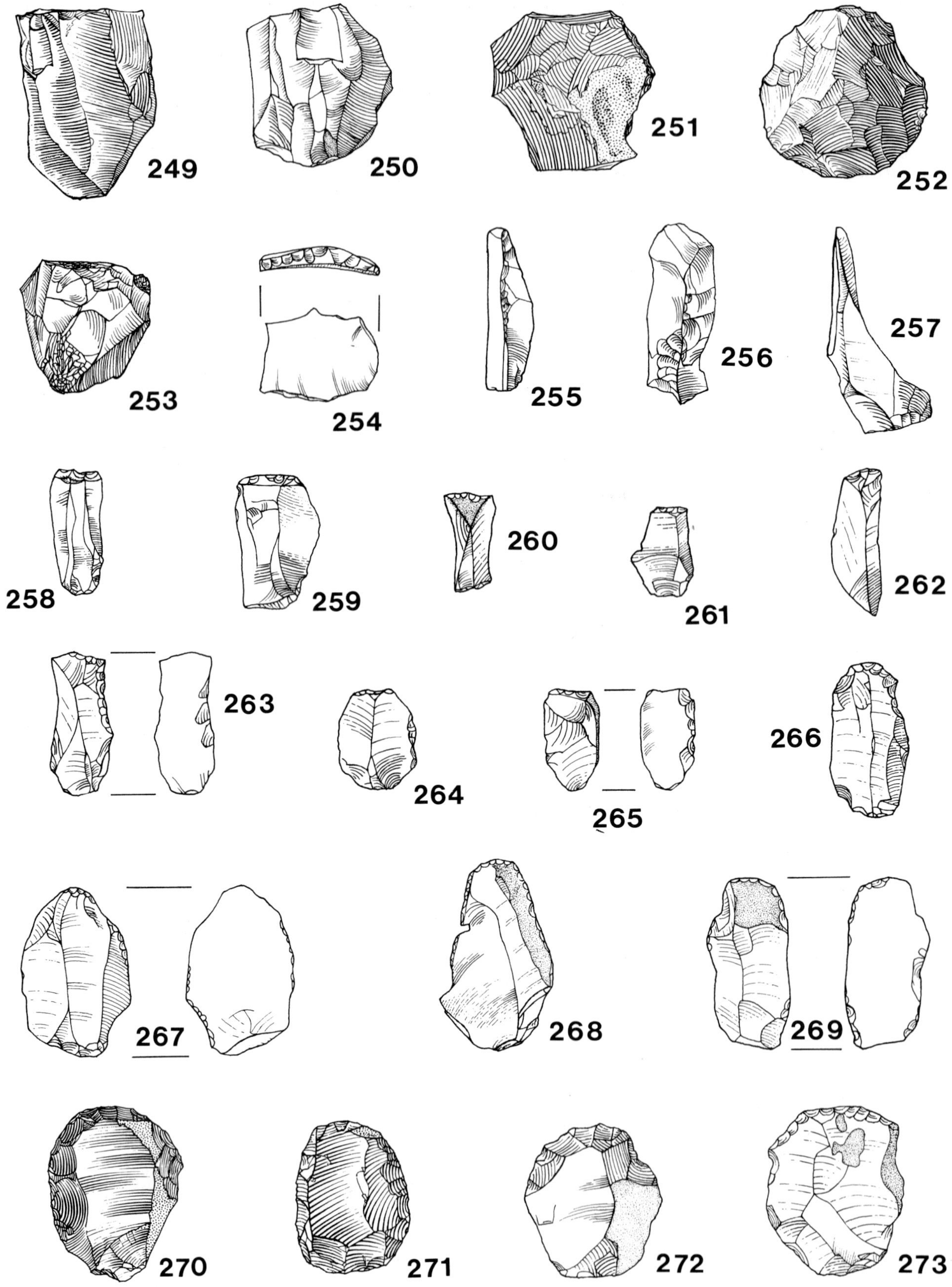

Fig. 40. *Prehistoric Flint (½), Darenth Roman Villa Site.*

b). CORES (172)

The 172 cores and core fragments can be broadly classified as:–

A (Single platform)
i flakes removed all round (3)
No. 249 ii flakes removed part of the way round (15)
B (Two platforms)
i parallel platforms (7)
ii one platform at an oblique angle (11)
iii platforms at right angles (9)
Nos. 250–1 C (Three or more platforms) (13)
No. 252 D (Keeled, including 'chopper' types) (8)
E (Keeled, but with one or more platforms) (1)
Shattered pieces off cores (99)
No. 253 Cores used as hammerstones (6)

The relatively high number of shattered pieces off cores can be attributed to the nature of the raw material, for much of the flint was probably surface collected and weakened by frost penetration.

c). CORE REJUVENATION/PREPARATION PIECES (37)

No. 254 Core tablets (8)
Nos. 255–6 Crested blades (22)
No. 257 Core rejuvenating flakes (7)

Only those rejuvenating flakes which can be ascribed to the working of cores have been counted. A greater number of flakes could perhaps have been included, but these have been omitted since they seem more likely to have been the result of axe or adze manufacture.

d). SCRAPERS (38)

The scrapers fall neatly into a number of distinct groups, as listed below:–

Nos. 258–262 Truncated/square-ended scrapers on blades or elongated flakes (5)
Nos. 263–265 Truncated/square-ended scrapers on flakes (3)
Nos. 266–269 Convex scrapers on blades and elongated flakes (4)
Nos. 270–278 Convex scrapers on thick squat flakes (9)
Nos. 279–282 Convex scrapers on small flakes whose breadth noticeably exceeds their length (4)
Nos. 283–284 Convex scrapers on small flakes (2)
Nos. 285–289 Scrapers on irregular flakes (11)

Included in this list is a group of five truncated scrapers on the end of blades which, more usually, would be described as truncated blades. They are, however, included here since they are indistinguishable, other than in their proportions, from the square-ended scrapers on truncated flakes.

Two of the irregular scrapers (Nos. 285 and 286) show two phases of working, although it is not beyond the bounds of possibility that some of the irregular retouch could have been the result of one flint crushing against another.

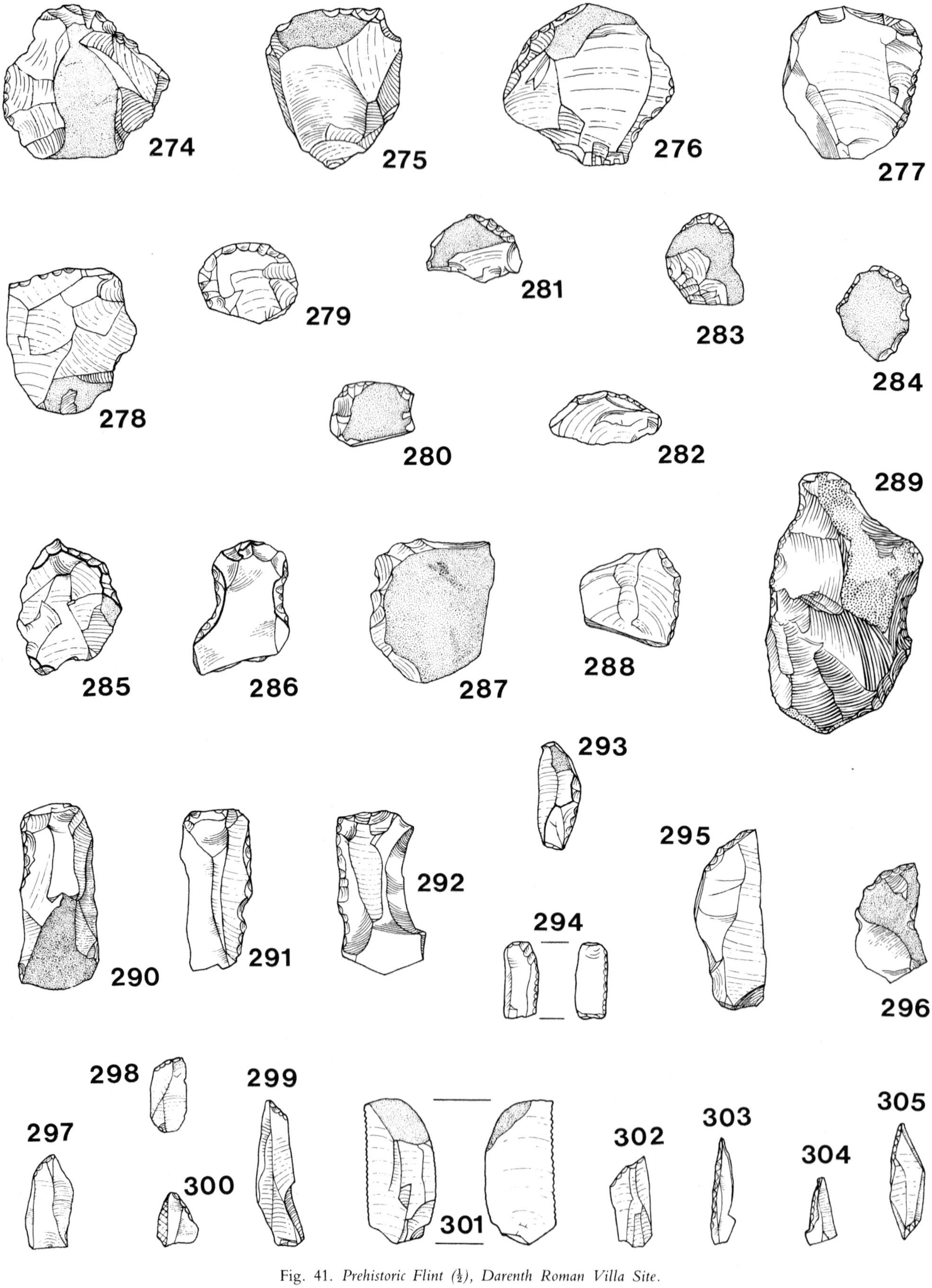

Fig. 41. *Prehistoric Flint (½), Darenth Roman Villa Site.*

e). BLUNTED-BACKED BLADES (5)

Nos. 290–293 Blunted down one edge only (4)
No. 294 Blunted down both edges (1)

Number 293 shows two phases of working, although the later retouch could be the result of accidental damage.

f). TRUNCATED BLADES (11)

Transversely truncated blades (5), (already listed under scrapers Nos. 258–262).
Nos. 295–300 Obliquely truncated blades (6)

Number 300 is notable for the high degree of polish on one of the blade facets, suggesting a previous use for the implement.

g). SERRATED BLADE (1)

No. 301 Only one example can be distinguished and this is in such poor condition that the serrations could have been the result of usage or accidental damage rather than deliberate retouch.

h). MICROLITHS (4)

No. 302 Obliquely blunted down part of one edge (1)
Nos. 303–4 Obliquely blunted straight down one edge (2)
No. 305 Obliquely blunted down part of one edge and across the base (1)

Of the two microliths which have been obliquely blunted straight down one edge, one (No. 303) has been damaged, perhaps by impact, whilst the other (No. 304) appears unfinished.

i). MICRO-BURINS (2)

Nos. 306–7 Although No. 306 is a typical micro-burin, No. 307 seems to have snapped at a somewhat higher point than anticipated so removing part of the microlith with it.

j). BURINS (10)

Nos. 308–9 Angular dihedral burins (5)
No. 310 Obliquely truncated burins (1)
Nos. 311–2 Busqued (3)
No. 313 Others (1)

Whilst the last mentioned implement has the appearance of a microlith which has broken during manufacture, it bears sufficient signs of its use as a burin for it to be classified here.

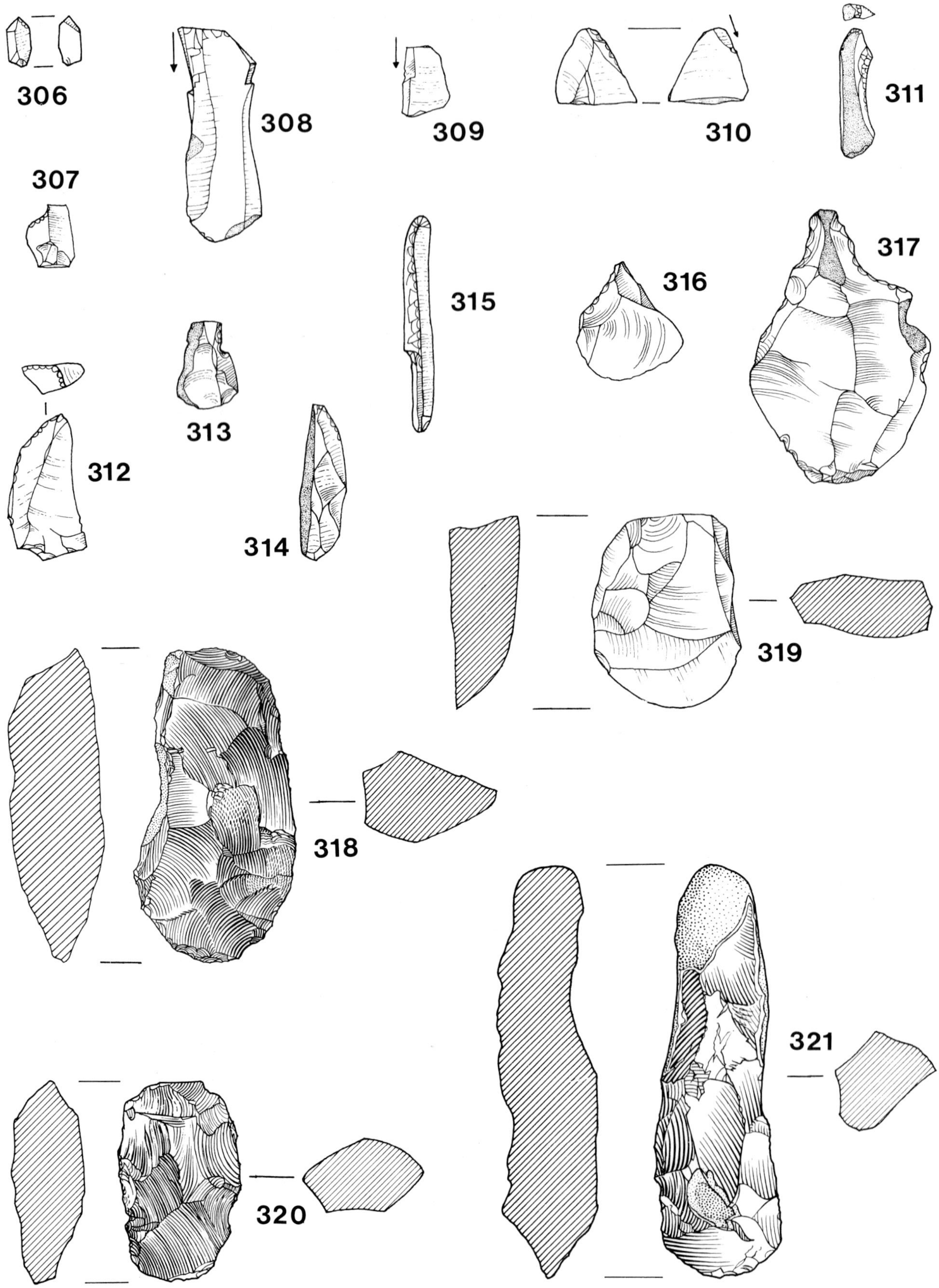

Fig. 42. *Prehistoric Flint (½), Darenth Roman Villa Site.*

k). BURIN SPALLS (2)

The small number of burin spalls detected is probably a reflection of the general absence of small flakes discovered during the course of the excavation.

l). GRAVERS (2)

Nos. 314–5 Into this category come two implements which, in other circumstances, might be considered as fabricators or miscellaneous tools. However, both are strongly reminiscent of the 'zinken' common in continental Hamburgian assemblages with their typical narrow scraper-like beaks. No. 315 is particularly interesting for it seems to have started life as a burin-spall, the careful retouch having been applied before the flake was struck to facilitate its removal. The tip of the implement was only then worked into its scraper-like form.

m). AWLS (4)

Nos. 316–7 Most are merely rough angular flakes which have been utilised with the minimum of additional work. Only No. 317 shows retouch on a substantial scale.

n). AXES (7)

Nos. 318–21	Tranchet (4)
No. 322	Others (1)
No. 323	Picks (1)
No. 324	Fragments (1)

All the above are typographically Mesolithic and five have tranchet cutting tips. No. 318 is a good example of a Mesolithic tranchet axe with its irregular, rhomboidal cross-section and somewhat sinuous outline. Nos. 319 and 320 show similar features but represent the last stages of an axe's life. No. 319 in particular has been sharpened and resharpened until it is no longer usable. No. 322 is probably Mesolithic also for, although it does not have a tranchet cutting tip, it is very similar in its general shape to the axes already described.
No. 321 is likewise somewhat different and reminiscent of a 'Thames Pick' in style, but somewhat smaller than is usual. The cutting tip is formed by a tranchet blow whilst the butt retains much of its original cortex so that the implement fits snugly into the hand. No. 324 is the broken butt of an axe, but it is not clear whether the implement fractured during the course of manufacture or use. No. 323 is typologically quite different and represents the broken end of a Mesolithic 'pick' its tip being formed by a tranchet flake on one side.

o). AXE SHARPENING FLAKES (3)

No. 325 Only three such flakes have so far been recognised.

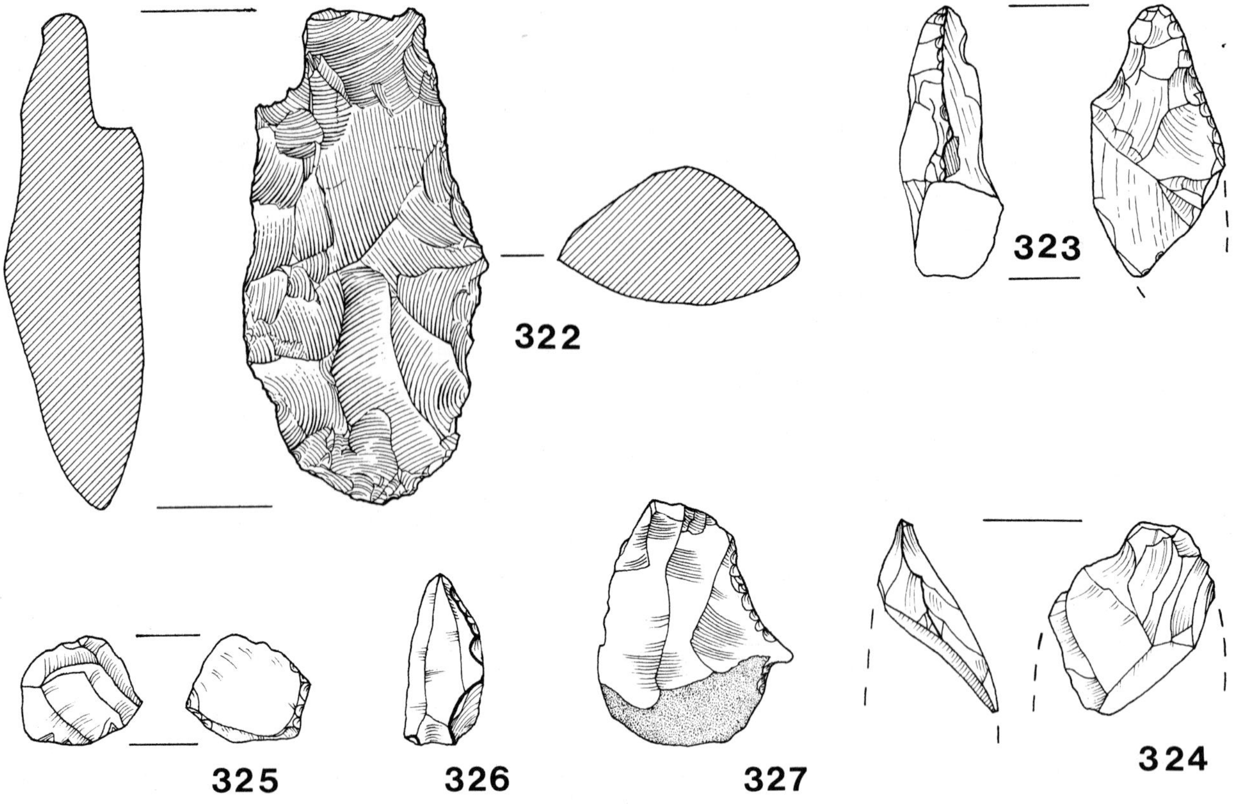

Fig. 43. *Prehistoric Flint* (½), *Darenth Roman Villa Site.*

p). MISCELLANEOUS RETOUCH (18)

Nos. 326–7 Included in this category are those pieces with secondary retouch, which cannot conveniently be placed elsewhere. The two examples illustrated are typical of this group.

q). BURNT FLINTS (108)

A total of 108 burnt flints were recovered from the excavation, 39 showing signs of having been worked.

CONCLUSIONS

Notwithstanding the fact that all the worked flints have been considered as a single group, attempts have been made to see if it is possible to recognise cultural or technological differences which could perhaps indicate the likely date range of the material, and to look for the production of specialised tool types which might suggest the nature and function of the site.

Since the industry contains a number of patinated and abraded pieces which show evidence of having been worked on more than one occasion (e.g. Nos. 285, 286 and 293) it seems clear that the site was occupied more than once. Certainly the presence of pottery fragments amongst the flintwork testifies to a certain degree of disturbance and the intrusion of later material. On the evidence of the flintwork alone, however, it is not possible to determine either the number of occupation phases represented or assign specific dates to them. As those artifacts which are noticeably patinated or abraded account for less than 1% of the total industry, it may well be that the bulk of the material is of the same date, but there is no way of proving this. Time has not been available to try and fit together the debitage in order to test the range of patination and abrasion on contemporary artifacts.

There are relatively few artifacts which are sufficiently distinctive to be dated. Although the presence of blades and blade-like flakes amongst the debitage suggests that at least part of the industry belongs to the Mesolithic, it must be remembered that such material is found in early Neolithic contexts also (Ref. 164). Only when it comes to an examination of the implements can one be more specific, and of those which are typologically indicative of a particular period all are of Mesolithic form. Amongst this diagnostic material are tranchet axes, axe sharpening flakes, microliths and micro-burins. This is not to say that the industry could not contain later pieces, merely that their presence cannot be detected.

The industry shows other interesting features, for example the proportion of flakes with evidence of use or secondary retouch is remarkably small, indeed much of the unspecialised chipping observed may have been the result of trampling underfoot at the time of manufacture or post-excavation damage. The ratio of tools to debitage is likewise small. Many of the larger flakes seem to have been the by-product of axe manufacture, a process which was certainly taking place on the site.

The overall impression given by the material is that whilst the site may have been visited by various groups over a considerable period of time, the bulk of the material is probably Mesolithic, and of one date. The relatively low number of tools and utilised flakes suggests a fairly short visit, or series of visits, to an area rich in local flint resources which could be exploited for the manufacture of tools. A number of the completed tools may well have been carried away from the site together with some of the finer blades.

It is difficult to be more specific about the date within the Mesolithic. The microliths are too few in number and too unspecialised to be of help. What evidence there is suggests that there are few industries of early Mesolithic date in Kent (Ref. 165) and certainly the rather 'Thames Pick' – like tranchet axe (No. 321) could belong to the latter part of the Mesolithic period.

(8). PREHISTORIC POTTERY (Fig. 44, Nos 328–333b)

By Dr. I.F. Smith.

Diagnostic sherds in this small assemblage suggest activity on the site during the first half of the second millennium bc. Four fragments, all from different vessels, can be attributed to the Fengate style of Peterborough ware; characteristic features are the collar and short neck of No. 328 (almost certainly not from a Bronze Age collared urn) and the lightly incised decoration on Nos. 329–331. No. 332 can also be classed as Peterborough ware, although the position of the finger-tip impression – on the body rather than the neck – is unusual. Two sherds (Nos. 333a and 333b) are less easy to place and could derive either from Peterborough vessels or from domestic beakers. The six remaining fragments, not necessarily contemporary with the rest, are unclassifiable.

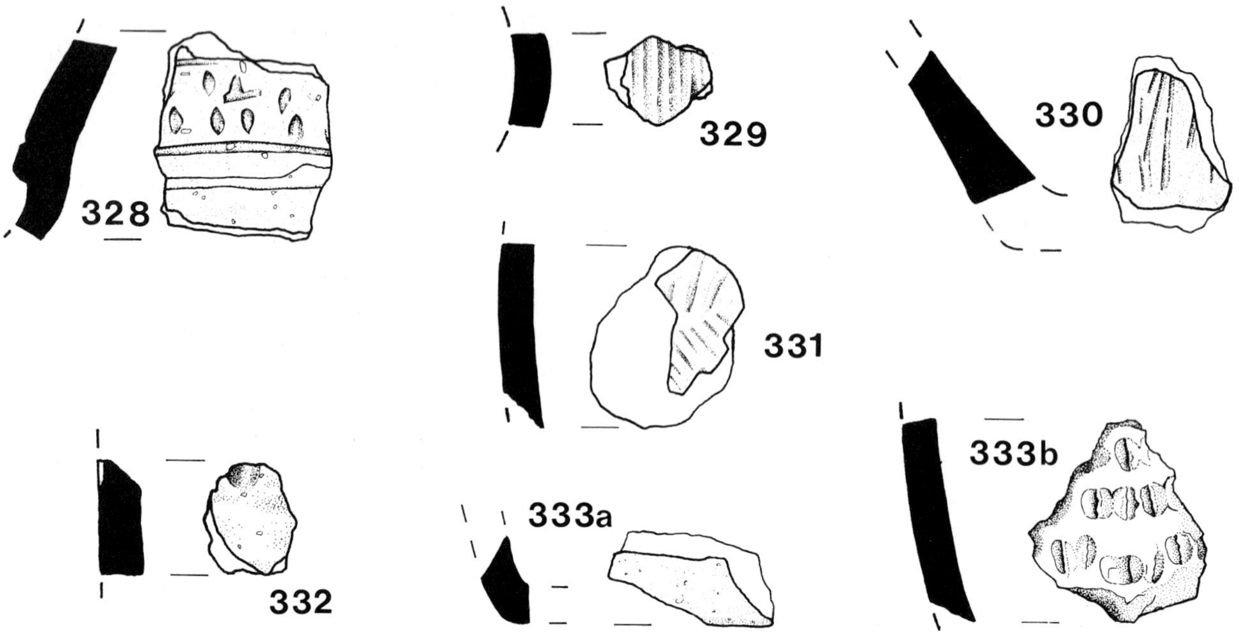

Fig. 44. *Prehistoric pottery* (½), *Darenth Roman Villa Site.*

PETERBOROUGH WARE OF THE FENGATE STYLE.

No. 328 Part of a collar and short concave neck; both the rim and the base of the collar (which apparently consisted of a narrow applied strip) broken off. Decoration on collar consists of two rows of finger-nail impressions above a narrow horizontal groove. No clear indications of decoration on the somewhat irregular outer surface of the neck. Both surfaces reddish-brown with darker patches; 'greasy' fabric, laminated in section, contains particles of shell up to 5 mm. in size, mostly well concealed. From Roman North Ditch, F5 (DRV–413).

No. 329 Small sherd from a concave neck, decorated externally with vertical lines lightly drawn with a comb-like implement. Exterior pale red, interior dark; fabric similar to that of No. 328, but also contains a few very small flints. From gullies F19 and F20 (DRV–470).

No. 330 Sherd from just above a thick flat base; outer surface decorated with vertical and oblique lines similar to those on No. 329. Exterior pale red, interior dark; fabric contains fine grog and rare particles of flint. From the Peat Deposit, F11 (DRV–430).

No. 331 Sherd from a rounded body; surviving part of outer surface decorated with shallow incised lines apparently forming part of a herring-bone motif. Exterior bright red, interior dark; soft laminated fabric contains grog and rare flints. From Field South of Villa (DRV–444).

PETERBOROUGH WARE

No. 332 Small body sherd carrying part of a single deep finger-tip impression. Exterior pale red, interior dark; slightly gritty fabric contains particles of calcined flint, generally under 3 mm. in size, and fine sand. From Post-hole of Saxon Structure, F23 (DRV–486).

PETERBOROUGH WARE OR DOMESTIC BEAKER

No. 333a Sherd from a basal angle; undecorated. Exterior pale red, interior dark; fabric contains sand, occasional fine flints and numerous pellets of red iron ore. From above Roman Chalk Raft 3 (DRV–411).

No. 333b Body sherd decorated with irregular zones of paired fingernail impressions, with pronounced rustication. Exterior reddish-brown, interior dark; gritty laminated fabric contains abundant rounded and sub-angular quartz grains up to 0·5 mm. in size. From Roman Water Channel F14 (DRV–468).

(9). LATE BRONZE AGE AND IRON AGE POTTERY (Fig. 45).

By Peter Couldrey, B.Sc.

A total of 158 sherds, weighing 1174 grams and representing about 49 vessels, was recovered. Nine vessels are illustrated (Nos. 334–342). These have been grouped into two chronological phases: the first belonging to the Late Bronze Age/Early Iron Age (c. 900–600 B.C.) and the second is tentatively assigned to the Middle pre-Roman Iron Age (c. 300–50 B.C.). Most of the sherds were very small and abraded and only one pit (Feature 33) produced a sufficient quantity of recognisable forms for dating purposes. This has been dated to the Late Bronze Age/Early Iron Age and a distinction in fabrics has been used to identify the Middle pre-Roman Iron Age phase.

The estimate of the number of vessels is based on a minimum number distinguished by form, fabric and extreme variations of wall thickness. When dealing with coarse pottery however, details of fabric and wall thickness can vary within one vessel and such an estimate is hazardous. For this reason, the number of vessels is not used in any statistical analysis of the material.

Each vessel was numbered and a record made of the weight, wall thickness, number of non-fitting sherds and fabric group. A catalogue containing this information for all the pottery is kept with the finds from the site.

FABRICS

The fabrics fall into six main groups and are characterised by their primary inclusions.

Fabric A:
Flint tempered vessels. This group is generally well fired, hard and the colours vary from brown to dark grey. It is sub-divided according to the size of the inclusions.
A1 Sparse or common inclusions of less than 1 mm., with rare inclusions of up to 2 mm.
A2 Moderate to abundant inclusions up to 2 mm., with rare inclusions up to 4 mm.
A3 Common to abundant inclusions up to 4 mm., with rare inclusions up to 5 mm.

Fabric B:
Shell tempered vessels. The quality of firing is variable and the colours range from brown to dark grey. Some surfaces are covered with slurry; some have been wiped, and many are rough. The group is sub-divided according to the size of inclusions.
B1 Common to abundant inclusions up to 3 mm. with sparse inclusions of iron oxide up to 1 mm.
B2 Abundant inclusions up to 3 mm. with sparse to moderate inclusions up to 5 mm.
B3 Moderate inclusions up to 5 mm. with sparse inclusions up to 8 mm.
B4 Moderate inclusions up to 8 mm. with sparse inclusions up to 12 mm.

Fabric C:
Shell and flint tempered vessels. This group is generally well fired, hard and the colours vary from orange-brown to dark grey. Some surfaces have been wiped, but most have been left rough. It is sub-divided according to the size of inclusions:
C1 Moderate inclusions of shell up to 2 mm, and sparse inclusions up to 7 mm., with sparse to moderate inclusions of flint up to 0·5 mm.
C2 Common inclusions of shell up to 5 mm, and moderate to sparse inclusions up to 9 mm., with moderate to common inclusions of flint up to 2 mm.
C3 As for C2, but with common inclusions of iron oxide up to 1 mm. One example of this fabric, a large storage jar (No. 338) was found to contain a fragment of a rim of a thin-walled vessel in Fabric F3 embedded within its wall. Apart from this example there was no other visible evidence for the use of grog; but it seems possible that this fabric was derived from old Fabric F bowls being ground down and mixed with Fabric B.
Samples of shell from Fabrics B and C were shown to Dr. John Cooper of the British Museum (Natural History) who identified them as belonging to the bivalve *Corbicula cordata,* derived from the black shelly clays of the Woolwich Beds. The nearest outcrop of Woolwich Beds occurs two kilometres to the north-east in Lords Wood.

Fabric D:
A sandy matrix containing flint and iron oxides. This group is generally well fired and the colours vary from brown to dark grey. The surfaces have been smoothed and some have been burnished. It is sub-divided according to the size of inclusions.
D1 Moderate to common inclusions of flint up to 0·5 mm. with moderate to common inclusions of iron oxide up to 0·5 mm.
D2 Sparse to moderate inclusions of flint up to 2 mm. and moderate inclusions of iron oxide up to 0·5 mm.
D3 Sparse inclusions of flint up to 2 mm. and sparse inclusions of iron oxide up to 1 mm.

Fabric E:
A sandy matrix with vegetable tempering and some flint. The quality of firing, range of colours and surface treatment is extremely variable.
E1 Common voids up to 7 mm. long, representing burnt out vegetable tempering.
E2 Common voids up to 3 mm. long and sparse to moderate inclusions of flint up to 0·5 mm.
E3 Common voids up to 9 mm. long and flint inclusions: moderate to common up to 2 mm. and sparse up to 5 mm.

Fabric F:
Fine fabrics in which quartz accounts for a high proportion of the tempering. Vessels in the fabrics are well fired; have smooth surfaces and are coloured dark grey to black throughout.
F1 Common inclusions of white translucent quartz between 0·2 mm. and 0·3 mm. and sparse inclusions of orange-brown translucent quartz between 0·5 mm. and 1 mm.
F2 As for F1, except the orange-brown quartz grains are between 0·3 and 0·5 mm.
F3 Common to abundant inclusions of white translucent quartz up to 0·5 mm. and inclusions of flint: sparse between 0·5 mm. and 1 mm. and common up to 0·5 mm.
F4 As for F3, but includes sparse to moderate inclusions of flint up to 2mm.

CATALOGUE OF ILLUSTRATED POTTERY

Nine sherds with identifiable forms or decoration are illustrated (Fig. 45, Nos. 334–342). In the description which follows colours are described verbally and with the use of Munsell colour codes which appear in parentheses.

Pit South of Main Trench (F33) (DRV–445)

No. 334 A vessel of shell tempered fabric with finger-tip decoration on both the top and outer edge of the rim, and on the shoulder. The external surface has been smoothed, though shell protrudes; and the internal surface is rough. The core is dark grey (N3) and the surfaces vary from dark grey to brown (N3–2.5YR5/6). (Fabric B3).
No. 335 An everted rim with flat top in hard shell and flint tempered fabric. The core is black (N2) and the surfaces vary from light brown to orange-brown (7.5YR6/5–2.5YR5/8). The surfaces have been wiped but the tempering protrudes (Fabric C3).
No. 336 A flat-topped rim in shell tempered fabric. As a result of flattening the rim, clay overhangs the internal surface and part of the external surface. The core is black (N2), and the surfaces are orange-brown (2.5YR4/4–10R5/6). (Fabric B2).
No. 337 A fragment of bevelled rim from a wide-mouthed vessel (or lid) in fine flint and quartz tempered fabric. The external surface is hard and smooth, but the internal surface is badly worn. The sherd has been fired black (N2) throughout. (Fabric F3).
No. 338 A flat base of a storage jar in shell and flint tempered fabric. The surfaces appear to have been wiped with grass. The outside of the base however, is covered with fragments of calcined flint. The core is black (N2) and the surfaces are brown (7.5YR6/4) with grey (10YR5/1) patches. (Fabric C2).

Unstratified South of Main Trench (DRV–444).

No. 339 A fragment of rim with finger-tip decoration on the sides in shell and flint tempered fabric. The core and external surface are dark grey (N3) and the internal surface is brown (5YR6/4). (Fabric C2).

Pre-Roman land-surface (F32). (DRV–436).

No. 340 A fragment of a carinated bowl in fine flint and quartz tempered fabric. The surfaces are smooth and hard and the sherd is black (N2) throughout. (Fabric F3).
No. 341 A fragment of plain rim in flint and sand tempered fabric. The top has been smoothed down to overlap the external surface. The angle and diameter are uncertain. The colour varies from brown to grey (5YR7/6–5YR4/1) throughout. (Fabric D2).

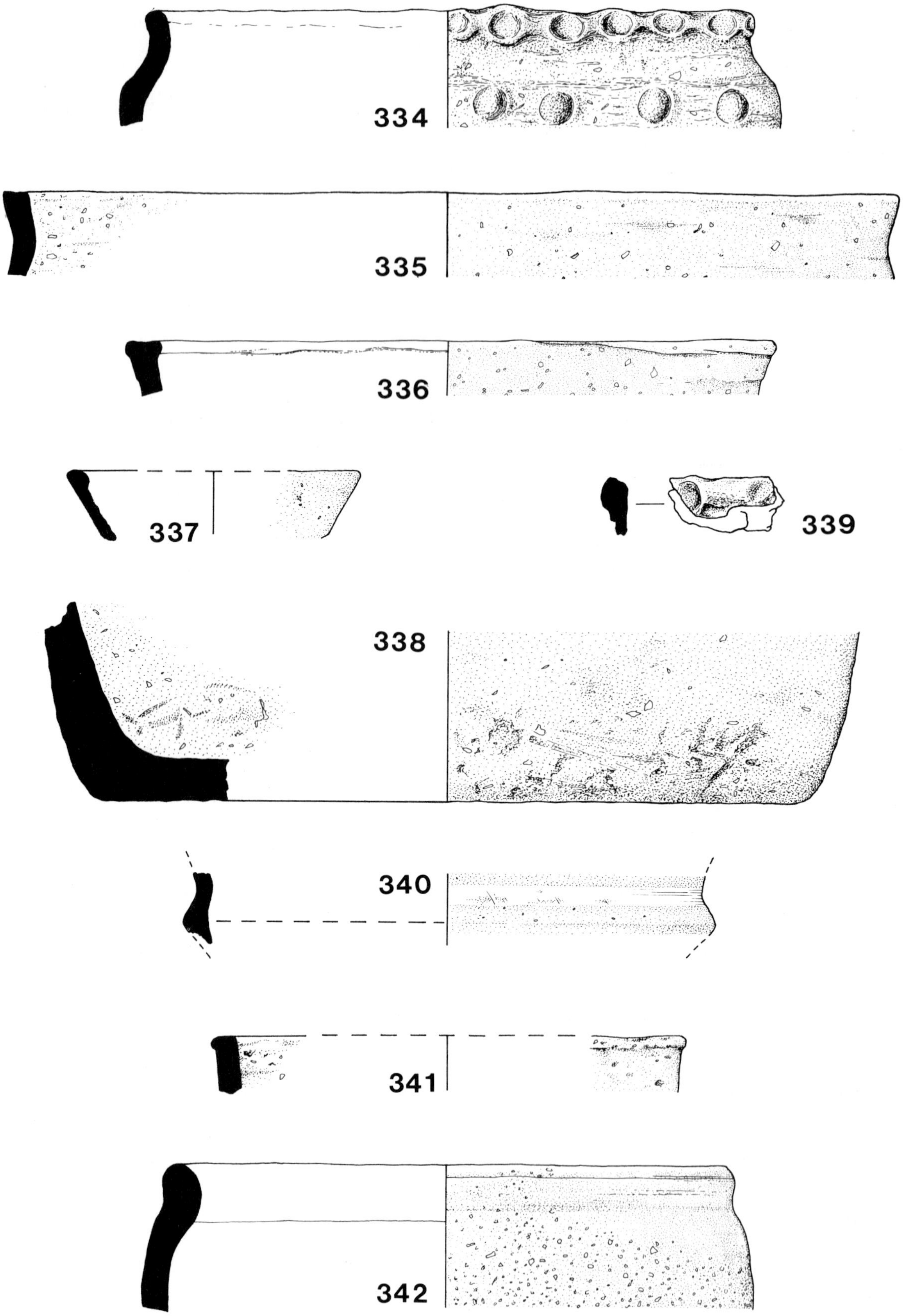

Fig. 45. *Late Bronze Age and Iron Age Pottery (½), Darenth Roman Villa Site.*

Black loam over peat (F11). (DRV–429).

No. 342 A vessel with a thick bead rim in hard shell tempered fabric. The core is black (N2); the internal surface brown (7.5YR7/4) and the external surface black (N2) with a patch of brown (7.5YR7/4). Both the surfaces have been wiped horizontally and the external surface, though worn, shows signs of having been coated with slurry. (Fabric B1).

DISCUSSION

Most of the vessels from this site are extremely fragmentary and the number of recognisable forms is small. For this reason no attempt will be made to provide an exhaustive list of parallels. Most references will be restricted to recently published examples from nearby sites, in order to establish an indication of chronology. The group with the largest number of recognisable forms (Feature 33) will be considered first and others will be compared with it.

The shouldered jar with finger-tip decoration (No. 334) is a well known form and examples are known from Petters Sports Field, Egham (Ref. 169), Runnymede Bridge (Ref. 170), Weybridge (Ref. 171), Orsett (Ref. 172) and Bridge, Kent site 8 (Ref. 173). In a recent discussion of Later Bronze Age pottery in Lowland England (Ref. 174) Barrett has argued for an increasing use of decoration, beginning in the Thames Estuary during the ninth century B.C. and becoming more widespread by the eighth century B.C. This form and a fragmentary incised design (not illustrated) may be attributed to Barrett's group of 'decorated assemblages'.

Wide-mouthed bowls or lids with bevelled rims (No. 337) are not common, but a similar example may be cited from Runnymede Bridge (Ref. 175). They are better known on the continent where they are found in late Urnfield groups dating between about 1000 and 700 B.C. – for example at Choisy-au-Bac, 'La Bouche d'Oise' in northern France (Ref. 176).

The presence of a large number of calcined flint fragments on the base of a storage jar (No. 338) as a result of standing the vessel on a bed of flints during manufacture, has been recognised in Late Bronze Age contexts at Mucking (Ref. 177), Runnymede Bridge (Ref. 178), Green Lane, Farnham (Ref. 179), Weybridge and Ivinghoe Beacon (Ref. 180).

The pot also contained fragments of thin-walled and carinated forms (not illustrated) in Fabrics F1 and F3; but their small size prevents reference to close parallels. The remaining forms (Nos. 335 and 336) are simple and of little chronological value.

From the parallels cited above, the fill of Feature 33 can be placed between about 900 and 600 B.C. Many of these forms may have had a long life. The lack of other sites in West Kent producing closed groups with material of this period and the small size of this sample, does not permit close dating of this group. The chronology of other deposits however, is less certain.

The black loam over the peat (F11) contained a vessel with a thick bead rim (No. 342). This form is not common in Late Bronze Age/Early Iron Age contexts, but examples have been recorded at Runnymede Bridge (Ref. 181) and Bridge, site 8 (Ref. 182) and, in the absence of evidence to the contrary, it is possible to consider this to be contemporary with the fill of Feature 33.

The pre-Roman land surface (F32) produced two identifiable forms: the carinated bowl (No. 340) could be attributed to the Late Bronze Age/Early Iron Age but the plain rim (No. 341) could date from almost any time during the Iron Age. Examination of the fabrics from this level shows that this material may be distinguished from that in other deposits. Table H shows the distribution of fabric by total sherd weight and average sherd weight from each deposit. Comparison of the pottery from F33 and the pre-Roman land surface reveals that, apart from Fabric A, the distribution of fabrics is almost mutually exclusive. Those from the pre-Roman land surface are predominantly sandy with fragments of flint and vegetable tempering (Fabrics D and E) and these are absent from the pit. The exceptions (one sherd of Fabric B2 and one of F3) may be regarded as residual.

The use of sand tempering is common on later sites in West Kent. In particular, sandy fabrics have been found associated with footring bowls of the third to first century B.C. Use of a similar fabric does not necessarily imply contemporaneity, and more evidence is required before a local sequence of fabrics is established. Nevertheless, the average weight of sherds from the pre-Roman land surface (Table H) shows that all the sherds are worn. A possible explanation is that this deposit contains material derived from the Late Bronze Age/Early Iron Age settlement, represented by Feature 33 and a later, possibly Middle pre-Roman Iron Age site.

	TOTAL WEIGHT (gm.)							AVERAGE SHERD WEIGHT (gm.)						
Features	F5	F26	F11	F32	F33	Unst.	F27	F5	F26	F11	F32	F33	Unst.	F27
Fabric														
A1				27	13		20				5·4	4·3		20·0
2					9							3·0		
3				33							3·7			
B1	265	120	47				12	37·9	40·0	47·0				12·0
2				2	129						2·0	3·5		
3					98							8·9		
4					145							16·1		
C1			6		12					6·0		6·0		
2					315							26·3		
3					26							13·0		
D1				1							1·0			
2				28							3·1			
3				5							5·0			
E1				6							3·0			
2				18		1					3·0		1·0	
3				50							3·8			
4							5							5·0
F1					1							1·0		
2					22							22·0		
3				3	13						3·0	3·3		
4					18							18·0		

Table H – The total weight and average sherd weight for each fabric type within Features.

(10). THE SAXON POTTERY (Fig. 46).

By John Willson.

The excavation at Darenth in 1972 produced only a limited amount of fragmentary Saxon pottery, which appears to fall into three basic fabrics and which are briefly described below.

In total some 62 sherds of Saxon pottery were recovered from both stratified and unstratified contexts on the site and these represent a minimum of nine vessels (Nos. 343–351). Only one certainly related group was located and that was from Saxon Hut A. Some 40 sherds of Saxon pottery were recovered from within its filling and sherds of all three fabric groups were present. Only two sherds of Fabric A were present, both undecorated (Nos. 343 and 344). Eleven sherds of Fabric B representing at least two vessels (Nos. 345 and 346) and 27 sherds of Fabric C representing at least five vessels (Nos. 347 to 351) were also found. Clearly the Fabric C, hand-made, grass-tempered wares predominate, but the presence of other fabrics allow only a generally wide date-range of fifth and sixth centuries A.D.

FABRIC A – Burnished hard sandy ware.

The fabric is generally of a hard, dense black-brown sandy consistency, with small amounts of fine grit and grass added as additional tempering agents.

Only four sherds of this ware were found and these represent a minimum of three vessels. They appear to have been made on a slow wheel and carefully finished. Similar parallels at St. Peter's, Kent and at Spong Hill, North Elmham, Norfolk, give a date-range of fifth and sixth centuries A.D. The external surfaces are generally burnished and decoration only appears in two cases. One vessel has slightly wavy horizontally incised lines on its shoulder (No. 343), whilst the other vessel is carinated, with burnished incised horizontal curves above the carination giving a 'swagged' look to the vessel's wall (No. 344).

FABRIC B – Sandy ware.

Generally a black and more noticeably sandier fabric than Fabric A with some grass tempering present. The surfaces are uneven and show tubular pockmarks where the grass has burnt out during firing. The vessels appear hand-made and show mild burnishing in general to exterior surfaces. Some 21 sherds were recovered and these represent a minimum of two vessels, consisting of an outcurved rim cooking-pot (No. 346) and a single wide bowl or dish (No. 345).

Similar vessels from Mucking, Essex and Caistor-by-Norwich, Norfolk appear to date to the fifth and sixth centuries A.D.

FABRIC C – Grass-tempered Ware.

This fabric is the true grass-tempered ware. It is generally of a dense black or dark grey-brown fabric with considerable amounts of grass or chaff added as a tempering agent. The whole, or large areas of the surface are very vesiculated where the tempering has burnt out during firing, and a rough burnishing to external areas is often visable. None of the sherds recovered showed any signs of decoration, all were roughly finished, of inferior quality and were clearly hand-made.

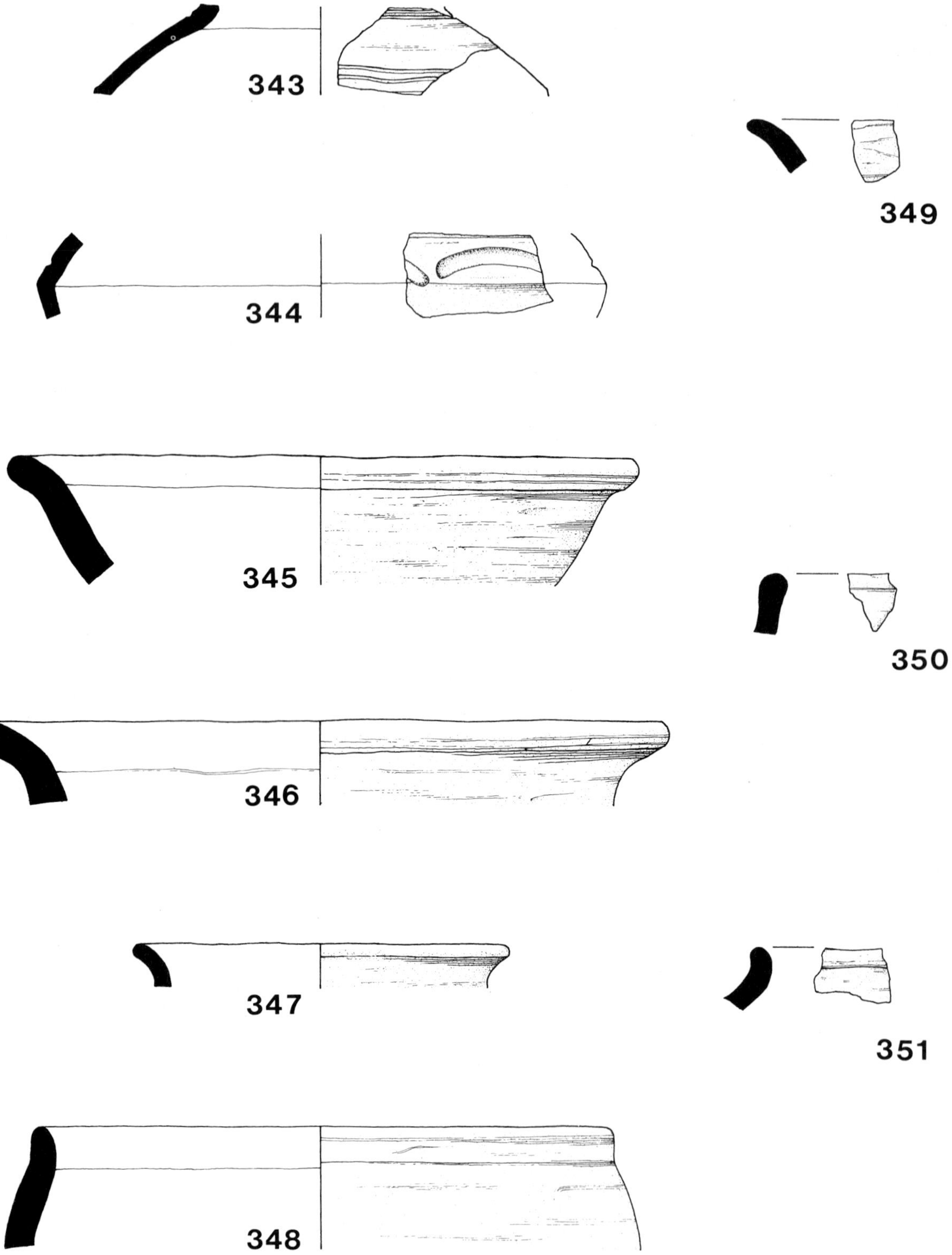

Fig. 46. *Anglo-Saxon pottery (½), Darenth Roman Villa Site.*

In all some 37 sherds were recovered and these represent a minimum of five vessels all of which have been illustrated (Nos. 347 to 351). All are simple cooking-pots with plain outcurved or almost upright rims and can be paralleled at Darenth and Keston, in Kent and at Mucking, Essex, where they appear to range in date from the fifth to six centuries A.D.

CATALOGUE OF THE ILLUSTRATED ANGLO-SAXON POTTERY

From Unstratified Contexts (DRV–452 and 464).

No. 343 Wall sherd (rim missing) of a slow wheel made, narrow necked jar of sandy ware (Fabric A). Burnished finish, decorated with a zone of horizontal wavy grooves on neck and another zone on shoulder. This fragment appears to be part of a vessel that has hollow bosses at intervals on the shoulder. It can be compared to a vessel from St. Peter's, Kent (Ref. 183) and probably dates to the fifth and sixth centuries A.D.

No. 344 Wall sherd (rim missing) of a slow wheel made, carinated jar of sandy ware (Fabric A). Burnished above the carination and decorated with a row of arched grooves with a horizontal groove above. A vessel from the cemetery at Spong Hill, North Elmham (Ref. 184) is somewhat similar and appears to date to the fifth and sixth centuries A.D.

From Roman Water Channel. F14 (DRV–465).

No. 345 Hand-made wide bowl, or dish with a slightly outcurved rim of sandy ware (Fabric B). Black fabric and surface. Very similar vessels from a Saxon grubenhaüs at Mucking, Essex (Hut 26, No. 414a) are dated to the fifth century A.D. (Ref. 185).

From Saxon Hut A. F.27 (DRV–489 and 493).

No. 346 Hand-made cooking-pot with a thick outcurved rim of sandy ware (Fabric B). Black fabric and a buff-brown surface. A parallel for form, shape and date can be found in a vessel from Caistor-by-Norwich (Ref. 186) dated to the fifth and sixth centuries A.D.

No. 347 Small hand-made cooking-pot, with outcurved rim of grass-tempered ware (Fabric C). Black fabric, black-brown surface. Similar vessels from a Saxon grubenhaüs at Mucking, Essex (Ref. 185 – Hut 26, No. 416e and 418b), are dated to the fifth century.

No. 348 Hand-made cooking-pot with a slightly outcurved rim of grass-tempered ware (Fabric C). Dark grey-brown fabric and surface. A similar vessel from Darenth (West Kent No. 461) (Ref. 187) is dated probably to the sixth century A.D.

No. 349 Outcurved rim fragment from a hand-made, probable cooking-pot of grass-tempered ware (Fabric C). Black-brown fabric and a black surface. Similar to No. 347 fifth century A.D.

No. 350 Hand-made cooking-pot, with a plain upright rim of grass-tempered ware (Fabric C). Black dense fabric with a black-brown surface. Probably a similar vessel to one from Keston (West Kent No. 464) (Ref. 187), where it is dated circa A.D. 500.

No. 351 Hand-made cooking-pot, with a plain upright rim of grass-tempered ware (Fabric C). Dense black fabric and surface. Similar to No. 350, circa A.D. 500.

CHAPTER IV

THE ARCHBISHOPS OF CANTERBURY'S PALACE AT OTFORD

SUMMARY

Large-scale rescue-excavation by the Kent Unit ahead of housing development located the east side of an 11th–12th century moat that had enclosed the manor-house of the Archbishop of Canterbury. A collapsed wooden revetment had been sealed when the moat was filled during the late-14th century and the site extended, probably by Archbishop Courtenay. A larger moat had then been dug to the east and enclosed major buildings, of which a domestic masonry building, about 17 m. long with a lateral garderobe turret, was found built over the filled early moat.

About 1514 Archbishop Warham began his grand palace, covering some 163 m. by 97 m. (about 1·30 hectares). This swept away the masonry building and many of the medieval buildings and also levelled the late-14th century moat. Only the Great Hall and Chapel were retained.

Warham's palace included a great four-sided block of buildings, framing courtyards, built across and beyond the medieval manor-house, which incorporated his principal buildings. Major east and south ranges were found, each about 11 m. wide and divided into large rooms. These joined at a massive stone corner-tower some 13 m. square and were flanked by broad, shallow moats, later filled. Elaborate drains and culverts carried storm-water and ground-water to flush a four-shafted garderobe in the South East Tower into a wide sewer.

Northwards a great Main Court, flanked by long galleries and large corner towers, contained the minor buildings. This court was entered through a monumental double-fronted gatehouse. The completed palace was one of the great buildings of the Realm, rivalling Hampton Court built on the orders of Warham's rival, Cardinal Wolsey! The palace passed to Henry VIII in 1537 who expended large sums on it, but subsequent surveys showed increasing decay and the palace was in a ruinous state by the 17th century.

CONTENTS

A. INTRODUCTION

This site (N.G.R. TQ. 5282–5916) lies in the parish of Otford, Kent close to the village centre and only about 100–200 m. south of the parish church. The original village, greatly expanded in the 20th century, lay on gently rising ground above the east bank of the River Darent at the south end of the valley cut by the river through the North Downs. More specifically it sits astride the Pilgrims' Way, an ancient track of uncertain origin, where this crosses the valley floor. Until 1974, Otford came under the Sevenoaks Rural District Council, but it now forms part of the much larger Sevenoaks District Council.

The total palace site (Fig. 47) appears to cover an area of just over one hectare (nearly 3 acres) and occupies both open ground and private gardens. Almost half of the north gallery of the Main Courtyard survives to a substantial extent, including the North West Tower (Plate XVIII) to a height of about 11·50 m. and most of the North West Gallery to a height of at least 3·00 m. Substantial masonry also projects from the side of a culverted stream within the back-gardens of Nos. 5–11 Bubblestone Road whilst the corresponding front-gardens all contain upstanding masonry to a maximum height of about 3·00 m. The site lies on dense Gault Clay, with a shallow water-table and at an elevation of about 65 m. O.D.

(1). The Threat to the Site

Although the various upstanding walls had long been known, no large-scale archaeological excavation had ever been carried out. The northern part of the area had long been scheduled as an Ancient Monument and in 1951–4, Mr. F. Pateman carried out Sunday morning excavations on 'Becket's Well', a stone-lined reservoir, some 250 m. to the east. A trench dug by members of the Otford Group in the back-garden of No. 5 Bubblestone Road in 1969, revealed a short length of sewer containing six lead Papal seals.

By 1973 planning permission had been given for four detached houses on lightly wooded waste-ground on the north side of Bubblestone Road immediately to the east of No. 11. From what could be seen of the masonry which projected through the soil and from a casual drawn survey made some years earlier, it was clear that this was the site of the south-east corner of the Tudor Palace.

The local Otford Archaeological Group did limited rescue excavation here at weekends in February and early March, 1974, finishing on 10th March. The builder, Foven Construction Ltd., started on 11th March and began uprooting trees and prepared to level the site. Unfortunately, the trial-digging was not notified to the full-time Kent Archaeological Rescue Unit or the Council for Kentish Archaeology, both organisations with excellent records of rescue and preservation. However, a private individual, concerned at the pending destruction of this important site, contacted the Kent Unit and the C.K.A and thus the site was then fully excavated and eventually saved from almost total destruction.

An immediate visit by the writer (11th March) revealed the outstanding potential of the area and that the contractor's plant was removing trees across small sections of exposed masonry. An immediate appeal brought a 24-hour stay and the Ancient Monuments Inspectorate, Dept. of the Environment, was immediately notified and asked to consider site-purchase. Dr. C. Young of the D.O.E. reached the site the following day and discussed the situation with the builder and the Otford Historical Society, though no member of the Unit was then present. By the end of the week the D.O.E. decided that a proper excavation of the threatened area was needed so that the situation could be fully assessed. The Department specifically requested the Unit to undertake the work, an offer that was eventually accepted. A second site-meeting was held when the situation was explained to the builder and terms agreed.

The excavation began on 26th March, 1974, the agreed date, by which time the builder had already laid the foundations of the first house immediately to the east. It was agreed that the work would be limited to five weeks, to be completed by 30th April. A decision was promised on the purchase and if none was taken by that date then building work would continue across the whole site (Refs. 188 and 189).

(2). Aims and Methods

With the threat of total destruction it was essential to recover the maximum information possible in the available time. The first task was to move tools and equipment to the site from the Unit's bases at Dover and in West Kent. The next was to call up all available members of the Unit, both full-time and part-time and then to invite the member-groups of the C.K.A. to join in. The local Otford Group was formally invited to join the operation, under normal conditions and it was most pleasant that two members of the Group, John Pyke and David Gayfer, willingly accepted this invitation. Apart from a bucket of pottery no other finds from the initial work were ever handed over though it is clear that other objects were recovered (Ref. 190).

The work lasted for 36 days, with some staff sleeping on site. The tree-stumps, topsoil and disturbed deposits were removed over the whole site by mechanical means and under tight supervision. It was also possible to machine-cut narrow trenches across the deep water-filled sections of silted ditches that underlay much of the site. This initial work was continued by extensive hand-excavation of stratified deposits and this was substantially completed in five weeks (Plate XIX). The detailed recording of the excavation, was carried out simultaneously with the digging and often required the pumping out of flooded areas (Plate XX).

Equally important was preservation. The Unit invited local members of both the House of Lords and the House of Commons, district and county councillors and also leading members of the Ancient Monuments Inspectorate, to the site. A special 'Open Day' (28th April) for the public, on what was a compact and difficult site, attracted 2,464 visitors. These were given enthusiastic lectures and encouraged to write their thoughts to their appointed representatives. Their reaction was otherwise entirely spontaneous and the necessary letters duly arrived. On 30th April local officers agreed in principle that the site should be purchased, just as the deadline was reached. The full Sevenoaks District Council met on 7th May and unanimously agreed the purchase. Subsequently, a large part of the site was purchased (for about £35,000) from the builder, with half the cost being met by the Department of Environment (Ref. 191). It was then possible to continue with some additional recording and to open to local schools for four days. A final public open-day was held on 19th May; the masonry covered and backfilled on 20–21st May, the area raked level on 21st May and seeded on 23rd May 1974.

The excavation archive for this five-week excavation consists of 19 plans and sections, 127 recorded contexts, 138 photographs, 36 boxes of finds and the site-notebook. Of this archive seven of the eight large-scale sections, six of the minor sections, three small-scale plans, three large-scale plans and 23 photographs are published here. The pottery has been sorted into 14 groups, reflecting the known periods and phases, and also classified into broad fabric-types. Most of the significant vessels are illustrated as these also form the main dating evidence and include important groups. Apart from the egg-shells and fragments of some 40 shoes, the latter mostly illustrated here, little environmental or organic material was recovered.

The post-excavation archive contains a summary of the pottery by context and group and the correlation of sections and plans. The archive is on short-term storage in the Kent Unit's security-controlled headquarters at Dover Castle where it may be consulted on request. Its final destination should be Maidstone Museum, with copies placed in the National Monuments Record.

(3). Acknowledgements

With a major project such as the Otford Palace excavation, thanks are due to many people and organisations who all helped in a variety of ways to bring the operation to such a highly successful conclusion. Thanks must firstly be given to the people who carried out the work. In all 98 full-time, part-time and volunteer archaeologists took part in this intensive excavation, the majority coming from the Kent Archaeological Rescue Unit and the West Kent Archaeological Group. However, under the umbrella scheme of the C.K.A., another eight local groups joined in the operation at different times. These were the Dover, Darent Valley Archaeological Training School, Otford, Reculver, Springhead, Sittingbourne, Thameside and Upchurch groups, all of whom are gratefully thanked here.

Of the various supervisors Edna Philp, Trevor Dennis, Derek Garrod and Andrew Norris, all deserve a special word of thanks. Of the diggers, it is not possible to name them all, but 17 deserve a special word of thanks for their extended efforts on this complicated site. These include Misses J. Dunmore and A. Borthwick, Mrs. P. Crozier and J. Newbery and Messrs. T. Allen, P. Ayres, D. Bolton, T. Emms, R. Dowling, P. Grant, N. Lake, B. Langridge, L. Murrell, R. Mummery, K. Nicol, E. Taylor and E. Tullett.

The tolerance of the directors of Foven Construction Ltd., must be acknowledged as must the financial support of the D.O.E., at whose specific request the work was undertaken. As regards the campaign to preserve the site from destruction, although organised from the site, several people deserve special mention for their work behind the scenes. In particular to Major-Gen. Viscount Monckton of Brenchley, Sir J. Winnifrith, Sir J. Rodgers (Member of Sevenoaks) and the late Lt. Col. Arnott Johnson (Chairman, C.K.A.), all of whom raised the matter with the Environment Minister. The Sevenoaks District Council must be fully acknowledged and congratulated for its support and agreement to buy the site. Here the vision of Miss Parrett and Mr. D.A. Clarke (Chief Executive Officer) were of particular importance. The help of Mr. Dennif and Mr. Walton, for the K.C.C., is also gratefully acknowledged. So, too, is the active support of the officers of the Council for Kentish Archaeology throughout the project and also to several members of the Otford Historical Society and local residents who encouraged the preservation aspect of the scheme. Thanks are also due to Mr. and Mrs. A.D. McDowell, for allowing access to their land.

Of specialist help Miss Deborah Kahn has reported on the Romanesque Capital; Mr. Derek Garrod on the post-medieval pottery; Mr. Peter Keller on the medieval pottery; Mr. Keith Parfitt on the small-finds and building materials; Mr. John Thornton on the leather and Mr. John Willson on the Roman pottery. Mr. Ralph Mills and Mr. Jonathan Joy have drawn all the small-finds, pottery and leather. Mr. Michael Dutto and Mr. Trevor Woodman have drawn the excellent sections and plans from the original site-drawings. The writer wishes to express his thanks to everyone concerned for their splendid support.

B. RECORDS RELATING TO THE SITE

By Christine Rosa

The earliest manor-house on the site may have been built by Archbishop Lanfranc (1070–89), though direct evidence is lacking. Certainly the manor of Otford is listed in the Domesday Survey (1086) as being held by the Archbishop of Canterbury and then being valued at £60 (Ref. 192) and thus one of the larger in the county. Local authors, however, believe in the existence of an earlier, undocumented Saxon hall at Otford and suggest that Lanfranc repaired and possibly extended the existing buildings to his own requirements (Ref. 193). Little else is known about the manor during the eleventh and twelfth centuries other than it continued to be held by the Archbishops of Canterbury. Thomas Becket's name was given to a well in the grounds which excavations in 1951–4 showed to be of 14th century date although an earlier flint structure discovered below could date back to Becket's time (Ref. 194). A trench dug in 1969 revealed six lead Papal *bullae,* one of Pope Lucius III (1181–5) and five of Urban III (1185–7) (Ref. 195).

Archbishop Boniface (1241–70) made additions to the manor and during the reign of Henry III he built a new hall. Henry's reign however, was a period of considerable unrest and civil war broke out causing damage to episcopal properties in Kent. Otford took its share as the accounts of Robert Kilwardby (1272–8), the ultimate successor to Boniface, seem to show. Repairs were found necessary to the hall, the Lord's chamber, the stables, the granary, the oxhouse and the sheepfolds. Altogether a sum of £7.6s.8$\frac{3}{4}$d. was spent (Ref. 196). Further repairs still were undertaken in 1288–9, this time by Archbishop Pecham (1279–92). The same set of accounts also notes the building of a new house with a turret (Ref. 197).

The early and mid-fourteenth century continued to see minor repairs and some rebuilding and in 1348, the see of Canterbury being vacant, Edward III spent his Christmas at Otford, passing the time with numerous banquets, plays and dances. Then, in 1381 disaster seems to have struck Otford again. This time it may have been due to the Peasants' Revolt. Otford was almost certainly attacked and evidence of this is found in the accounts for 1382–3, prepared for Archbishop William Courtenay. An interesting item noted is payment for 30s. 11$\frac{1}{2}$d. for smithing and ironworking caused by carriage of materials for repair-work. A total of £13.17s.0d. was spent in renewing and repairing roofs, buildings, gates, fences, tables, desks and chairs. Courtenay also left his own addition to the manor, by building a magnificent new hall to replace the 13th century structure erected by Boniface (Ref. 198).

By the end of the fifteenth century the Manor probably had an entrance on all four sides. In 1410–11 a new bridge was built on the south side (Ref. 199). In 1431–2 an east gate is mentioned (Ref. 200) and in 1439–40 a new entry to the west of the Lord's chamber (Ref. 201), but the start of the 16th century was to bring about a devasting change to the manor of Otford and very few of the medieval structures were to survive.

In 1514 Archbishop Warham completely redesigned Otford, demolishing most of the existing buildings and putting in their place a magnificent Tudor Palace. His building accounts for this period unfortunately have not survived, but one of his letters to Erasmus shows that only the walls of a hall (Courtenay's) and a chapel, survived of the original structure (Ref. 202) and Lambard, 50 years later, believed that Warham spent £33,000 on the palace.

Fittingly, the new palace was used for entertaining important guests. In 1518 Cardinal Campeggio remained for two days at the palace, in 1519 Henry VIII stayed there, whilst in 1520 both the King and his wife, Catherine of Aragon, visited before crossing to France. Princess Mary spent the Autumn of 1532 and the summer of 1533 in residence at Otford and Knole and wrote several letters from Otford in 1533 (Ref. 203).

After Warham's death the palace passed to Thomas Cranmer (appointed Archbishop 1533), but in 1537 the latter was obliged to surrender Otford and other property to King Henry VIII. He did so reluctantly and suggested that it was "too small a house for his majestie". The King is reported to have replied "Marye; I had rather have it than this house (meaning Otford), for it standith of a better soile. This house standith lowe, and is rewmatike, like unto Croydon, where I colde never be withoute sykenes. And as for Knoll (it) standeth on a sounde, perfaite, holesome grounde. And if I should make major abode here, as I do suerlie mynde to do nowe and than, I myself will bye at Knolle, and most of my house(hold) shall by at Otteforde". Henry soon ordered a complete survey of the Palace. This Survey gives an indication of its size and splendour (Ref. 204). Entry was through the twin-towered gatehouse of fifteen rooms. This gave access to a large inner courtyard enclosed to the west and east by galleries and to the south by the main buildings containing a total of 71 rooms which included the great Halls, staterooms, the chapel, towers and domestic quarters. Formal pleasure gardens were set out on the western side and to the east were the kitchen gardens. The palace stood in its own parkland which included ponds and a deer park.

In 1542 Sir Richard Long was appointed keeper of the mansions and gardens of Otford and Knole (Ref. 205). Between 1541 and 1546 he received from the Treasurer of the Augmentations over £2,000 for building-work and repairs at Otford and Knole, of which over half must have been spent at Otford. In 1541 a sum of £152 was paid direct to the King's Chief Carpenter, John Russell, who was in charge of work at that date. It is thus clear that the King paid out very considerable sums of money for work at Otford, but after his death the palace soon decayed. In a survey of 1548, for Edward VI, it was discovered that the great hall, presence chamber and many other rooms were in decay due to defective lead on the roofs. These repairs were estimated at about £106 (Ref. 206).

During the short reign of the young King Edward, the manor was taken by Dudley, Earl of Warwick, who installed his son-in-law, Sir Henry Sidney, as steward (1551) but it is unlikely that any repairs were undertaken and in 1552 the property was returned to the King.

A survey of 1573, by virtue of a Royal Commission to three local gentlemen (George Milton, William Lambarde and Thomas Wotton), Lewis Stockett, the Queen's Surveyor of Works and Thomas Fludd, the surveyor of the Royal estates in Kent, showed that the estimated cost of repairs had risen to £1629.9s.10d! This survey provides important details as to the layout of the palace and even lists a school-house butting onto the Great Chamber (Ref. 207).

In 1576 repairs to gutters and roofs actually cost £14.5s.4d. and some 20 years later the whole building was found to be in great decay. Even so Sir Henry Sidney had been prepared to finance the repairs at his own cost, in return for ownership of the park and manor, but this was steadfastly refused by Queen Elizabeth. In 1594 Henry's son, Robert Sidney, made another offer for the house and this was again refused. Finally, in 1601, Robert Sidney was granted the house and park (the Lordship remaining with the Crown until the 19th century). Within a few years Sidney was financially insolvent and the palace was left to decay and be robbed of stone and timber. This process continued throughout the centuries until now very little remains to remind us of the once magnificent palace.

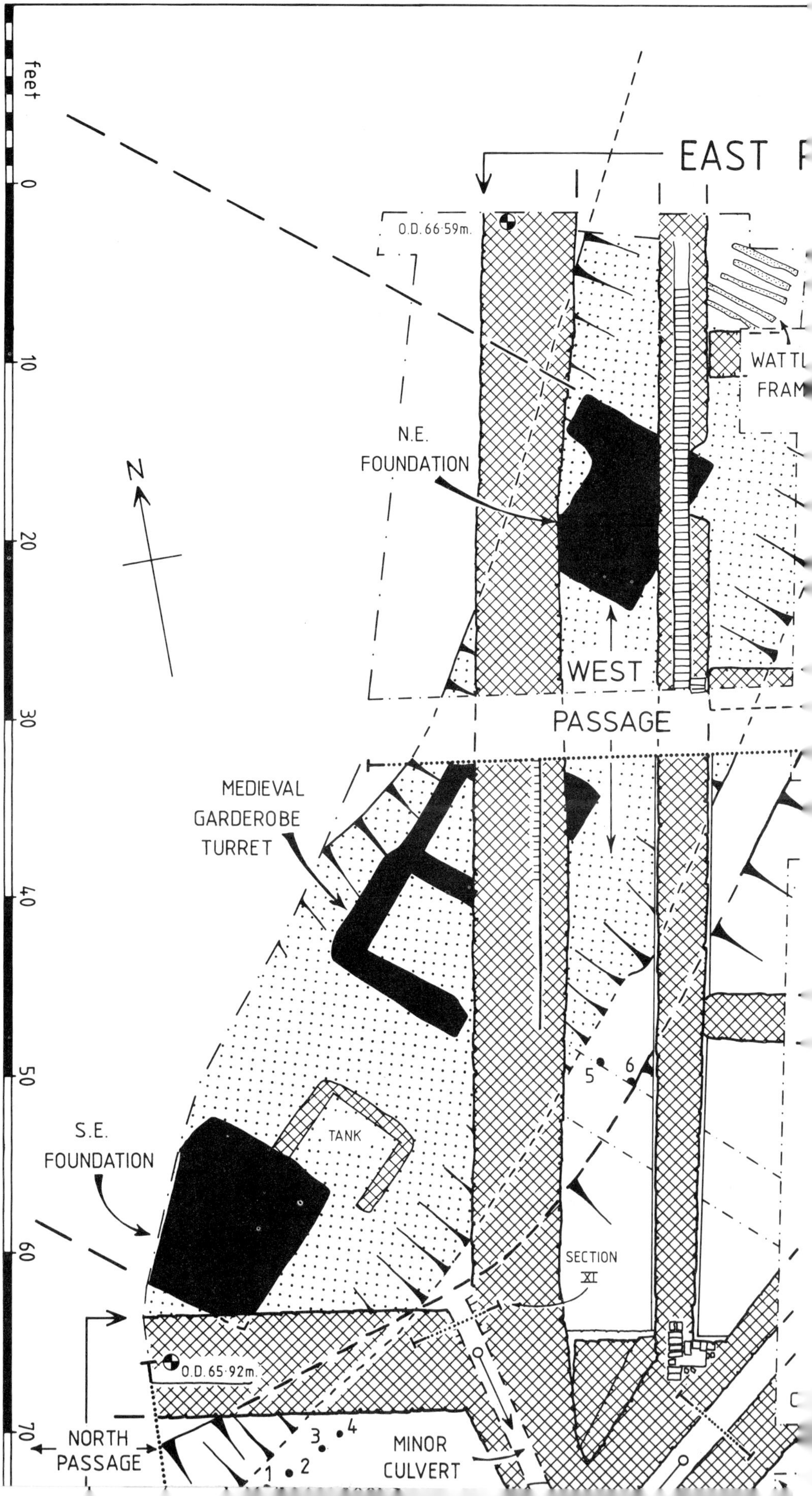

feet
0
10
20
30
40
50
60
70
EAST
O.D. 66·59m.
N.E.
FOUNDATION
N
WEST
PASSAGE
MEDIEVAL
GARDEROBE
TURRET
S.E.
FOUNDATION
TANK
5
6
SECTION
XI
O.D. 65·92m.
NORTH
PASSAGE
1
2
3
4
MINOR
CULVERT

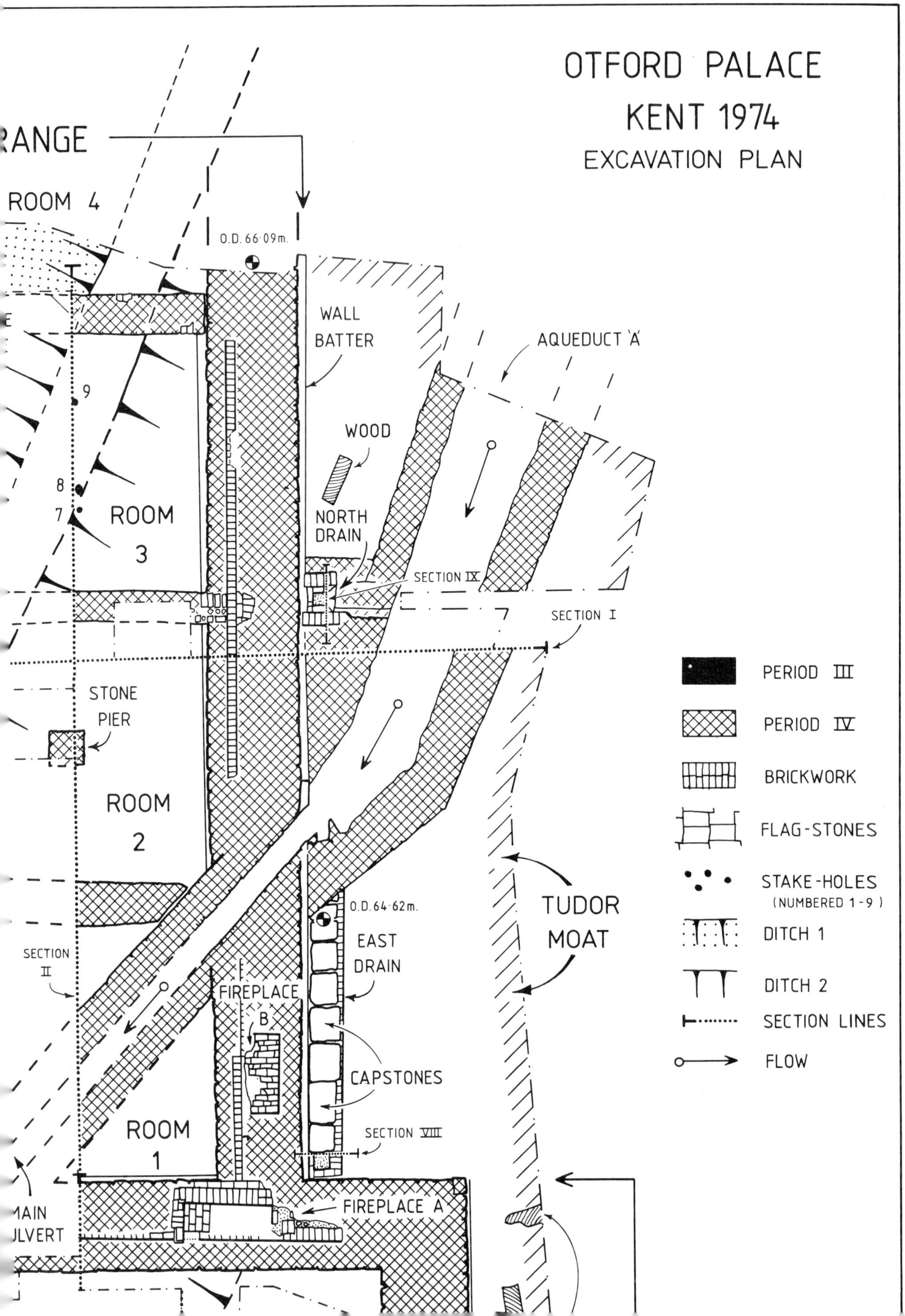

OTFORD PALACE
KENT 1974
EXCAVATION PLAN
RANGE
ROOM 4
O.D. 66·09m.
WALL
BATTER
AQUEDUCT 'A'
WOOD
NORTH
DRAIN
ROOM
3
SECTION IX
SECTION I
STONE
PIER
ROOM
2
O.D. 64·62m.
EAST
DRAIN
TUDOR
MOAT
SECTION
II
FIREPLACE
B
CAPSTONES
ROOM
1
SECTION VIII
FIREPLACE A
MAIN
CULVERT
PERIOD III
PERIOD IV
BRICKWORK
FLAG-STONES
STAKE-HOLES
(NUMBERED 1-9)
DITCH 1
DITCH 2
SECTION LINES
FLOW

C. THE EXCAVATED STRUCTURES (Fig. 48)

The main structural features across the site were the South and East Ranges and the South East Corner-tower of the Tudor Palace. There were, however, other major and minor features, both earlier and later in date than the palace and thus the structures from the whole site are described in chronological order. Four periods have been identified:–

PERIOD I – Romano-British (building materials and finds only).
PERIOD II – 12–13th century manor-house (Moat, wooden revetment and pottery).
PERIOD III – 14th century manor-house (Moat, stake-holes, masonry building and finds).
PERIOD IV – The Tudor Palace (structures and finds).

PERIOD I – Romano-British

No trace of a Romano-British structure was found on this site, but fragments of Roman tile, *opus signinum,* pottery and a single bronze brooch were recovered from various deposits, mostly medieval and post-medieval.

The underlying soil on the site, seldom seen and always beneath water-level, was a hard grey-white clay (Gault Clay). Over most of the excavated area this had been cut into by the medieval moats (Ditches 1 and 2) and the Tudor moat. At the extreme north-west corner of the site, however, it was capped by a deep layer of a cream coloured granular material, very similar to crushed tufa. It seems likely that this was natural tufa forming in this low-lying area beneath the Downs, though not yet set into a compact bed. This material was in turn capped by layers of fine brown loam. Here three deposits produced twelve small sherds, representing a minimum of four vessels of which three were Romano-British and the fourth probably medieval.

The earliest ditch located on this site, that identified as marking the south-east side of the Norman manor-house (see below), contained about 20 fragments of Roman tile, including tegulae, imbreces and combed flue-tile. Another 34 fragments of tile, some 36 potsherds and two fragments of *opus signinum,* also of Roman date, were recovered from various parts of the site in medieval or later contexts.

The absence of stratified Roman deposits on this particular site, taken with the presence of some 90 objects of Roman date, strongly suggests that a corresponding site existed nearby. Indeed it seems likely that the builders of both the manor-house and the later palace were taking materials from a nearby Roman building. There is in fact some evidence for such a Roman building about 250 m. north-east of this site. Here in 1934 Mr. F. Godwin carried out some trial-trenching and noted many broken Roman tiles, mortar and rubble but no walls surviving (Ref. 208). In the absence of proper recording, or of vertical soil sections or of detailed plans it is difficult to be certain as to what he actually found. It is likely, however, that he was near or within a badly robbed Roman building and that he was unable to distinguish robber-trenches or foundations.

PERIOD II – The 12th and 13th Century Manor-House

(a). THE EARLY MOAT (Ditch 1 on all plans).

The earliest archaeological feature located on this site was a ditch running diagonally across the north-west corner of this site on a north-east by south-west axis. This was traced for 24 m., but it clearly continued in both directions. Its outer, east lip was seen in four places and its inner west lip in three places. It was 5·75 m. wide and had sloping sides and a largely flat base (Fig. 50, Section I).

It had a minimum depth of 70 cm. and its primary fill consisted of a dense brown mud-silt some 35 to 50 cm. thick, that contained fragments of small branches and pottery.

This primary mud-silt was examined in 13 places, but seldom to any large extent owing to the large areas of overlying masonry. However, some 106 potsherds were recovered and these represent a minimum of 15 vessels of which ten are illustrated (Nos. 352 to 361). These include shell-loaded cooking-pots, probably dated 1250–1350 and at least two decorated jugs, probably dated 1300–1350.

The primary mud-silt in the ditch was everywhere sealed by deep deposits of grey-white clay and loam and it is clear the the ditch was deliberately filled in one operation. This material also extended beyond the outer lip of the ditch on the northern part of the site (Fig. 51, Section II) and provides evidence of a large-scale site-levelling operation. The amount of soil involved was considerable and it had the effect of raising the level of the general area by almost one metre.

The dumped material was examined in 19 places and this work produced 123 medieval potsherds from a minimum of 16 vessels, of which three are illustrated (Nos. 362 to 364). Apart from several Romano-British sherds all the pottery seems to date from the second half of the 13th and the first half of the 14th centuries. It includes fragments of eight jugs and seven cooking-pots, six of the latter being shell-loaded. Two of the jugs, which probably date from the middle of the 14th century, appear to be the latest dateable objects from the dumped soils. This demonstrates that the levelling took place no earlier than about the middle of the 14th century.

It seems highly probable that this large operation took place at the same time as the excavation of Ditch 2 (see below). This new ditch was dug immediately east of Ditch 1 with its centre-line very roughly 8 m. beyond the centre-line of Ditch 1, but only one metre separating it from the outer lip of that ditch. Indeed it is likely that much of the clay used to fill Ditch 1 and to level up the surrounding area was obtained when Ditch 2 was dug.

It seems likely that this original ditch here (Ditch 1) represents the wet moat enclosing an early manor-house. In plan it appears to curve marginally to the south-west, thereby suggesting that it helped enclose an area to the north-west. That was anyway the focal point of the later sites and in the absence of corresponding early structures in the excavated area, there can be little doubt that any related structures stood to the west, or north-west. The ditch appears to have silted to a depth of about 50 cm. and was probably still open during the 13th and first half of the 14th centuries, if the domestic pottery discarded in the silt is a representative guide. This early ditch was clearly abandoned no earlier than the mid-14th century, presumably when the area of the manor-house was extended and rebuilding took place. This rebuilding took place no later than the late-14th century for about then a substantial masonry structure (see below) had been built across the filled-in ditch. The North-east Foundation of this structure contained a fine early-12th century stone capital (No. 446). Clearly this had been taken from an earlier building and incorporated as rubble in an inverted position in the foundation (Plate XXV). The probability is that it came from one of the principal buildings forming part of the Norman manor-house, though other less likely possibilities must be considered.

Of additional interest was a deposit of late-11th or early-12th century domestic rubbish that came from the extreme west edge of the site, partly beneath both the 14th century masonry and the South Range of the Tudor Palace. The pottery from here had been disturbed by the earlier excavation and technically must be treated as unstratified. Fortunately, part of the same deposit was recorded in the foundation-trenches of an extension to the adjacent No. 11 Bubblestone Road by John Pyke in 1978, working in co-operation with the Kent Unit. He has kindly supplied details to show that the pottery from this deposit, mostly from a depth of about 70–90 cm., includes shell-loaded cooking-pots of 12th century date. This largely confirms the dating recovered during the official excavation in 1974 and suggests that domestic rubbish was being dumped here during the 12th century, probably away from principal buildings, though perhaps in the general vicinity of the kitchen.

(b). THE WOODEN REVETMENT (Fig. 49).

Lying on the primary mud-silt at the bottom of Ditch 1, were the remains of a small timber frame (Plate XXI). This consisted of at least five square-sectioned posts (Table A), evenly spaced out and joined by thin wattles interwoven between them. The whole structure was found lying almost horizontal, but it was clear that it had once stood vertically near the junction of the west side of the ditch with the bottom. This precise position was covered by the wall of the Tudor passage on the west side of the East Range and thus it was not possible to locate *in situ* any posts, or even broken post-stumps.

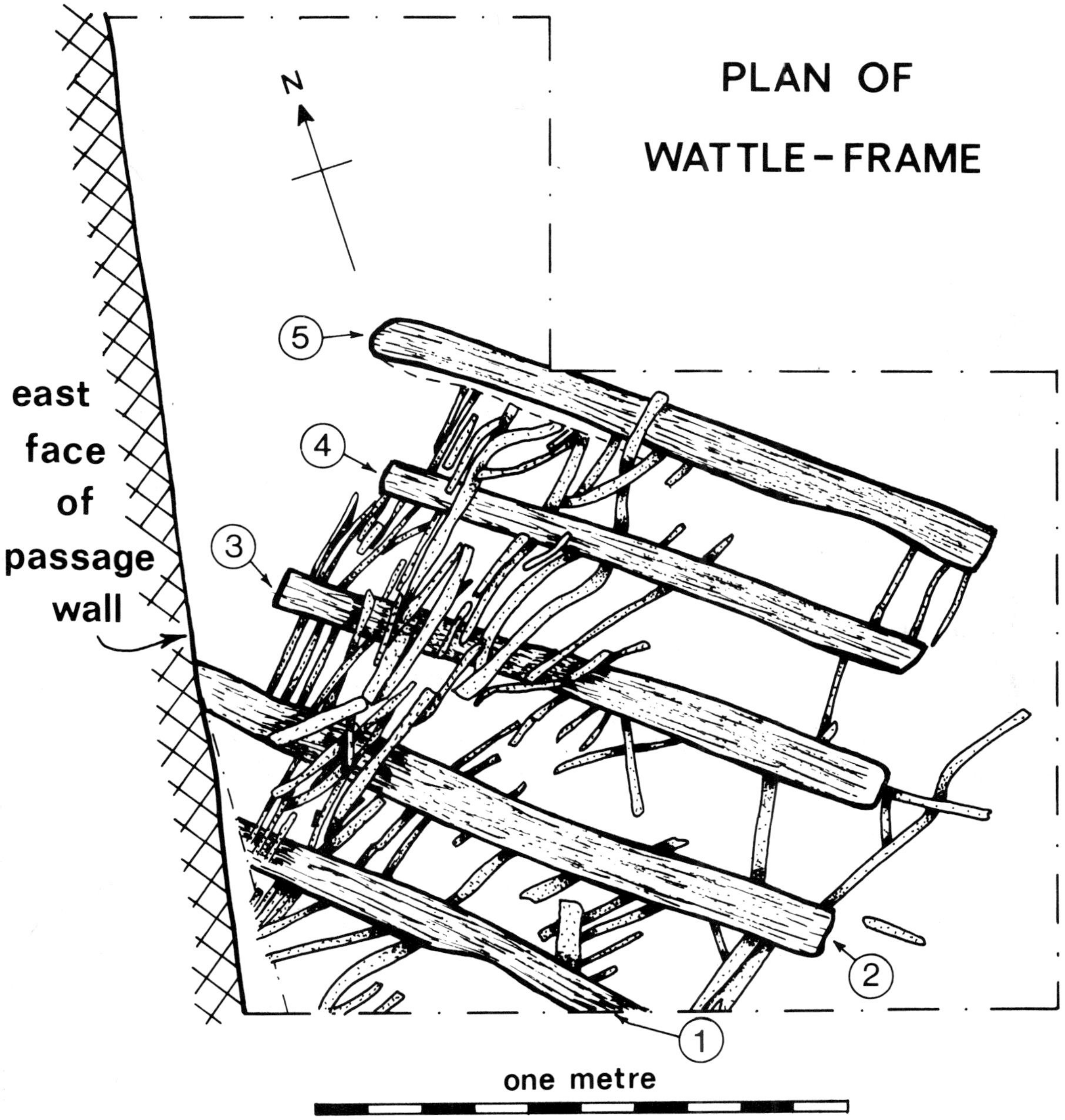

Fig. 49. *Plan of collapsed wooden wattle revetment found in the bottom of the Early Moat (Ditch 1), Otford Palace.*

The posts were between 0·82–1·30 m. in length, but these are minimum lengths and none was probably smaller than 1·06 m. in total length. They were all 7–9 cm. wide and 3–5 cm. in depth with the broad surfaces facing outwards. The wattles were circular and mostly 1–2 cm. in diameter. All the wood was soft and partly rotted due to its having been below water-level for at least 600 years. None was lifted and it remains exactly as found, where it will continue to be preserved by the ground-water.

It seems clear that this vertical framework had supported a section of the west bank of the first ditch. The space between it and the lip of the bank had been packed in part, at least, with rubble, as this was found lying on the collapsed wood. It may have served as a small jetty, or landing-stage, or simply to revet a short section of bank. More than this cannot now be said.

	Length	Width	Depth
Post 1	82 cm. (min.)	8 cm.	3 cm.
Post 2	130 cm. (min.)	9 cm.	4 cm.
Post 3	120 cm.	9 cm.	5 cm.
Post 4	106 cm.	7 cm.	4 cm.
Post 5	121 cm.	9 cm.	5 cm.

Table A – Posts of Wooden Revetment

PERIOD III – The 14th Century Manor-House

(a). THE 14TH CENTURY MOAT (Ditch 2 on all plans).

The excavation showed that the Early Moat (Ditch 1) on this site was clearly filled, levelled and replaced by a much larger moat (Ditch 2), dug immediately to the east. Its inner lip lay just one metre beyond the outer lip of the earlier moat and roughly parallel to it. Presumably both ditches were dug broadly concentrically to a common point.

The new ditch was traced for 28 m., running roughly north-east by south-west across the centre of the site. The west lip was seen in five places and the east lip in one place only, the latter within the area of the great Corner-tower of the Tudor Palace. Its width was 9·50 m. and its sides sloped evenly at about 40° to create a flat bottom about 5·50 m. wide. Its depth was 1·60 m. (Figs. 50 and 51, Sections I and II).

Its filling consisted mostly of mixed loams and clays, mainly tipped in from the north-west side. These contained large numbers of broken medieval roof-tiles (No. 449) and pottery. In some 14 deposits examined a total of 214 potsherds, represented a minimum of 47 vessels, of which 13 are illustrated (Nos. 369 to 381). The bulk of this pottery dates from the 13th to 15th centuries, but three of the sherds are from stoneware mugs of early-16th century date. It seems clear from all this that the ditch was deliberately filled at one attempt, with large quantities of derived soil containing earlier domestic rubbish being thrown in at the same time. Indeed the quantity of roof-tile fragments strongly suggests that an adjacent building was then being demolished. The general absence of mortar in the ditch-fill may indicate that such a building may have been largely timber-framed, or else that any masonry was carefully removed for incorporation in other structures.

In all probability the deliberate ditch-filling and the presumed demolition of an adjacent building formed part of a single operation which, judging by the circumstantial evidence and the stoneware sherds, almost certainly formed part of the massive Tudor redevelopment that spread across the whole area at the beginning of the 16th century.

(b). THE STAKE HOLES

Nine small stakes, or stake-holes, were found at different points just above or below the inner west lip of the 14th century ditch. The four at the south end (SH 1–4) formed a straight line and were spaced at intervals of 44, 68 and 39 cm., respectively. The others (SH 5–9) were variously aligned, but it is likely from their broad similarity that all nine stake-holes related to a single scheme (see Table B). In general these were circular, mostly 8–9 cm. in diameter and, where examined, had been hammered some 40–50 cm. into the ground. It must be that several, if not many, more stake-holes had once existed along this edge, but if so, these were either destroyed by the later Tudor masonry or were under blocks of soil not excavated. Several of the stakes had been driven into the ground at about 15–20° from the vertical and these leaned outwards towards the centre of the ditch.

It seems likely that these stakes formed part of a continuous, or largely continuous, line of small posts set as a fence along the inner lip and side of the ditch. Their modest size does not suggest that they formed part of a defensive network, but more probably a barrier along the edge of the wet moat. This might serve to prevent domestic animals from straying into the moated area and also to keep out animals, both wild and domesticated, that were not wanted within the enclosure. To some extent this would also deter casual human intrusions.

Stake-holes	Section	Diameter	Depth	Angle
1	Circular	8 cm.	Not exc.	Vertical
2	Circular	17 cm.	Not exc.	80°
3	Circular	8 cm.	Not exc.	70°
4	Circular	8 cm.	Not exc.	Vertical
5	Square?	9 cm.	Not exc.	75°
6	Circular	9 cm.	67 cm.	75°
7	Circular	6 cm.	45 cm.	Vertical
8	Circular	17 cm.	50 cm.	75°
9	Circular	9 cm.	40 cm.	Vertical

Table B – Details of stake-holes on west side of 14th century Moat (Ditch 2)

(c). THE MASONRY BUILDING

Three large blocks of masonry, not physically connected, but clearly forming part of an integral structure were found close to the north-west corner of the site. These lay on a north-east by south-west line and are marked on the plan (Fig. 48) as South East Foundation, Medieval Garderobes and North East Foundation.

These three structures spanned a total length of 16·65 m. and all sat along and over the filled early ditch (Ditch 1). All were in turn cut through, in part at least, by the massive Tudor masonry, of the early-16th century. They also sat about 3 m. to the west of and largely parallel to the inner lip of the large 14th century ditch (Ditch 2) to which they must have related. Indeed the associated finds, particularly the pottery from the two garderobe shafts, makes it virtually certain that the masonry is of 14th century date. In detail the South East Foundation was 2·95 m. long, the space between it and the central garderobes was 3·20 m., the garderobes were 4·80m. in overall length, the space beyond was 2·90 m. and the North East Foundation was 2·80 m. in length. It seems probable, on this limited evidence, that the three structures represent the south-east length of a substantial domestic masonry building (see discussion p. 165).

South East Foundation

This was a massive rectangular block of ragstone rubble set in a hard pale yellow mortar. It was 2·95 m. by 2·50 m. and survived about 50 cm. high. It had no dressed faces and it must be that it represents a massive foundation for a largely, or partially, free-standing structure. The south corner of this structure had been enveloped by the South Range of the Tudor Palace and a small tank butted to its damaged north face.

North East Foundation (Plate XXIV)

A broadly similar and almost certainly corresponding structure was found to the north-east. This was also built of ragstone rubble set in a hard pale yellow mortar. It was 2·80 m. by 2·45 m. and survived three courses high to a height of about 50 cm. What survives must also represent a massive foundation. There were two extra points of interest. A small rectangular projection some 74 cm. long and about 60 cm. wide was found on the north-west side of this structure and clearly formed an integral part of it. There was just a hint that another similar projection had existed at its south-west corner, but this was masked by the large wall of the Tudor East Range. Careful examination of the north face of this foundation revealed that a fine early-12th century capital had been incorporated within it (Plate XXV, No. 446). This had been placed in an inverted position and it is certain that it represents re-used material. Slight traces of the mortar on its original internal surfaces were creamy-white, whilst that of the foundation was a pale yellow. The narrow internal wall of the passage of the Tudor East Range had been laid across this earlier masonry which was here considered as an adequate foundation.

The Garderobes (Turret) (Plates XXII and XXIII)

Roughly midway between the two massive masonry foundations was an E-shaped structure consisting of two rectangular chambers, both open on the south-east side. The walls were built of ragstone in yellow mortar, but they were of variable thickness. In general the south-west wall was about 58 cm. wide, the central wall was about 42 cm. wide and the north-east wall about 90 cm. wide. The long west wall was 40–60 cm. wide. The overall length of the structure was 4·80 m., the overall width about 2·70 m. and both chambers were about 1·45 m. in internal width. The walls survived to a height of about 70 cm. and both chambers had been cut through by the massive west wall of the East Range of the Tudor Palace (Fig. 50, Section I).

The internal faces of both chambers were roughly finished and it seems clear that both were intended to be open to a depth of about 1·00 m. below contemporary ground level. The north-east angle had been lined with squared ragstone blocks of which two survived (Plate XXIII). It seems certain that they represent the lower sections of a pair of garderobe shafts that probably served a two-storey structure, as at other medieval sites (see discussion) where they are described as garderobe turrets. Those at Otford were within 3·00 m. of the edge of the ditch (Ditch 2) and were thus at the extreme east end of the site, at a point that probably facilitated easy clearance.

The filling of the two chambers consisted of a mixture of grey clays and mortar-specks, several potsherds and two largely complete vessels. In all some 73 potsherds were recovered and these represent a minimum of seven vessels, of which four are illustrated (Nos. 365–368). These include small shell-loaded sherds and the two largely complete pots. The latter seem to be of late-14th or early-15th century date. In addition the filling also contained four partially complete avian eggs. Three of these were probably domestic fowl or small duck-eggs and the fourth, much larger, probably a goose-egg (see specialist report). These were probably lost or laid in the disused shafts at the end of the 14th century or at the beginning of the 15th century. It is tempting to imagine that geese and ducks living on the adjacent moat found the partially filled garderobe shafts, conveniently open towards the water, a highly satisfactory nesting-box.

The base of the chambers was covered by a thin band of stone-chippings, probably dropped during their construction. Clearly the whole structure had been superseded by the construction of the Tudor Palace in about 1515.

PERIOD IV – The Tudor Palace

It was clear from the outset that the major structures on this site were those relating to the great Tudor Palace, conceived and built by Archbishop Warham in about 1515. These superceded all the other structures and ditches found on the site. The various structural elements are dealt with below, beginning with the great Corner-tower and the two adjoining main ranges.

It is also clear that the first part of the building programme involved site-levelling and some demolition of existing structures. The 14th century moat (Ditch 2) was filled with large quantities of mixed soil containing broken roof-tiles and also domestic rubbish including pottery (see above).

In places the moat was filled and levelled with about 1·50 m. of soil. This elevated platform was then cut away, substantially in places, to allow for the constuction of the main walls of the new building. On completion of at least part of the masonry walls, mostly placed well forward from the trench faces, the voids left behind the new masonry were backfilled with soil, again often containing tile and pottery. Subsequently, some layers of soil were spread across the internal area to help provide a level surface. The finds from the infill of the foundation-trenches and from the levelling layers, all effectively part of the same operation, may be treated as a single group. In some 29 deposits were 325 sherds representing a minimum of 41 vessels, of which ten are illustrated, (Nos. 382 to 391). Of these the great majority seem to be medieval jugs, cooking-pots and bowls of the 13th to 15th centuries. However, fragments of three Tudor stoneware mugs were found in the foundation-trenches and clearly help date the construction work to the 16th century. Several other fine ware vessels from these deposits are also probably of early-16th century date. These deposits also produced fragments of roof-tiles (Nos. 447 and 448), floor-tiles (Nos. 454 and 455), a red-deer antler (No. 462) and a broken Roman brooch (No. 461).

(a). THE SOUTH EAST TOWER (Figs. 52 and 53, Sections III and IV)

The excavation revealed that the extreme south-east corner of the palace complex had been marked by a great square stone tower (Plate XXVI). This had been laid out with considerable precision for it was 12·70 m. on its north-south axis and 12·68 m. on its east-west axis. Its south, east and north walls, some 1·70 m., 1·68 m. and 1·72 m. respectively at ground-level, were all thus intended to be much the same thickness. However, the west wall had been increased to 2·53 m., no doubt to facilitate the inclusion of the four-shafted garderobe (see below). The Tower had been divided internally by a wall 78 cm. wide, to create largely equal north and south rooms. The north room was 8·47 m. by 4·23 m. internally and the south room 8·47 m. by 4·27 m. internally. The detailed north-south measurements across the tower were as follows:–

South wall foundation thickness	=	1·70
South room width	=	4·27
Internal wall foundation thickness	=	0·78
North room width	=	4·23
North wall foundation thickness	=	1·72
Total	=	12·70 m.

The walls were all built of ragstone rubble set in a hard cream-white mortar. The external facing consisted of finely cut squared blocks (Plate XXVII), mostly ragstone laid in even courses and very finely jointed. Nor were all the outer faces vertical. Those on the south and east sides were battered at about 85° (that is about 5° from the vertical) in effect to create a high, marginally battered plinth. No trace of floors survived and the only brickwork remaining *in situ* were small strips along the west and north sides. Here only a single brick course survived, but it shows that the brickwork on the west side was almost flush with the masonry, whilst on the north side the brickwork was about 60 cm. less in thickness than the underlying masonry. This seems to suggest that the masonry was in fact a high stone plinth, upon which sat a largely brickwork superstructure. This is the pattern of the surviving North West Tower, though not one employed externally along the South Range. It is very likely that this tower, with its massively thick walls, was at least two-storeys high, though third and fourth-storeys are also possible.

The only detail of interest was the base of a brick-lined fireplace (Fireplace A) slightly east of the centre of the north wall. The brickwork at the back of this was 42 cm. wide, at the front 16 cm. wide, whilst there were traces of sandstone side linings. The base, heavily burnt, was of bricks laid north-south across the width of the main wall. Even though the brickwork was severely damaged the fireplace length had been about 1·70 m. and its width about 52 cm. The overall thickness of the north wall would, therefore, have been about 1·10 m.

It seems probable that access to the north room was from the north-west corner at the junction of the passages from the two ranges. Access to the south room was probably from the north room through a doorway in the narrow dividing wall. The large external drain on the south side of this tower is described below.

(b). THE SOUTH RANGE (Fig. 54, Section V)

Whilst the great square tower dominated the south-east corner of the Tudor complex, the south side was occupied by a massive range. The outer wall of this has always been visible in part in the front gardens of Nos. 5–11 Bubblestone Road where it could be traced, with small gaps, for at least 60 m. Quite predictably the range extended into the area threatened by the development. Here a 7 m. length was uncovered and this represented the eastern end of the range where it joined the South East Tower. For the first time it was possible to excavate part of this structure and to record details. It was found to have been built right across the filled-in moat of the 14th century manor-house (Ditch 2) and even partly across the Early Moat (Ditch 1).

The range had an overall width of 10·28 m. and this was divided internally into rooms with a passage along their northern side. Only part of one room (Room 5) was found, but the extreme eastern end of the range was found to contain an elaborate garderobe structure (see below).

The following dimensions were recorded across the South Range:–

South Foundation thickness	=	1·93
Room 5 width	=	4·53
Internal Foundation width	=	0·90
North Passage width	=	1·24
North Foundation thickness	=	1·68
Total	=	10·28 m.

The masonry of the outer wall was substantially the same as the South East Tower with which they formed an integral part and there can be no doubt that they were part of a single grand scheme. The north wall of the South Range was virtually the same size as three of those of the South East Tower, but the external south wall was some 20 cm. wider.

As with the South East Tower the floors had been removed and some evidence of the brick

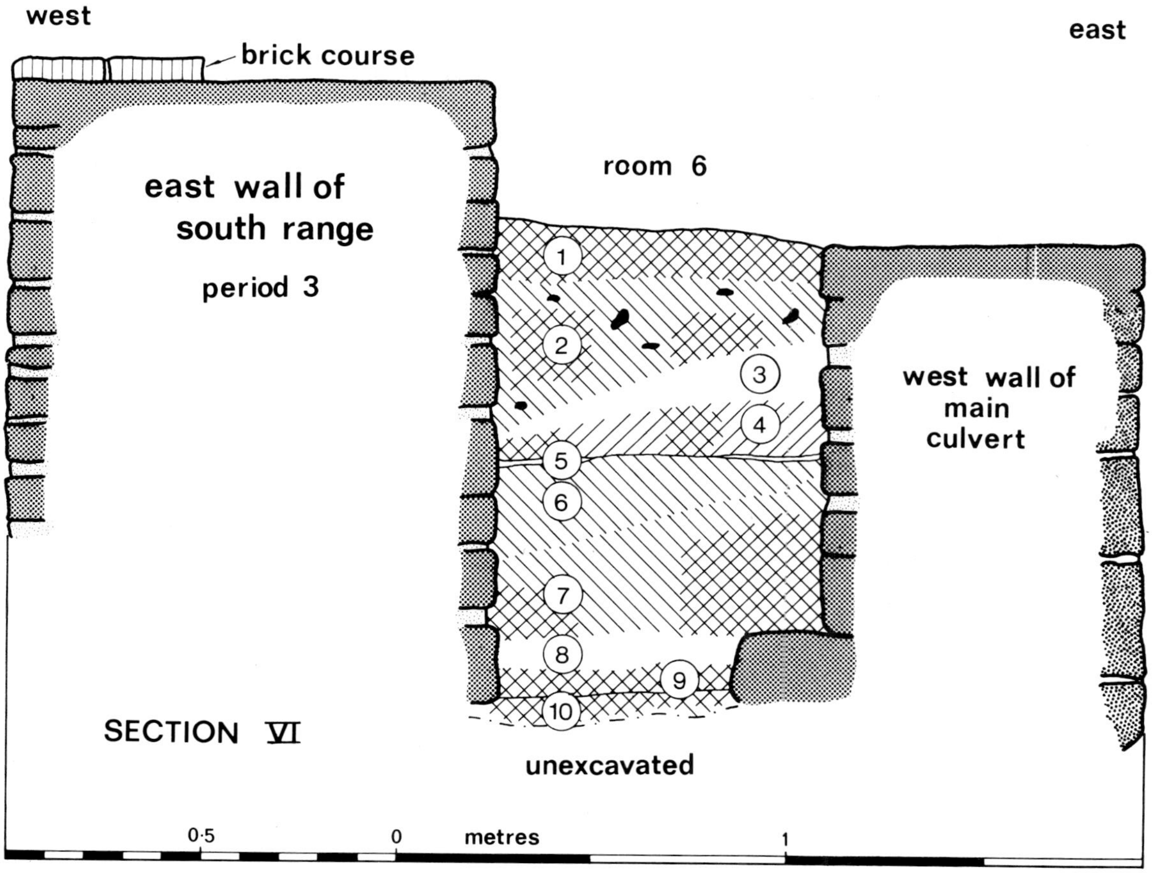

Fig. 55. *Section VI through Room 6, Otford Palace.*

superstructure had survived. This revealed a single course of brickwork on the inner face of the south wall set back about 50 cm. from the stone foundation. This suggests that the superstructure itself was no more than about 1·40 m. in width. The wall between Room 5 and the north passage consisted of two rows of red brick and thus had a total width of about 25 cm. The wall on the east side of Room 5 consisted of two lines of bricks, laid end to end which thus had a width of 50 cm.

What is less certain is the function of the small unit, Room 6 on the plan (Plate XXVIII), framed between Room 5 and the South East Tower and next to the garderobe area. This had substantial stone foundations on all four sides and clearly this was a deliberate part of the original plan. This created a small rectangular chamber, about 1·92 by 0·70 m. in plan, with the masonry foundations still surviving to a depth of 1·50 m. (Fig. 55, Section VI). The chamber had no openings at foundation level and it is clear from the soil deposits over the ragstone offset of the east wall that both walls were built free-standing. The construction mortar (L.9) was then sealed by dumps of grey clay and loam (L.7 and 8) which were in turn sealed by a line of yellow mortar droppings (L.6). This was sealed by successive dumps of soils, mortar and light rubble (L.1–5). Seventeen sherds of pottery from five vessels were recovered from the dumped soil and all appear to be of medieval date and thus derived from adjacent areas. To judge by the brick walls on the west and north sides it is likely that this constituted a small room. If similar brick walls had existed on the east and south sides then a small room about 2·50 by 1·70 m. could be indicated. Just possibly this could have extended over the water culverts and into the west wall of the South East Tower. Whatever the original size it was clearly a deliberate construction, undertaken for some very specific purpose. Its position, adjacent to the junction of the passages in the East and South Ranges must be significant and the most likely explanation is that it had supported a staircase to provide access from the passages to the upper floors.

(c). THE EAST RANGE (Figs. 50 and 51, Sections I and II)

It was clear from the start of the excavation that much of the threatened area was occupied by a substantial part of the East Range of the Tudor Palace (Plate XXIX). Detailed excavation showed that this had formed an integral part of the original Tudor Palace, having been constructed in one operation with the great South East Tower and the South Range. Indeed the South and East Ranges had been laid out at right-angles to each other. The entire section of the range that was excavated sat along the filled-in medieval ditches (Ditches 1 and 2).

The East Range was largely similar to the South Range, for it had a series of rooms flanked by a narrow passage, the latter on the inner (west) side of the range. The East Range was, however, about 1·20 m. wider than the South Range. The following dimensions were recorded across its width:–

West Foundation	=	1·65
West Passage	=	1·50
Internal Foundation	=	0·77
Room width	=	5·78
East Foundations	=	1·78
Total	=	11·48 m.

Three complete rooms and part of a fourth were revealed (Rooms 1–4 on the plan). The following measurements were recorded along their common north-south axis:–

Width Room 1	=	4·96
Internal Foundation	=	0·75
Width Room 2	=	4·97
Internal Foundation	=	0·60
Width Room 3	=	5·04
Internal Foundation	=	0·70
Width Room 4	=	2·00 min.
Total	=	19·02 m.

It seems clear that the rooms were intended to be of similar size, though it is just possible that a single long room was planned at the outset. The foundations of the dividing walls between the rooms all butted to the main walls and had clearly been added at some subsequent stage, most probably shortly after the main foundations were laid. Room 2 contained a small rectangular foundation close to the centre of the room. This was about 75 by 65 cm. and may have supported a central pier.

Room 1 had been provided with a wide fireplace (Fireplace B) within the thickness of its eastern wall. Only a single course of burnt red bricks survived and these suggested a fireplace of some 1·52 m. in length and about 67 cm. wide, set back well into the thickness of the wall. No trace of fireplaces was found in the other rooms. What must be significant is that the fireplace in Room 1 was very adjacent to the fireplace (Fireplace B) in the north room of the South East Tower, the two being less than two metres apart. It seems highly probable that the vertical flues above these fireplaces eventually joined within a largely common brick stack that projected from the roof at the junction of the tower and the East Range.

Traces of the bottom course of brickwork survived in places on most of the foundations.

Generally these consisted of a single line of red bricks laid with heads outwards, but offset inwards from the face of the masonry foundations. These demonstrated that the internal faces, at least, were brick-lined and that the actual finished room sizes were slightly larger than that suggested by the foundations. From this it is possible to suggest that the following dimensions were the intended sizes above ground:–

west-east

west wall	=	1·10
west passage	=	2·30
internal wall	=	0·25
Room 3	=	6·30
east wall	=	1·40
Total	=	11·35 m.

south-north

Room 1	=	5·20
internal wall	=	0·60
Room 2	=	5·00
internal wall	=	0·50
Room 3	=	5·00
internal wall	=	0·70
Room 4	=	2·00 (min.)
Total	=	19·00 m.

(d). SOUTH DRAIN (Figs. 53 and 56).

The great South East Tower was flanked on its outer south side by a substantial brick-built drain, capped with 17 large ragstone blocks. This served three rectangular outlets at the east, centre and west side of the south face of the tower (Plate XXX). These outlets probably mark the positions of vertical lead-pipes that had been fixed to the external face of the building and whose function was to carry stormwater from the adjacent roofs. No trace of any pipes survived, but it is highly likely that these would have been removed at an early stage in the demolition. The drain dropped westwards to the south-west corner of the tower where it turned through the sewer wall and fed into the sewer itself, no doubt to aid the flushing of the garderobe system.

In detail the drain had been built on a substantial base set in the moat against the face of the tower (Sections IV and VII). This was constructed of soft claystone packed behind five courses of blocks. The drain itself was lined with bricks and capped by stone. Internally the drain was mostly 20–24 cm. high and about 25 cm. wide. The east outlet was brick-built 50 cm. deep and 24 cm. square in plan. The centre outlet (Section VII) was brick-built 43cm. (min.) deep and 25 cm. square. The west outlet was brick-built, 75 cm. (min.) deep, only 25 by 18 cm. in plan and was positioned directly above the outlet into the sewer. The outfall opening was 25 cm. wide and 24 cm. high.

The capstones varied in size. The lengths were 58–88 cm., the widths 37–60 cm. and the depths 15–30 cm.

(e). EAST DRAIN (Plate XXXI and Fig. 57).

This was constructed in a similar manner to the South Drain. It had been added to the outside east wall of the East Range in the angle formed by the range and the short north wall of the Corner-tower. Its function was to serve a single rectangular outlet which must have marked the position of one, or more, vertical water-pipes that carried storm-water from the roof. The drain carried this water down at an angle into the moat at exactly the point where aqueduct 'A' entered the East Range and in this way helped flush the garderobe system. It was built on a base of claystone blocks, some 70 cm. wide which rose at an angle from the bed of the moat at the north end to a maximum height of 60 cm. at the south end.

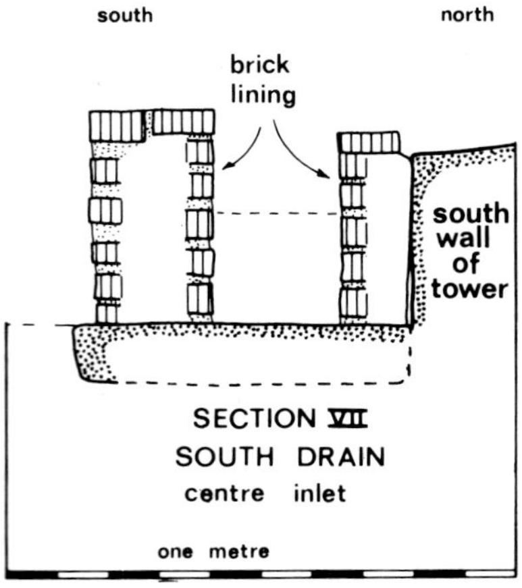

Fig. 56.

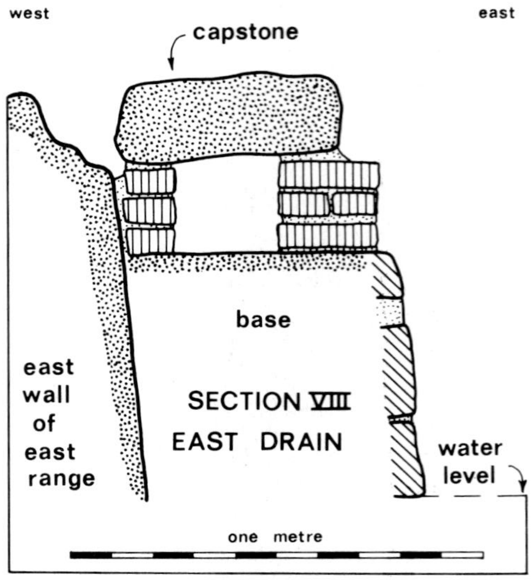

Fig. 57.

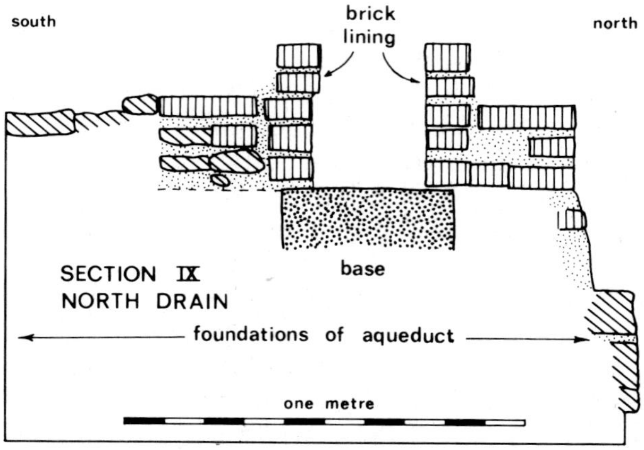

Fig. 58.

Figs. 56–58. *Sections VII–IX, Otford Palace.*

In detail the drain was 6·70 m. long and built of three courses of bricks capped by a line of nine large sandstone blocks (Section VIII). The internal width of the drain was 24–26 cm. and the internal height 23–24 cm. The brick outlet was 38 cm. high and 33 by 25 cm. in plan. The capstones were 52–88 cm. long, 25–63 cm. wide and 12–25 cm. high.

(f). NORTH DRAIN (Fig. 58, Section IX).

A single drain outlet, perhaps one of a series at regular intervals along the external faces of the main ranges, was found on the east face some 11 m. north of the Corner-tower. It must mark the position of a single downpipe which fed into the drain and then directly into the aqueduct. It was brick-lined on three sides and this lining survived five courses high. The drain was built on a large sandstone slab set on the side of the aqueduct. It was 44 cm. deep and 26 by 30 cm. in plan. The side walls were 38 cm. in width.

(g). THE TANK

Close to the internal angle formed by the walls of the South Range and the East Range was a small stone-lined tank built of claystone blocks (Plate XXXII). It had been built into the ground with one side touching the South East Foundation of the 14th century manor-house, though judging by the way the latter had been cut at this point it is likely that this was largely accidental. The tank was 1·38 by 1·30 m. in plan internally, its walls were 25–30 cm. thick and it survived to a height of only 50 cm.

Its filling consisted of light brown loam containing chalk-specks, mortar, tile (Nos. 450 and 451) and four sherds of pottery, from a minimum of two vessels. Two sherds appear to be medieval and two sherds are from small stoneware jugs of the first half of the 16th century. It seems probable that this small tank was constructed specifically within the corner of the courtyard that was flanked by the South and East Ranges. It may have served a variety of functions.

(h). THE GARDEROBE SYSTEM (Fig. 59).

A complex system of garderobe shafts and culverts and a massive sewer outlet were found at the east end of the South Range at a point where it joined the great South East Tower (Plate XXXIII). Here the shoots of four rectangular garderobe shafts were found within the thickened west wall of the tower, where they presumably serviced the upper floors. In detail these had brick bases, about 0·90–1·75 m. long by just 75 cm. wide that sloped away from the tower at an angle of about 35°. These were separated from each other by narrow walls just 25 cm. wide, built of finely dressed ragstone blocks (Plate XXXIV). These walls survived three courses high and extended in length from between 1·00–1·80 m. The whole area of the four shafts created a space within the west wall of the tower about 3·75 m. long and at least 2·00 m. wide.

The four shoots spilled westwards into a large rectangular area about 3·50 by 2·98 m. within the thickness of the masonry at the east end of the South Range. The main part of this area was occupied by a massive masonry pier some 3·05 by 1·45 m. in plan and surviving 58 cm. high. This was enclosed by brick-based channels on its west, north and east sides some 70, 61 and 83 cm. wide, respectively. The faces of the masonry on the west and north sides was neatly dressed and it is clear that the channels were designed to take water. Indeed they were flooded throughout the excavation.

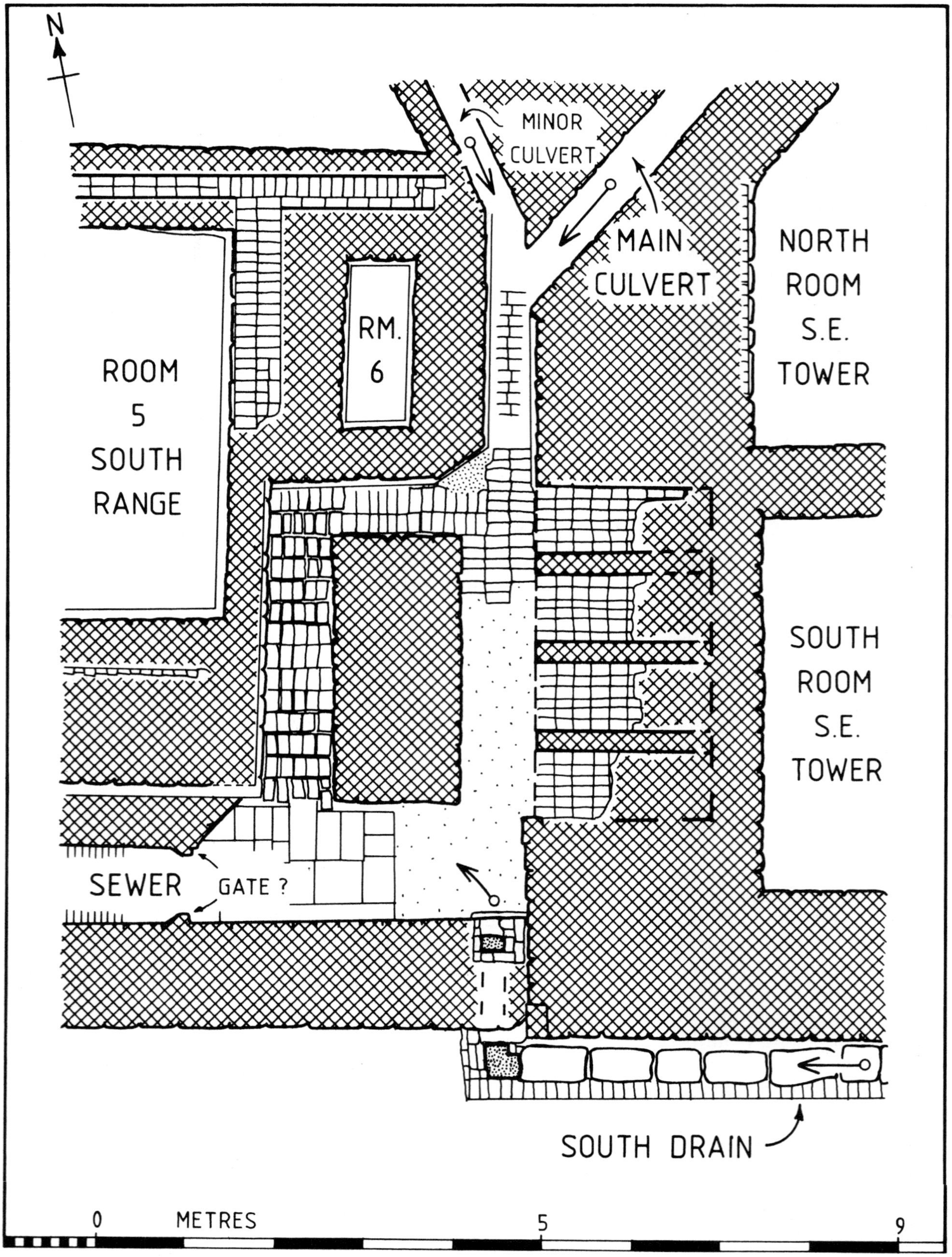

Fig. 59. *Plan of Tudor Garderobe area, Otford Palace.*

(i). MAIN CULVERT (Figs. 51 and 60, Sections II and X).

At the north-east corner of this rectangular structure there was a brick-based inlet culvert, some 35–50 cm. wide, that had been carefully constructed partly through the north-west corner of the great South East Tower (Plate XXXV). It continued diagonally through Room 1 of the East Range until its inlet, carefully constructed, broke through the outer east wall. It was clearly integral with the main walls and had thus formed part of the original Tudor scheme in this area. Its walls were of ragstone, at least 60 cm. wide, it had a mortared base, a minimum depth of 90 cm. and a total length of 14·50 m. It remained flooded throughout the excavation and its purpose was clearly to provide water to flush the garderobe area. This water was supplied from a large vaulted conduit built across the moat (see below). It is likely that the main culvert was capped with large flat stones, no trace of which survived.

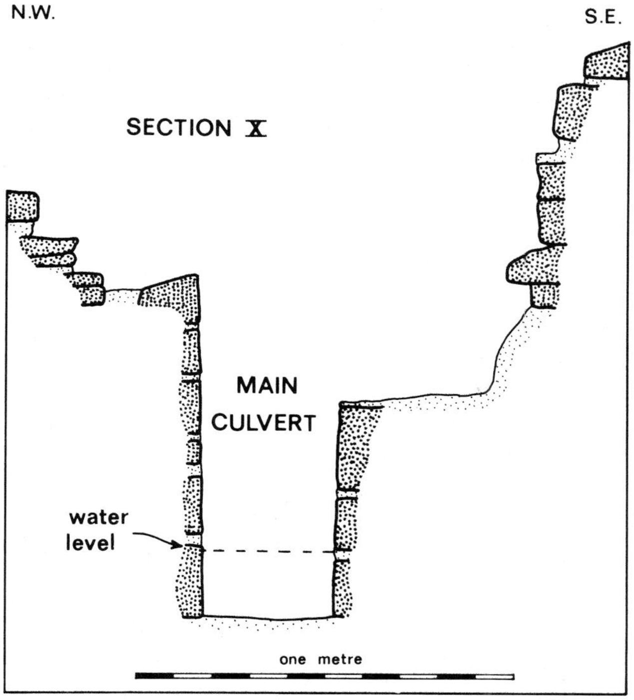

Fig. 60. *Section X through Main Culvert, Otford Palace.*

(j). MINOR CULVERT (Fig. 61).

The main culvert through the East Range was joined by a similar, smaller culvert about 2 m. from where it flowed into the garderobe area. This smaller culvert was 35 cm. wide, 4·90 m. long and at least 60 cm. deep. It had vertical sides, a flat base and its sides were lined with brick and ragstone (Section XI). It originated at the precise internal junction of the South and East Ranges where it had a brick-lining. It seems very likely that this served another vertical drainpipe placed in this corner and that the water it carried also helped flush the garderobe system. It is also likely that this minor culvert was capped with large flat stones, subsequently robbed.

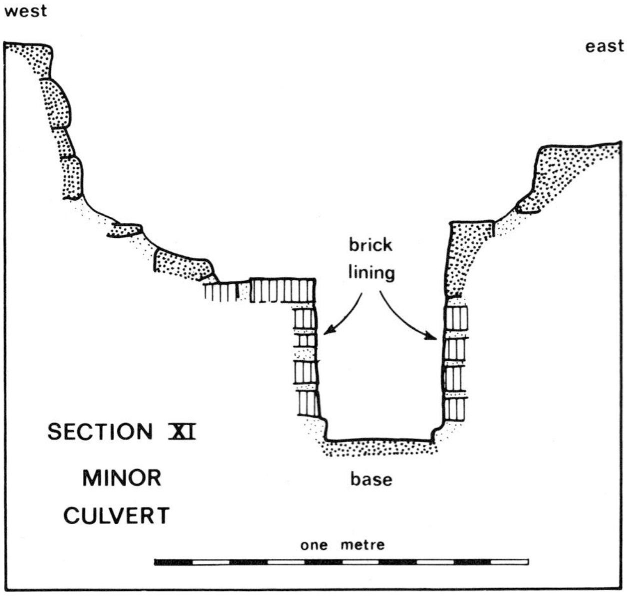

Fig. 61. *Section XI through Minor Culvert, Otford Palace.*

(k). THE SEWER (Fig. 54, Section V).

A substantial stone-built sewer had been added to the external face of the South Range to take away the effluent from the garderobe system. This had stone-built walls, the northern one 70 cm. wide and the southern one 1·20 m. wide. Both walls stood 1·15 m. high and it is likely that these were either capped or vaulted. The southern wall butted to the short west face of the South East Tower and the total length found was nearly 6 m., though clearly this sewer extended further to the west.

Both walls were lined internally with bricks at the base and squared masonry above. The wall-cores were of claystone rubble set in yellow mortar. The width of the channel between the walls was 84 cm. and its base of red bricks laid longitudinally. These sloped down from both sides to create a shallow gully at the centre. Most of the brickwork in the sewer was coated with a hard layer of lime, probably redeposited through water-action. The sewer was filled with demolition rubble.

Of special interest were two vertical stone jambs (Plate XXXVI), one on each side, close to the entrance to the sewer channel. These rose to the full height of the surviving masonry, had a total width of 20 cm. including a chamfer and projected 8 cm. into the channel. In this way the pair of jambs reduced the width of the channel to 68 cm. and there can be little doubt that they were intended to support some sort of frame or door. There was in fact clear evidence that a hinged structure had at sometime been inserted here. An L-shaped iron pivot, some 2 cm. in diameter and 3 cm. high, had been built in the south-east angle of the jamb. This stood vertically some 3 cm. from the wall face, 7 cm. from the jamb and 27 cm. above the floor. A socket for a corresponding pivot was detected 50 cm. higher up the wall and in this there were traces of a lead-plug. It seems clear that a gate or frame probably swung on a pair of iron pivots here and its purpose was to restrict entry, or the flow, along the sewer channel.

(l). AQUEDUCT 'A' (Fig. 50, Section I).

This was located in the north-east corner of the site where it crossed the wide moat diagonally and butted to the outer wall of the East Range. It was a large structure and had been 3·30 m. in overall width. Its central channel had been about 1·00 m. wide, but its flanking masonry had been robbed away leaving a ragged channel about 1·70 m. wide. What survived of the side walls, built of claystone rubble set in yellow mortar, was about 80 cm. wide. The structure was traced for about 9·00 m. Although badly robbed there were slight traces of an internal lining of red bricks and even a slight suggestion that the original structure had been vaulted over, also in brick. It would then have resembled the surviving vaulted channel (Aqueduct 'B'), probably of the same date, that carried the outfall from the adjacent lake across the site and is situated only about 40 m. to the north (Fig. 63).

It is clear that this large walled channel was built specifically to carry a significant volume of natural water from the area of the present lake to the East Range. Its south-west end coincided exactly with the large culvert constructed under the East Range which helped supply water to flush the garderobe system. It seems certain, therefore, that the large brick-lined structure was in fact an aqueduct that formed a vital element in the drainage arrangements of the south-east corner of the Tudor Palace. Indeed taken with the other aqueduct, the drains, the sewer and the wall-pipe outlets it is clear that the whole drainage arrangements formed part of a sophisticated system.

(m). THE TUDOR MOAT (Figs. 50, 53 and 54, Sections I, IV, V).

It was immediately clear that the external walls of the South East Tower, the South Range and the East Range were flanked by deposits of mud-silt at a level at least 1·00 m. lower than the presumed floor-levels within the structures. This mud-silt was found to contain some fine pottery and leather shoes (see below) of 16th century date and it is clear that this water-laid deposit was forming during this time. There can be little doubt that this was part of a broad moat that encompassed the Tudor Palace on at least parts of the south and east sides. All trenches in this area remained flooded throughout the excavation.

On the east side the mud-silt was traced for at least 8 m. from the outer walls and a single trench close to the south-east corner of the palace, failed to locate an outer edge within 12 m. of the walls. On the south side (S.IV) only a minimum width of 2·55 m. was obtained and if the moat here was 10 m. or more wide, then its outer edge must lie under the north footpath of Bubblestone Road.

The mud-silt was generally up to 35 cm. deep near the walls and here contained three large squared timbers, that were left *in situ*.

Excavation in eight areas produced 133 potsherds, from a minimum of 36 different pots, of which 18 are illustrated (Nos. 392 to 409). The pottery included 20 stoneware mugs, five small cups similar to Cistercian Ware, various sandy wares and medieval vessels. The 25 stonewares and Cistercian-type Wares all seem to date from the first half of the 16th century. The sandy wares are difficult to date accurately, on their own merits, but their direct association here with a greater number of vessels of the first half of the 16th century suggests that they too are of much the same date. Certainly, none of the pottery from the mud-silt in the moat need be any later in date than about 1550.

What is very interesting is that ten of the small mugs and cups were found almost complete and it is clear that these had been thrown into the moat. These are generally the best quality Tudor wares found on the site and it is unusual that these should have been lost whilst still complete. The fact that these are all small drinking vessels may be significant and it is tempting to suggest that these were thrown out of the windows and into the moat during the bouts of secular celebration. However, several equally likely, though far less popular, circumstances may have been the cause! Similarly, about 40 (Nos. 463 to 482) leather shoe fragments found at various points in the mud-silt, seem to suggest that disused footwear was frequently cast out of the windows.

The silt was generally covered by a deep dump of cream clay and soil that had been deposited to fill in the moat and raised the level of the ground. In five areas some 51 potsherds were recovered and these represent a minimum of eight vessels, of which four are illustrated (Nos. 410 to 413). Most appear to be jugs and seem to date from the second half of the 16th century. One small sherd, which may be of 17th or 18th century date, is probably intrusive considering the absence of similarly dated material from this area. The pottery from this dumped clay suggests that the moat could not have been filled before the latter part of the 16th century. The general absence of later material, however, suggests that the levelling probably took place not much later. This accords well with the pottery from the mud-silt forming in the bottom of the moat and everywhere sealed by the dumped infill, none of which needs to be later than the middle of the 16th century. The demolition rubble lay over the clay dump and it seems likely that the moat was deliberately filled, during the latter part of the 16th century or early in the 17th century. Just why this was done is difficult to determine, but possibly the wet moat had become stagnant or had presented other problems and it was decided to fill it in. Significantly, or not, the Tudor moat across the front of Hampton Court was filled during the time of Charles II.

(n). 19TH CENTURY PIT IN SOUTH EAST TOWER (Fig. 53, Section IV).

A large rectangular pit was found in the south room of the South East Tower, close to the internal dividing wall. This had vertical sides and a flat base. It was at least 2·80 m. long and about 1·25 m. wide and at least 65 cm. deep. On its bottom were traces of decayed organic matter. Lying on this was a badly decayed wooden frame, consisting of four short parallel cross-members which supported the remains of five long irregular planks..The cross-members were generally 0·78–1·09 m. in length, 8–17 cm. in width and 1–8 cm. in depth. The planks were 1·85–2·25 m. long, 16–28 cm. wide and 1–2 cm. in depth. The filling of the pit above the frame consisted of mixed brown loam which contained several clay-pipe stems and a bowl (No. 460) of 19th century date. Exactly what function this pit served is difficult to gauge, but the absence of demolition rubble and the 19th century material show that it was dug several centuries after this part of the palace was demolished.

(o). THE DEMOLITION OF THE TUDOR PALACE.

It seems clear from the extant records and maps that the palace had a short life and that demolition largely took place in the 17th century. Certainly the 1869 1st Edition 25″ map by the Ordnance Survey shows only a few wall-stubs in the southern part of the site (Plot 133).

The excavation showed that demolition had been systematic with superstructures removed almost down to foundation level. Only occasionally did the bottom one or two courses of brickwork survive. There was comparatively little rubble and mortar on the site, considering the size of the structures, though in places this was found up to 30 cm. deep. In general the robbed culverts, sewer and aqueduct contained mixed soil and rubble (No. 452).

Small quantities of pottery were found in the robbed features and in the demolition rubble. From twelve deposits came 101 sherds representing a minimum of 20 vessels, of which three are illustrated (Nos. 414 to 416). Nine of these vessels are of medieval date, six are stoneware mugs of the 16th century and the rest date from 16th to 19th centuries. Presumably the earlier pottery was derived from nearby. The soil sealing the demolition rubble contained 17 sherds from five vessels, only two of which are illustrated (Nos. 417 and 418). The pottery seems to be of 16th century date and includes fragments of four stoneware mugs.

The unstratified deposits on the site produced 455 potsherds from a minimum of 53 vessels of which 27 are illustrated (Nos. 419 to 445). These largely match the pottery from many parts of the site. They included six Romano-British, at least 20 medieval and at least 20 post-medieval vessels, the latter including at least six stoneware mugs. The medieval pottery includes the group of late-11th or early-12th century cooking-pots, all of which were handed over in a bucket by a very young schoolboy, from the previous excavation on the site. The unstratified deposits also included several medieval glazed floor-tiles (Nos. 456 to 459).

INTERPRETATION OF MAJOR SECTIONS (In order of deposition)

SECTION 1 (Fig. 50 East-West through East Range).

Layer 1	Excavation, February 1974.
2	Topsoil deposits.
3	Robber-trench of aqueduct.
4–11	Demolition rubble and soil.
12–13	Clay, loam and rubble fill of robbed aqueduct.
13A	Clay fill of Tudor Moat.
13B	Mud-silt. Primary deposit in Tudor East Moat.
14	Thin band of brick and tile dust. Seals foundation-trench, and probably represents 16th century construction-level.
15	Brown loam, mortar-specks and tile fragments. Fill of foundation-trench of west wall of East Range.
16–20	Loam and clay soils containing roof-tiles and occasional mortar-specks. Fill of wide foundation-trench of east wall of East Range cut through fill of Ditch 2.
21–25	Grey and brown clays and loams containing large numbers of roof-tiles, some flint and sandstone. Fill of Ditch 2.
26–39	Grey and cream clay dumps over the primary mud-silt of Ditch 1, probably derived from the excavation of Ditch 2 and raising ground-level by about 1·00 m. or more.
40	Mud-silt in bottom of Ditch 1.
41–45	A succession of apparently natural deposits of brown, grey and cream silts and clays, Cut by Ditch 1.

SECTION II (Fig. 51, N-S along East Range).

Layer 1	Excavation February 1974.
2	Topsoil deposits.
3	Loam forming over demolition rubble.
4–5	Demolition rubble, mortar and loam.
6	Clay dump over robbed culvert.
7–10	Clay, loam and rubble fill of robbed Main Culvert.
11–12	Clay and tile fill of wall-trench of north wall of South East Tower.
13–39	Clay, loam, silt, flint and tile fill of Ditch 2 which raised ground-level by about 60 cm. Oblique section along length of ditch.
40–47	Dumps of clay east of Ditch 1 (just off section) to raise general level of area by about 1·00 m.

SECTION III (Fig. 52, E-W through South East Tower).

Layer 1	Topsoil deposits.
2–3A	Demolition rubble.
3B–3C	Clay. Fill of Tudor East Moat.
3D	Mud-silt. Primary deposit in Tudor East Moat.
4–6	Clay and loam. Tudor levelling layers.
7	Red brick dust. 16th century construction-level.
8–9	Loam and clay levelling layers.
10–15	Clay and loam fill of foundation-trench of west wall of South East Tower.
16–22	Clay, loam and tile fill of foundation-trench of east wall of South East Tower.
23–27	Clay, loam and tile. Fill of Ditch 2.
28	Clay. Upcast from Ditch 2.
29	Dark-brown loam. Buried land-surface?
30–31	Grey clays. Natural soils?

SECTION IV (Fig. 53, N-S, through South East Tower).

Layer 1	Excavation February 1974.
2	Topsoil deposits.
3A	Brown loam. Fill of 19th century pit.
3B	Clay and loam. Minor feature cutting L–25.
4–6	Demolition rubble.
7–11	Loam, clay and rubble. Material dumped to fill Tudor Moat.
12	Mud-silt. Primary deposit in Tudor South Moat.
13–17	Clay and loam. Tudor levelling layers.
18–22	Clay deposits. Fill of foundation-trench, south wall, South East Tower.
23	Clay. Fill of foundation-trench, internal wall, South East Tower.
24	Clay. Fill of foundation-trench, north wall, South East Tower.
25–26	Clay, loam and tile. Fill of Ditch 2.
27	Clay. Upcast from Ditch 2.
28	Dark brown loam. Buried land-surface?
29–32	Clay and loam. Natural soils?

SECTION V (Fig. 54, N-S through South Range).

Layer 1	Topsoil deposits.
2	Soil formed over demolition rubble.
3	Demolition rubble.
4–6	Loams and clays. Material dumped to fill South Moat.
7	Demolition rubble.
8–10	Loams, mortar and rubble. Fill of robbed sewer.
11	Lime encrustation. Natural deposit forming in base of sewer.
12	Mud-silt. Primary deposit in South Moat.
13	Stone-blocks and grey clay. Packing of sewer wall.
14–22	Loam, clay, stone and tile. Fill of foundation-trench, south wall, South Range.
23–28	Loam, clay and tile. Fill of Ditch 2.
29–30	Clay and flints. Dump over primary mud-silt in Ditch 1.
31	Mud-silt. Primary fill of Ditch 1.

D. DISCUSSIONS

(1). The Implications of the Evidence.

(a). ROMAN AND MEDIEVAL.

Whilst no Roman structures have ever been recorded on the palace site a limited amount of Roman material, including pottery, roof and hypocaust tile, small pieces of *opus signinum* and a bronze brooch, from the site strongly suggests the presence nearby of a Roman building. This almost certainly lay about 250 m. north-east of this site where abundant Roman building debris was found in 1934.

No material of Anglo-Saxon date has so far come from the palace area. Few early documents exist, but certainly by 1086 the Archbishop of Canterbury held the Manor of Otford and it is possible that he, or another, had a residence at Otford. If so, this has never been found and if it had existed then it is likely that it stood on or near the site occupied by the later medieval manor-house and the Tudor Palace. Clearly no details of any possible Saxon structure can be offered at present.

It seems probable from various post-Conquest references that the Archbishop of Canterbury's manor-house was established on the site no later than the end of the 12th century. Significantly, the large-scale excavations produced some evidence to support this view. A wet moat (Ditch 1), some 5·75 m. wide and traced for some 24·00 m. across the north-west corner of the excavation, contained 13th century pottery in its primary filling. Immediately to its west a dump of domestic rubbish was found to contain 11th-12th century pottery, whilst a fine 12th century capital was found re-used in a 14th century foundation. No other 11th-12th century building materials were found across the site.

The ditch appears to curve to the west and there seems little doubt that the ends continued to both north and south (Fig. 62). Indeed it seems likely that the ditch would have completed a circuit to the west and that it would have enclosed any early manorial buildings, in much the same way as did the later medieval and Tudor layouts. The domestic rubbish would then lie at the extreme east end of such an area. The stone capital, if from the manor-house site as seems likely, suggests at least one masonry building of good quality that was demolished no later than the 14th century. The Papal bulls (dated 1181–7) may well have arrived in such a building, though the Seals could have been discarded then, or at any time later. By 1274 a hall, the Lord's Chamber, stables, a great granary and oxhouse were being repaired and it is reasonable to suppose that most of these had been built in Norman times. More repairs of these buildings and new work took place in 1288–9, 1322–3 and 1355–6. Clearly, by the mid-14th century the moated manor-site was of some considerable scale and local significance.

To judge by the evidence in the ground, major rebuilding took place during the second half of the 14th century. Certainly the earliest moat (Ditch 1) was filled; a new masonry range built across the filled-in ditch and a new, bigger moat (Ditch 2) dug to enclose a larger area on the east side by the end of the 14th century. Presumably the original area was no longer adequate and more, or larger, buildings were then required. It is not known if the enclosed area was increased on all sides, but an enclosed area of about half an hectare (say one-two acres) seems probable (Fig. 62). What is significant also is that the historical record shows large-scale repair-work in 1382–3, by Archbishop Courtenay, following possible extensive damage during the Peasant's Revolt of 1381. Certainly the battlements and buttresses of a new hall are recorded and also new palings round the moat. It seems probable that the new moat, the new masonry building and the various documented repairs all formed part of the William Courtenay scheme. The evidence on the site shows that a large building was laid out on a south-west by north-east axis, at least 16·65 m. long and containing a pair of masonry garderobe shafts flanking the newly dug moat. Along the inner lip of the ditch was a line of large stakes and there is a good chance that these are those mentioned in 1382–3. Otherwise the manor-house might have followed the broad arrangement used in the 14th century, as for example at the comparable site at Charing (Ref. 209).

However extensive and grand the late-14th century manor-house may have been it was clearly far from adequate for Archbishop Warham about 130 years later. Otford was certainly chosen for the site of his grand new palace, in preference to his otherwise largely comparable sites at Wrotham, Maidstone and Charing.

(b). TUDOR (Fig. 63).

Largely as a result of the major excavation it is now possible to consider the Tudor Palace complex as a whole. The short lengths of extant masonry and limited information from surviving records all add useful details.

The palace was clearly a much larger and more pretentious structure than the medieval manor-house that preceded it. The manorial buildings were largely swept away and the ditches partly, or entirely, filled. Only the Great Hall and the Chapel are recorded as having been retained. It seems that these two structures were regarded as of major importance and sufficiently grand and sound to be incorporated into the new layout. Indeed the survival of these buildings to some extent then dictated the broad planning of the Tudor Palace, for they determined the location of the principal buildings. Once the principal buildings were fixed the rest of the layout was bound to follow.

It is also clear that the main axis of the Tudor Palace lay roughly north-south, on a centre line that passed close to the west end of the parish church (Fig. 47). It seems likely that this was anyway an important alignment in medieval times, though one largely lost since the demolition of the palace. The overall length of the Tudor Palace on this main north-south axis was about 163 m. (about 535 ft.), whilst the shorter east-west width seems to have been about 97 m. (about 318 ft.). Allowing for the asymmetrical layout the various structures alone covered an area of about 1·30 hectares (over 3 acres), which would have been vastly increased by the enclosing moat and adjacent gardens.

The Main Courtyard and its Buildings.

In detail the Tudor Palace was almost certainly divided into two main elements. One, with the principal buildings ranged round one or more courtyards, lay south of the small stream that still bisects the site, which was largely the site of the manorial buildings. The second main element lay exclusively north of the small stream and consisted of a massive new Main Courtyard, about 75 m. (about 246 ft.) square in internal area, flanked by long galleries on at least its west, north and east sides. The various 16th century surveys show that the galleries were of two-storeys and it seems likely that their roof-lines followed their main axes. One survey, at least, records this as the Base Court or Inner Court, with an Outer Court situated beyond the Main Gatehouse towards the church. Preference is here given to the simple term of 'Main Courtyard' as the most meaningful compromise.

The north gallery of this Main Courtyard contained an impressive twin-towered Great Gatehouse (of which the bottom storey of the west tower still survives) and is recorded in the Survey of c. 1540 as containing 15 rooms. The surviving tower is about 15 by 7 m. in plan. Allowing for a wide single carriageway with projecting jambs the total width of the gatehouse was probably about 22 m. It is also very likely that it projected above the adjacent galleries with a third-storey to create a grand and imposing main-entry to the palace. Certainly the palaces at Hampton Court (Ref. 210) and Nonsuch (Ref. 211) were provided with grand entrances in this manner. The whole gatehouse seems to have been built in brick with stone-linings, stone quoins at its angles and diaper patterns in the brickwork. Its towers had half hexagonal fronts and small external stair-turrets at the rear (Plates XXXVII and XXXVIII).

Flanking the Great Gatehouse on both sides were long two-storeyed galleries, almost certainly of similar length and scale. That on the west side partially survives (Plate XXXIX), though the original upper-storey is a modern replacement. This North West Gallery is about 27 m. in length, about 4·10 m. in width and is today divided into three small cottages. The Survey of c. 1540 describes it built of stone and timber and offers measurements at variance with what survives. Its brick superstructure sits on a ragstone plinth about 1·00 m. high and contains nine openings. Two more are largely hidden by an added chimney-stack and all are shown completely blocked in an 18th century print. The same print shows the upper-storey to be missing and the ground-floor to be thatched. Subsequently, the upper brick-storey was rebuilt, a new roof constructed and five of the blocked openings partially unblocked and framed.

The north-west corner was high-lighted by a fine three-storeyed brick tower, which substantially remains (Plate XVIII) and is the finest upstanding section of the palace that survives. Though long a neglected ruin it was roofed and repaired in 1982. It is basically heptagonal in plan and measures about 10 to 8 m. It has a stair-turret at its south-east junction with the North West Gallery that gave access to all its floors. On its south side is a rectangular extension that seems to have served as a garderobe shaft. The tower, which survives to a height of 11·50 m. is brick-built above a high ragstone plinth. Its openings are stone-lined and its angles are quoined with stones of alternating sizes. The brickwork contains clear diaper patterns, created by the use of much darker headers. Internally, there are at least three fireplaces and sockets for floor joists.

It is clear from the 1573 Survey that a North East Gallery ran eastwards from the Great Gatehouse and that a large North East Corner-tower formed part of the original scheme. It is highly probable that both the gallery and the tower matched their counterparts west of the gatehouse and these are shown thus on the reconstructed plan (Fig. 63). A check on the masonry wall east of the gatehouse shows that it incorporates a 20 m. length of original Tudor stone wall. This has the familiar high stone plinth and traces of a single brick pier that may have separated two window-openings. Most of the original wall here, however, survives at least 2 m. high and although no other openings are obvious, the wall is largely covered by ivy. The internal face of the wall is brick-lined.

Of the West Gallery almost nothing survives above ground, although its line is certainly reflected by a marked change in ground-level. Of special significance is a stub of masonry which projects from the west end of the extant North West Gallery and is clearly an integral part of it. It clearly represents part of the internal east wall of the West Gallery and its line shows that the two ranges met at an angle of about 84°. It has a width of 75 cm. and a high stone plinth matching that of the North West Gallery. The width of the missing West Gallery is less certain. It seems likely that it was at least the same width (4·10 m.) as the North West Gallery, whilst if its outer west wall lined up with the outer wall of the tower then its width could have been about 6·50 m., and it is shown thus on the overall plan. The tower itself was clearly an extension of this range for it was not built parallel to the Great Gatehouse. The West Gallery may have had a maximum length of about 75 m. and is described in the 1573 Survey as "one long gallery with lodgings adjoining". From this it seems likely that it contained a long passage, which gave access to several rooms situated along the outer, west side.

Of the East Gallery there is again very little evidence. It has been assumed that this lay parallel to the West Range and about equidistant from the Great Gatehouse and this is how it is shown on the overall plan. The 1573 Survey states "one longe gallerye from the sayde Towre southward with IX lightes uppon the estsyde thereof". Again it may be assumed that it contained a long passage flanking a series of rooms which, if the windows (lightes) truly reflect the rooms, could have been nine in number. The length of this range was probably a maximum of 80 m. The Survey of c. 1540 states that the east and west galleries were 228 ft. and 304 ft. in length and whilst a differential length seems clear it is difficult to reconcile these measurements so precisely given.

From all this it seems that the Main Courtyard was designed as a separate and spacious unit, entirely north of the present stream. It no doubt contained the lesser buildings. To judge by the axes of the North and West Galleries the Main Courtyard was not itself square in plan. Certainly its main axis seems to be some 7° west of that of the ranges containing the principal buildings south of the stream, though cleverly the East and West Galleries appear to be still largely parallel.

The Principal Buildings.

It seems clear from the various contemporary surveys that the principal buildings formed part of an extensive complex of structures with at least one large courtyard. It seems equally certain that these lay south of the small stream across the site, very largely over and beyond the area of the medieval manor-house. The Survey of c. 1540 records a complex of '71 chambers' with galleries, towers and turrets of stone and variously roofed with lead or tile. The major excavation in 1974 showed that the south-east corner was dominated by a large square tower, 12·70 m. in plan and probably the three-storeyed tower mentioned in the 1573 Survey. The excavation also showed that large, broad ranges sprang from the tower to frame part of a rectangular courtyard with a length of at least 17 m. The great East Range, some 11·50 m. wide and probably two-storeys high, was excavated for nearly 20 m. whilst crop-marks suggest that its total length was not less than 45 m. The walls had massive broad stone-footings which in part cut through and across the medieval foundations and the filled-in moats. The external plinths and faces, where these survive, were of ragstone, whilst the internal walls were either brick-built or brick-lined over stone foundations. Internally, it contained a range of apartments about 6·00 by 5·00 m. in size, flanked by a passageway about 2·30 m. wide.

The excavation also revealed part of the South Range, about 10·50 m. wide and certainly exposed for about 7 m. in length. This, too, contained a passage flanking a room, or rooms. The line of its external south wall can still be traced for another 23 m. through the front gardens of Nos. 9 and 11 Bubblestone Road, to a point where a small projecting three-sided bay, 5 m. wide, seems to mark a major structural variation in the plan. The external wall beyond the bay then steps northwards, reduced in thickness, where it can be traced for about another 37 m. The wall re-aligns though the gardens of Nos. 5 and 7 four times in this length to finish with a sharp corner and an increased width at its south-west end (Plate XL). These re-alignments could suggest a variety of structural variations and functions, whilst the total length of the south side of the palace comes to about 85 m. The surviving masonry in the gardens of Nos. 5–11 Bubblestone Road varies in height from about 30 cm. to about 3·00 m. with the higher lengths generally towards the west end. The external faces are of ragstone throughout, with both vertical and slightly battered elevations. A weathered stone moulding occurs for a short length near the west end, whilst the general similarity of the masonry strongly suggests that all these masonry elements formed part of the overall Tudor scheme. Certainly the external south-west corner is remarkably similar in constructional detail to the corners of the great South East Tower and a similar South West Tower may be indicated.

The projecting stone bay, only about 5 m. in width, may have contained a corner-stair or may simply represent projecting windows. Somewhere along this frontage there may have been an entry, though no obvious trace survives. Internally, traces of brickwork survive showing that the interior was brick-lined. In one place twelve courses of brickwork survive and at least one ragged wall-stub suggests an internal division.

What appears to be the outer walls of the West Range, can be seen in the garden of No. 5 Bubblestone Road and these suggest a total length of about 50 m. At least two alignments are suggested with the northern one lining up reasonably well with the West Gallery of the Main Courtyard. Various other isolated lumps of masonry survive, though these allow a variety of reconstructions. What is significant is that the West Range does not form a right-angle with the South Range, but swings westwards by a total of 108°. Presumably, the precise arrangement was dictated by topographical features, or perhaps a desire to give this range a south-west aspect.

It seems clear that the North Range was the major range of the whole complex, to judge by both its size and general location and it seems to have joined both the East and West Ranges at about 80°. Its overall length seems to have been about 90 m. and certainly its surviving masonry is most impressive. What makes this both difficult to see and somewhat unusual is the fact that although the masonry is almost entirely below ground it is exposed as much as 2 m. in height along its north face. It seems clear that this masonry originally flanked a deep water-channel or moat, that was about 4 m. wide and which carried the natural stream across the site and could also mark the site of the medieval north moat. The bottom of this water-channel is marked by a narrow culvert, still in use today, but it seems clear that in Tudor times the water was intended to spread across the whole width of the channel, with the stone walls flanking its southern side and a brick-wall, of which traces can still be seen, flanking its northern side. Of special interest are five large stone buttresses that rise from the bed of the channel and may have extended up much of the height of the North Range. Three have truncated ends and two are square-ended and it is possible that others once existed. Traces of three or four large masonry projections also flank the stream and these may represent window-bays running up the height of the buildings much as suggested by the Survey of c. 1540. Whilst it is difficult to conjecture more detail with certainty, it must be that this range contained an entry, linking the Main and inner courtyards. The central axis of the Main Courtyard seems the most likely position and this anyway largely coincides with the centre-point of the North Range. If a gate existed here then a bridge with abuttments would be necessary and indeed the Survey of c. 1540 records a wooden bridge somewhere along the North Range passing beneath the 'forefront of the gallerye'! In fact some of the projecting masonry here could be part of this. In addition the 1573 Survey suggests that the Great Hall stood in this range and that it had at least four buttresses on its south side. It is possible that some of the large buttresses flanking the water-channel corresponded to buttresses on the north side of this building, though several other possibilities also need to be considered.

The Survey also records the Grete Chamber, the Presence and Privye Chamber, the Greene Gallerye, schole house, a Chappell, Great Kytchen and various lodgings, all of which were within the ranges of the principal buildings. No precise plan can be deduced from the Survey and only planned, properly-conducted excavations in the future will add any significant information. Nor do various walls shown on early maps, particularly the First Edition Ordnance Survey, 25-inch, produce conclusive evidence. Clearly, only when the houses in Bubblestone Road have served their full time will it be possible to consider properly all the buried structures in this area.

Beyond the main buildings ranged around the various courtyards were the other elements relating to the Tudor Palace. A wet moat was found on the east and south sides during the 1974 excavation and at one point this seemed to be at least 8 m. wide. Beyond were gardens, farm buildings and an extensive Park. Of special interest were the drainage and water-channels. These were supplied by springs on marginally higher ground to the east. One source fed Becket's Well, established in medieval times, continued by the Tudors and still flowing today. The Tudors certainly built at least two vaulted brick aqueducts, the one discovered on the excavation (marked A on Fig. 63) and the other (marked aqueduct B on Fig. 63) still functioning. The former brought fresh water from the direction of Becket's Well diagonally through the East Range to flush the large four-shafted garderobe into the gated sewer. The vertical down-pipes on the superstructure were cleverly linked to this system.

The functioning aqueduct still brings constant clear water from a small lake fed by Becket's Well. The aqueduct travels underground for more than 50 m. following three main alignments and incorporating both Tudor and modern features. The Tudor sections are vaulted in brick and mostly about 1·50 m. high and rather less than 1·00 m. wide. It also includes a stone-vaulted chamber that may have formed part of the East Range. The water in this particular aqueduct continued westwards to feed the culverted stream that flanks the north side of the North Range and effectively divides the site.

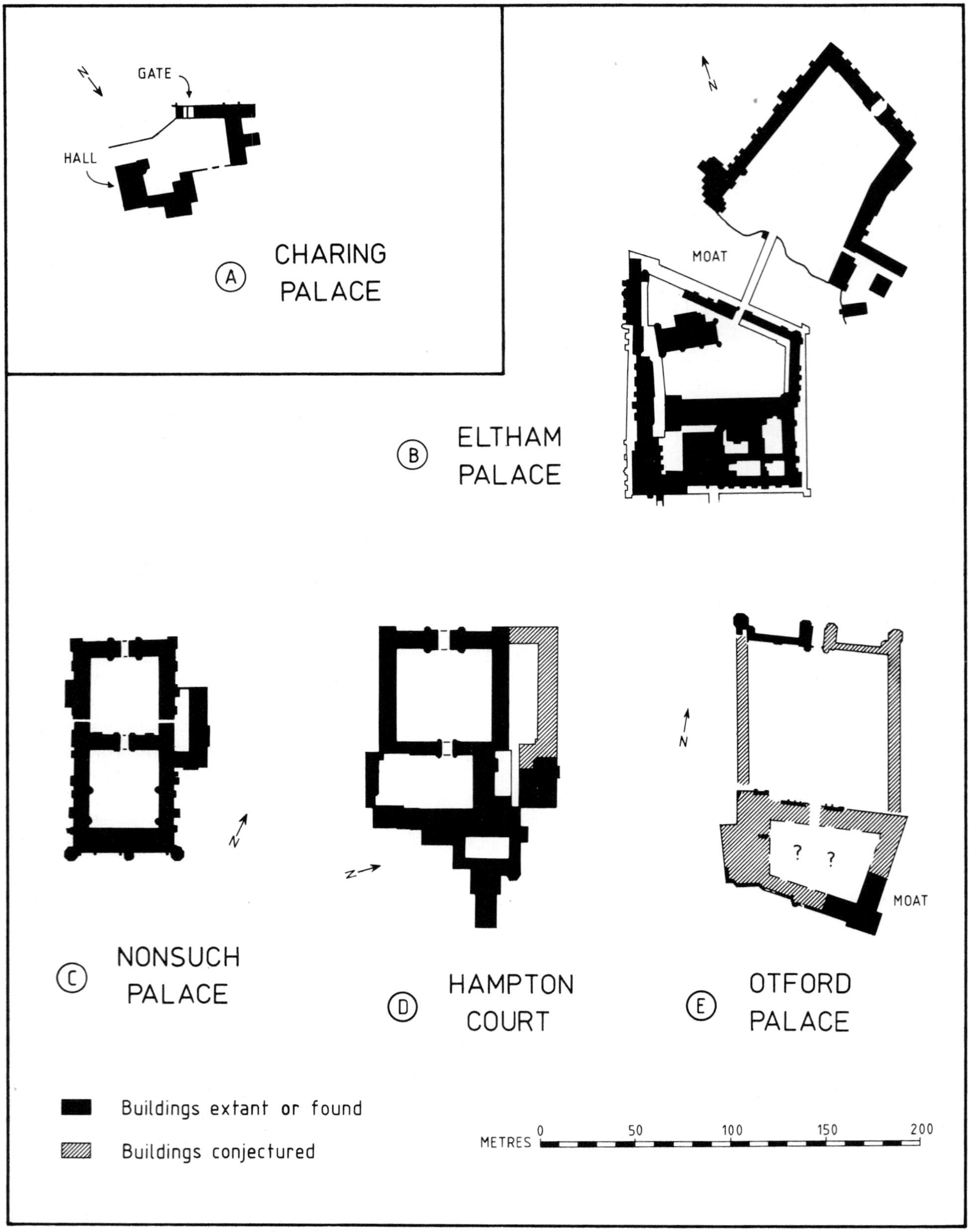

Fig. 64. *Comparative block-plans of Medieval and Tudor palaces.*

(2). A Comparative Study

(a). THE ARCHBISHOP'S MANOR-HOUSE.

Whilst not much is known of the definitive plan of the medieval manor-house at Otford, details from records and from the excavation give some idea of the scale and importance of the buildings. There can anyway be little doubt that the size and extent of the Archbishop's manor-house at Otford were scarcely less than his other manor-houses in Kent at Charing, Maidstone and Wrotham. The best known plan of these is that of Charing (Fig. 64, A) where most of the major elements likely at Otford, such as the Great Hall, kitchens, gatehouse, Chapel and West Range are known. The plan at Charing includes buildings of late-13th to late-15th century date, much the range of those at Otford and although the precise plan and details would almost certainly differ, the broad form and scale may offer a reasonable comparison. The buildings at Charing cover a minimum area of about 80 m. by 60 m. (about half an hectare) and are generally ranged around a large courtyard.

The only medieval building (the Masonry Building) found at Otford, or rather part of the south-east side of it, was traced for about 17 m. It could have extended to the north-east and to the south-west, though the line of the corresponding moat (Ditch 2) would have set close limits. Similar double garderobe shafts to those found here occur elsewhere in medieval buildings and useful parallels occur at Dartington Hall (about 1388–1400) and at the Hospital of St. Cross, Winchester (c. 1445) (Refs. 212 and 213). At both sites the shafts occupy the long side of apartment-blocks which formed part of important groups of buildings. This could also be the situation at Otford and if so, then the walls found were part of a range with a main south-west by north-east axis. If a courtyard existed north-west of this building, as seems likely, then some general estimate can be made of the location of the other principal buildings. The large masonry bases might then have supported the corners, as their basic shape suggests, with their great size reflecting the instability of the underlying infilled moat (Ditch 1). It has also been suggested that the masonry bases may have been built to support chimney-stacks and this possibility must be considered.

To this can be added the moat, found on the east side, but probably enclosing the site on all four sides. The documentary evidence mentions gates and bridges and these may have existed on two or more sides. In addition a small section of a medieval drain was found in 1969.

(b). THE ARCHBISHOP'S PALACE.

As regards the great Tudor Palace of Archbishop Warham there are, predictably, few buildings in West Kent that can compare. The more obvious comparisons within a distance of 32 km. (20 miles) at Otford are the Palaces at Eltham (Ref. 214), Greenwich (Ref. 215), Hampton Court and Nonsuch.

The Royal Palace at Greenwich as revealed by excavation was largely the work of Henry VII about A.D. 1500. Much of the plan is not known, but it seems clear that at least three main ranges framed a large courtyard and the total area was probably about 78 m. by 78 m. (256 ft.). More helpful is Eltham (Fig. 64, B) where the truncated plan is reminiscent of Otford. There, most of the known plan dates from the time of Edward IV (1461–83) and Henry VII (1485–1509). The area enclosed by the great moat is about 125 m. (410 ft.) by about 90 m. (295 ft.) and thus covers an area somewhat smaller than Otford. It, too, had a main northern entrance, which gave access to a Great Courtyard beyond the moat, which had ranges of buildings on all sides. Like Otford its principal buildings (other than its Chapel) were in the southern half of the site and framed around several courtyards. It, too, had replaced earlier medieval buildings on the same site.

The plan recovered in 1959 of Nonsuch Palace (Fig. 64, C), started by Henry VIII in 1538, is also useful. The area covered by the buildings and courtyards there was 115 m. (377 ft.) by 73 m.

(240 ft.), much less than Otford, though perhaps its buildings were more compact. It, too, had a main north entrance which gave access to outer and inner courtyards with ranges of buildings on all sides. Where Nonsuch Palace differed from Otford, Eltham and Hampton Court, was its symmetrical balanced planning. Indeed, it is said to be a vital building in the history of early Renaissance Architecture in England. Its grand south front had octagonal projecting corner towers and the palace had complex water-supply and drainage arrangements. In plan the projecting towers are reminiscent of the North West Tower at Otford, though Otford can never have matched the splendour of Hoefnagel's drawing of 1582. Significantly, the south front at Otford (at 85 m.) was the same size as the splendid front at Nonsuch (also 85 m.).

Of special interest and significance is Hampton Court (Fig. 64, D), started by Cardinal Wolsey in 1515 and like Otford built over a pre-existing moated manor-house. At Hampton the main gatehouse was on the west side and this gave access to a rectangular Outer Court some 50 m. (164 ft.) square, thus much smaller than the Main Court at Otford. Both the main courts at Hampton and Otford were flanked by long galleries and lodgings. At Hampton the principal buildings were placed beyond an inner gatehouse and were ranged around an Inner Court and various lesser ones, probably much as conjectured for Otford. Excluding the projecting chapel at the east end the overall length at Hampton Court was about 129 m. Including the conjectured offices on the north side the overall width was about 102 m. (335 ft.).

What becomes clear from this is that Otford Palace (Fig. 64, E) was designed and laid out on a scale that could compare with even the largest contemporary palaces in England. In area alone (163 by 97 m.) it covered a greater area than either the slightly later Renaissance Nonsuch Palace or the moated area of the slightly earlier Eltham Palace. It clearly approached the area of Hampton Court and seems to have been started at very much the same time! Indeed this comparability in terms of both time and scale seems to be further evidence of the rivalry between the Cardinal and the Archbishop.

William Warham had become Archbishop in 1503 and Lord Chancellor in about 1504. His new palace at Otford seems to have been under construction in 1514, but he found the political pressures too great and resigned as Chancellor in 1515, but continued as Archbishop. Significantly, Thomas Wolsey who succeeded him as Lord Chancellor acquired the site of Hampton Court in 1514 and by 1515 work had already begun on his Palace. Politically, at least, the two men were rivals and it now seems likely that this rivalry was also being expressed in architectural terms on the ground. Although the cunning of Cardinal Wolsey was to leave him largely omnipotent, the older Archbishop Warham was not to be totally eclipsed.

Warham was able to entertain Cardinal Campeggio at Otford for two days in 1518 and in 1520 Henry VIII and Catherine of Aragon stayed at Otford whilst *en route* for the Field of the Cloth of Gold. Wolsey for his part had also planned and furnished Hampton Court on the grand scale and in 1527 he entertained there the French Ambassador with his retinue of 400 when a treaty was signed between England and France.

Of special interest in these matters is a letter from Warham to Wolsey, written in the winter of 1522–3, which explained how his physician had considered him unfit to travel to attend Wolsey. He had added his thanks to Wolsey for his advice to live on high and dry ground, as at Knole (Otford was low and wet), and for his offer of accommodation at Hampton Court! No doubt Wolsey had made the offer tongue-in-cheek, but with the very clear implication that his Hampton Court was much superior to Warham's Otford! The rivalry had not many years to run. Wolsey died in disgrace in 1530 and Warham of old age in 1532, no doubt with a small degree of satisfaction. Only Henry was the real victor. He took Hampton Court in 1527 and Otford Palace in 1537 and held them until his own death in 1547. Only the spirit of Wolsey could, perhaps, claim the final satisfaction. The mighty palace at Otford has now largely disappeared, whilst Hampton Court remained a Royal Palace for another 200 years and survives today as a tourist attraction of international significance. But for the quirks of history and the saturated ground at Otford the roles could well have been reversed and little Otford today might yet have had one of the finest palaces in the realm!

E. THE EXCAVATED OBJECTS

(1). THE MEDIEVAL POTTERY

By Peter Keller.

Some 1,230 potsherds of medieval date were recovered from the excavation and these represent 173 vessels, of which 56 have been illustrated (Figs. 65–70). Although no exhaustive study of this material has been attempted it has been possible to classify the pottery into seven main fabric-types (Table C) ranging in date from the late-11th to the 15th centuries.

Fabric	Cooking-Pots	Bowls/ Dishes	Jugs	Other	Total Pots	% Pots
Fabric 1	35	–	–	–	35	20
Fabric 2	38	10	–	–	48	28
Fabric 3	27	7	–	1 curfew	35	20
Fabric 4	10	–	14	–	24	14
Fabric 5	–	–	23	–	23	13
Fabric 6	–	–	7	–	7	4
Fabric 7	–	–	1	–	1	c.1
TOTALS	110	17	45	1	173	100%

Table C. Types of medieval pottery vessels, arranged by fabric.

The vessels from Otford do not form a large group and in all probability may not be representative of the whole site. However, a few useful comments can be made.

The material from Otford shares similar characteristics with material found at nearby Eynsford Castle, approximately 5 miles north of Otford, excavated by S.E. Rigold on behalf of the then Ministry of Works. Mr. Rigold has dated the Eynsford pottery mainly on historical evidence and offered fairly precise dates. Elsewhere it is almost certain that the forms and fabrics continued well beyond the rigid dates offered at Eynsford (Ref. 216).

It can be seen from Table C that 68% of the vessels from Otford are shell-filled wares (Fabrics 1–3) and are either cooking-pots or bowls. No jugs are present. The pottery is almost certainly a local product but as yet there has been no kiln or kilns identified producing shell-filled wares in the area. Perhaps these have yet to be located. It is highly probable that a single kiln or kilns was supplying both Eynsford and Otford and perhaps other sites too. The sandy ware products of Fabric 4 are cooking-pots and jugs whilst the finer wares including the glazed ware products are exclusively jugs. It is odd that the products of the Limpsfield kilns, only about ten miles to the west are not represented in the Otford assemblage.

MEDIEVAL FABRIC 1 – Coarse Heavily Shell-Filled Fabric.

Some 276 sherds represent 35 vessels (20%). These are coarse, hard, crudely made vessels of a heavily shell-filled fabric with approximately 55 medium to large grits per square inch (2·5 $cm.^2$). Fifteen have been illustrated (Nos. 419 to 430 and 443 to 445). They have a soft, almost soapy texture with generally a light grey to grey core and an external surface from orange-brown to various shades of grey, all of which appear to be cooking-pots. The rim profiles fall into roughly four categories: (i) slightly everted, clubbed rim with almost flat top, Nos. 419, 425 and 443. Similar profiles occur from Phase W at Eynsford Castle (Ref. 216, W4 and W5), where they are dated late-11th century. (ii) Simple everted rims, straight or nearly so, Nos. 426, 427, 429 and 445. These are reflected in Eynsford Phase X (X4 and X5) dated to *c.* first half of the 12th century. Possible parallels occur at Canterbury (Ref. 217 from Group III). Nos. 420, 424 and 430 may be a more upright, slightly thickened version of this group. (iii) Curved rim with squared top sometimes producing an inner bead, Nos. 421, 422 and 423 and similar forms occur in early wares from Eynsford (L4) and are there dated to the mid-12th century. (iv) Everted, beaded, one example No. 428 is similar to a vessel from Eynsford (XI). Locally produced pottery of this nature cannot be dated precisely. At Eynsford the 'early shelly wares' are dated mainly on historical evidence to the late-11th to early-12th century. However, at Southampton (Ref. 218), Kings Lynn (Ref. 219) and Cheddar (Ref. 220) stylistically similar vessels with closely resembling rim forms and fabrics to those at Otford are more broadly dated to the 11th to 12th centuries and later. In view of this the Fabric 1 ware at Otford is here broadly dated to mid-11th to mid-12th centuries.

MEDIEVAL FABRIC 2 – Hard, Moderately Shell-Filled Fabric.

Some 361 sherds represent 48 vessels (28%). These are generally a harder, better fired, well-made vessel than that of Fabric 1 of a lightly shell-filled fabric with approximately 30 small to medium grits per square inch (2·5 $cm.^2$). Sixteen have been illustrated (Nos. 352 to 358, 362, 369, 370, 375, 377, 382, 383, 431 and 432). The texture, although of slightly harder quality to Fabric 1 is still fairly soft and somewhat soapy to the touch. Generally they have a light grey to grey core and the external surfaces from buff-brown through various shades of grey to almost black, some heavily encrusted with soot (Nos. 353, 355, 356 and 358). About 80% (38 vessels) of the pottery recovered in this group represent cooking-pots. The rim profiles fall into broadly three categories: (i) Up-turned with undercut flange and squared or slightly concaved top. Nos. 352, 355, 356, 362, 370 and 431. No. 352 may be a slightly earlier example, compare similar vessels from Eynsford (B5) mid to late-13th century. No. 431 has been pricked to prevent cracking during firing. (ii) Up-turned, almost horizontal with upper bevel. Nos. 353, 357 and 375. (iii) Tapered flange, Nos. 358 and 369; these may well be a product of chance, perhaps a too prominently fashioned bevel, than by design. Nos. 352, 353, 355, 357, 369 and 375 have vertical applied thumb-strip and/or regular latitudinal striations, sometimes these may be quite faint that they can only be seen from certain angles. Although there is not enough wall to determine the decoration of Nos. 356, 358, 362, 370 and 431, it is highly probable that they too were decorated in similar fashion. The pot profile, as reconstructed from Nos. 352 and 355 can be seen to have a bulbous body, its girth greater than the rim and base diameters and a sagging base, although it may not be typical of all. Nos. 352, 355, 356, 357, 358, 362, 370, 375 and 431 have similar forms and rim profiles occurring at Rochester (Ref. 221), Canterbury and Eynsford in the late-13th to early-14th centuries. Similar examples occur at Joyden's Wood (Ref. 222) where Dr. D.G. Dunning has dated them to A.D. 1280–1320.

The remaining 20% (ten vessels) are bowls and dishes. The bowls have a greater rim diameter than body and base. The rim profiles have flanged, either level topped with upper bevel, (Nos. 377 and 382) level-topped and undercut flange, (No. 383), or the flange slightly upturned as No. 432. All have thumb-strip and/or latitudinal striations decorating the body. No. 383 is a finer quality vessel with no noticeable shell-filling and thus may be slightly later in date. The rims appear to conform with vessels from Joyden's Wood, (Group 2) also for cooking-pots, where they are dated to A.D. 1280–1320. Similar examples occur at sites already mentioned above and are dated to the late-13th to early-14th century. The Otford Fabric 2 ware may have continued well into the 14th century.

MEDIEVAL FABRIC 3 – Hard Sandy Fabric with Light Shell-Filling.

Some 329 sherds represent 35 vessels (20%). These are of a harder more sandier fabric than Fabrics 1 and 2, and have less shell-filling with up to 25 small to medium grits per square inch (2·5 cm^2). Nine have been illustrated (Nos. 360, 376, 384, 386, 387, 388, 389, 390 and 433). These are generally a better quality version of Fabric 2 where the forms and profiles are almost identical. The core can be seen to be from light grey to grey and the surface buff through to various shades of light grey. About 77% (27) of those recovered are cooking pots, Nos. 376, 384 and 433 with flanged rims either bevelled as No. 376 or recessed, as No. 384. All have applied thumb-strip and/or latitudinal striations. About 20% (seven) are bowls, Nos. 386–389. All have slightly downturned flanges and with the exception of No. 386, have thumb-pressed decoration. Only No. 387 has body decoration in the form of latitudinal grooving. At least one pot-lid has been identified (No. 360) and one sherd is almost certainly part of a curfew (No. 390).

Similar forms and fabrics can be compared from Eynsford Castle, Phase D, where they are dated no later than A.D. 1312 when occupation ceased on the site. The form probably continued well into the 14th century elsewhere as at Dover (forthcoming). Joyden's Wood also has similar forms occurring in the early 14th century. The Fabric 3 ware from Otford, stylistically similar to products from Eynsford, almost certainly continued well into the 14th century alongside Fabric 2.

MEDIEVAL FABRIC 4 – Sandy Fabric.

This group comprises non-glazed sandy wares, of which 126 sherds represent 24 pots (14%). Of the vessels, six are illustrated (Nos. 363, 371, 372, 373, 385 and 391). These are generally hard, well-made, sandy vessels, buff through to orange-pink to various shades of grey outer surfaces with orange-pink to grey core. Fourteen (58%) are jugs, with small triangular rims with level top as Nos. 363, 371 and 391, one thumb-pressed base, No. 372, 'rod handles', Nos. 373 and 385 and a 'strap' handle, No. 363. Nos. 363, 371 and 391 (though No. 363 is slightly coarser) appear to have close parallels in Phase D at Eynsford to c. A.D. 1300–1312. Other local examples can be found at Joyden's Wood and Dartford (Ref. 223). The remaining 42% (ten vessels) are either cooking-pots or small jars. The dating of this group appears to be contemporary with that of Fabrics 2 and 3; that is late-13th to mid-14th century.

MEDIEVAL FABRIC 5 – Glazed Sandy Fabric.

Some 93 sherds represent 23 pots (13%). These consist of a hard sandy fabric with one or both surfaces wholly or partly glazed. Five have been illustrated (Nos. 359, 361, 364, 365 and 374). The glazes vary from yellow through green to browns combined with coloured slips. All are jugs. Nos. 359, 364 and 374 are lead-glazed, simulating metallic vessels and the surfaces have been decorated with applied strips and pellets usually forming linear and geometric patterns. Similar vessels have been found in London (Ref. 224), there broadly dated to the 14th century. Nos. 359 and 364 show small pellets of lead adhering to the pot surface. It would appear that instead of just lead-salt, free-lead was also added to the glaze. The lead particles would have melted during firing (lead having a low melting point) and whilst cooling resolidified into small globules. Similar lead-glazed vessels were found at Faversham Creek 1965 (Report forthcoming) where S.E Rigold provisionally dated them to the 14th century. At least three Grimston-type decorated jugs are represented and one has been illustrated (No. 365) and can be dated to the 14th century.

MEDIEVAL FABRIC 6 – Finer Wares.

A total of 44 sherds represent seven vessels (4%) and consist of a much finer quality, generally cream to off-white, less sandy fabric containing very fine black flint grits and particles, here confined to jugs. Four are illustrated (Nos. 366, 367, 368 and 378). All are stylistically similar to the products of the kiln at Cheam (Ref. 225) where large numbers of jugs, bowls and pipkins etc. were made. Much of that kilns' wares were sent to London. Although these may not be products of the Cheam Kilns certain characteristics e.g. fabric, form and decoration are similar with the Cheam products and probably date to the 15th century.

MEDIEVAL FABRIC 7 – Finer Ware – Imported.

This fabric is represented by one sherd (No. 442), in all probability an import from Northern France. This is of a hard, slightly sandy light grey fabric with very small dark inclusions and has applied decoration of rouletted strip. It closely resembles Rouen-type ware and compares with similar wall sherds found at Kings Lynn (Ref. 219) in Period II contexts dated 1250–1350.

(2). THE POST-MEDIEVAL POTTERY

By Derek Garrod.

A total of 313 sherds was found during excavation and these represent a minimum of 68 vessels of which 37 have been illustrated (Figs. 65–70). Although no definitive study has been made on the post-medieval pottery, it can be divided into four main fabric-groups of which two are subdivided.

Fabric Group	Type	Sherds	Vessels	% Vessels
1A	Raeren Stoneware	144	29	43·0
1B	Cologne Stoneware	5	1	1·5
1C	Frenchen Stoneware	1	1	1·5
2	Hard Fine White Wares	15	2	3·0
3	Sandy Wares	56	17	25·0
4A	Hard Red Wares	82	14	20·0
4B	Crumbly Red Wares	10	4	6·0
Total		313	68	100·0

Table D – Classification of post-medieval pottery from Otford Palace.

POST-MEDIEVAL FABRIC – GROUP 1A – Raeren Type Stone Ware (Nos. 379–81, 392–400, 410, 414, 417–8, 435–6).

This is the predominant group in the post-medieval layers, a minimum of two jugs and 27 mugs being identified. All have typical frilled bases and upright rims; the fabric is generally hard grey with a range of surface or glaze colours from buff to grey or brown with mottled patches of either appearing on the same vessel. Most are unglazed on the inside surface indicating an upside-down position in the kiln, during firing. On some, the bases can be clearly seen to be joined to the walls and the frilled edge is where they have been pinched together.

Mugs and jugs of this type are found on most early-16th century sites. They were first imported into this country in the late-15th century and were most common in the first half of the 16th century. They are now regarded as type-fossils of any site of that date. They have been found at and dated from the following sites:–

1. Farnham Castle, Surrey, from the well in the keep dated 1521 (Ref. 226).
2. Hareplain Kiln, Biddenden, Kent; suggested date first quarter of the 16th century (Ref. 227).
3. Southampton, Pit 4B, National Provincial Bank site dated early-16th century (Ref. 218, p. 163).

What is of special interest is that three of the illustrated vessels (Nos. 379–381) came from the fill of the 14th century Moat. They should therefore have been discarded at the time of the construction of the Palace in about 1515–1520. Another nine (Nos. 392–400) of those illustrated came from the fill of the Tudor Moat and should therefore date from about 1520–1550.

POST-MEDIEVAL FABRIC – GROUP 1B – Cologne-Type Stoneware (No. 440).

Only one vessel of this type was found, unfortunately fragmentary and only the base and a few wall sherds were recovered. The fabric is hard light grey with a sandy surface; this is red-brown inside with a golden-brown glazed exterior. The base is plain and unornamented, but the sides are decorated with trailing vines and oak leaves.

Small jugs and mugs of this type have been given a date range of 1520–1540 by German scholars but an example for stratified deposits at Wharram Percy (Ref. 228), dateable to circa 1510, suggests a possible earlier date.

The Otford example seems to be unusual in that it has a very plain base and lacks the normal beaded external profile, common to most Cologne wares. They have been found at Farnham Castle from a well in the keep and dated 1521 and at Kings Lynn (No. 377, p. 280) dated early-16th century.

POST-MEDIEVAL FABRIC – GROUP 1C – Frenchen-Type Bellarmine Stoneware (No. 434).

Only one example of this type was found. It is a rim and neck with part of a facemask. The fabric is hard dark grey with a light to dark brown inner-glazed surface; the exterior is mottled brown and white with an orange peel surface. The very debased mask suggests a date around the second half of the 17th century. It is very similar to an example from Southampton (Ref. 218, No. 1254, Aberg Canute's Palace, Pit 2) dated late-17th century.

POST-MEDIEVAL FABRIC – GROUP 2 – Fine White Ware (No. 409).

This ware is represented by two vessels. The fabric is hard white in colour with a smooth surface. One vessel, a bowl or jug base, is ornamented with vertical black stripes and these are covered with a thin pale green glaze. The rest of the vessel is plain. The other vessel is too fragmentary to illustrate or identify. It is small with very thin walls, the exterior being covered by an even, deep green glaze. These may come from Surrey kilns.

POST-MEDIEVAL FABRIC – GROUP 3 – Sandy Wares (Nos. 406–7, 412, 416 and 441).

This is a group of a minimum of 17 vessels of which four are almost identical beakers with small pulled spouts. The remainder, where large enough for identification, would seem to consist mainly of jugs.

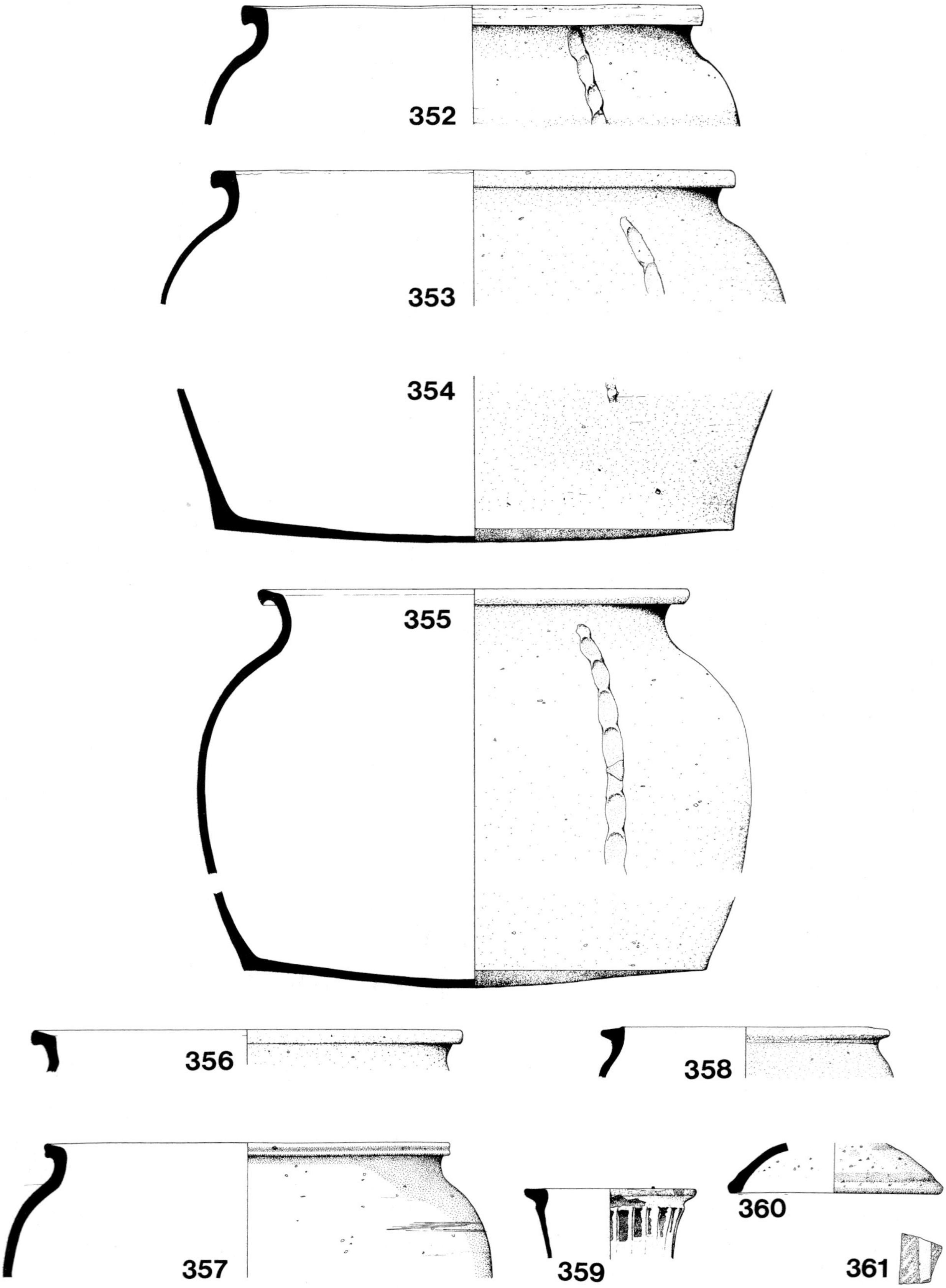

Fig. 65. *Medieval pottery (¼), from fill of Early Moat, Otford Palace.*

The fabric is tempered with fine dark specks of quartz sand and is mainly light grey in colour, though some vessels show an even colour right through. Surface colours vary from light grey to buff and pale orange. Three vessels are part-glazed in green or yellow.

These vessels may be the products of one or more local kilns. The colour variation reflects uneven firing conditions with varying degrees of oxidisation.

POST-MEDIEVAL FABRIC – GROUP 4A – Hard Redwares (Nos. 401–2, 404, 411, 413, 437 and 439).

This group is represented by 14 vessels and includes four posset cups of Cistercian type; the remainder consists of jugs, dishes and cooking-pots. The fabric is hard and red and breaks with a clean fracture, though some examples have bands of grey. The surface is fairly smooth. Seven vessels are glazed in a range of colours including brown, purple, green and yellow.

POST-MEDIEVAL FABRIC – GROUP 4B – Redwares (Nos. 403, 408 and 415).

This group is represented by four vessels and in external appearance resembles Group 4A. The fabric is red or grey with red-brown surface, but it breaks with a crumbly fracture. The groups consists of two jugs, one dish and one two-handled posset cup of Cistercian type. One jug (No. 405) has a red fabric and a grey surface and is covered in a pinky-cream slip.

The above two groups are clearly the products of a number of kilns. The posset cups vary and only two have the true purple colour common to Cistercian Ware. Another which has six applied yellow clay spots has a distinct brown tinge to the glaze, similar to another, too fragmentary to illustrate. The remaining vessel, although of similar fabric and shape, has a very different light brown clear glaze and is probably the product of yet another kiln. The remaining domestic wares, although of similar fabric, vary in glaze or surface texture and indicate equally varying sources as seen in the posset cups.

The manufacture of pottery cups in this country was introduced towards the end of the 15th century. The cups from Farnham are somewhat similar to those from Otford and are thought to have a terminal date towards the middle or second half of the 16th century. The Otford group, associated as they are with many Raeren drinking mugs, probably date from the first quarter of the 16th century.

CATALOGUE OF THE MEDIEVAL AND POST-MEDIEVAL POTTERY (Figs. 65–70)

Fill of Early Moat (Ditch 1), (OTP–19, 30, 56, 82 and 104).

No. 352 Cooking-pot with slightly upward turned, undercut squared rim. Fabric 2, dark grey surface and core. Vertical applied thumb-strip and regular latitudinal striations starting from shoulder. Similar to No. 353. The rim profile can be seen to be similar to Eynsford No. B5 (Ref. 216), classified as thick squared rims, of slightly earlier date. Mid to late-13th century.

No. 353 Cooking-pot with horizontal flanged rim with upper bevel. Fabric 2, dark grey surface, sooted exterior and grey core. Vertical applied thumb-strip and regular latitudinal striations. Similar to Eynsford Castle No. B12, also Moat Farm, Leigh (Ref. 229) No. 38. Late-13th to early-14th century.

No. 354 Sagging base of large cooking-pot. Fabric 2, dark grey surface, sooted exterior and grey core. Vertical applied thumb-strip and faint latitudinal striations. Similar vessels can be seen from Eynsford. Early-14th century.

No. 355 Cooking-pot with slightly upward turned, flanged undercut rim, with upper bevel and slightly concaved top. Fabric 2, grey surface, heavily sooted exterior and grey core. Vertical applied thumb-strip and regular latitudinal striations. Late-13th to early-14th century.

No. 356 Slightly upward-turned flanged rim of cooking-pot. Fabric 2, grey-brown surface, sooted exterior and grey core. Similar to No. 432. Compare Rochester No. 76 (Ref. 221). Similar forms occur at Canterbury (Ref. 217) and also at Joyden's Wood (Ref. 222). Late-13th to early-14th century.

No. 357 Cooking-pot with almost horizontal flanged rim. Fabric 2, dark grey surface and grey core. Regular latitudinal striations starting from shoulder. Sooted exterior. Late-13th to early-14th century.

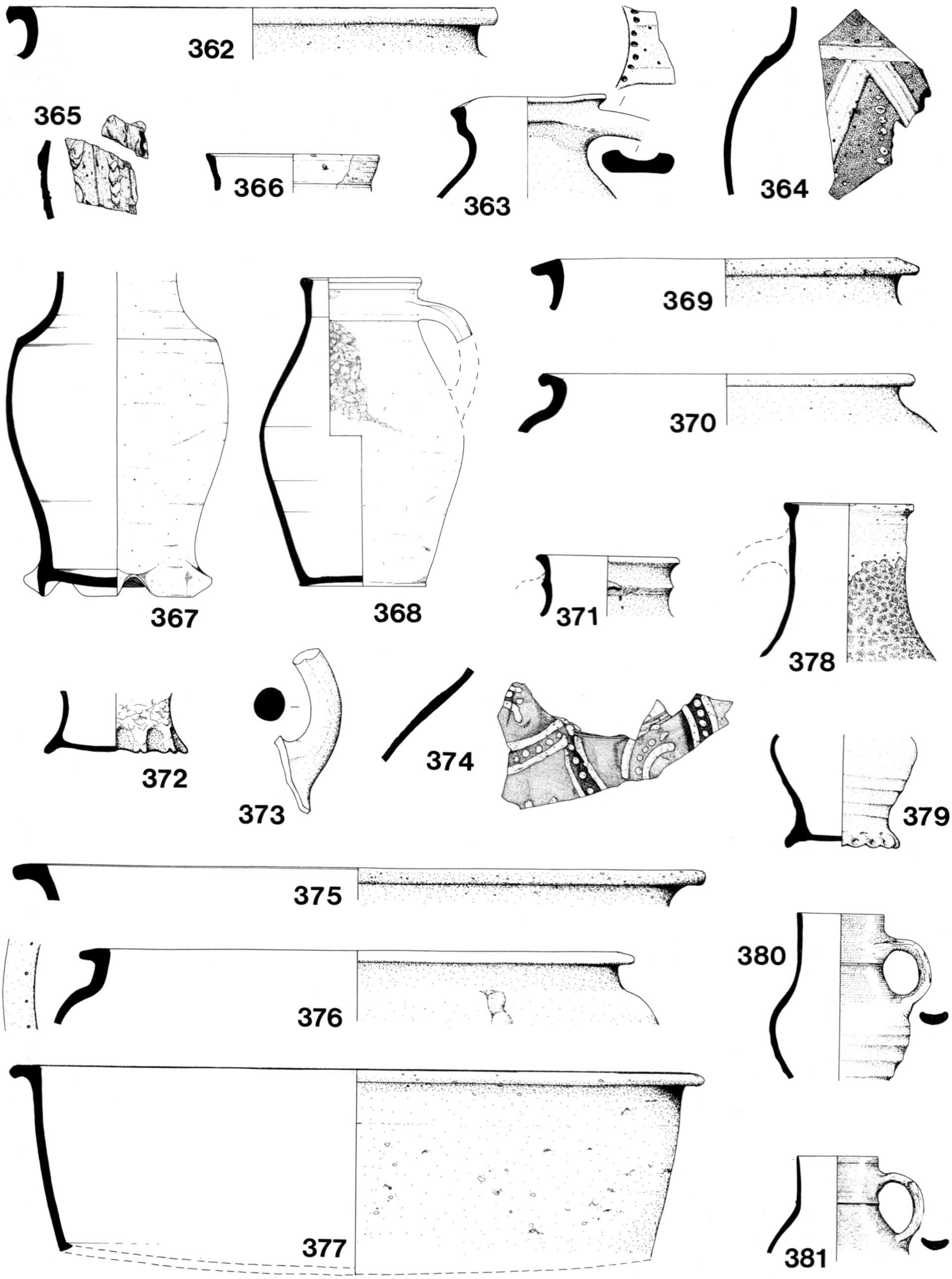

Fig. 66. *Medieval and post-medieval pottery (¼), from dump over Early Moat, medieval Garderobe turret and 14th century moat, Otford Palace.*

No. 358 Tapered flanged rim of cooking-pot. Fabric 2, dark grey to black surface and grey core. Similar to Eynsford Castle No. B2. Mid to late-13th century.

No. 359 Triangular flat-topped rim of jug with shallowly hollowed neck. Fabric 5, orange-brown surface, light grey core. Applied, light green glazed vertical strips starting from neck over mottled brown lead-glaze. Simulating metal vessels. The external surface is pitted with small lead-pellets. 14th century. Compare London Med. Cat. No. A27515 (Ref. 224).

No. 360 Rim of pot-lid. Fabric 3, grey surface and dark grey core.

No. 361 Wall sherd of probable jug. Fabric 5, orange-brown surface and grey core. Applied vertical white-glazed strip over orange-brown glaze.

Dump Over Early Moat (Ditch 1). (OTP–61, 70 and 125).

No. 362 Horizontal flanged undercut rim with slight upper bevel of cooking-pot. Fabric 2, dark grey surface and grey core. Late-13th to early-14th century.

No. 363 Small triangular flat-topped rim of jug with hollowed neck and stabbed strap-handle. Fabric 4, light grey surface and grey core. Compare Dartford No. M.S.1 (Ref. 223), where similar vessels were found to those from Eynsford in phase D. Early-14th century.

No. 364 Part of neck and body of probable jug. Fabric 5, grey surface and core. Mottled brown lead-glazing on surface over which a green glazed decoration has been applied. This consists of a vertical row of 'pimples' between two diagonal bands joining a green glazed neck-band. Similar to No. 359. 14th century.

Medieval Garderobe Turret, (OTP–64 and 78).

No. 365 Wall sherd of jug in Fabric 5. Grey core, cream-buff surface with external overall light olive-green glaze with dark green speckles. Applied strips and scales decorate the surface. Stylistically similar to Grimston ware decorated jugs found at Kings Lynn (Ref. 219). Compare Kings Lynn No. 19 (Fig. 91) found in Period II Phase 3 context, dated to the 14th century.

No. 366 Flat-topped rim of Cheam type jug in Fabric 6. Pinky-buff core and fabric. Splash of light green glaze on external surface and rim top. Probably 15th century.

No. 367 Jug with frilled base in Fabric 6. Light grey core, buff-brown surface. This appears to be a rather unusual form of which the present writer has been unable to find any parallel. The finer quality product and form suggests a probable 15th century date.

No. 368 Cheam type jug in Fabric 6. Light cream-grey core, cream-buff surface. 'Bib' of mottled green and brown glaze on upper portion of vessel opposite rod-handle. Compare similar vessels from Smithfield, London, Med. Cat. No. A24924. 15th century.

Fill of 14th Century Moat, (OTP–7, 8, 9, 10, 38, 54 and 89).

No. 369 Downturned flanged rim of cooking-pot or jar. Fabric 2, dark grey surface and grey core. Faint latitudinal striations below rim. Similar to No. 358. Mid to late-13th century.

No. 370 Cooking-pot with horizontal, flanged, undercut rim. Fabric 2, grey surface and core. Late-13th to early-14th century.

No. 371 Outcurved, flat-topped rim of jug with hollowed neck and external rib. Fabric 4, grey surface and light grey core. Similar to Eynsford No. D42. Early-14th century.

No. 372 Thumb-pressed base of jug. Fabric 4, orange-brown surface. Thick cream-white slip on exterior.

No. 373 Rod-handle of jug. Fabric 4, orange-brown surface, light grey core.

No. 374 Wall sherd of jug in Fabric 5. Grey core, light grey-brown surface. External light green lead-glaze. Applied decoration of strips and pellets, combined with coloured slips of yellow and dark brown. Stylistically similar to London Cat. No. A27515 (Med. Cat. plate LXIII). 14th century. Similar to No. 359.

No. 375 Almost horizontal flanged rim with slight upper bevel of bowl. Fabric 2, dark grey sooted exterior, buff-brown interior surface and grey core. Faint latitudinal striations below rim. Late-13th to early-14th century.

No. 376 Cooking-pot or large jar with horizontal flanged, pricked rim with upper bevel. Fabric 3, light grey surface and core. Vertical applied thumb-strip starting on shoulder. Compare Eynsford No. D19, from dismantling Phase D. Early-14th century.

No. 377 Large bowl with horizontal flanged rim with prominent upper bevel. Fabric 2, dark grey surface and grey core. Faint latitudinal striations below rim. Late-13th to early-14th century.

No. 378 Jug in Fabric 6. Light cream-buff core and surface with a suggestion of a creamy-yellow slip over external surface. Large 'bib' of mottled yellow and green glaze on upper portion of vessel opposite stabbed rod-handle. Compare Cheam Series A, (Ref. 225), 15th century.

No. 379 Mug with frilled base of stoneware hard grey fabric, light brown surface, patchy salt-glaze.

No. 380 Mug with vertical rim and handle of stoneware, hard grey fabric, grey surface, salt-glazed outside only.

No. 381 Jug with vertical rim and handle of stoneware, hard grey fabric, grey-brown surface, salt-glazed.

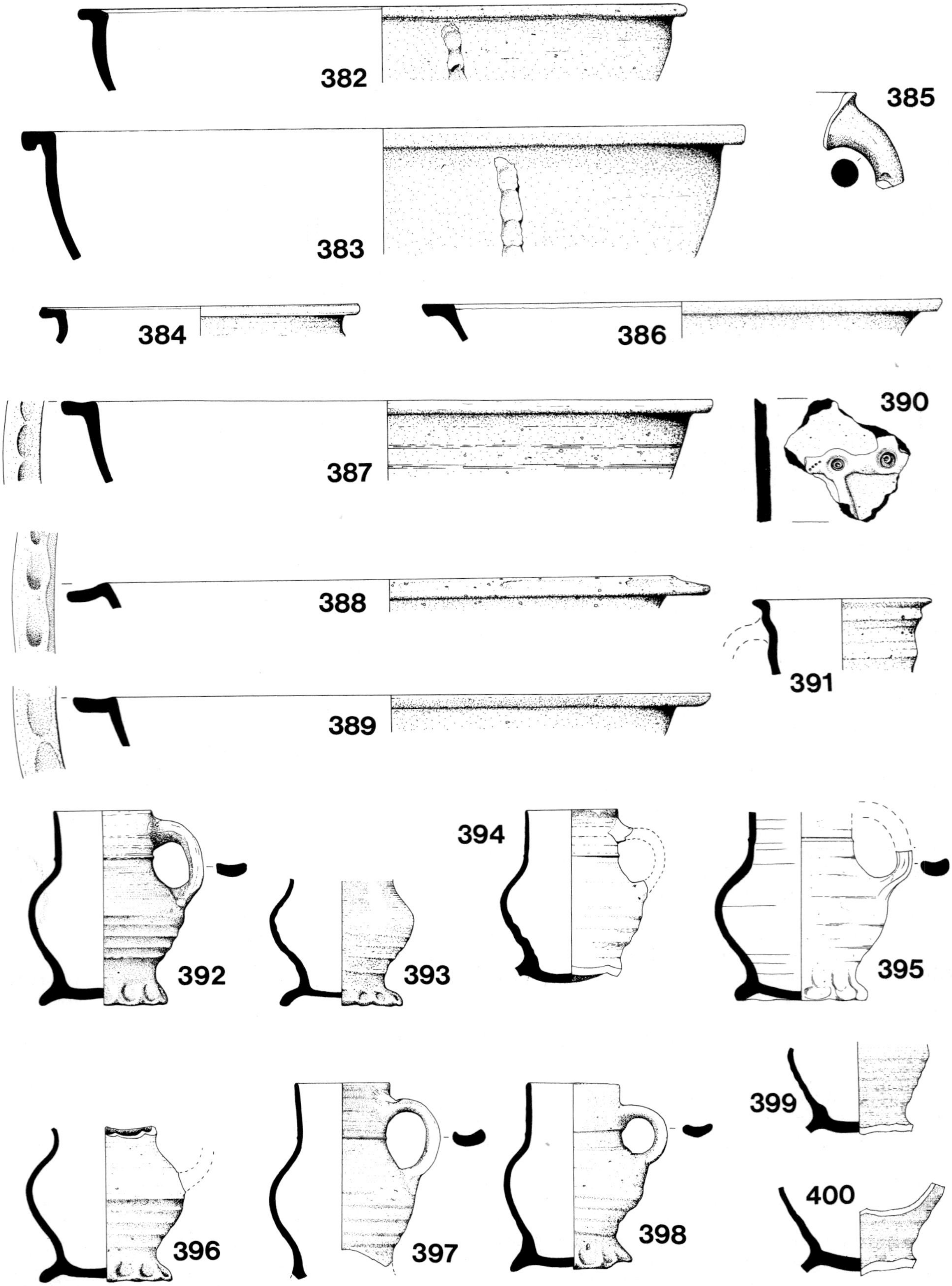

Fig. 67. *Medieval and post-medieval pottery (¼), from Tudor levelling and Tudor Moat. Otford Palace.*

Tudor Levelling, (OTP–27, 60, 65, 71, 72, 80 and 91).

No. 382 Horizontal flanged rim with upper bevel of probable bowl. Fabric 2, dark grey surface and grey core. Vertical applied thumb-strip starting from below rim. Late-13th to early-14th century.

No. 383 Large bowl with horizontal flanged rim. Fabric 2, dark grey surface and grey core. Vertical applied thumb-strip and faint latitudinal striations below neck. Late-13th to early-14th century.

No. 384 Horizontal flanged, thumb-indented rim of cooking-pot. Fabric 3, buff-brown exterior. Grey interior surface and core.

No. 385 Rod-handle of jug. Fabric 4, orange-brown surface, grey core.

No. 386 Horizontal flanged rim with lower bevel, of bowl with slight internal bead. Fabric 3, buff-brown surface and core. Early-14th century.

No. 387 Slightly downturned flanged, thumb-indented rim with lower bevel of bowl. Fabric 3, grey surface and core. Parallel latitudinal grooves on body. Similar to Nos. 388 and 389.

No. 388 Down-turned, thumb-indented flanged rim of probable bowl. Fabric 3, grey surface and core. Similar to Eynsford No. D23, from Rigold's dismantling Phase D. Early-14th century.

No. 389 Slightly downturned flanged, thumb-indented rim of probable bowl. Fabric 3, grey surface and core. Similar to Nos. 387 and 388. Early-14th century.

No. 390 Sherd of probable curfew. Fabric 3, dark grey-black core, grey to buff surface. Applied strips decorating surface having been pressed at intervals using a circular or tubular tool. Late-13th to early-14th century. A similarly decorated curfew was found in Southampton No. 40, there the excavator has dated it to probably the 12th century. The Otford example may be considerably later.

No. 391 Outcurved flat-topped rim with hollowed neck of jug. Fabric 4, grey surface and core. Early-14th century.

Mud-Silt in Tudor Moat, (OTP–33, 39, 44, 63 and 102).

No. 392 Mug with vertical rim and frilled base of stoneware. Hard grey fabric, mottled grey-brown salt-glazed outside only.

No. 393 Mug with frilled base of stoneware. Hard grey fabric, brown surface, salt-glazed outside only.

No. 394 Mug with vertical rim and frilled base with edges deliberately removed, of stoneware. Hard grey fabric, grey surface, salt-glazed outside only.

No. 395 Mug with vertical rim and handle with frilled base of stoneware, hard pale grey fabric, pinky-buff inner surface; outer whitish-grey with thin sheen of salt-glaze.

No. 396 Mug with frilled base of stoneware. Hard grey fabric, brown surface salt-glazed outside only.

No. 397 Mug with vertical rim and frilled base of stoneware. Hard light grey fabric, light brown surface salt-glazed lightly inside and out.

No. 398 Mug with vertical rim and frilled base of stoneware. Hard grey fabric with rough surface, mottled grey-brown salt-glazed outside only.

No. 399 Mug with frilled base with edges deliberately removed, of stoneware. Hard grey fabric, light brown surface salt-glazed outside only.

No. 400 Mug with frilled base with edges deliberately removed, of stoneware. Hard light grey fabric, light brown surface salt-glazed outside only.

No. 401 Posset cup of Cistercian type with upright rim and two handles. Hard red fabric with red-brown surface, inner and outer surfaces covered with purplish-brown glaze flecked with yellowish-white specks, stopping short of base on outer surface.

No. 402 Posset cup of Cistercian type, base and handle. Hard red fabric, inner and outer surface covered in light brown glaze which stops just short of base on outer surface.

No. 403 Posset cut of Cistercian type, base and walls, two loop handles. Red fabric with red-brown surface covered with black-brown glaze, flecked with yellowish-white specks which stops short of base on outer surface. Decorated with six applied, slightly indented yellow/brown glazed roundels around body.

No. 404 Posset cup of Cistercian type, base and handle. Hard red fabric with red-brown surface, inner and outer covered with purplish-brown glaze flecked with yellowish-white specks.

No. 405 Jug with upright and flattened rim and handle. Orange-red fabric with grey surface covered in thick pinky-cream slip. Similar in shape to Kings Lynn Jug No. 25, p. 236. Bourn-type ware. Dated to 16th century.

No. 406 Jug base of sandy ware. Light grey fabric with a pink to buff sandy surface.

No. 407 Slightly splayed jug rim of orange sandy ware with a thin coat of pale buff slip covered with a pale yellow glaze.

No. 408 Base of cooking-pot or jug of red fabric, Group 4B, the edges of which show a very rough crumbly fracture. The surface is fairly smooth and the inside is partly covered by a light brown glaze.

No. 409 Base of jug of fine white fabric with painted vertical black stripes, thinly covered with pale green glaze; the remainder of vessel is left plain.

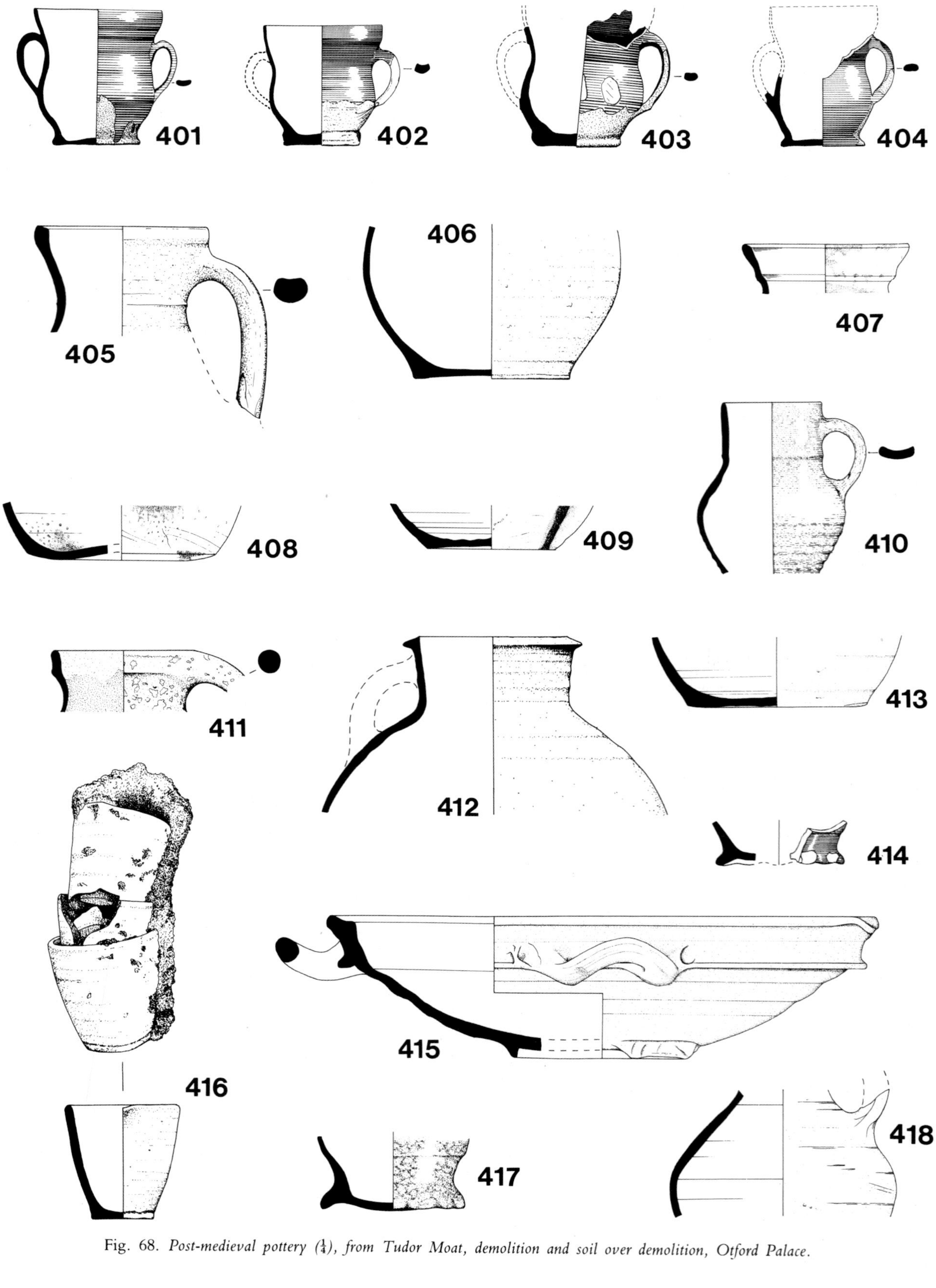

Fig. 68. *Post-medieval pottery (¼), from Tudor Moat, demolition and soil over demolition, Otford Palace.*

Dumped Upper Fill of Tudor Moat, (OTP–35, 52 and 55).

No. 410 Mug with vertical rim and frilled base of stoneware. Hard grey fabric, mottled grey-brown surface salt-glazed outside only.

No. 411 Jug with vertical rim and part of rod-handle of hard red ware. Red fabric (Group 4A) with rough surface and patchy brown glaze inside, overlaid by yellow glaze around rim. A broadly similar jug was found at Southampton (Ref. 218) dated 16th century (Pot No. 690, page 107).

No. 412 Jug with angular rim of sandy ware. Pale red fabric with buff sandy surface, decorated with four ribs around neck.

No. 413 Jug base of hard red fabric with bands of grey. Surface pinky-red with slightly sandy texture.

Demolition of Tudor Palace. (OTP–57 and 97).

No. 414 Frilled base of stoneware mug. Hard grey fabric. Surface light grey with iron flecks inside, brown outside. Salt-glazed.

No. 415 Dish with fattened and slightly upturned rim with lower flange and looped-handle of redware. Hard grey fabric with red surface, splashed with yellow-brown glaze mainly on lower inside face. A similar vessel came from Brentford (Ref. 230 No. 4, page 109).

No. 416 Four almost identical beakers or measures with vertical rims and small pulled spouts of sandy ware, of which two have grey and two have buff fabric with a smooth surface. Found cemented together and lifted as a group.

Soil over Demolition, (OTP–3).

No. 417 Mug with frilled base of stoneware. Hard grey fabric, grey-brown surface salt-glazed on outside only.

No. 418 Part of large jug with handle of stoneware, hard grey fabric, grey inner surface with slightly mottled light and darker brown outer, salt-glazed all over.

Unstratified, (OTP–1, 2, 4, 9 and 40).

No. 419 Cooking-pot or jar with everted 'clubbed' rim. Fabric 1, orange-brown surface, grey core. Similar to Eynsford No. W5, there dated late-11th century, although the rim is slightly smaller – this may be a varient. At Otford a broader date of mid-11th to mid-12th century is offered.

No. 420 Cooking-pot or jar with upright slightly thickened rim. Fabric 1, grey exterior, buff-brown interior surface with grey core. Early to mid-12th century.

No. 421 Cooking-pot with squared top rim. Fabric 1, grey-brown surface and grey core. Similar to Nos. 422 and 423. Early to mid-12th century.

No. 422 Curved rim with squared top and small internal bead of cooking-pot or jar. Fabric 1, dark grey surface, grey core. Similar to Eynsford No. L4, there dated late-11th century to early-12th century. At Otford a broader date of mid-11th to mid-12th century is offered.

No. 423 Cooking-pot with curved rim and square top with small internal bead. Fabric 1, grey to grey-brown surface with traces of internal sooting, grey core. Similar to No. 422. Mid-11th to mid-12th century.

No. 424 Cooking-pot or jar with almost upright thickened rim with slight external bead. Fabric 1, reddy-brown exterior, grey interior surface and grey core. Early to mid-12th century.

No. 425 Cooking-pot with slightly out-turned 'clubbed' flat-topped rim. Fabric 1, grey external surface, grey-brown internal surface and grey core. Similar to Eynsford No. W4 there dated late-11th or early-12th century. Here dated broadly mid-11th to mid-12th century.

No. 426 Cooking-pot or jar with simple everted rim. Fabric 1, orange-brown surface with slight traces of external sooting, grey core. Similar to No. 427. Early to mid-12th century.

No. 427 Out-turned slightly thickened everted rim of cooking-pot. Fabric 1, dark grey surface, soot encrusted interior and grey core. Similar to Eynsford No. X4. Early to mid-12th century.

No. 428 Cooking-pot or jar with everted beaded rim. Fabric 1, orange-brown surface and grey core. Similar to Eynsford No. XI. Early to mid-12th century.

No. 429 Cooking-pot with simple everted rim with slightly concaved top. Fabric 1, grey external surface, grey-brown internal surface and grey core. Similar to Eynsford No. X5. Early to mid-12th century.

No. 430 Cooking-pot or jar with almost upright thickened rim with convexed top. Fabric 1, grey to grey-brown surface and grey core. Early to mid-12th century.

No. 431 Cooking-pot or jar with undercut flanged, pricked rim. Fabric 2, grey-brown surface and blue-grey core. Late-13th to early-14th century.

No. 432 Probable bowl with slightly upward flanged rim. Fabric 2, grey-brown exterior, buff-grey interior and grey core. Vertical applied thumb-pressed strip and regular latitudinal striations. Late-13th to early-14th century.

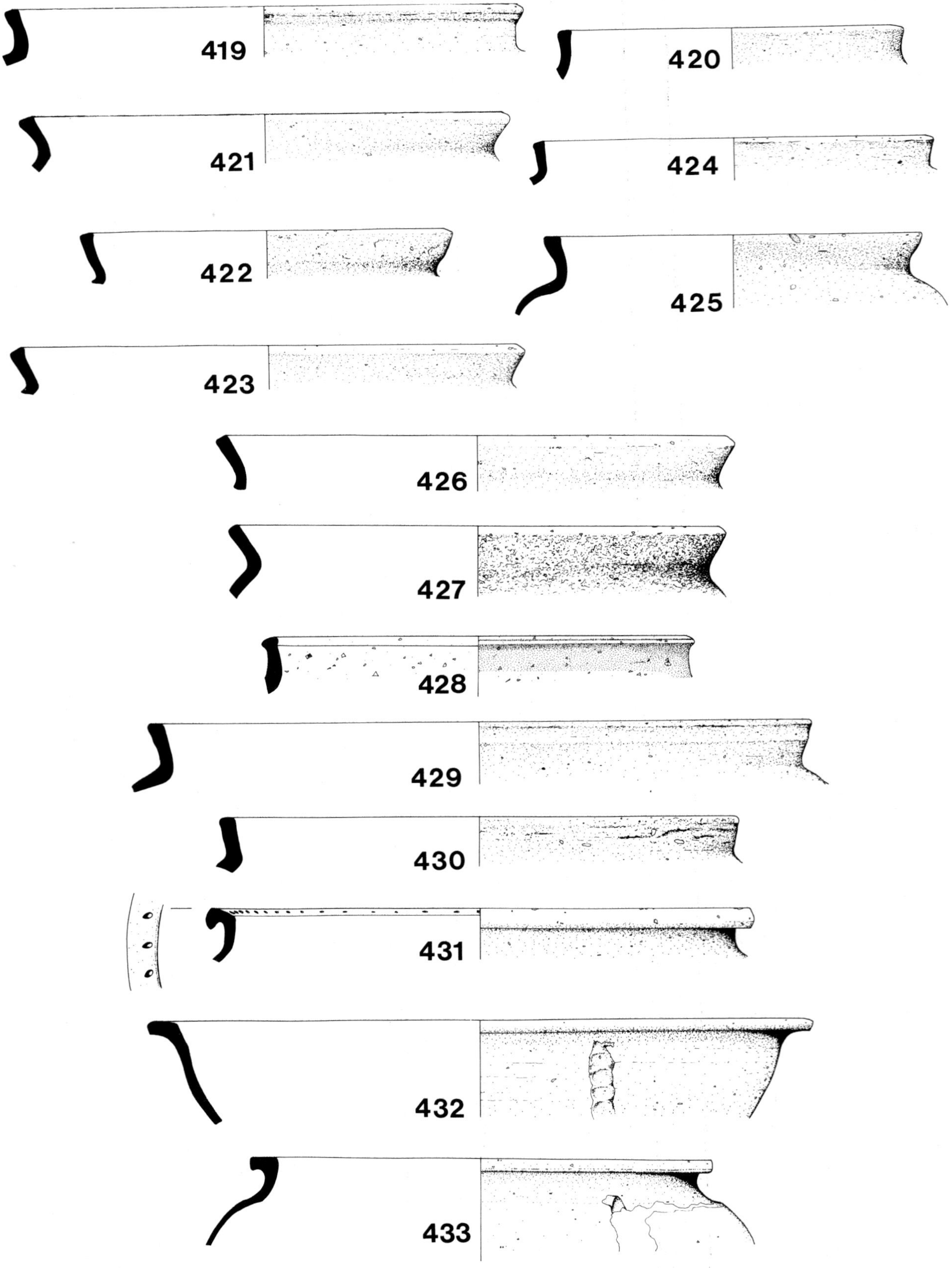

Fig. 69. *Medieval pottery (¼), from unstratified deposits, Otford Palace.*

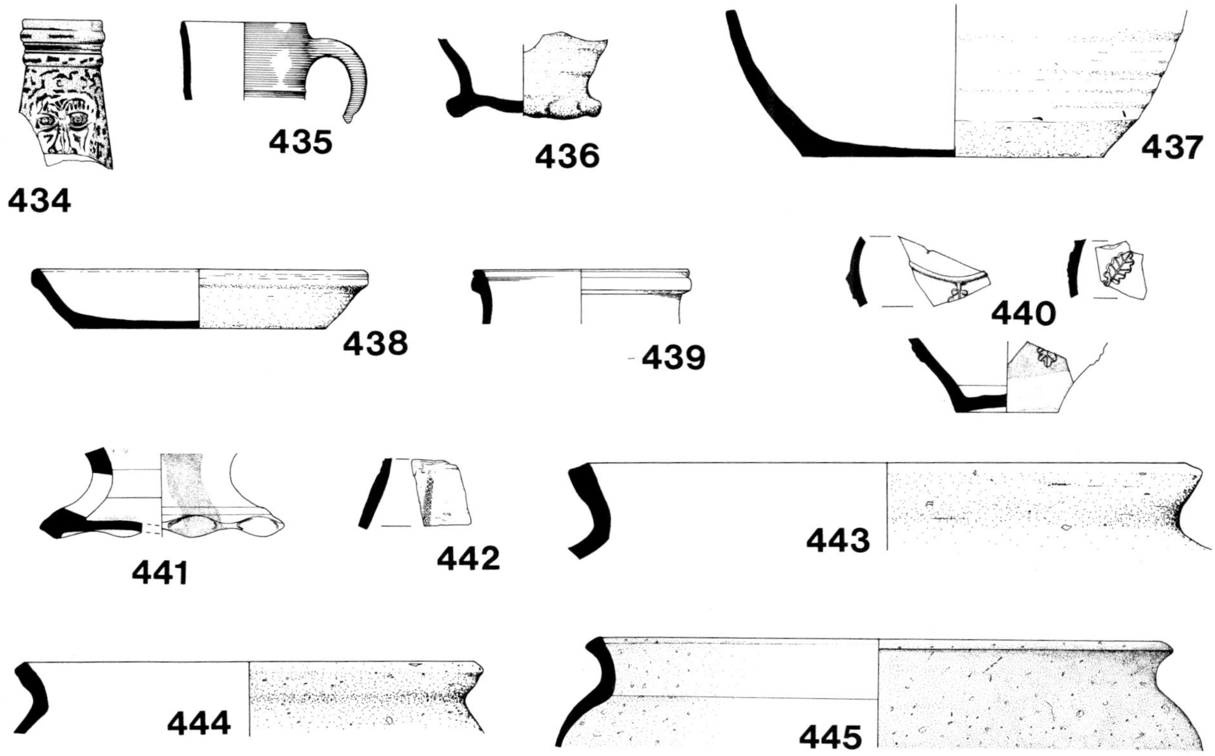

Fig. 70. *Medieval and post-medieval pottery (¼), from unstratified deposits, Otford Palace.*

No. 433 Cooking-pot with horizontal flanged rim. Fabric 3, with grey surface and core. Vertical applied thumb-strip and regular latitudinal striations. Compare Canterbury No. 35 (Ref. 217). This example also has fine grit on the interior confined to the upper portion of the vessel. Second half of the 13th century.

No. 434 Bottle with ringed neck of stoneware. Hard grey fabric, mottled grey-brown surface salt-glazed only thinly on inner surface. Decorated with face mask.

No. 435 Mug with vertical rim and handle of stoneware. Hard grey fabric and surface salt-glazed.

No. 436 Jug or mug with frilled base of stoneware, hard pale buff to grey fabric, surface light brown to grey, salt-glazed.

No. 437 Base of cooking-pot of sandy ware. Hard orange fabric with bands of grey, smooth surface.

No. 438 Flat-bottomed dish with outward leaning sides and almost vertical rim of sandy ware, buff sandy fabric with smooth surface and slight incised lines on outer lip.

No. 439 Jug with upright rim with external overhanging rib in redware. Orange fabric with smooth red surface, inside covered with slightly speckled brown glaze.

No. 440 Mug or jug base and wall sherds of stoneware, light grey fabric with lightly glazed red-brown inner surface. Outer, light golden-brown with whitish speckles near base, salt-glazed; decorated with trailing vines and oak leaves.

No. 441 Base of sandy ware. Pale orange fabric with yellow-buff outer surface. Thumbed or frilled edges with a knife cut aperture on one side. Part glazed with pale green glaze.

No. 442 Wall sherd of probable Rouen-type jug. Light grey core and surface with light green glaze. Applied rouletted strip decoration. Compare similar sherds from Kings Lynn, Nos. 7–17 (Fig. 101), there dated 1250–1350.

No. 443 Cooking-pot with everted slightly concaved rim. Fabric 1, grey exterior, grey-brown interior surface and dark grey core. Similar to Eynsford No. W5, there dated late-11th to early-12th century. At Otford broadly dated mid-11th to mid-12th century.

No. 444 Cooking-pot with simple everted, almost straight rim. Fabric 1, dark grey, heavily sooted exterior, grey-brown interior surface and grey core. Similar to Eynsford No. X4. Early to mid-12th century.

No. 445 Everted flattened rim of cooking-pot. Fabric 1, grey core, light grey-brown surface. Similar to Nos. 427 and 424. Early to mid-12th century.

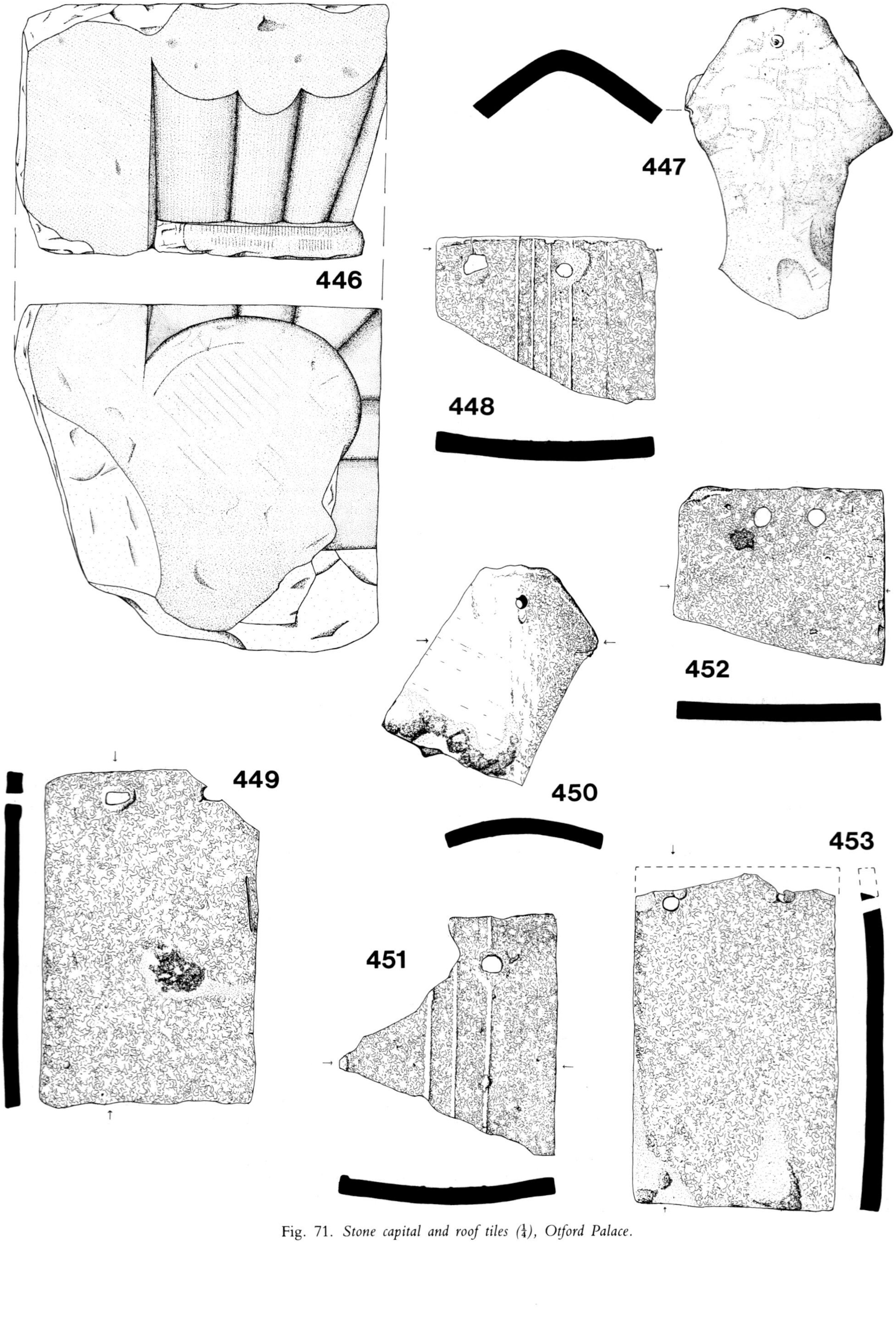

Fig. 71. *Stone capital and roof tiles* (¼), *Otford Palace.*

(3). THE ROMANESQUE SCALLOP CAPITAL (Fig. 71, No. 446).

By Deborah Kahn.

This is an interesting example of a scallop capital, carved on two sides. This form of capital is a refinement in the cushion capital, a type used frequently in Romanesque buildings in England, but not in Normandy before the Conquest. It is thus usually assumed that the cushion capital had been introduced to England in the Anglo-Saxon period, probably from Germany. This particular scallop capital has a trefoil form, that is with the central cusp or shield dipping lower than the flanking shields. Such capitals, though larger and of slightly more sophisticated design, were used in the crypt at Canterbury Cathedral which was built during Archbishop Anselm's episcopate (1093–1109) during the priorate of Ernulf (1096–1106). By analogy this scallop capital probably dates to the first quarter of the twelfth century (Refs. 231 and 232).

The capital is of considerable interest as the only known piece of masonry from the manor-house at Otford of the Romanesque, or as it is also known, the Anglo-Norman period. The so-called Jew's house in Lincoln, which dates to the end of the twelfth century is among the few houses to survive from the period in England. This has a carved doorway and carved, shafted windows on the first floor. The Otford capital is only sculpted on two sides, the rest of it was left rough and was presumably embedded in the wall. It may have come from a doorway, but its diminutive size (19 by 18 cm.) suggests that it was more likely used in a window. In the twelfth century the capital was probably brightly painted though no trace of paint survives.

This capital was found in an inverted position in the North-east Foundation of the 14th century manor-house, where it had been used as rubble (OTP–127).

(4). ROOF TILE (Fig. 71).

By Keith Parfitt B.A.

The excavations at Otford produced a large amount of broken medieval roof-tile. The largest group came from the Tudor levelling deposits and is presumably derived from earlier buildings on the site. A total of some 161 tile fragments were retained for study. The bulk is of the well-known peg-tile variety, with two holes at one end, through which wooden pegs were driven to hold the tile in place. Traces of white mortar on many of the tiles indicate that they were also mortared in place on the roof. The peg holes in the tiles include both round and square forms.

The tiles are generally of an orange-red sandy fabric, with a few examples being over-fired to a dark grey-brown colour. In width, the tiles vary from 14·4 to 16·5 cm. (5·7 to 6·5 ins.), averaging 16 cm. (6·3 ins.). Only four tiles were sufficiently complete to allow their lengths to be measured. These varied from 24·8 cm. (9·8 ins.) to 26·8 cm. (10·6 ins.). The tiles are mostly 1·2 cm. (0·5 ins.) thick. A few tiles have splashes of green-brown glaze on their surfaces and many have vertical ridges on their upper side, formed during the manufacturing process. In addition to peg-tiles, two other tile types occur. Fragments of three ridge-tiles are present in the collection and there are two hip-tiles, one with its original iron nail still in place.

It seems reasonably certain that these roof-tiles were produced fairly locally. Three medieval tile kilns have been excavated in this part of West Kent, at Keston (Ref. 233), Hartley (Ref. 234) and Addington (Ref. 235), all between six and eight miles from Otford. At least two of these sites appear to have been making tiles of a very similar form to those discovered at Otford and it is just possible that one of them supplied some of the tiles used here. The kiln sites seem to have been working sometime during the 13th to 15th centuries but appear to have been abandoned before the great Tudor rebuilding at Otford. It seems likely that other tile kilns remain to be found in the area.

No. 447 Incomplete hip-tile, of orange sandy fabric. There is a single nail-hole at the top, which still contains the original iron nail used to hold the tile in place. There are traces of a grey-white mortar on the under side. From the Tudor levelling layers. (OTP–83).

No. 448 Incomplete peg-tile, in orange sandy fabric, with two sub-square peg-holes and four vertical ridges on the upper surfaces. From Tudor levelling layers. (OTP–80).

No. 449 Virtually complete peg-tile, measuring 25·00 by 15·80 cm. The peg-holes are roughly square and one has partly broken away. The tile is of an orange-red sandy fabric and has traces of cream-white mortar adhering on the lower part of the upper surface and on the under side. From fill of 14th century moat. (OTP–8).

No. 450 Incomplete hip-tile of orange sandy fabric, of similar type to the last. There is a single round nail-hole at the top. Traces of white mortar occur on the lower part of the upper surface. From Tudor tank. (OTP–31).

No. 451 Incomplete peg-tile of orange-red sandy fabric. One square peg-hole remains and there are three vertical ridges on the upper surfaces. From Tudor Tank. (OTP–31).

No. 452 Incomplete peg-tile, in orange-red sandy fabric, with two closely spaced, round, peg-holes. Slight traces of white mortar on the upper surface. From final Demolition layers. (OTP–90).

No. 453 Almost complete peg-tile of hard sandy fabric, with red-brown surfaces and dark grey core. The two peg-holes are circular; one, partly broken away, does not go through the full thickness of the tile. There are traces of yellow-white mortar on the lower part of the upper surface and on the underside of the tile. From the Tudor Moat. (OTP–33).

(5). THE GLAZED FLOOR TILES (Fig. 72).

By Keith Parfitt, B.A.

The site produced 21 pieces of glazed floor tile, 20 of these are of medieval date and one fragment is of post-medieval, Delft ware, type (No. 459). No complete tiles were recovered and over half are unstratified. Many of the fragments are small and damaged and none was found *in situ,* all the stratified examples coming from Tudor or later levels. Thirteen of the medieval tile fragments are plain with, often rather worn, glazes mainly dark green or light green and a few of brown or yellow. Six pieces have inlaid motifs in cream slips. (Nos. 454–458) and one other small fragment has traces of a raised relief pattern (not illustrated).

Most of the tiles are too fragmentary for any accurate assessment of their size. One plain, almost complete example, with a yellow-green glaze measures 13·8 cm. (5·5 ins.) square and a decorated tile (No. 458) was probably also square, the one surviving side, measuring about 13 cm. (5 ins.). Another decorated tile (No. 456) appears to have been just over 10·5 cm. (4 ins.) square, a size frequently occurring in medieval floor tiles. All the medieval tiles are of a red (generally fairly hard) sandy fabric often with a grey core. At least two of the tiles (Nos. 456 and 457) can be closely paralleled, both in fabric and design by material produced in kilns at Tyler Hill (Ref. 236), just outside Canterbury, some 37 miles to the east and there seems little doubt that this was their place of manufacture. Some of the other floor tiles are likely to be from this source. The Tyler Hill kilns were in use throughout the 13th and 14th centuries. Other extensive kilns producing a range of glazed floor tiles existed at Chertsey Abbey, Surrey, in the 13th century. This production centre lies some 30 miles north-west of Otford, but none of its products have been identified on the present site.

There seems little doubt that the medieval floor tiles recovered from Otford are derived from the medieval manor-house, which preceded the Tudor Palace. The existence of tiled floors within this building would be entirely in keeping with its status.

The Delft ware tile, unfortunately not from a stratified context, presumably comes from the Tudor Palace. It is likely to be of 16th or possibly 17th century date.

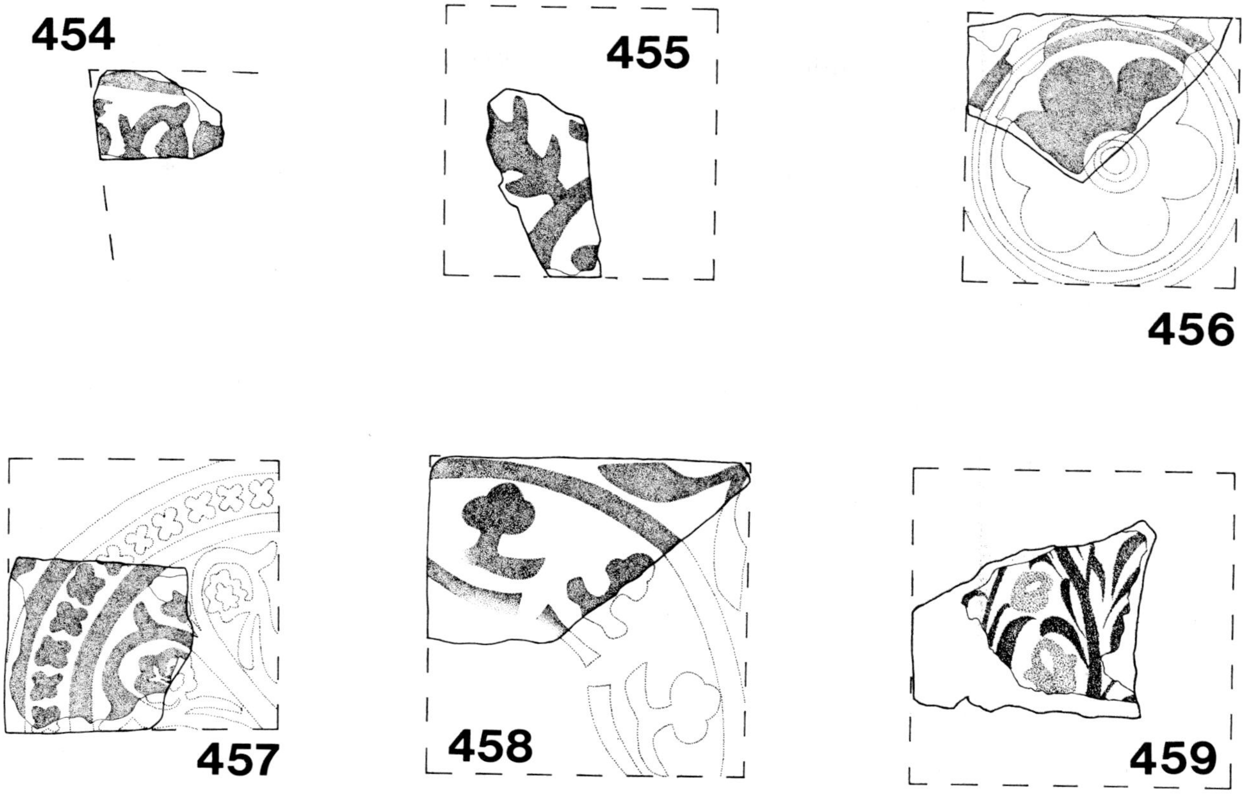

Fig. 72. *Floor Tiles (⅓), Otford Palace.*

CATALOGUE OF GLAZED FLOOR TILES

No. 454 Small fragment, of orange-red sandy fabric, with good orange-brown glaze over an inlaid, cream slip, motif. From Tudor levelling (OTP–83).

No. 455 Small fragment, of orange sandy fabric with a thin orange-brown glaze over an inlaid, cream-yellow slip, motif, possibly part of a crude oak-leaf. From Fill of Tudor foundation-trench. (OTP–37).

No. 456 Nearly half of a diagonally bisected tile, in an orange-red sandy fabric, with a thin olive-green glaze over an inlaid, cream slip, motif. The somewhat chipped motif appears to be part of a six foil within a double circle. Very similar motifs were found on tiles at Faversham Abbey (Type 97) (Ref. 237) and these are likely to have been made at Tyler Hill (Ref. 236). The Otford tile was also probably made at Tyler Hill. Unstratified. (OTP–1).

No. 457 Part of a well-worn tile in a hard red sandy fabric, with a grey core. A very thin green-brown glaze seals an inlaid, cream slip, motif. The motif consists of a series of small saltires set between arcs, enclosing a stylized foliage design. The design and fabric can again be paralleled by material from Tyler Hill, (Type 13) and Faversham Abbey (Type 99). Unstratified. (OTP–1).

No. 458 Incomplete tile of sandy red fabric, with a grey core. A thin patchy, olive-green glaze covers an inlaid, cream slip, motif, consisting of an arc, with external trefoil, enclosing two small stylized foliage designs. Unstratified. (OTP–26).

No. 459 Delft ware tile of fairly smooth cream-pink fabric. The painted design consists of two purple flowers and traces of a third, with dark blue foliage, on a light blue-grey background. Unstratified. (OTP–1).

FINDS REPORTS 6–9

The following specialist reports have been produced on microfiche and are to be found in the envelope attached to the inside back cover of this volume.

(6). The Romano-British Pottery by John Willson. (Nos. M13 and M14).
A short report on 36 sherds of pottery of 2nd–4th century date, probably derived from the adjacent Roman site.

(7). The Small Finds by Keith Parfitt (No. M15).
Short notes on a Roman cross-bow brooch, a clay pipe-bowl and a small red deer antler (Fig. 73, Printed).

(8). The Avian Egg-shells by Carole Keepax (No. M16).
A note on the remains of four eggs from a late-medieval deposit, one a goose egg and the others probably from domestic fowls.

(9). The Leather by John Thornton (Nos. M17–22).
A detailed report on 21 fragments of leather found in the Tudor Moat (Figs. 74 and 75 Printed). All were parts of early-16th century welted shoes and the numerous repairs suggest a shoe repairer, or shoemaker, on the site.

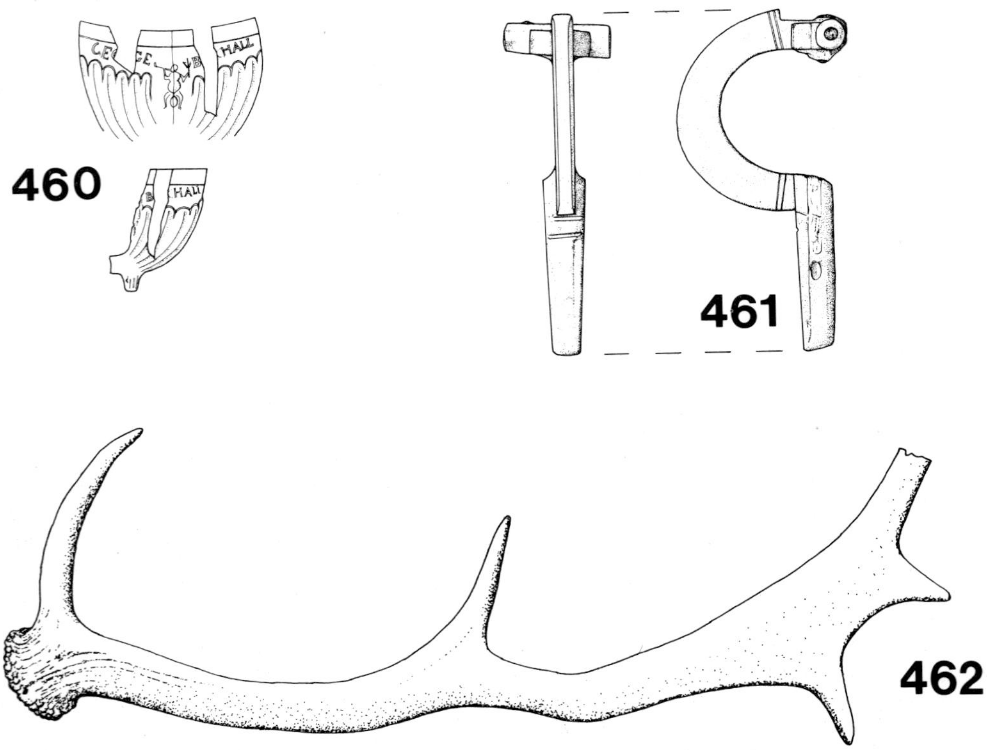

Fig. 73. *Clay pipe ($\frac{1}{1}$), bronze brooch ($\frac{2}{3}$), and an antler ($\frac{1}{3}$), Otford Palace.*

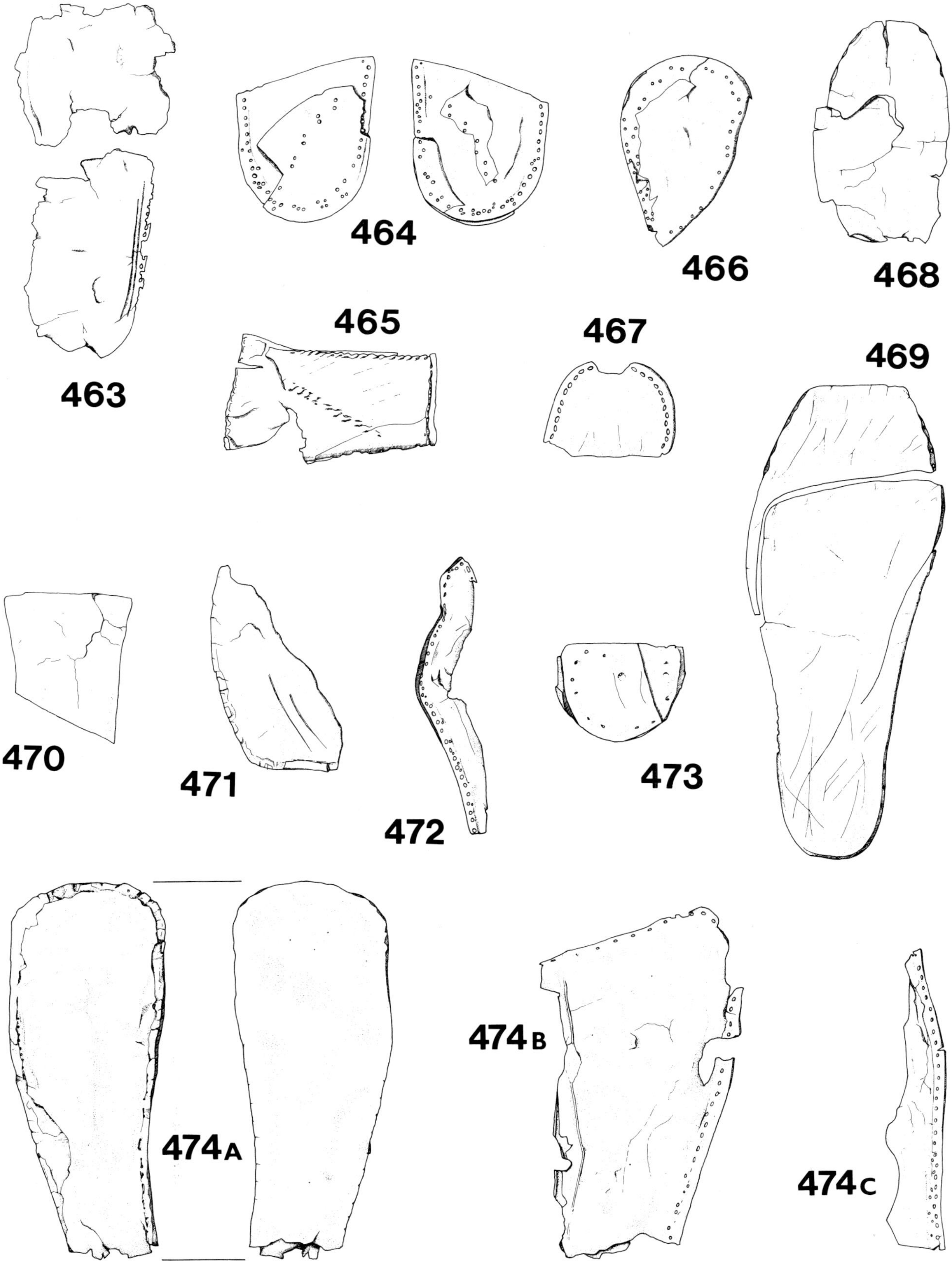

Fig. 74. *Fragments of Tudor leather shoes* (⅓), *Otford Palace.*

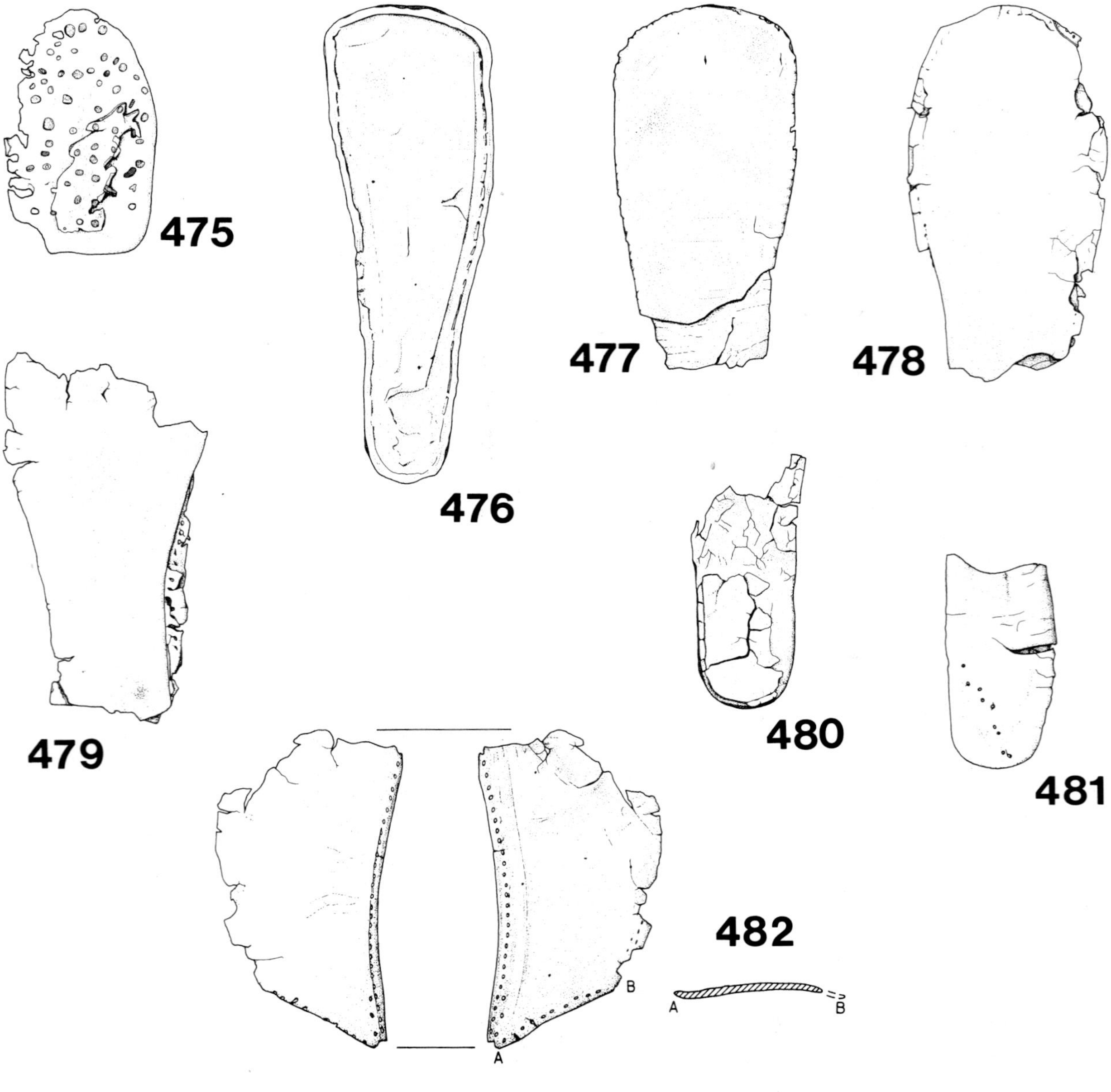

Fig. 75. *Fragments of Tudor leather shoes (⅓), Otford Palace.*

BIBLIOGRAPHICAL REFERENCES

REF. NO.	SUBJECT	AUTHOR	PUBLICATION
1	Kent Rescue-work	Cook, N.C. and Jessup, R.F.	*Arch. Cant.*, LXVIII (1954), p. 1.
2	Kent Rescue-work	Frere, S.S.	*Excavations on the Roman and Medieval Defences of Canterbury*, (1982), p. 17.
3	Kent Rescue-work	Philp, B.J.	*Arch. Cant.*, LXXI (1957), p. 167.
4	Formation of C.K.A.	–	*Kent Arch. Review*, No. 50 (1977), p. 229.
5	Polhill Excavation	Philp, B.J.	*Excavations in West Kent 1960–1970*, (1973), p. 164.
6	Faversham Excavation	Philp, B.J.	*Excavations at Faversham 1965*, (1968).
7	Radfield Excavation	Mills, H.P.	*Kent Arch. Review*, No. 14 (1968), p. 10.
8	Motorway Archaeology	*Ed.* Rosa, C.	*Kent Archaeology 1972–1982*, p. 20.
9	Darenth Villa Excavations	Philp, B.J.	See Ref. 5, p. 119.
10	Darenth Sewer Excavations	Davies, H.	*Kent Arch. Review*, No. 29 (1972), p. 267.
11	Darenth Sewer Excavations	H.M.S.O.	*Arch. Excavations 1972*, (1973), p. 57.
12	Darenth Sewer Excavations	–	Forthcoming.
13	Motorway Archaeology	Philp, B.J.	See Ref. 8. p. 20.
14	Prehistoric settlements	S.E.R.C.	*S.E. Regional survey*.
15	M20 Swanley-Kingsdown	H.M.S.O.	*Arch. Excavations 1975*, (1976), p. 122.
16	Iron Age Pits (beehive)	Cunliffe, B.	*Iron Age Communities in Britain*, (1974), p. 168.
17	Iron Age Pits	Reynolds, P.J.	*Iron-Age Farm; The Butser Experiment*, (1979), p. 77.
18	Iron Age enclosures	–	See Ref. No. 16, p. 161.
19	Little Woodbury	Bersu, G.	*Proc. Prehistoric Soc.*, No. 6 (1940), p. 30.
20	Evolution of enclosures	Harding, D.W.	*The Iron Age in Lowland Britain*, (1974), p. 21.
21	Tollard Royal enclosure	Wainwright, G.	*Proc. Prehistoric Soc.*, No. 34, (1968), p. 102.
22	Rotherley enclosure	Pitt-Rivers, A.	*Excavations in Cranbourne Chase*, Vol. 2, (1888).
23	Woodcuts enclosure	Pitt-Rivers, A.	*Excavations in Cranbourne Chase*, Vol. 1, (1887).
24	Down Barn West enclosure	Fowler, *et al.*	*Wilts. Arch. Mag.*, 60, (1965), p. 52.
25	Worthy Down enclosure	Dunning, G. *et al.*	*Proc. Hants. Field Club*, 10, (1929), p. 178.
26	Casterley Camp enclosure	Cunnington, M.E. and B.H.	*Wilts. Arch. Mag.*, 38, (1913), p. 53.
27	Langford Downs enclosure	Williams, A.	*Oxon.*, 11–12, (1946–7), p. 44.
28	Tallington enclosure	Simpson, W.G.	*Rural settlement in Roman Britain*, (1966), p. 15.
29	Colsterworth enclosure	Grimes, W.F.	*Problems of the Iron Age in Southern Britain*, (1958), p. 23.
30	Survey of sites	C.B.A.	*C.B.A. Research Report*, No. 48. (1982), p. 40.
31	Beard Mill, huts	Williams, A.	*Oxon.*, 16, (1951), p. 5.
32	Stanlake, huts	Riley, D.	*Oxon.*, 11–12, (1946–7), p. 27.
33	Huts	–	See Ref. 20, p. 43.
34	Cereals	–	See Ref. No. 16, p. 167.
35	Kent farmsteads	Caesar, J.	*The Conquest of Gaul, V.*
36	Hampshire farmsteads	Hall, R.T.S. and Shennan, S.J.	*Archaeology of Hampshire*, Monograph No. 1, (1981), p. 37.
37	Sutton-at-Hone farmstead	Mynott, E.	*Kent Arch. Review*, No. 38 (1974), p. 226.
38	Lullingstone Park farmstead	Horner, G.K.	*Arch. Cant.*, LXXX (1965), pre. lii.
39	Lullingstone Park farmstead	Horner, G.K.	*Arch. Cant.*, LXXXI (1966), pre. lix.
40	Fawkham farmstead	Jessup, R.F.	*Arch. Cant.*, LIV (1941), p. 74.
41	Potin coins	Mack, R.P.	*The Coinage of Ancient Britain* (1953), p. 8.
42	Iron brooch	–	See Ref. 20, p. 188.

43	Dagger chape	Jope, E.M.	*Proc. Prehistoric Soc.*, No. 27 (1961), p. 307–43.
44	Borden, reels	Worsfold, F.H.	*Arch. Cant.*, LXI (1948), p. 148.
45	Rim-and-base equivalents	Orton, C.	*Mathematics in Archaeology*, (1980), p. 162–167.
46	Iron Age Pottery	Tyers, P.A.	In *Skeleton Green*, (1980), by C. Partridge. Britannia Monograph Series No. 2, p. 102–3.
47	Camulodunum, Iron Age pottery	Hawkes, F.C. and Hull, M.A.	*Camulodunum*. (Repts. Res. Comm. Soc. Ant. No. XIV).
48	Iron Age Pottery	Tyers, P.A.	*Aspects of the development of the late La Tène and early Roman pottery industries of Britain and Gaul*. University of Wales Ph.D. Thesis (1981).
49	Iron Age Pottery	Cooper, J.	*Sussex Arch. Collections*, Vol. 115 (1977), p. 124.
50	Grog-tempered pottery, 'Belgic'	Thompson, I.	*B.A.R.* No. 108 (1982).
51	Pottery, 'Wealden' Culture	Ward-Perkins, J.B.	*Archaeologia* 90, (1944), p. 144–146.
52	Pottery, everted rim jars	Drury, P.J.	*C.B.A. Research Report* No. 26, (1978), p. 54.
53	Stone Castle Quarry, Greenhithe pottery	Detsicas, A.P.	*Arch. Cant.* LXXXI, (1966), p. 136 and Figs. 3 and 4.
54	Caesar's Camp, Keston, pottery	Piercy-Fox, N.	*Arch. Cant.*, LXXXIV, (1969), p. 185–199, and Fig. 5.
55	Crayford pottery	Ward-Perkins, J.B.	*Proc. Prehistoric Soc.*, No. 4 (1938), p. 163 and Fig. 9.
56	Hulbery and Oldbury, pottery	–	See Ref. No. 51, p. 160, Fig. 12 and p. 172, Fig. 18.
57	Saucepan pot	Cunliffe, B.	*Iron Age Communities in Britain*, (1978), (2nd edition), p. 45–48.
58	Calfstock Lane, Farningham, pottery	Philp, B.J.	See Ref. 5. p. 111, Fig. 34, No. 307.
59	Dragonby, Lincs., pottery	May, J.	*Prehistoric Lincolnshire*, (1976), Fig. 94, 5.
60	Oldbury, pottery	–	See Ref. No. 51, p. 160, Fig. 12, 15.
61	Mucking, pottery	Jones, M.U. and W.T.	In *Recent Archaeological Excavations in Europe*, R. Bruce-Mitford, (Ed.). (1975), p. 133.
62	Caburn, pottery	Curwen, E. and E.C.	*Sussex Archaeological Collections*, Vol. 68, (1927) pl. XVI, 167–173.
63	Greenhithe, pottery	–	See Ref. No. 53, p. 153, Fig. 4, No. 33.
64	Oldbury, pottery	–	See Ref. No. 51, p. 160, Figs. 12, 11.
65	Mucking-Crayford style	–	See Ref. No. 57, p. 52.
66	Hawk's Hill, pottery	Hastings, F.A.	*Surrey Archaeological Collections*, LXII, (1965), p. 20, Fig. 8, 26.
67	Bishopstone, pottery	Bell, M.	*Sussex Archaeological Collections*, Vol. 115, (1977), p. 117, Fig. 54, 95.
68	Greenhithe, pottery	–	See Ref. No. 53, p. 153, Fig. 4, Nos. 25 and 26.
69	Caesar's Camp, Keston	–	See Ref. No. 54, p. 191, Fig. 5, No. 11.
70	Stamped and grooved decoration	Elsdon, S.	*B.A.R.*, No. 10, (1975), p. 18–24.
71	Canvey Island, stamped decoration	Drury, P.J. and Rodwell, W.J.	*Essex Archaeology and History*, No. 5, (1973), p. 76, Fig. 14, 45.
72	Lincolnshire, stamped decoration	–	See Ref. No. 70, p. 42.
73	Canvey Island, decoration	–	See Ref. No. 71, p. 76, Fig. 14, 44.
74	Little Waltham, pottery	–	See Ref. No. 52, p. 74, Fig. 48, 192.
75	Aylesford, pottery	–	See Ref. No. 50, p. 601, No. 786.
76	Southend, pottery	–	See Ref. No. 50, p. 825, Fig. 71a, 719.
77	'Belgic' wheel-thrown pottery	–	See Ref. No. 50, p. 21
78	Gun Hill, Essex, pottery	–	See Ref. No. 71, p. 81, Fig. 16, 83.
79	Mucking-Crayford style	–	See Ref. No. 57, p. 52.

80	Calfstock Lane, pottery		See Ref. No. 5, p. 111, Fig. 34, Nos. 288–311 and p. 113–117..
81	Franks Hall, Farningham, pottery	Meates, G.W.	*Arch. Cant.*, LXXVI, (1961), pre. 1.
82	Farningham Roman Villa	Meates, G.W.	*Arch. Cant.*, LXXXVIII, (1973), p. 1–21.
83	'Belgic' pottery in West Kent.	–	See Ref. No. 50, p. 11.
84	Essex, pottery	–	See Ref. No. 50, p. 10–11.
85	Oldbury, pottery	–	See Ref. No. 51, p. 160, Fig. 12, 19 and 20.
86	Greenhithe, pottery	–	See Ref. No. 53, p. 155, Fig. 5, Nos. 36–44.
87	Little Waltham, fabrics	–	See Ref. No. 52, p. 56.
88	Petrological examination	Peacock, D.P.S. and Williams, D.F.	See Ref. No. 52, p. 58.
89	Pottery fabrics	–	See Ref. No. 50, p. 11–12 and p. 7, Map 2.
90	Skeleton Green, pottery	Tyers, P.	See Ref. 46, p. 102–3.
91	Animal Bones	Jones, R.T., Wall, S.M., Locker, A.M., Coy, J. and Maltby, M.	*Ancient Monuments Laboratory. D.o.E. Computer Based Osteometry. Data Capture User Manual 1.* Ancient Monuments Laboratory Report No. 3342, (1978).
92	Animal Bones	Getty, R.	*The Anatomy of the Domestic Animals.* Vols. 1 and 2 (Sisson and Grossman, 5th edition), (1975), p. 872.
93	Animal Bones	Maltby, M.	*Balkesbury Camp Metrical Archive,* (unpublished).
94	Animal Bones	Matolsci, J.	*Historische erforschung der Korpergross des Rindes aus Grund von ungarischem Knockenmaterial.* In Zeitschrift f. Tierzuchty. u. Zuchtungsbiol. Hamburg. Vol. 87, (1970), p. 89–137.
95	Animal Bones	Clayson, A.T.	*Animal and Man in Hollands Past.* Palaeohistoria, Vol. XIII, A and B, (1967).
96	Animal Bones	Fock, J.	*Metrische Untersuchungen an Metapoden einiger Europaischer Rinderrasen Dissertation,* Munchen, (1966).
97	Animal Bones	Harcourt, R.A.	*Journal of Archaeological Science,* Vol. 1 (1974), p. 151–175.
98	Animal Bones	Getty, R.	See Ref. 92, p. 1544.
99	Seeds	Clapham, Tutin and Warburg.	*Flora of the British Isles,* (1962).
100	1894–5 Excavations	Payne, G.	*Arch. Cant.*, XXII, (1897), p. 49.
101	1969 Excavation	Philp, B.J.	See Ref. No. 5, p. 119.
102	Darenth Villa 1972	Philp, B. and E.	*Archaeological Excavations in the Darent Valley,* (1974), p. 7.
103	Darent Valley operations	Philp, B.J.	*Current Arch.*, No. 38 (1973), p. 89.
104	Ickham Watermill	Young, C.J.	*Collectanea Historica,* (K.A.S.), (1981), p. 32.
105	1982 Survey	Black, E.W.	*Arch. Cant.*, XCVII, (1981), p. 159.
106	Bignor	Winbolt, S.E.	*V.C.H. Sussex,* Vol. III (1935), p. 20.
107	Brading	Price, J.E. and F.G.	*Remains of Roman Buildings at Morton near Brading,* (1881).
108	Woodchester	Lysons, S.	*Roman Antiquities discovered at Woodchester,* (1797).
109	Winkel-Seeb	Drack, W.	*Helvetia Archaeologica,* 15 (1973).
110	Multiple house villas	Smith, J.T.	*Studies in the Romano-British Villa,* (1978), p. 154.
111	Rockbourne	Morley-Hewitt, A.T.	*Roman Villa, West Park, Rockbourne, Hants.* (1971).
112	Eccles	Detsicas, A.	*Arch. Cant.* LXXXVII, (1972), p. 103.
113	Chedworth	Goodburn, R.	*The Roman Villa of Chedworth,* (1972).
114	1969, Anglo-Saxon at Darenth	–	See Ref. No. 5, p. 155.
115	Chalton, Hants	Addyman, P. and Leigh, D.	*Med. Arch.*, Vol. XVII (1973), p. 1.

116	Bishopstone, Sussex	Bell, M.	*Exc. at Bishopstone, Sussex., Sussex Arch. Coll.* Vol. 115 (1977), p. 193.
117	Lower Warbank, Keston, hut	–	See Ref. No. 5, p. 156.
118	Lower Warbank, Keston, hut	Philp, B.J.	*Kent Arch. Review,* No. 25 (1971), p. 131.
119	Frank's Hut	Philp, B.J.	*Med. Arch.,* Vol. XX (1976), p. 164.
120	Dover Huts	Philp, B.J.	*Kent Arch. Review,* No. 45 (1976), p. 122.
121	Canterbury Huts	Frere, S.S.	*The Civitas Capitals of Roman Britain,* (1966).
122	Canterbury Huts	Blockley, K.	*Arch. Cant.,* XCVI (1980), p. 405.
123	Mucking site	Jones, M.U.	*Ant. Jnl.,* LIV, part II, (1974), p. 183.
124	Chalton, Hants	–	See Ref. No. 115
125	West Stowe Site	West, S.E.	*Med. Arch.,* Vol. XII (1968), p. 161.
126	Richborough	Bushe-Fox, J.P.	*Excavation of the Roman Fort at Richborough IV,* (1949), p. 145, No. 192. (Repts. Res. Comm. Soc. Antiqs. No. XVI).
127	Wingham, Saxon	Jenkins, F.	*Arch. Cant.,* LXXXII (1967), pre. lx.
128	Milton Regis, Saxon	Hawkes, S. and Grove, A.	*Arch. Cant.,* LXXVIII (1963), p. 22.
129	Chatham, Saxon	–	*V.C.H.,* Kent Vol. I (1908), p. 375.
130	Chatham, Saxon	Douglas, J.	*Nenia Britannica,* (1793), p. 1. *ff.*
131	Jutes in East Kent	Hawkes, S.	*C.B.A. Research Report,* No. 48 (1982), p. 67.
132	Battle of Crayford	–	*The Anglo-Saxon Chronicle, A.D. 457.*
133	Cliffe Anglo-Saxon settlement	–	*Roch. Nat.,.* Vol. 6 (1924), p. 53.
134	Northfleet Anglo-Saxon settlement	Burchell, J.P.	*Ant. Jnl.,* 28 (1948), p. 186.
135	Dartford Anglo-Saxon settlement	Tester, P.	*Arch. Cant.,* LXX (1956), p. 256.
136	Orpington Cemetery	Tester, P.	*Arch. Cant.,* LXXXIII (1968), p. 55–104.
137	Cliffe Cemetery	Smith, C.R.	*Arch. Cant.,* XIII (1880), p. 562.
138	Higham Cemetery	–	See Ref. No. 129, p. 385.
139	Horton Kirby Cemetery	Priest, S.	*Trans. of the Dartford District Arch. Soc.* Vol. VIII (1938), p. 14.
140	Deleted		
141	Samian	Oswald, F. and Pryce, T.D.	*Introduction to the study of Terra Sigillata,* (1920).
142	Glass	Harden, D.	*Archaeologia,* XCVII (1959), p. 204.
143	Patch-Grove and related pottery	–	See Ref. No. 5, p. 60–61.
144	Shell-tempered pottery	–	See Ref. No. 5, p. 61.
145	Southwark, Roman pottery	Sheldon, H. *et. al.*	*Southwark Excavations 1972–74,* Parts I and II (1978).
146	West Kent, Roman pottery	–	See Ref. No. 5, p. 92–153.
147	Rochester, Roman pottery	Harrison, A.C. and Flight, C.	*Arch. Cant.,* LXXXIII (1968), p. 55–104.
148	Greenhithe, Roman pottery	Detsicas, A.P.	*Arch. Cant.,* LXXXI (1966), p. 136–190.
149	Richborough III, Roman pottery	Bushe-Foxe, J.P.	*Excavations of the Roman Fort at Richborough, Kent, III,* (1932). (Repts Res. Comm. Soc. Antiqs. No. X).
150	Bekesbourne, Roman pottery	Tatton-Brown, T.	*Arch. Cant.,* XCVI (1980), p. 27–57.
151	Faversham, Roman pottery	Philp, B.J.	*Excavations at Faversham 1965,* (1968), p. 76–84.
152	Oxfordshire, Roman pottery	Young, C.J.	*The Roman Pottery Industry of the Oxfordshire Region,* (1977), B.A.R. No. 43.
153	Joyden's Wood, Roman pottery	Tester, P.J. and Caiger, J.E.L.	*Arch. Cant.,* LXVIII (1954), p. 167–183..

154	Dover, Roman pottery	Philp, B.J.	*The Excavation of the Roman Forts of the Classis Britannica at Dover 1970–1977,* (1981), p. 207–249.
155	Richborough II, Roman pottery	Bushe-Fox, J.P.	*Excavations of the Roman Fort at Richborough, Kent II,* (1928). (Repts. Res. Comm. Soc. Antiqs. No. VII).
156	Roman pottery, Northern Britain	Gillam, J.P.	*Types of Coarse Pottery in Northern Britain,* (1970).
157	Richborough IV, Roman pottery	–	See Ref. No. 126, Various types.
158	Canterbury, Roman pottery	Jenkins, F.	*Arch. Cant.,* LXIII (1950), p. 109.
159	Mortarium	Hull, M.R.	*The Roman Potter's Kilns of Colchester,* (1963). (Res. Rept. Comm. Antiq. Soc. No. XXI), Fig. 89, No. 74 and Fig. 87 Nos. 3–4.
160	Antler tools	Philp, B.J.	*Kent Arch. Reviews,* No. 32 (1973), p. 47, No. 2.
161	Antler tools	–	See Ref. No. 5, p. 153, Fig. 46, Nos. 453–455.
162	Stamped tile	–	See Ref. No. 5. p. 140 and 153, Fig. 46, Nos. 456–457.
163	Stamped tile	Lowther, A.W.G.	*A Study of the patterns on Roman Flue Tiles and their Distribution,* p. 15, Fig. 17.
164	Mesolithic Flints	Pitts, M.W. and Jacobi, R.M.	*Jnl. Archaeol. Science,* No. 6 (1979), p. 163–77.
165	Mesolithic Flints	Jacobi, R.M.	See Ref. No. 131, p. 14.
166–168 not used			
169	Pottery, Egham	O'Connell, M. and Needham, S.	*London Archaeologist,* Vol. 3, No. 5 (1977), p. 123–130.
170	Pottery, Runnymede Bridge	Longley, D.	*Runnymede Bridge 1976: Excavations on the site of a late Bronze Age Settlement,* Research Volume, Surrey, Arch. Soc. No. 6 (1980).
171	Iron Age pottery, Weybridge	Hanworth R. and Tomalin, D.J.	*Brooklands, Weybridge: The excavation of an Iron Age and Medieval site, 1964–5 and 1970–71,* Research Volume, Surrey Arch. Society No. 4 (1977).
172	Iron Age pottery, Orsett	Barrett, J.	*Proc. Prehistoric Soc.,* No. 44 (1978), p. 268–288.
173	Iron Age pottery, Bridge Kent	Macpherson-Grant, N.	*Arch. Cant.,* XCVI (1980), p. 133–183.
174	Iron Age pottery, Lowland England	Barrett, J.	*Proc. Prehistoric Soc.,* No. 46 (1980), p. 268–280.
175	Iron Age pottery, Runnymede Bridge	–	See Ref. No. 170, Fig 19, 5.
176	Iron Age pottery Choisy-au-Bac	Freidin, N.	*B.A.R.* International, No. 131 (1982), Fig. 17, No. 4.
177	Iron Age pottery, Mucking	Jones, M. and Bond, D.	*B.A.R.,* No. 83 (1980), p. 471–482.
178	Iron Age pottery, Runnymede Bridge.	–	See Ref. No. 170, p. 65.
179	Iron Age pottery, Green Lane, Farnham	Elsdon, S.	*Surrey Arch. Colls.,* No. 73 (1982), p. 127–139. Fig. 4, No. 11.
180	Iron Age pottery, Weybridge	–	See Ref. No. 171, p. 24, No. 23.
181	Iron Age pottery, Runnymede Bridge	–	See Ref. No. 170, Form 7 (b).
182	Iron Age pottery, Bridge, Kent	–	See Ref. No. 173, Fig. 19, No. 120.
183	Saxon pottery, St. Peter's, Kent	Evison, V.	*A Corpus of Wheel-Thrown Pottery in Anglo-Saxon Graves,* (1979), p. 30, Fig. 18C.
184	Saxon pottery, North Elmham	Hills, C.	*East Anglian Archaeology,* Report No. 6, Norfolk. Spong Hill (1977), p. 131, No. 1380.

185	Saxon pottery, Mucking, Essex	Jones, M.U.	*Berichten Van de Rijksdienst voor het Oudheidkundig Bodemonderzoek,* (1969), p. 145 and 151.
186	Saxon pottery, Caistor-by-Norwich	Wilson, D.	*The Archaeology of Anglo-Saxon England,* (1981), p. 296, Fig. 7.4, No. 4.
187	Saxon pottery, West Kent	–	See Ref. No. 5, p. 155–163.
188	Excavation	Philp, B.J.	*Kent Arch. Review,* No. 36 (1974), p. 192.
189	Excavation	Philp, B.J.	*Post-Med. Arch., Vol. 9, (1975), p. 254.*
190	Trial-Excavation	Ward, C.	*Arch. Cant.,* LXXXIX (1974), p. 199. This contains major errors of interpretation and is now entirely superceded.
191	Preservation	Mynott, E.	*Kent Arch. Review,* No. 37 (1974), p. 195.
192	Otford in Domesday	Ragg, Rev. F.W.	*V.C.H. Kent,* Vol. III (1932), p. 210.
193	Building by Lanfranc	Clarke, D. and Stoyel, A.	*Otford in Kent,* (1975), p. 47.
194	Becket's Well	Pateman, F.R.	*Arch. Cant.,* LXX (1956), p. 172.
195	Papal bullae	Chewley, G.	*Kent Arch. Review,* No. 20 (1970), p. 3.
196	Accounts for repairs (1273–4)	–	B.M. Add., MS., 29794 M7 (Kilwardby ministers accounts 1273–4).
197	Accounts for repairs (1279–92)	–	L.P.L., MS., 830.
198	Hall and repairs (1382–3)	–	L.P.L., MS., 835.
199	New bridge 1410–1411	–	L.P.L., MS., 846.
200	East gate 1431–1432	–	L.P.L., MS., 860.
201	New Entry 1439–40	–	L.P.L., MS., 865.
202	Letter from Warham to Erasmus	*Ed.* Allen, P.S.	*Erasmi Epistolae* (1910), v. 352 (1st Dec. 1523).
203	Letters – Princess Mary	Gairdner, J.	*Letters and Papers, Foreign and Domestic (Henry VIII),* Vol. VI, (1882), Nos. 550, 1473, 1474 and 1475.
204	Survey c. 1540	Ward, G.	*Otford Notebook II,* p. 4. (In Sevenoaks Library) from original copy by Major C. Hesketh.
205	Building Work	Brodie, R.H.	*Letters and Papers, Foreign and Domestic (Henry VIII),* Vol. XVII (1900), No. 1258, p. 691.
206	Expenditure	Colvin, H.M.	*History of the Kings Works,* Vol. IV, 1485–1660 (Pt. II), (1982), p. 217–9.
207	Survey 1573	Hesketh, C.	*Arch. Cant. XXXI* (1915), p. 18. For detail with extracts only in Gordon Ward's Otford Notebook No. II, p. 110.
208	Roman Site	Godwin, F.	*Arch. Cant.,* XLVII (1935), p. 36.
209	Charing Palace	Kipps, P.K.	*Arch. Jnl.,* 90 (1933), p. 78.
210	Hampton Court	Chettle, G.H.	*Hampton Court Palace,* (1971), H.M.S.O.
211	Nonsuch Palace	Biddle, M.	*Med. Arch. IV.,* (1960), p. 151.
212	Dartington Hall	Emery, A.	*Arch. Jnl.,* CXV (1958), p. 184.
213	Hospital of St. Cross, Winchester	Pantin, W.A.	*Med. Arch.,* III (1959), p. 249.
214	Eltham Palace	Emery, A.	*Arch. Cant.,* LXXIV (1960), p. 99.
215	Greenwich Palace	Dixon, P.	*Excavations at Greenwich Palace, 1970–1* (1972). Interim Report.
216	Medieval Pottery, Eynsford Castle	Rigold, S.E.	*Arch. Cant.,* Vol. LXXXVI (1971), pp. 149–170.
217	Medieval Pottery, Canterbury	Frere, S.S.	*Arch. Cant.,* Vol. LXVIII (1954), pp 126–138.
218	Medieval pottery, Southampton	Platt, C. and Coleman-Smith, R.	*Excavations in Medieval Southampton 1953–69* (1975), Vol. 2. The Finds.
219	Medieval pottery, Kings Lynn	Clarke, H. and Carter, A.	*Soc. for Med. Archaeology,* Monograph No. 7, (1977).
220	Medieval pottery, Cheddar	Rahtz, P.	*B.A.R.* No. 65, (1979).

221	Medieval pottery, Rochester	Flight, C. and Harrison, A.C.	*Arch. Cant.*, Vol. LXXXIII (1968), pp. 93–99.
222	Medieval pottery, Joyden's Wood	Caiger, C. and Tester, P.J.	*Arch. Cant.*, Vol. LXXII (1958), pp. 31–39.
223	Medieval Pottery, Dartford	Mynard, D.C.	*Arch. Cant.*, Vol. LXXXVIII (1973). pp. 187–199.
224	Medieval Pottery, London	London Museum	*Medieval Catalogue, London,* 1954: Reprint 1967. pp. 224–228.
225	Medieval Pottery, Cheam	Marshall, C.J.	*Surrey Arch. Coll.*, Vol. XXXV, pp. 79–97.
226	Post-Medieval Pottery Farnham Castle	Moorhouse, S.	*Surrey Arch. Coll.*, Vol. LXVIII (1971), pp. 39–55.
227	Post-Medieval Pottery, Biddenden	Kelly, D.B.	*Arch. Cant.*, Vol. LXXXVII (1972), pp. 159–175.
228	Post-Medieval Pottery, Wharram Percy	Hurst, J.G.	Report Forthcoming.
229	Post-Medieval Pottery, Leigh	Parfitt, J.H.	*Arch. Cant.*, Vol. XCII (1976), p. 190.
230	Post-Medieval Pottery, Brentford	Canham, R.	*2000 years of Brentford,* H.M.S.O. (1978), p. 109.
231	Norman Capital	Zarnecki, G.	*English Romanesque Sculpture 1066–1140,* London, (1951).
232	Norman Capital	Zarnecki, G.	*Later English Romanesque Sculpture 1140–1210,* London, (1953).
233	Tile Kiln, Keston	Philp, B.J.	*Kent Arch. Review*, No. 33 (1973), p. 79.
234	Tile Kiln, Chapel Wood, Hartley	Philp, B.J.	See Ref. 5, p. 220.
235	Tile Kiln, Addington	Philp, B.J.	*Kent Arch. Review*, No. 50 (1977), p. 237.
236	Tile Kiln, Tyler Hill	Philp, B.J.	*Kent Arch. Review*, No. 36 (1974), p. 175.
237	Floor Tiles, Faversham	Philp, B.J.	*Excavations at Faversham 1965,* (1968), p. 49.
238	Avian Egg-shells	Keepax, C.A.	*Jnl. of Arch. Science*, No. 8, (1981), p. 315.

Plate II. *The long south-east arm of the South East Ditch, Iron Age site at Farningham Hill.*

Plate III. *The short north-east arm of the South East Ditch, Iron Age site at Farningham Hill.*

Plate IV. *The South Ditch and the South Entrance, Iron Age site at Farningham Hill.*

Plate V. *The North West Ditch under excavation, Iron Age site at Farningham Hill.*

Plate VI. *The south end of the North West Ditch and the South West Entrance, Iron Age site at Farningham Hill.*

Plate VII. *The North East Entrance and flanking ditches, Iron Age site at Farningham Hill.*

Plate VIII. *Pits 16–18 from the east, Iron Age site at Farningham Hill.*

Plate IX. *Pit 13 with its bottom post-hole, Iron Age site at Farningham Hill.*

Plate X. *Layer of discarded pottery in Pit 16, Iron Age site at Farningham Hill.*

Plate XI. *Post-holes and gully in the Hut Area, from the North, Iron Age site at Farningham Hill.*

Plate XII. *The Contractor's sewer-pipe approaching the Darenth Roman Villa.*

Plate XIII. *Roman Chalk Rafts (Features 2 and 3), Darenth Roman Villa site.*

Plate XIV. *Roman Oven (Feature 6), Darenth Roman Villa site.*

Plate XV. *Excavation in progress looking south, Centre Area, Darenth Roman Villa site. A marks the Roman water-channel (Feature 14), B marks the Roman Boundary wall (Feature 22) and the figures mark some of the Saxon post-holes (Feature 23).*

Plate XVI. *The north-west corner of 'Room 65', Darenth Roman Villa site.*

Plate XVII. *South Area, section across Saxon Hut B (Feature 28), Darenth Roman Villa site.*

Plate XVIII. *The North West Tower, Otford Palace.*

Plate XIX. *The Otford Palace site on completion by the kent Unit in five weeks.*

Plate XX. *Work in progress, Otford Palace.*

Plate XXI. *The collapsed Wooden Revetment in the bottom of the Early Moat (Ditch 1), Otford Palace.*

Plate XXII. *The foundation of the Garderobe Turret of the Medieval Building, cut by the Tudor East Range, Otford Palace.*

Plate XXIII. *The north-east angle of the Garderobe Turret of the Medieval Building, cut by the Tudor East Range, Otford Palace.*

Plate XXIV. *The North East Foundation of the Medieval Building cut by the walls of the West Passage of the Tudor East Range, Otford Palace.*

Plate XXV. *12th century capital incorporated as rubble in North East Foundation of Medieval Building, Otford Palace.*

Plate XXVI. *The Tudor South East Tower, Otford Palace.*

Plate XXVII. *The ragstone face of the east side of the Tudor South East Tower, Otford Palace.*

Plate XXVIII. *Room 6 at the extreme east end of the Tudor South Range, Otford Palace.*

Plate XXIX. *The East Range of the Tudor Palace, from the south-east, Otford Palace.*

Plate XXX. *East outlet of Tudor South Drain, Otford Palace.*

Plate XXXI. *East Drain with large capstones, flanking the external wall of the Tudor East Range, Otford Palace.*

Plate XXXII. *Stone-lined tank at junction of Tudor South Range and East Range, Otford Palace.*

Plate XXXIII. *The flooded Tudor Garderobe outlets from the south, Otford Palace.*

Plate XXXIV. *The outlet shoots at the base of the four-Shafted Tudor Garderobe, Otford Palace.*

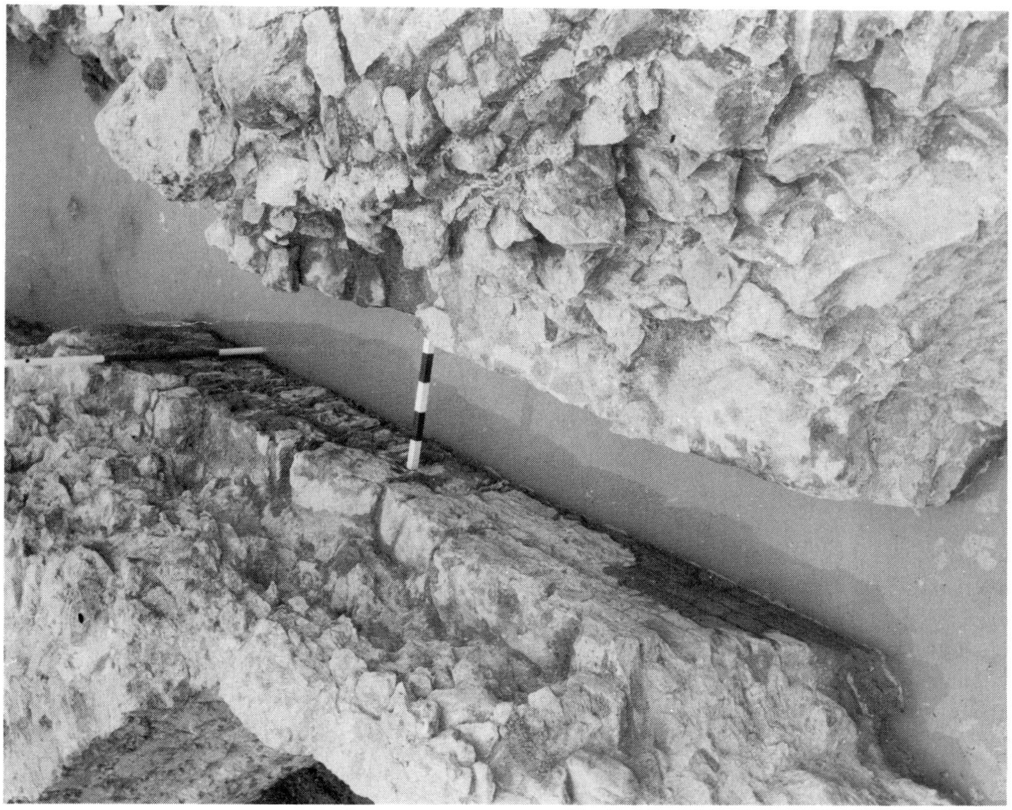

Plate XXXV. *Main Culvert Passing outer wall of Tudor East Range, Otford Palace.*

Plate XXXVI. *Stone jambs of the flooded Tudor Sewer, Otford Palace.*

Plate XXXVII. *North elevation of west side of Tudor Main Gatehouse, Otford Palace.*

Plate XXXVIII. *South elevation of west side of Tudor Main Gatehouse, Otford Palace.*

Plate XXXIX. *South elevation of Tudor North West Gallery, Otford Palace.*

Plate XL. *South West corner of Tudor South Range in Bubblestone Road, Otford Palace.*

INDEX

LIST OF SUBSCRIBERS

1. Mr. S. Burden, Headcorn.
2. Mr. J.E. Moorhouse, Banchory, Scotland.
3. Mrs. N.M. Roberts, Faversham.
4. Mr. E.G.F. Briggs, Bromley.
5. Mr. R.C. Fendt, Keston.
6. Mr. J.M. Dennis-Purves, Beckenham.
7. Miss C. Pegram, Bromley.
8. Mr. R. Tollfree, Bromley.
9. Mr. W. Fairhead, West Wickham.
10. Mr. L.F. Johnson, London.
11. Mr. P. Grant, Bromley.
12. Mrs. P. Maddison, Lewisham.
13. Mr. F.G. Rundall, Farningham.
14. Mr. J. Willson, Whitfield.
15. Mr. G.W. Church, Bromley.
16. Mr. A.E.A. Wild, Orpington.
17. Mrs. S. Edwards, Catford.
18. Mr. M.W. Meekums, Petts Wood.
19. Miss J.M. Albery, Farningham.
20. Mr. C.M. Martin, Sidcup.
21. Mr. T.C. Woodman, Bromley
22. Mrs. M.A. Brown, Dover.
23. Mrs. J. Alpin, Mersham.
24. Mr. M. Godfrey, Keston.
25. Wing Commander G.T. Wynne-Powell, Beckenham.
26. Mr. A.G. Scott, St. Leonards, East Sussex.
27. Mr. C.R. Baker, Dartford.
28. Mr. E.W. Black, London.
29. Miss C. Rosa, Ramsgate.
30. Mr. A. Gidlow, Faversham.
31. Mrs. W. Williams, Dover.
32. Mr. D. Garrod, Welling & Cairo.
33. Mr. M. Dutto, Dover.
34. Mr. P. Keller, Dover.
35. Mr. K. Parfitt, Polhill.
36. Mr. R. Mummery, Worcestershire.
37. Mrs. P. Barrett, Whitfield.
38. Mr. B. Stocker, Dover.
39. Miss A. Button, Bromley.
40. Mrs. P. Crozier, Bromley.
41. Mr. C.I.B. Philp, West Wickham.
42. Mr. C.J.B. Philp, West Wickham.

Also:

43. Passmore Edwards Museum, London.
44. West Kent Archaeological Group.
45. Orpington and District Archaeological Society.
46. Dartford District Archaeological Group.
47. Kent Archaeological Trust.
48. Thameside Archaeological Group.
49. Springhead Excavation Group.
50. Dover Archaeological Group.
51. Darent Valley Archaeological Training School.